CROMWELL
TO
CROMWELL

D1099547

CROMWELL
TO
CROMWELL

Reformation to Civil War

JOHN SCHOFIELD

The History Press

For Nicola and Richard

First published 2009
This edition published 2011

The History Press
The Mill, Brimscombe Port
Stroud, Gloucestershire, GL5 2QG
www.thehistorypress.co.uk

British Library Cataloguing in Publication Data.
A catalogue record for this book is available from the British Library.

ISBN 978 0 7524 5968 4

Printed in Great Britain

CONTENTS

LIST OF ILLUSTRATIONS

19. Prince Henry of Wales, eldest son of James and Anne. He died of typhoid in 1612 aged eighteen, leaving his less gifted brother Charles (the future Charles I) as heir to the throne. (THP Archive)
20. Portrait engraving of Francis Bacon. (THP Archive)
21. Charles I and Henrietta Maria. (THP Archive)
22. Print of a Van Dyck painting of Charles I, reproduced by Hollar at the time of the king's execution in 1649. (THP Archive)
23. Charles I, from the engraving by William Hole, 1625. (Author's Collection)
24. 'The Sovereign of the Seas' from the engraving by John Payne, 1637. (Author's Collection)
25. John Hampden, from Nugent's *Life of Hampden*. (Author's Collection)
26. John Pym, from a miniature by Samuel Cooper. (Author's Collection)
27. Oliver Cromwell, from a miniature by Samuel Cooper, in the Baptist College at Bristol. (Author's Collection)
28. Statue of Oliver Cromwell, by Thorneycroft, erected at Westminster in 1899. (Author's Collection)
29. John Milton, from an engraving by Faithorne. (Author's Collection)
30. Charles II in middle age. (THP Archive)
31. Coronation of Charles II in Westminster Abbey. (THP Archive)

PREFACE

This work is a sequel to the recent biography of Thomas Cromwell. It examines how the principles of the Reformation changed and evolved in England, in some cases out of all recognition.

English reformers in the 1530s, led by Cromwell, had a near reverence for kingly rule and authority. Resisting the king was tantamount to resisting God. Even on a matter of conscience, the will of the king should prevail. Yet just over 100 years later, Charles I was called the 'man of blood', and *Oliver* Cromwell famously declared that 'we will cut of his head with the crown on it'.

Now the core question – how did we get from A to B? How did the deferential Reformation become a regicidal revolution? This book is one man's quest for an answer.

That answer, so I am persuaded, cannot lie entirely in Ship Money, or Archbishop Laud or even in the disdain Charles I showed for Parliament. These are the immediate causes of the Civil War; but something else, something deeper, must account for the difference in psyche and mindset between the deferential reformers of the 1530s and the godly revolutionaries of the 1640s.

This is a big subject, but knowing how readers and publishers appreciate brevity, I have aimed for a succinct account that highlights the salient and most significant developments in church, state and society between the two Cromwells. This book is not a general narrative of the Tudor and early Stuart periods; rather it concentrates on the core question above and selects the most germane material.

This work focuses on England. Events in Scotland and Ireland will be treated as and when they are relevant to the main subject, but details of the Scottish and Irish reformations are left to those more qualified to discuss them.

Regarding terminology, the words 'evangelical', 'reformer' and 'Protestant' are used interchangeably to avoid repetition, 'evangelical' being understood in its sixteenth-century sense, meaning Gospel. The 'new learning' was another term used in Tudor times to describe Protestantism.

If the early sections of Chapter 2 read like a résumé of Thomas Cromwell's life, this is because I cannot assume that all those who pick up this book have read the previous one. Apologies to those who find this material rather familiar, but it would hardly do to begin with Cromwell's fall.

ACKNOWLEDGEMENTS

My thanks to Tony Morris, who, when I was thinking about doing something on these lines but had only fuzzy ideas, suggested the title and has been supportive ever since.

Inexpressible thanks for the labours of S.R. Gardiner over a century ago in producing what must be one of the greatest achievements ever in historical writing. If, in the sections on the Stuarts, his name appears more frequently in the notes than any other, that implies no disrespect to modern authorities. They have been consulted as well, and most of them recommend reading Gardiner anyway.

I am grateful to all other scholars who have studied and written about the Tudors and the Stuarts. A great deal of material has been consulted for this work, but it is impracticable to list every remotely relevant or worthwhile article, book or monograph, and there is no point in padding out the footnotes and bibliography simply to try and impress.

Thanks to Newcastle University and particularly Professor Tim Kirk, Head of the School of Historical Studies, for accepting me as a guest member and visiting scholar, thereby allowing me to do the necessary research for this book; and to the staff of Newcastle and Durham University libraries. Also to John Cannon, Emeritus Prof. at Newcastle, for kindly offering to read through the manuscript and for his many helpful suggestions, and to Simon Hamlet, Abigail Wood and their colleagues at The History Press for bringing the work into print.

1

THE EUROPEAN BACKGROUND,
1517–31

LUTHER

On a late spring evening, on 4 May 1521, a mystery visitor arrived under escort at Wartburg Castle near Eisenach in Germany. He was ushered into a room hastily prepared for him, and given books, paper and a writing table. The castle's occupants were told that a certain Knight George (*Junker Jörg*) would be staying with them for a short while. Only a carefully select few knew his real name – it was Martin Luther, the notorious heretic and excommunicate.

Luther had been at the diet of Worms in obedience to a summons from the Holy Roman Emperor, Charles V. In the emperor's presence Luther defended his writings and refused to recant when directed to do so. For this he was placed under the imperial ban, though Charles did honour his promise of safe conduct, and Luther was allowed to return home. For his own protection, however, and with the knowledge of Frederick the Wise, Elector of Saxony where Luther lived, Luther's friends staged a mock kidnap and spirited him away to Wartburg. With a beard to help his disguise, he remained several months there in seclusion from the outside world, concentrating on his translation of the New Testament and many other writings.[1]

Safe though he was in Wartburg, at least for the time being, Luther knew that his struggles with opponents were far from finished. 'We must resist that most atrocious wolf with all our strength', he urged his friend, George Spalatin, referring to his old adversary on the indulgence crisis, Cardinal Albrecht.[2] Rumours soon reached him of disturbances among students, artisans and peasants, supporting Luther and hostile to the German clergy. The authorities were seriously alarmed. Among Luther's Wartburg works was a commentary on the *Magnificat*, and one line of Mary's song – 'He has put down the mighty from their thrones' – may have struck his mind (Luke 1:52). But if Luther was ever tempted to take advantage of the simmering unrest in Germany by calling the people to arms, he resisted it. Troubled by reports of strife in his native Wittenberg, in December 1521 he composed his *Sincere admonition … against insurrection and rebellion.* Luther was convinced that divine judgement was about to fall on the papist kingdom, and if the pope and his cardinals were afraid of risings throughout Europe, then that served them right for having corrupted the Gospel. Nevertheless, Luther would never endorse insurrection, either for the sake of religion or in any other cause. Insurrection lacks all discernment: for 'when Mr Mob breaks loose he cannot tell the wicked from the good, he just lays about him at random'. Therefore, said Luther:

> I am and always will be, on the side of those against whom insurrection is directed, no matter how unjust their cause. I am opposed to those who rise in insurrection, no matter how *just* their cause, because there can be no insurrection without hurting the innocent and shedding their blood [emphasis mine].

In times of trial or persecution, Luther appealed to Christian readers to commit matters to God and wait patiently on Him. The way to defeat the pope and his bishops is to continue the work already begun, to preach and believe the Gospel – 'better this way than a hundred insurrections'. Rebellion is the devil's work, cunningly contrived to disgrace the Gospel.[3]

The Reformation that Luther had begun was primarily a controversy over St Paul, and particularly Paul's great theological treatise, the epistle to the Romans. For years Luther had been immersed in Paul's writings before being convinced that the medieval Roman Church of his time, with her Masses, penance and indulgences, had become the bastion of a false and corrupted Christianity. Justification by faith alone was no mere theological theory; it was a way of salvation radically at odds with the one taught by the church's leaders: a gift of divine grace, freely offered, received by faith, impossible to earn by any good work or human merit. This discovery led Luther to attack the Roman Mass, clerical celibacy, traditional teaching on penance and papal authority in the church. But he did not attack the authority of kings and civil powers.[4]

Luther's spiritual trials and breakthroughs have been admirably and exhaustively explained by his definitive modern biographer, Martin Brecht, so they can be passed over very quickly here.[5] Besides, Luther's teaching on salvation and justification quickly became a Protestant consensus. But there was something else in Paul's epistle that would exercise the minds of generations of Protestants throughout Western Europe in diverse ways, namely the apostle's directive in Romans 13 to the church to honour and obey the civil power. This will be the chief subject of this book: the various reformers' views on church and state, and the curious, frequently difficult connection between reform and revolt; how these views changed and evolved as the sixteenth century unfolded; how religious reform sometimes leads to strife and sometimes does not; how some reformers befriend the state while others set themselves against it; and so on.

This was a slightly uncertain area for the Reformers, because whereas the New Testament is quite definite on matters of theology and doctrine, that is not always the case with secular affairs. The men who wrote the New Testament could not foresee either the conversion of Constantine or the collapse of the Roman Empire. Consequently, they did not give precise instructions on how a Christian kingdom should be constituted; they probably never expected to see such a thing on earth. Reformers who believed in the primacy of Scripture, therefore, had no conveniently itemised list of Scriptural commands on this subject that they were supposed to follow, which left them feeling their own way to some extent.

When Luther returned to Wittenberg he set his face against religious and political radicalism in his Invocavit sermons. He put a summary and permanent end to outbreaks of image-smashing in Saxony. He forcefully reminded some of his more zealous brethren of the need for patience when introducing even necessary reforms. The need of the hour was for good preaching to win the hearts and minds of the people to the new faith. Allowing the laity to receive the wine as well as the bread at communion was right and good, but *compelling* it would merely be a new form of legalism. Even the hated Mass should be reformed by persuasion rather than by force. The sermons made a strong impression, and Luther won over most of his hearers.[6]

Along with his chief ally and co-worker, Philip Melanchthon, Luther now began building the evangelical church, and reforming the University of Wittenberg to become a centre of evangelical education and scholarship. Luther was also putting together his ideas on church and state, and he made the second as well as the first an institution of divine authority. What motivated him to do so was his deference to Scripture and the call of the apostles to the church to be subject to the civil power, for it is ordained of God to govern the world (Romans 13:1–7; 1 Peter 2:13–17). On a personal level Luther had no love and precious little respect for most of Christendom's princes. Affairs of state, he noted, 'are usually administered by those least capable of the task'. Civil government among the heathen was just as good as and probably better than in much of Western Christendom, which, in Luther's opinion, was singularly unlucky with its rulers: 'very few princes are not fools or scoundrels', and a prince is 'a rare prize in heaven'. However, the world is an evil place and deserves its bad princes. 'Frogs must have their storks' (this from the Aesop fable, where the greedy frogs demand a king, and for their troubles they get a stork which eats them all up).[7]

Luther knew where the hearts of far too many princes lay:

> If they would so manage that their dancing, hunting and racing were done without injury to their subjects, and if they would otherwise conduct their office in love towards them, God would not be so harsh as to begrudge them their dancing and hunting and racing. But they would soon find out for themselves, if they gave their subjects the care and attention required by their office, that many a fine dance, hunt, race and game would have to be missed.[8]

But despite his generally poor view of Christendom's political leaders, Luther could not ignore the commands in the New Testament to honour the civil power. So he accepted the legitimacy of princes, their right to rule, their usefulness in keeping civil peace and restraining evil. Rulers were entitled to obedience from all their subjects, including the clergy, in civil affairs. The authority of the princes, however, did not allow them to bind consciences or determine articles of faith; so when German princes like Duke George tried to suppress Luther's New Testament, their mandates were invalid and may be ignored. Luther never required unconditional obedience to princes. At Worms he had effectively been ordered to recant in the presence of the emperor, but he did not do so. In matters of faith and conscience, 'God must be obeyed rather than men' (Acts 4:19; 5:29). So the Christian may refuse to obey a command from a ruler to take part in idolatrous worship, and if the consequences are imprisonment or worse, they must be patiently endured. On no account, however, no matter what the circumstances, should the Christian resort to insurrection.

Luther accepted the right of a Protestant nation to defend itself if it came under attack from a Catholic power, but he would not support an attack in the other direction in the cause of religion. Luther would, and frequently did, fight fiercely with his pen, but he would not use the sword in the cause of the Gospel. He did not object on principle to a Christian joining the army and serving his prince as a soldier in a just war, repelling an invader or maintaining civil peace at home; but he should never contaminate the name of Christ by stirring up or joining rebellion. All this is far more than a concern for law and order, though that is involved. This is *sola fides* – faith alone – applied to the political sphere. It is a trust in God, who, perhaps despite appearances, is neither idle nor indifferent to human affairs. God has promised to hear the cry of the afflicted – 'Vengeance is mine, I will recompense' (Romans 12:19) – and He should be trusted to deal with tyrants in His own way. The private citizen, especially if he is a Christian, has no right to do God's avenging work for him. Rebellion will always cause massive harm and do no good.

Luther was not the first man in Western Christendom to mull over the meaning of Romans 13, but few doctors of the church before him had so strongly emphasised the civil power as a divine ordinance. Luther was rebutting papal claims to temporal sovereignty, and also developing his so-called 'two kingdoms' theme – the spiritual and secular, both divinely ordained. The first, covering matters of faith and conscience, was largely the responsibility of the church, while the second was instituted to deal with civil affairs. Because the civil power was ordained of God, as Paul says, it could not be intrinsically evil, so Luther had no objection to a Christian becoming a civil officer, magistrate or a prince. This meant that a Christian could straddle both kingdoms, but this was not a crude attempt to get the best of both worlds; Luther's wish was that princes would not oppress their subjects for the sake of conscience, while the evangelical church would accept the authority of princes in civil affairs, and not interfere with it as the popes and bishops had done. Church and state could then coexist reasonably harmoniously and with mutual respect, each in its own sphere free from uncalled-for intrusion by the other.

The much talked-about 'two kingdoms' idea has often been critiqued for being a little too theoretical and impracticable for the sixteenth century, when most princes coveted some degree of control over the church. Imagine, for example, suggesting to King Henry VIII that affairs of the church were none of his business. Others have also noted that in later Lutheran church settlements the prince was frequently the head, nominally at least, of the state or territorial church. Complications could also arise if someone prominent in the church was appointed to a leading role in the civil arena. Whatever its anomalies, however, the 'two kingdoms' was a genuine attempt to define the roles of church and state clearly. It also excluded any idea of a rule of the godly or the 'elect' on earth, or a millennial golden age. Luther did not expect the two kingdoms one day to merge into one. From now until the end of time, the church must take the civil power as she finds it: sometimes it would be favourable to evangelical religion, sometimes not. The church will have to suffer patiently where necessary; but she should not clash with, rise in rebellion against, or seek to dominate the state.

The Lutheran Reformation was a spiritual event. Luther's mission, as he saw it, was to restore and proclaim the Gospel that the medieval church had lost; he was not a political or social reformer. As he said: 'It is not in my power to fashion the hearts of men … I can go no further than the ears; their hearts I cannot reach … We should preach the Word, but leave the results to God's good pleasure.'[9] Luther hoped, of course, that the Gospel would produce fruit before long: a more virtuous society, greater charity and love to neighbour, less greed in commerce, better conditions for the poor, and so on. As a general rule, however, he was content to concentrate on the spiritual message of salvation and faith in Christ, and let it bear its own fruit in its own way in its own time.

For agitators and radicals of all kinds, whether political or religious, Luther had neither time nor patience, only exasperation and contempt. His innate conservatism made sure that there was no root-and-branch reform to the liturgy or the structure of the church. A visitor to Wittenberg in 1522 who went to Sunday services might have been forgiven for thinking that not a lot had happened recently. Many saints' days and feast days, though admittedly not all, were kept. Images, crucifixes and candles still adorned the interior of the church; priests dressed for the most part as priests had always dressed; and although a discerning listener would notice a few small changes, much of the liturgy was unaltered. No major difference would be apparent until the sermon began: and then a new Gospel would be heard, a new way of salvation, a gift of God to be received by faith in Christ the Mediator and Redeemer; while pilgrimages, monasticism, praying to saints, vows of celibacy, and all talk of earning or meriting grace would be roundly condemned. If our imaginary visitor had made Wittenberg his home, over the next few months and years he would have seen more reforms to the external worship and life of the church: the laity receiving bread and wine rather than bread only at communion; a new liturgical order of service for the Mass; priests marrying and raising families; congregational singing accompanying the traditional liturgy; and the use of the German language in services without the traditional Latin being completely abolished. But these changes were brought in gradually, after explanation and persuasion in sermons, so as not to alarm the good citizens unnecessarily.[10]

The Reformation of the church under Luther may be likened to a house undergoing a change of ownership. The papacy, the cardinals and the medieval scholastic theologians were turned out of doors; the apostles were put in the best rooms, and their writings made the title deeds; while the church fathers, at least up to the time of St Augustine, were accepted as honoured guests. But much of the furnishing was retained. The beauty of holiness – church artwork, images, sacred music and liturgy – Luther preserved, with certain modifications. He even sought to improve on it. A deep lover of music, who wrote some of the first evangelical hymns and melodies, it irked him to think that the pope might have all the best tunes; so he worked closely with two musicians of the Elector's chapel, Conrad Ruppsch and Johann Walther, to see 'all the arts, especially music, used in the service of Him who gave and made them'.[11] So the house was left substantially intact. Then along came a man who wanted to raze the entire building to the ground.

THE REFORMER AND THE REVOLUTIONARY

One of Luther's fiercest early non-Romanist opponents was Thomas Müntzer. At first he appeared to be on Luther's side, because he supported

Luther during the Leipzig dispute with the Roman theologian John Eck in June and July 1519. The main subject debated at Leipzig, however, was not the doctrine of justification by faith or the righteousness of Christ, but the more political issue of papal supremacy in the church. This, Luther had argued, had no Scriptural foundation, though at this stage he might have been prepared to accept the pope as chief pastor of the Western church, provided the pope allowed the Gospel to be freely proclaimed. Müntzer was impressed with the force of Luther's arguments, but there is little evidence that he was ever equally drawn to Luther's revised beliefs on justification. Luther himself would later say, from his limited contacts with him, that although Müntzer and his ilk may have taken the name of Christ, they actually denied Him as the Mediator. In Luther's view this would make Müntzer not just a bad Christian, but downright *un*christian.[12]

A distinctive feature of Müntzer was his forthright, unapologetic claim to be 'filled with the Spirit', a conviction his biographer has dated to sometime between May 1519 and July the following year. Müntzer had immersed himself in German mysticism, particularly the works of the medieval writer John Tauler, and the theology of baptism of the Spirit. This was something distinct from normal Christian baptism, and also from conversion. At the risk of over-simplifying an intricate subject, it might be described as a spiritual transformation, frequently accompanied by a vision or some ecstatic encounter, which lifted the 'spirit-filled' person to a higher level of holiness, joy and zeal than ordinary believers reached. Luther had also read Tauler in his early days, but he had moved on since then, and he never claimed to be 'spirit-filled' in this sense.[13]

The Leipzig debate had also renewed Müntzer's interest in church history. He was fascinated by the ideal of an early pristine, apostolic church, in which visions, prophecies and revelations were presumed to be normal. But according to Müntzer, the church 'remained a virgin only until the time of the death of the disciples of the apostles; after that she became an adulteress'. Müntzer believed the moment had now arrived to restore the church to her past spotlessness, and remove the corrupt tares from the pure wheat. He had been reading the parable in St Matthew's Gospel, and like many of his time he was convinced that the end times were close at hand (Matthew 13:24–29, 36–43). He seems, however, to have overlooked the fact that in the parable the task of uprooting the tares is assigned to the angels (the harvestmen), not to the church (the servants). Nevertheless, based on Tauler's mysticism, on an idyllic depiction of early church life, and the pressing need to purge the tares out of the kingdom of God, Müntzer's radical spiritual renovation was complete.[14]

Müntzer, therefore, was a man of a different spirit from Luther. Luther's conversion and his Reformation breakthrough was the outcome of intensive soul exercises and Bible study. Müntzer did not, of course, deny the value of the Bible, but in his *Prague Protest* of 1521 he attacked priests of the Roman Church, and implicitly Luther as well, for their reliance on Scripture alone. 'All true parsons must have revelations', said Müntzer, which 'these damned parsons [the priests] falsely deny'. He also condemned the clergy's exploita- tion of the poor, but soon he was back to his favourite theme: 'The office of the true shepherd is simply that the sheep should all be led to revelations and revived by the living voice of God.' Müntzer decried the idea of faith received solely from the written Word – 'what kind of assurance of faith is this which comes from books?' Such notions are 'more insane than insanity itself'.[15]

Müntzer was drifting further and further away from Luther. He reproached Luther and his friends for their 'ignorance of the living Word'; they should strive instead for 'gifts of prophecy'. Müntzer also condemned priestly mar- riage, now allowed in Wittenberg, and he accused the Lutherans of exalting marriage above true sanctification, and of making marriage 'Satan's brothel'. Sexual relations, he said, even between lawfully married couples, hamper true holiness; the soul needs to be free from such 'lower passions'. It is not clear why Müntzer was getting so pent up about marriage, especially as Luther was still single and still expecting to remain that way. Whatever his reasons were, as Müntzer's biographer has noted, these are not the words of a former disciple of Luther now growing to maturity and finding his own spiritual feet. This was a man who may have once moved within Lutheran circles, but did so only fleetingly, and without ever making his home there.[16]

Müntzer led an itinerant life in 1522, wandering from Erfurt to Nordhausen, then to Halle, before settling at Allstedt in spring 1523. There his controver- sial preaching drew large crowds, many crossing the border from nearby Catholic territories. When Ernest Count of Mansfeld forbad his subjects from attending Müntzer's fiery sermons, Müntzer wrote to the count calling him a 'heretical knave and extortionist' for having forbidden the 'Holy Gospel'. If the count did not repent, Müntzer would 'write books against you and have them translated into many tongues, calling you a miserable and stupid man to the Turks, Heathen and Jews'. Müntzer was not afraid of rulers and princes: he warned them that 'I shall deal with you a hundred times more severely than Luther dealt with the pope'. The letter is signed ominously: 'Thomas Müntzer, a destroyer of unbelievers.'[17]

But Count Mansfeld, like Duke George of Saxony, who had likewise for- bidden his subjects in Sangerhausen from listening to Müntzer, remained firmly attached to the medieval faith and opposed to the Reformation.[18] Crucial for Müntzer would be the attitude of the Dukes of Electoral Saxony who were supporting Luther. An opportunity came when Frederick the Wise and his brother John decided they would hear Müntzer speak for him- self at Allstedt castle. What they heard, in July 1524, was nothing less than a call to war.

Müntzer began in typical vein with another attack on Luther – 'Brother Fattened-swine and Brother Soft-life' – for rejecting visions and relying on the written Word alone. Müntzer saw ahead the transformation of the world, and the establishment on earth of a society where the elect are chosen to rule. 'It is true – and I know it to be true – that the Spirit of God now reveals to many elected pious people that a momentous, invincible, future reformation is very necessary and must be brought about.' He now turned to the book of Daniel, chapter 2, and the vision of the giant statute signifying the coming kingdoms of the world from Babylon to Persia, Greece, Rome and finally, according to Müntzer, the Holy Roman Empire of the sixteenth century. The smiting of the statute with a stone was a call to destroy the false kingdom of the world. So Müntzer urged Frederick and John to draw the sword. 'A new Daniel must arise … and go forth, as Moses teaches, at the head of his troops' (Deuteronomy 20:2). Müntzer may have had himself in mind at this point, though the dukes, both intelligent men, may have recalled that the Old Testament Daniel did *not* go forth in battle. Undaunted by embarrassing historical minutiae, however, Müntzer urged them to 'begin government at the roots … to drive Christ's enemies away from the elect, for that is your appointed task'. He despised the 'stale posturing about how the power of God should do it without your application of the sword … I, together with pious Daniel, bid the princes not to oppose the revelation of God'; otherwise, 'may they be strangled without mercy'. Müntzer called for holy war and the slaying of the 'godless rulers, especially the priests and monks'; the godless 'have no right to life except that which the elect decide to grant them'.[19]

Duke John then asked Müntzer whether he would debate theology with Luther. This invitation was declined. Luther was not sorry; by now he was convinced Müntzer was deranged. 'I cannot stand this spirit', he exclaimed; Müntzer must be either 'drunk or mad'.[20]

But Luther felt obliged to reply to Müntzer's address, and he did so in a letter to the Saxon princes at the end of July. Luther had no doubt that something sinister was afoot. 'After wandering around in waterless places, seeking rest but finding none, Satan had made himself a little nest at Allstedt' (Matthew 12:43). Luther scorned Müntzer's talk about the need for suffering to arrive at a purer life: for no-one 'has so much as touched him either with pen, mouth or fist'. His 'boasting about the Spirit meant nothing, for we have the word of John the apostle to test the spirits' (1 John 4:1). If Müntzer was 'filled with the Spirit', where were the fruits of the Spirit; where is the love, peace, patience, gentleness (Galatians 5:22) in destroying churches and smashing images, 'which the worst rascals on earth can do'. Luther urged the princes to act decisively with Müntzer if he carried on preaching violence.[21]

Luther and Müntzer are examples of two men each using the same simple little word 'faith', yet meaning entirely different things by it. Luther's faith was derided by Müntzer: 'It falls far short of the mark if one preaches that faith must justify us and not works.' A true Christian must suffer and be transformed, 'and thus he finally receives edification, even to the extent of the full return of the Spirit'. People like Luther 'have only poisoned the world more with their fictitious faith than the others [Catholics] had already done with their foolish works'. Müntzer praised those who are 'filled with an ardent and right serious zeal to uproot false Christians, to break, to scatter and destroy all their wicked faith'.[22] Müntzer was now admitting that no common ground existed between him and Luther.[23]

'The Christian faith is a certainty, based on Christ's Word and promise. If anyone is to hear this Word with a true and unfeigned heart, his ear must be cleansed of the clay of cares and lusts.' So spake Thomas Müntzer.[24] His first sentence is, on the face of it, pure Lutheran; but the second is decidedly anti-Luther. For Luther, a true and unfeigned heart can only be a *result* of saving faith, usually a long-term result. Müntzer had rejected Luther's faith *alone*, and was introducing preconditions for faith. In a strange way, he was more medieval than Lutheran in religion.

Besides a theological definition of faith, here was also a clash between the spiritual reformer, albeit a vigorous one, and the revolutionary. The mystical and apocalyptical Müntzer had, to quote Brecht, a 'mission of fighting all ungodliness and bringing judgement upon it'. Contrast Luther during his Invocavit sermons: 'I opposed indulgences and all the papists, but never with force; I simply taught and preached and wrote … then slept and drank beer with my friends Philip and Amsdorf.' For Luther, it was the Word of God that 'broke the papacy more than any king or emperor ever did'. Luther fought with his pen; Müntzer would use the sword as well.[25]

In July 1524 Müntzer was rousing his followers to cast aside all fear of godless rulers, for God 'intends to tear them up by their roots'; the time had come to purify themselves, to forsake material things, and a 'bloodbath' is about to come. Slowly and reluctantly the Lutheran princes were coming round to the view that armed force might be the only way to restrain Müntzer. Righteous teaching, reflected Frederick the Wise, will not threaten revolt or bloodbath; rather it would give 'honour and praise to God's Word and His Spirit'. In August orders were sent to the civil authorities in Allstedt banning Müntzer from seditious preaching. To his horror Müntzer heard that his printing press was to be closed. He was not formally arraigned, but life was becoming difficult for him, and on 7 or 8 August 1524 he left Allstedt furtively by night.[26]

Müntzer then made his way to Mühlhausen, an interesting choice. The city was in some turmoil due to the activity of a renegade monk called Heinrich Pfeiffer, who had quit his monastery and was preaching against priests, monks and nuns. Radical preaching was accompanied by the smashing of church images and altars. An attempt was made to set up an 'eternal covenant or league', effectively a rule of warrior saints like Müntzer and Pfeiffer in place of the existing council. Ten members of the council, as well as two mayors, were forced to flee. Müntzer failed, however, to win sufficient support among the populace, and once again he was forced to move on elsewhere.[27]

He arrived in Nuremburg in December. It had not soothed his restless spirit to learn that Luther's more light-hearted supporters had been mocking him, greeting each other jokingly with quips like: 'Has God spoken to you lately?', or 'Do you have the Holy Spirit?' Perhaps provoked by this, Müntzer took up his pen once more to reply to Luther's letter to the princes of Saxony. Luther was Dr Liar (*Dr Lügner*), for using Scripture 'in a most deceptive way', and Dr Mockery (*Dr Ludibrii*), a man with a 'contrived faith', and a 'cunning Scriptural thief'. Luther and his friends can do nothing except babble 'Believe! Believe!' Then they live in comfort and luxury. Müntzer was striving 'for the clear purity of the divine law', while the godless Luther 'perverted' it. (This is an attack on Luther's emphasis on justification by faith without the works of the law – Romans 3:28.) Luther, now 'Father Pussyfoot', fawns and flatters the 'godless rogues' (the princes), and tries to 'conceal himself beneath a false kindness of Christ'. All the while the 'pope of Wittenberg' enjoys life 'with his good Malvasian wine and his whores' banquets'. This 'blasphemous monk' tries to be a 'new Christ', and he has 'confused Christendom with a false faith'. And Luther 'did this for the sake of a fine thing – that priests might take wives'. Müntzer, revolutionary though he was, had all the antipathy of the papal clergy towards the marriage of priests; such carnal, earthly entanglements, in his opinion, were unworthy of a man of God.[28]

Shortly after this latest broadside against Luther, Müntzer and Pfeiffer returned to Mühlhausen, where activists had not given up trying to impose their form of godly rule on the people. Possessions of monks and nuns were confiscated, and Müntzer sought for himself a place on the council. He also carried on preaching, with the new demand that the people should give up their jewellery, their belongings and even their cash, else the Spirit of God 'would not dwell in them'.[29]

Authorities in church and state were becoming ever more alarmed, because Müntzer's radicalism was not confined to colleges, universities and lecture halls. Since the fourteenth century, Germany and central Europe had experienced sporadic disturbances among the peasant peoples. The Peasants' War of 1524–25 had begun in the Black Forest due to a complicated mix of causes. Poverty was one, though conditions varied from region to region; serfdom was a burning issue in Upper Swabia, though not in the Tyrol. Grievances were not just economic; they also included social, political and legal matters relating to community self-government, election of local civil officials and the independence of courts. Troubles quickly spread through much of Germany and Austria, though until March 1525 it was more a mass protest movement than a determined rebellion, with demands for social and economic reform rather than a call to arms. Even the word 'peasant' is a little misleading because some 'peasant' leaders were noblemen, craftsmen, clergy or civil officials.[30]

The Twelve Articles of the Upper Swabian peasants issued in March 1525, besides setting out some basic demands, were designed to enlist the support of the Wittenberg divines. They professed a loyalty to the Gospel and rejected violent rebellion. They opened with a demand that congregations be allowed to choose their own pastors. The peasants promised to pay the tithe, provided it was 'distributed to the people and paid to a pastor who clearly proclaims the Word of God'; anything left over should go to the poor. Remaining articles dealt mainly with social reforms – an end to serfdom, permission for the poor to hunt game and have access to woodland, relief from servile labour and punitive taxes, reform of corrupt laws and legal practice. The articles ended with a promise to withdraw any article not in accordance with the Gospel. Taken as a whole the articles seem an illustration of utter reasonableness, and they may have reflected a desire or expectation, following the Reformation, to see the establishment of a Christian commonwealth, more conformable to the spirit of the New Testament than hitherto. Next month, however, the peasants' moderate image was somewhat tarnished. When Count Ludwig von Helfenstein failed to put an end to unrest in Weinsberg, peasants who had supported the Twelve Articles carried out an act of exemplary popular justice by 'executing' the count and other nobles.[31]

Nevertheless, Luther was heartened when news reached him of peasants in Upper Swabia disbanding, accepting arbitration and agreeing to accept the authority of their lords pending discussions, while the lords in return renounced threats of penalties. Müntzer, however, was now urging the citizens of Mühlhausen to arm themselves in readiness for an attack from hostile princes, led by Duke George. In league with his friend Pfeiffer, Müntzer tried to gain control of the city council in Mühlhausen. As a result of their efforts, an ambitiously named 'Eternal Council' was elected. Duke George and Philip of Hesse, fearful of mounting unrest, decided that the state of affairs in Mühlhausen called for punitive action. Frederick the Wise, as usual more moderate, urged an end to the plundering of monasteries, and suggested the restoration of the former council and the banishment of Müntzer. Undeterred, Müntzer sought to rally support from neighbouring territories. His open letter to Allstedt, dated 26 April 1525, roused the godly in ever more militarily ecstatic tones: 'The whole of Germany, France, Italy is awake.' Three of the godly 'need have no fear of a hundred thousand … So go to it, go to it, go to it! … Pay no attention to the cries of the godless … show no pity … the time has come'. It bore a by now familiar signature: 'Thomas Müntzer, a servant of God against the godless.' That same day news reached him of an uprising in nearby Langensalza, and immediately he offered his support. This was declined, but the Salza rising was yet another ugly example of a seemingly unstoppable rush into conflict.[32]

In Wittenberg Luther had now heard about the Twelve Articles. He was not opposed to them in principle, but because of the growing unrest he was not entirely convinced by the evangelical protestations of the peasants either. Nevertheless, he decided to take the peasants' willingness to be guided and if need be corrected by Scripture at face value, hoping that things might yet turn out for the good. Luther's *Admonition to Peace* was printed on 6 May.

Despite misgivings regarding the peasants' good faith, Luther began with a scorching attack on Germany's rulers. 'We have no one on earth to thank for this disastrous rebellion except you princes and lords, and especially you blind bishops and mad priests and monks'. The princes were doubly guilty because besides resisting the Gospel they had callously exploited the poor. 'You do nothing but cheat and rob the people so that you may lead a life of luxury … The poor people cannot bear it any longer.' He rejected claims made by Romanist opponents that he and his preaching were to blame for all the trouble – 'I have striven against rebellion, and have energetically encouraged and exhorted people to obey and respect even you wild and dictatorial tyrants'. Therefore, blame the 'murder prophets' (he meant Müntzer and others), who 'have gone about among the people for more than three years, and no one has resisted and fought against them except me'. Luther urged the princes to be reasonable and not to use force: 'Do not start a fight … for you do not know how it will end … try kindness first'; otherwise you will risk kindling 'a fire which no one can put out'.

Luther then turned to the peasants, and although he had sympathy with many of their grievances, he warned them that 'all who take the sword will perish by the sword'. No one 'by his own violence shall arrogate authority to himself'; rather he should respect the authorities, as Paul commands (Matthew 26:52; Romans 13:1). The peasants cannot ignite an uprising and call themselves a 'Christian association', because a Christian can never be a rebel. Even bad rulers did not justify a bloody rebellion; better to suffer wrongs with patience, as Scripture commands (Matthew 5:39–41, 44; Romans 12:19). If the peasants were unwilling to keep these commands of Jesus and the Apostles, they should strike the word 'Christian' out of their title. Luther used his own experiences as an example of how to resist the mighty ones of the world: 'Pope and emperor have opposed and raged against me … but I have never drawn a sword or desired revenge'; yet God has 'preserved my life … and made my Gospel grow and spread'. Many rulers were indeed guilty of injustice, but Luther still clung to the hope that bloodshed might be prevented, else 'God will, as usual in these affairs, use one rascal to punish another'. If the peasants refused to listen to him, 'I shall pray for you, that God may enlighten you, and resist your undertaking'. Luther then turned once more to the princes, warning them that unjust rulers will not escape divine judgement for ever, for 'God hates both tyrants and rebels'. Critical and suspicious of both sides, Luther urged peace talks. The adversaries should draw back from the brink, else 'Germany will be laid waste'. And 'what have all these innocent women, children and old people, whom you fools are drawing with you into such danger, ever done to you? Why must you fill the land with blood and robbery, widows and orphans? … Beware, dear sirs, and be wise … You still have time to find a better way, by repenting before God, by reaching a friendly agreement, or even by voluntarily suffering for the sake of humanity'. If the protagonists paid no heed, 'I must let you come to blows; but I am innocent of your souls, your blood or your property'.[33]

But the chance for peace had now passed, and violence was escalating alarmingly. Castles, churches and convents were sacked, while Erfurt and Salzungen capitulated to the peasant forces. A serious illness to Frederick the Wise briefly threatened a political void in Saxony. Luther and Melanchthon then paid a visit to Eisleben in Thuringia, one of the worst affected areas, to set up a new school there; and they had ample opportunity to see and hear about the worsening situation for themselves. Luther's detachedness, and his heavily qualified support for the peasants' demands, had not been well received, and he suffered the unusual indignity of being interrupted by hecklers when he preached at Nordhausen. In Mühlhausen and the surrounding areas Müntzer's militia were on the rampage, plundering monasteries, castles and property and then carting the spoils back to their base camp.[34]

Luther's attitude was now hardening. Sometime between 6 and 10 May he wrote one of his most controversial tracts *Against the Robbing and Murdering Hordes of Peasants*. He did not renounce his *Admonition*, but he recognised how dangerously the situation had deteriorated. The peasants had broken their pledge to remain peaceful, and 'are robbing and raging like mad dogs'. Their Twelve Articles were 'nothing but lies presented under the name of the Gospel'. Luther blamed Müntzer, that 'archdevil ruling at Mühlhausen' for fanning the flames. Rebellion 'is not just simple murder; it is like a great fire which attacks and devastates the entire land', filling it with 'murder and bloodshed; it makes widows and orphans, and turns everything upside down like the worst disaster'. The contagion of revolt had to be destroyed. The following quoted words, frequently distorted, need to be taken in this context. Luther was mustering all good citizens to arms in *support* of the authorities in the face of rebellion; this is not a call for vigilante gangs to attack the innocent, or for anyone to exact private vengeance. 'Let everyone who can smite, slay and stab, secretly or openly … nothing can be more poisonous, hurtful or devilish than a rebel'. He must be killed like a 'mad dog … if you do not strike him, he will strike you and the whole land with you'. Most awful of all, these rebels 'cloak this terrible and horrible sin with the Gospel, call themselves Christian brethren … they become the worst blasphemers of God … under the outward appearance of the Gospel they honour and serve the devil'. Luther slammed the claims of some peasants' groups to common ownership of property and goods – 'They want to make the goods of other men common and keep their own for themselves. Fine Christians they are!' Yet even now Luther urged princes who were Christian to try one last time and 'offer the mad peasants an opportunity to come to terms'. Should that fail, let the prince 'swiftly take to the sword'. There should be no more parleying. 'This is the time of the sword, not the day of grace.'[35]

On 14 May the armies of Duke George, Philip of Hesse and the Duke of Braunschweig – 2,500 cavalry and 4,000 infantry – massed outside Frankenhausen, now defended by peasant armies. The princes called for Müntzer to be handed over, and for the peasants to surrender. Both demands were refused. The peasants, full of zeal but no match for superior government forces, were destroyed in a victory overwhelming for the princes, and decisive in the Peasants' War. The carnage of battle over, Müntzer was found hiding in an attic, and interrogated under torture by George and Philip. According to reports circulating shortly afterwards, Müntzer made a full confession, but this is far from certain; surviving statements of his suggest that he tried to justify himself. The 'spirit-filled', apocalyptic preacher was now a condemned man, executed at the end of May.[36]

Luther had no illusions about the nature of the conflict, nor regrets about the outcome. 'I killed Müntzer', he said. It was almost a boast, without a morsel of contrition. 'His death is on my shoulders [*Der tode ligt auff meim hals* – literally 'on my neck']. But I did it because he wanted to kill my Christ.'[37]

In some of our history books it is claimed that the peasant fighters were supporters of the Reformation, though why, in that case, they went on the rampage when Luther told them to settle down and be quiet is left unexplained. Many peasants, however, did come from areas that were at least nominally Lutheran. Maybe they did not fully understand Luther, maybe they cherry-picked some of his ideas and discarded others less convenient, or maybe they had become disenchanted with him, feeling he had let them down; the evidence does not allow us to apportion reasons precisely. But burdened with poverty and social injustice, the peasants knew that a reformation of the church was under way, and they apparently expected it to permeate into society as a whole, with economic, social and political reforms following on in train. When high expectations were disappointed, disillusionment set in and a spirit of violence was aroused. Radical apocalyptic preaching did the rest.

Luther's attitude throughout the troubles has caused controversy over the years. It saddened even some of his friends. One of these was John Rühl, the Mansfeld councillor, who warned him of the widespread feeling that he had connived at the slaying of the peasants. The princes were exacting a savage revenge on the defeated captives, and the unhappy Mayor of Zwickau noted

that 'Doctor Martin has fallen into great disfavour with the common people'.
The mayor commended Luther's *Admonition*, and he condemned Müntzer,
who had 'so pitiably misled the poor folk'. But he feared that Luther had
earned himself the reputation of the 'hammer of the poor' by calling for the
'private and public murder' of the peasants. 'Is the devil, and those who do
this, to be our Lord God?' There was no need, the mayor went on, for Luther's
'hasty tract … there was enough murdering of peasants already'. The mayor
agreed that, as a matter of principle, 'rebellion should be put down'; but Luther
had 'conceded too much to one side'. If only the princes had 'followed Martin's
advice [in the *Admonition*] and allowed some commissioners … to negotiate'.
The mayor's conclusion: 'Martin has not done well … he has written the truth
in condemning rebellion, but the poor have been greatly forgotten.'[38]

A biographer of Philip Melanchthon has agreed in substance with the
mayor. Dr James William Richard wished that princes and peasants alike had
heeded Luther's appeals before the troubles began; but although Luther's
concern that the Gospel should never be mixed with violence was entirely
genuine, Richard was disturbed by the call to 'smite, slay and stab'. He regretted, moreover, the undue weight given to Romans 13, as if the Bible had
nothing to say on the subject of civil government apart from the duty of the
subject to do as he is told. Another balanced judgement is that of Luther's
own biographer, who notes the lack of any real sympathy for the peasants and
the hardships they had to endure.[39]

Predictably, others took a different, less sympathetic line. Catholic opponents continued to blame Luther for all the ills of the world including the
violence, while the peasants accused him of betrayal, and their sympathisers
attacked him for excessive harshness. Through it all Luther remained unfazed.
When friends urged him to retract his words he refused, because 'a rebel is
not worth rational argument … you have to answer people like that with a
fist'. He scorned those who tried to lecture him about showing mercy, when
I 'have taught and written more about mercy than any other man in a thousand years'. God's mercy is indeed offered freely – to the weak, the penitent
and the humble; but violent and hardened men must face His wrath. A ruler
who strikes down men of blood, said Luther, commits an act of mercy, because
he protects good people seeking to live in peace. Luther shrugged off accusations that he was toadying to the princes – he had warned the princes against
exploiting the poor, and he would continue to do so. His only concession was
to stress that his book *Against the Robbing and Murdering Hordes of Peasants* was
directed specifically against those who had been actively taking part in violent
rebellion, and he condemned the wanton cruelty shown by some 'furious,
raving, senseless tyrants' against prisoners and others not directly involved.[40]

Martin Luther was a Professor of Theology, not Political Science. Perhaps he
was just not cynical enough, or calculating enough, to realise that most princes

would simply ignore his calls to look to the genuine needs of the poor, and then take him enthusiastically at his word when it came to rigorously suppressing disturbances. For Luther, the Peasants' War had been an unhappy and unwanted brush with German politics, and for much of the rest of his life his relations with the peasants were unsurprisingly strained. But of his unconditional opposition to insurrection, and of his words and writings during the conflict, he had no regrets.

ZWINGLI

Huldrych Zwingli was born in Wilderhaus, Switzerland in January 1484. Switzerland was then part of the Holy Roman Empire, though the imperial writ ran there only nominally. Zwingli was a gifted child with a good singing voice and an ear for music, a lover of nature and the countryside. At the universities of Vienna and Basle he studied the medieval theologians, the humanities and the classics, and he was parish priest at Glarus from 1506–16. Influenced by humanist luminaries like Erasmus and Reuchlin, he developed a love of the literature of ancient Greece and Rome, which stimulated in him a desire to learn Greek and Hebrew.

At this time Switzerland was an emerging European power. Many Swiss men fought as mercenaries in Europe's never-ending dynastic wars, some in the armies of Pope Julius II, and Zwingli acted as chaplain or 'field-preacher'. This experience made him think deeply about politics and international affairs. His growing conviction that mercenary service was immoral and unchristian was brutally reinforced at the battle of Marignano in September 1515, when the Swiss suffered a crushing defeat at the hands of the French. A Swiss patriot, Zwingli shared the sense of shock and humiliation felt by his countrymen; he also longed for Swiss unity.

More and more of his time he devoted to Bible study, now in the original Greek, using the new translation produced by Erasmus. Zwingli's reputation grew as a humanist, a preacher and a fine scholar with a keen insight into political and diplomatic affairs. Slowly but inexorably, Zwingli was losing his trust of the papacy and the medieval church, yearning instead for a return to the pure apostolic faith. He spent two years in Einsiedeln, where miraculous healing powers were ascribed to the 'black virgin'. Increasingly he distrusted medieval schoolmen and conventional piety. He was no plastic saint, however, and he freely and penitently confessed that he had yielded to the temptations of a harlot. It is a comment on the times that his fling was quickly forgiven and forgotten, and Zwingli was appointed foundation preacher at Zürich, beginning his ministry there on 1 January 1519.[41]

As well as opposing mercenarism, Zwingli was appalled by wars in Christendom. Much of this he blamed on the popes for inciting Europe's princes against one another. Only grace, he feared, could turn away the righteous wrath of God that would otherwise be poured out on the sinful people. While preaching in Zürich, he preferred to take themes from the Bible rather than stories of saints, the seven deadly sins or canon law. Soon Zürich closed its gates to the indulgence preachers, and Zwingli began putting church dogmas to the test of Scripture. Zwingli welcomed Luther's writings, now circulating freely in Zürich, and gradually Zwingli gained the confidence of the civil authorities. Luther, however, was not the only one to influence Zwingli in a Protestant direction, and maybe not even the chief influence; Erasmus had played a key part and so had the church fathers, particularly Augustine. Above all, it was many years of intensive study of the Bible that produced a fully evangelical Zwingli by 1522, three years after Luther's Reformation discovery. So far as is known, there is no direct equivalent of a dramatic 'Tower experience' in Zwingli's spiritual journey.[42]

It was during Lent 1522 that a sausage – surely the most notorious sausage in the history of the church – was reportedly eaten in defiance of the fasting conventions. Zwingli did not partake of the forbidden food himself, though he supported those who did. By now he was opposing compulsory clerical celibacy, and early that same year he secretly married Anna Reinhart, widow of Hans Meyer von Knonau. Outwardly Zürich was still Catholic, but support for Zwingli was growing. Soon pilgrimages, relics, the invocation of the saints and also images were renounced as Zwingli gradually persuaded the Zürich Council in favour of the Reformation. Altars were removed and monasteries closed with little opposition, and in 1525 Zürich abandoned the Roman Mass.[43]

Unlike Germany, the Swiss Reformation did not suffer greatly from social unrest, though when news of the German Peasants' War reached Zürich, the authorities were naturally concerned. Like all major Reformers, Zwingli preached the duty of obedience based on Romans 13:1, but he also urged the Zürich Council to treat the peasants humanely. The government promised to investigate the peasants' grievances, and it was this generally conciliatory attitude that did so much to prevent trouble. Zwingli championed social and economic justice as well as justification by faith. He praised farmers and all who worked for their living, and he condemned injustice to the poor. Politicians responsible for inflation, he recommended, deserved to be boiled in oil. (There is no evidence that this recommendation was ever taken on board by the Zürich legislature.) Despite his opposition to wars, however, he was not entirely averse to the use of military force if it would help to expand the Reformation, and he entertained ambitious plans to make Zürich the principal base of an evangelical Swiss confederation. He also founded a theological college known as the *Prophezi*, the main aim of which was to train men already learned in Hebrew, Latin and Greek for preaching and evangelising.[44]

Like Luther, Zwingli proceeded steadily, anxious not to upset the people with indecorously rapid changes to their long accepted religious way of life. Like Luther, he was taken to task by more enthusiastic colleagues for proceeding too slowly and with insufficient godly zeal. Again like Luther, Zwingli gave his people a Bible in their own tongue. The Zürich Bible of 1531, though it took advantage of Luther's translation, was no mere copy; it was the fruit of many years of Scripture study in the original languages carried out in Zürich. In addition to the basic text Zwingli wrote chapter summaries and compiled a huge concordance. Like Luther and Melanchthon in Wittenberg, Zwingli worked tirelessly to create a highly educated evangelical ministry, skilled in the Biblical languages and the liberal arts of rhetoric, dialectic and exegesis.[45]

Despite considerable common ground between Wittenberg and Zürich, it was not long before significant differences surfaced, not over the authority of Scripture, but the interpretation of it. One was the commandment from Exodus 20:4–5: 'Thou shalt not make unto thee any graven image or any likeness of anything … *Thou shalt not bow thyself down to them or serve them*' (italics mine). For Luther, this forbids making an image – implicitly the image of an idol or a false deity – with the specific purpose of rendering it the worship that is due to God alone. But it does not forbid images *per se*, especially as God elsewhere commanded Moses to make the cherubim and the serpent of brass (Exodus 25:18; Numbers 21:4–9). So, said Luther, images in churches were permissible and edifying, though in the era of Christian liberty not compulsory. Zwingli, however, read the text differently. Though opposed to mob iconoclasm and willing to be patient, in summer 1524 images and pictures were removed from Zürich churches as a matter of principle. Images were deemed to be a violation of the commandment; they invariably led to a false worship, and therefore had no place in a church. Besides, they taught nothing about Christ and faith. Zwingli had little time for the view, which Luther sometimes used, that an image of Christ or a Biblical event served as an aid to faith and devoutness, especially for poor people who could not read, impressing a Christian truth on the mind more lastingly than a sermon might be able to do. For Zwingli, right teaching comes from Scripture and preaching, not looking at pictures. Zwingli was no philistine – he loved art and music just as he devoured the classics – but he was decidedly uncomfortable about depicting the Deity in art, a scruple that never bothered Luther.[46]

Fortunately for the future of the arts in Protestant lands, Luther loved music deeply. It was the 'noblest of the arts … a gift of God next only to theology', with the power to 'give life to sacred texts and put evil spirits to flight'. But when Zwingli revised the Mass and the liturgy, he did not stop with the removal of images and the altar; he also excluded music. There were prayers, Bible readings and a sermon; the *Gloria* and Nicene Creed were recited, followed by the Lord's Prayer, then communion, a Psalm spoken and finally a blessing. But no singing. This did not become the norm in all Swiss Protestant churches – in Basle and St Gall they sang hymns and Psalms – but other states, like Berne, soon followed Zürich's example. As with images, Zwingli's dislike of the aesthetic in church cannot be ascribed to cultural philistinism. He was just as gifted musically as Luther, perhaps more so; he composed the stage music for a production of the *Plutus* of Aristophanes in 1531 in the original Greek. Yet there could be no place for music – Luther's 'handmaiden to theology' – in the Zürich churches. This ban lasted until 1598, when hymn singing was reintroduced mainly in response to the pleas of the congregation.[47]

It is just possible that Luther and Zwingli might have been able to agree to differ on images and singing in churches, but a more serious dispute soon emerged which did permanent damage to hopes of evangelical union. The Words of Institution in the Lord's Supper – 'This is my Body … This is my Blood' – were interpreted by Zwingli in the light of another text, John 6:63: 'The words I have spoken to you are spirit and life.' Therefore, and because Christ has ascended into heaven, there could be no real or substantial presence of Christ in the Eucharist. This, to Luther, reeked of dubious rationalising and philosophising, the sort of thing he despised. He took the Words of Institution on trust: the bread and the wine are truly and substantially the Body and Blood of Christ after consecration. There was no need to quibble over how this comes about; no one can explain the 'real presence' adequately; the point is that God is perfectly capable of doing what He promises (Romans 4:21). Regrettably for the Reformation, the Eucharistic controversy caused much bitterness and division, and was never resolved.[48] (Among English historians there is a tradition that this is largely Luther's fault for being too obstinate, which slightly overlooks the fact that when the two men met at Marburg, Zwingli dug his heels in just as much as Luther.)

Strange though it may be that such sharp differences could arise between two evangelical reformers, who had both devoted years of study to the same Scriptures and the same church fathers, there is nevertheless a degree of consistency in their differences. Unlike Luther, Zwingli took offence at the depiction of the Deity in an image, and of music in the service of God, and of the presence of Christ, except in a spiritual sense, in the bread and wine. Zwingli did not want the spiritual and material mixed together. Or rather, he did not like material things intruding into the spiritual. He was not the first in the history of Christendom to feel this way, nor the last. This spirit will be seen again in the England of Edward VI, and yet more strongly in the English Puritans.

Significantly for this story, Luther and Zwingli also disagreed on the subject of the relationship between church and state. In his formative years, Zwingli was more motivated than Luther by social justice and economic and political reform. Consequently, he was more receptive than Luther to a social aspect to the Gospel. Luther's background was almost exclusively theological – occupied with sin, penance, indulgences, grace and the righteousness of God. So it stayed for much of his life, despite the occasional tract on social or political subjects. But Zwingli was a politician as well as a pastor, with strong and clearly formed views on government and society. He distrusted monarchical rule on the grounds that the king invariably becomes corrupt or tyrannical; and on the rare occasion when a land is blessed with a good king, a bad one all too often succeeds him and undoes all his good work. Democracy too readily leads to confusion, even sedition. On balance Zwingli preferred an aristocracy, where a selection of the ablest minds in society are appointed to govern; though even this can quickly become corrupted if a selfish few rule in their own interests rather than for the common good. Progressively Zwingli developed his theocratic vision of society, with ruler and pastor working together in the kingdom of Christ, one by laws the other by preaching. This vision did not allow for a clear-cut distinction between church and state, like Luther's 'two kingdoms'. The pastor, in Zwingli's view, besides preaching grace and faith, should also attack greed, war, the mercenary system, and where necessary, monopolies and corporations believed to be harming the common good. A good pastor will criticise the prince not just for oppressing the Gospel, but also for oppressing the poor with unjust laws and taxes. Luther occasionally did this sort of thing, for example in his *Admonition* on the eve of the Peasants' War (see p. 25), and also when he suspected that suppliers, whether peasants or noblemen, were profiteering from shortages of food and driving up prices. Here he was using the pulpit to condemn iniquity in the land, but not seeking in any way to join the office of the ministry with that of the state. Luther's forays into politics were generally the exception rather than the norm.[49]

To buttress his vision of a truly Christian society, effectively an evangelical theocracy, Zwingli turned increasingly to the Old Testament and the examples there of the prophet and the king in the Israel of old. He held that 'in the *church* of Christ the office of the magistrate is as necessary as that of the prophet … the church cannot exist without the magistracy' (italics mine).[50] Making the magistrate an integral part of the church sets him apart from Luther, who preferred to see the church and state distinct. Unlike Zwingli, Luther did not expect to see an evangelical theocracy on earth.

The political element in Zwingli's personality then led him to mull over something unthinkable for Luther. With the vision of a united Protestant Switzerland in his sights, Zwingli resolved to spread the Word by all available means, including the sword. Sometime in 1527 he produced a detailed military plan to overcome resistance to the Reformation in neighbouring Swiss Catholic states. Zwingli did not believe in forced conversions, but open opposition to the Gospel seemed intolerable. By now Swiss Protestant cities, including Zürich, Berne and St Gall, had formed the Christian Civic Union, and Zwingli was closely involved in politics and negotiations for alliances. At the diet of Baden in 1528 he demanded that Catholic states should allow evangelical preaching. In response the Catholics sought Austrian support and formed the 'Christian Alliance'.[51]

Tensions between the two sides rose quickly. A flashpoint occurred in May 1529 when the evangelical pastor, Jakob Kaiser, took a wrong turning while on a journey and strayed unintentionally into Catholic territory, where he was arrested and executed. Even though Protestant Berne urged restraint, Zürich mobilised for war. Zwingli drew up plans for an attack, though he hoped that a convincing show of force might be enough to compel Catholic states at least to allow free evangelical preaching. Zürich's aggressive stance paid off: with no prospect of aid from Austria, the Swiss (Catholic) Christian Alliance made hasty peace overtures. Though there had been little real fighting, Zwingli's demands were almost those of a conqueror: the Bible should be preached in every Swiss state, the Austrian alliance must end, foreign pensions should be annulled, while compensation payments had to be made to Zürich to cover the costs of raising an army, and to provide for the surviving family of Jakob Kaiser. These terms were far more than the other side could accept, but to Zwingli's disappointment the Protestant alliance agreed on a compromise: though the Austrian alliance was ended, Swiss territories and parishes would decide their own form of worship, and compensation claims were submitted to arbitration. The treaty also included a rather hopeful call for an end to victimisation, slander and defamation, but it laid down no measures to enforce this effectively.

Before long each side was accusing the other of breaking its treaty obligations. Zwingli's life had now reached a crisis point. Angry at the denial of his demand that Catholics should be compelled to allow unfettered evangelical preaching, his thoughts turned once more to war. This time, unusually for him, he found himself opposed not only by Protestant Berne, but also by a significant faction in his native Zürich. Given the divisions in the Protestant ranks, a blockade of Catholic states was imposed as a kind of compromise. Zwingli did not like this either; far better, he thought, that men should fight on the battlefield than women and children starve through sanctions. His astute political antennae sensed that sanctions risked handing the initiative to the enemy, who would then be able to decide whether and when to fight. In this he was soon proved right. Fearing the possibility of starvation, the Catholic states launched a surprise attack. Zürich, hamstrung by internal divisions and low morale, proved to be fatally ill-prepared. At the battle of Kappel on 15 October 1531, Zwingli and his group fought bravely, but Zwingli was wounded, recognised by his foes and killed, his body then quartered and burned, mixed with dung. Before dying he was reported to have said: 'You may kill the body but you cannot kill the soul.' The story survived that his heart, like Joan of Arc's, escaped the flames.

In December the Zürich Council negotiated a settlement that granted it political and ecclesiastical independence, an impressive diplomatic achievement seeing that it had just lost the war. It was agreed that each Swiss state would choose its own religion, though whereas Catholics in Protestant states would enjoy freedom of worship, little reciprocal provision was made for Protestants in Catholic areas. This was the price that Zürich had to pay for defeat. Henry Bullinger, who had all along opposed the war, was chosen as Zwingli's successor, and he remained for forty-five years the widely respected chief pastor of Zürich. The debacle of Kappel left Zürich in a state of shock, with many blaming Zwingli personally for the disaster, and it is a tribute to Bullinger's leadership that no serious demand was raised to undo the Reformation.[52]

Luther was dismayed when news of Kappel reached him. It struck him as a divine judgement on Zwingli; he feared for Zwingli's soul, and attacked those who were making a martyr of him. He adapted the Gospel text – 'Zwingli drew the sword; and all who take the sword shall perish by the sword' (Matthew 26:52).[53] What he meant was that those who take the sword *unlawfully* shall perish by it. Those *entrusted* with the sword – the ordained princes and magistrates – are entitled, even commanded, to use it to keep the peace and punish lawbreakers; but this was not the responsibility of churchmen and pastors, not according to Luther.

Zwingli's war policy was abandoned for good by Zürich after his death. It had been born of a zeal for the godly, evangelical society he dreamed of. It was not as radical or aggressive an idea then as it may seem now. In the late medieval age, the continent of Europe was seldom at peace for long. Kings like Henry VII of England, who had little taste for military glory and preferred domestic stability instead, won neither love nor a good reputation for doing so. Far more exciting was a call to arms in a good cause, and the exhilaration of the battlefield, and the prospect of thanksgivings and celebrations for a victorious peace. Luther, not Zwingli, was the reformer going against the grain of his times. But Luther's view prevailed, and became the model for Protestants throughout Europe, including England.

strict financial policy assiduously. Another who discerned this unappealing side of Henry's character was Thomas More, the humanist scholar. Henry was wont to converse affably with More with the royal arm round More's neck, but More was under no illusions; Henry, he confessed wryly to a friend, would not hesitate to have his head if it 'could win him a castle in France'.[1]

And Henry lost little time in going to war for castles in France. Joining forces with Ferdinand of Aragon and the Emperor Maximilian in the Papal League against France, Henry's armies succeeded in capturing Tournai; but the grand plans of the allies were frustrated by divisions among them, problems of communications, suspicions and mutual recriminations. It was not long before Ferdinand defected and concluded a treaty with France. Then Maximilian backed away from a planned attack on Milan, complaining that money owed him by Henry had not arrived. Meanwhile at home an English force had routed an invading Scottish army at Flodden, a stunning victory that eclipsed all Henry's deeds on the continent. Nevertheless, in 1514 Henry was able to make peace with France on fairly favourable terms, having at least made some mark on the European stage.

Henry's church policy was broadly orthodox, though mingled with a dash of nationalism even in the early years of his reign. In 1485, the year the Tudor dynasty began, the Lord Chief Justice of England declared that the king was accountable directly to God. Common law and parliamentary statute were already held to be superior to the canon law of the medieval church. Henry VIII, in 1515, boasted that 'kings of England in time past have never had any superior but God only'; and he was determined to 'maintain the right of our crown and of our temporal jurisdiction as well in this point as in all others'.[2]

In England as in Europe, the authority civil rulers exercised over church appointments was growing, even though English bishops were still appointed by Rome, often after being nominated by the king in return for a favour from Rome. These developments in England reflected a European trend, where a certain tension existed between the advocates of papal primacy and the conciliarists – those who held that the ultimate authority in the church lay in a General Council rather than in the papacy. Despite all Rome's efforts, the writings of the fifteenth and early sixteenth centuries show that the issue of final authority in the church was still not entirely resolved. The papacy had the edge, but its victory was not decisive. To consolidate its power base, the papacy made deals and alliances with Europe's princes, who gratefully seized the opportunities this afforded to increase their own power in church affairs. By the end of the fifteenth century it was already possible to think in terms of a national or territorial church, though functioning within, and still integrally part of, Western Latin Christendom, with Rome as the spiritual centre.[3]

Despite this royal flexing of muscle in matters of church authority and jurisdiction, no serious official threat to religious orthodoxy existed in England, as the authorities' response to Luther amply demonstrated. On Sunday 12 May 1521, the Lord Chancellor Thomas Wolsey, the king's chief minister, led a solemn procession through the streets of London to preside over a ceremony at St Paul's, where Luther was formally anathematised, and as many of his books as Wolsey's men could find were ceremonially burned. Bishop John Fisher, probably England's most able theologian, delivered a sermon defending papal primacy, attacking justification by faith alone, and rejecting Luther's claim to an 'exclusive interpretation of Scripture' regardless of the fathers, the councils, the church and everyone else.[4]

For some time King Henry had been coveting a title akin to the 'Most Christian King' of France or the 'Most Catholic King' of Spain. 'Defender of the Faith' was considered by the pope as early as 1516, but it had not been officially granted, and somewhat to his chagrin Henry was still a mere 'Your Grace'. So Henry, inspired by Wolsey, decided he would ride to the defence of the Catholic church against the enemy. In spring of 1521, aided by a team of loyal divines, he composed his *Assertion of the Seven Sacraments* against Martin Luther generally, and chiefly Luther's most recent salvo against Rome, the *Babylonian Captivity of the Church*.[5]

The *Assertion* was a vigorous defence of the medieval faith, though using patristic rather than medieval authorities to support the author's arguments. It has suffered the indignity of being damned with faint praise by historians. 'Not a piece of theology of the highest order', said Prof. Scarisbrick. 'Not as bad as its Protestant detractors made it out to be', said Prof. Tjernagel, and he was trying his best to be fair to Henry. It may justly be said that the *Assertion* generates more heat than light. Henry fumes and splutters a lot against Luther – this enemy of the church, this 'hellish wolf', and so on – but he rarely says anything insightful and he frequently misses the point. Luther was charged with establishing the 'grace of baptism for a free liberty of sinning', preaching faith to 'defend an evil life', and making faith a 'cloak for a wicked life'.[6] This is all nonsense, and it provoked Luther into a furious reply that ridiculed Henry's pretensions to theological expertise, calling him a 'stupid king', a scribbler, an ass, a buffoon, a liar, a blasphemer, a feeble and unworthy opponent despite all his bombast and bravado. Henry was scandalised and hugely offended, but the hostility of the excommunicate Luther only confirmed the king's essential orthodoxy in the eyes of Roman divines, and he was duly awarded the title 'Defender of the Faith', one which British sovereigns bear to this day.

So relations between Luther and England had got off to a spectacularly unpromising start. Further anti-heresy measures, including book burning, were then set in train by Wolsey and the church authorities. However, as a thoughtful observer at Worms allegedly noted, burning Luther's books was a lot easier than driving his ideas out of men's hearts, and it was not long before an evangelical underground movement began in England. Its leading light was William Tyndale, an outstanding linguist, scholar and later Bible translator, though in 1524 he was forced to flee to the continent for his safety. Despite this, evangelical material continued to find its way into England, and the authorities failed to crack the underground network. The most common route was via the great trading city of Antwerp, from where books were smuggled into England in bales of cloth and other merchandise. The profits of the trade in books and other goods ensured that the authorities in Antwerp turned a blind eye to heretical material, and five editions of Tyndale's New Testament were printed in Antwerp between 1527 and 1534, giving a total of around 3,000 copies. Bishop Cuthbert Tunstall ordered the ceremonial burning of Tyndale's New Testament when illegal copies were found in London, and Wolsey asked the Regent of the Low Countries to search for Tyndale and have him arrested. Thomas More's cultivated humanist learning deserted him as, first in print and then in power as Lord Chancellor, he raged furiously against both Luther and Tyndale.[7] Yet Tyndale survived, sheltered by friends, and the anti-Lutheran energies of the English government were distracted by a crisis at home, known as the King's Great Matter.

By the late 1520s the court of King Henry VIII was gripped with talk and expectation of reform in church and state, though reform of a different kind from that of Luther or Zwingli. Henry had one daughter, Mary, by his marriage to Catherine of Aragon, but no son and heir, and he was seeking to divorce his wife and marry Anne Boleyn, the latest royal mistress. It was an issue fraught with theological, constitutional and diplomatic ramifications. Henry based his moral case on texts from the book of Leviticus, which appeared to forbid sexual relations or marriage to a brother's wife on pain of childlessness (Leviticus 18:6, 20:21; Catherine's first husband was Henry's elder brother, Arthur, who died tragically young in 1501). The exact meaning of these texts, and their relevance in the Christian era, were disputed; but for the most part Henry's divines supported him, and the pope was applied to for a dispensation. It is possible that Rome might have been prevailed upon to grant this, but for one fact: Catherine's nephew was Charles V, the Holy Roman Emperor, and the most powerful prince in Christendom, whose troops in May 1527 bloodily sacked Rome and carried off the pontiff as prisoner. He was released not long after, but the point was well made: the pope could not gratify Henry without risking the wrath of Charles.[8]

Negotiations with Rome were dragging on seemingly interminably, but a crucial turning point occurred in summer 1529. Catherine's case was being heard in the London Blackfriars in the presence of Wolsey and Cardinal Campeggio, in England representing Rome. On 30 July Campeggio insisted on an adjournment until October, following Roman custom. This was more than Henry could bear; he was now convinced that Rome and the emperor were combining to thwart him. A few days after Campeggio's bombshell, however, a hitherto little-known Cambridge don named Thomas Cranmer dined with Edward Foxe and Stephen Gardiner, two prominent members of the king's divorce team. Cranmer then made a suggestion that would endear him to the king for as long as Henry lived: instead of fruitlessly pursuing his case through Rome, let the king seek the considered opinions of scholars among Europe's universities. It was a typical academic's idea. What made it even more appealing was the fact that the respected University of Paris had already debated the affair and had found, albeit by a slender majority, for Henry.[9] The king seemed galvanised. His boldness and his opposition to Rome now increased to the point where he could even admit that Luther's attacks on papal power contained some truth, though he was still far from agreement with Luther on justification by faith, the sacraments and other important points. Henry told Charles's ambassador, Eustace Chapuys, that he would begin reforming the English church. Foreign ambassadors were also reporting that the king and his nobility were arranging to extend royal control over the church, including the monasteries and church property.[10]

Apart from Catherine, the chief casualty of the Great Matter was Wolsey, whose failure to secure the divorce had displeased Henry and infuriated Anne Boleyn. Wolsey was sent north to York where he might have been allowed to live out his last days undisturbed; but incriminating letters, suggesting unauthorised contacts with foreign courts, were subsequently found in the possession of his doctor. Wolsey was summoned back to London. His death at Leicester on 29 November 1530 may have spared him the mortification of having to answer charges at a trial for treason. Cranmer, by contrast, advanced further in Henry's favour when he, along with Edward Foxe and others, produced the so-called *Collectanea* in 1530. Its aim was to justify the English Crown's pre-eminence over the church in England from diverse historical sources. These sources varied from the lofty Councils of Nicea (AD 325), to King Wambar summoning bishops to Toledo (589), and the extract from the Council of Carthage that no one, not even the bishop of Rome, was entitled to bear the title of 'universal bishop'. To Henry's delight it claimed that the king was God's vicar in England, and consequently the English church enjoyed a large amount of ecclesiastical independence from Rome. Early evidence supporting all of this was unearthed in an epistle of Eleutherius, Bishop of Rome to King Lucius of Britain in AD 169, authorising him to 'rule your kingdom', for 'you are God's vicar' there.[11]

Meanwhile, forbidden literature, chiefly Tyndale's Bible, continued to be smuggled into the country, defying the efforts of men like Wolsey and More, and Bishops Tunstall and Stokesley, to suppress it. The evangelical underground movement was growing, numbers being added daily. Tyndale's New Testament was read furtively in homes, in universities and even in monasteries by scattered groups of men and women eager to receive the new learning. What the movement lacked, however, was a powerful leader who could direct and energise it, and even influence the king himself in a reformist direction.

THE ROYAL SUPREMACY

Following Wolsey's demise, the chief men around the king were Thomas Boleyn (Anne's father), Thomas Howard, Duke of Norfolk, and Thomas More, now Lord Chancellor. Thomas Cranmer, Archbishop of Canterbury, and Thomas Audley, Speaker of the House, were rising stars, both strong supporters of the king's cause. But the most impressive of Henry's band of Thomases was still feeling his way cautiously in the corridors of power.

Thomas Cromwell was a man of humble birth and background, but formidable energy and intellect. An accomplished linguist and collector of works of art, his interests spanned the range of the humanities and also theology, in which he was more than a match for Henry's bishops and divines. He had been a Member of Parliament, and a prosperous lawyer and merchant in Wolsey's service. After the cardinal's fall, Cromwell's abilities as an administrator impressed the king, and he began to advance steadily in Henry's favour. In early 1531 he was appointed to the king's council. That year, unknown to the king, Cromwell converted to the Lutheran faith, and with the help of close allies like Stephen Vaughan, Robert Barnes and Christopher Mont, Lutheran writings like the Augsburg Confession and Philip Melanchthon's *Apology* were smuggled into England. This was dangerous work in the early 1530s, when More and Bishop Tunstall were waging war on Lutheran heresy, and only a consummately streetwise operator could have negotiated political advancement and spiritual conversion as adeptly as Cromwell did.[12]

Cromwell was also able to offer his experience as a lawyer and parliamentarian to help the king's constitutional cause. Fortified by the favourable response of Europe's universities, most of whom supported him in his Great Matter, Henry proceeded to strengthen his control over the English church. In the parliamentary session beginning in January 1532 Annates – payments that new clerical incumbents paid to Rome – were abolished and transferred to the Crown. The bill's preamble warned defiantly that if Rome threatened excommunication or interdiction, then the king and country may 'without any scruple of conscience … lawfully to the honour of Almighty God … continue to enjoy the sacraments, ceremonies and services of the holy church'. After lively debate, especially in Commons, the bill passed successfully.[13] Then on 15 May 1532, Henry became effectively Head of the Church in England when he compelled the clergy to surrender their legal independence to him in a move that came to be known as the 'Submission of the Clergy'. This was a bridge too far for Thomas More, who resigned as Lord Chancellor, and was soon replaced by Audley.[14]

Events in England were placing an ever greater strain on Henry's relations with Charles V, Catherine's nephew; but European power politics played into Henry's hands. Charles's chief international rival was King Francis of France. Francis was delighted to see the rift opening up between Charles and Henry, and he decided he could widen it even further. An Anglo-French summit was arranged in Calais in October 1532, and Francis welcomed Henry with lavish fanfare and ceremonial. Anne accompanied Henry, acting as if she was already queen according to several observers – she danced with Francis at one of the banquets held in honour of the guests. Sometime during the talks between the two kings, a plan was laid. It is likely that Francis, not Henry, was the mastermind. Francis encouraged Henry to marry Anne. This would create, certainly for as long as Catherine lived, an irresolvable enmity between Henry and Charles. No longer would Francis fear an Anglo-Imperial alliance against him. A subsidiary element of the plan was that Francis would try and bring about reconciliation between Henry and the pope. This part of the plan came to nothing, because Francis had underestimated the strength of English nationalism. It was, however, not as far-fetched an idea as it may sound; it was reported in diplomatic circles that the pope was not necessarily as hostile to Henry as his public stance suggested, and that pressure from Charles was the main reason preventing Rome from accepting Henry's case. Nor was it entirely a piece of Gallic cynicism, because Francis really did make some effort to persuade the pope to look more favourably on Henry's case.[15]

After bidding Francis farewell in November, Henry returned to England and married Anne, though the date of this marriage is disputed. Edward Hall, the Tudor historian, tells us there was a secret marriage in November, though according to other witnesses it did not take place until January the following year.[16] More important than the exact date is the fact that by early 1533 Henry and Anne were married, and Anne was pregnant. The dearly longed-for male heir was in the womb. But Anne was not yet crowned and Henry was still legally married to Catherine, so a series of major constitutional measures were hastily enacted to legitimise the marriage and the heir. The Act of Restraint of Appeals, drafted by Cromwell, prohibited appeals in all marital cases to Rome. The act rehearsed the historical case of the king's independence from Rome presented in the *Collectanea*; it gave Henry the constitutional jurisdiction he wanted to decide all church affairs, and particularly his Great Matter, in England. By 7 April 1533 it had passed both houses. About the same time Convocation discussed the Aragon marriage. Lords and Commons gave assent to Henry. On 23 May at Dunstable, Cranmer formally declared Henry's marriage to Catherine contrary to divine law and therefore invalid. In a lavish coronation ceremony, Anne was crowned queen on 1 June 1533.[17]

Henry now mulled over the name he should give to his heir – he decided it would be Edward or Henry. Lacking modern medical techniques, the anxious king was consulting physicians and astrologers about the sex of the child. All assured him the child would be a son. Then all these diviners, as well as the expectant father, were nonplussed on 7 September when Anne gave birth to a girl.[18]

Henry controlled his disappointment well, and Princess Elizabeth received a royal christening. No record survives of what happened to those badly mistaken physicians and astrologers, but it apparently never occurred to Henry that another daughter signified divine disfavour on his second marriage or his breach with Rome. That winter he told Chapuys that he was ready to 'throw off allegiance to the Holy See', and that he now disowned the section in the *Assertion* defending papal authority.[19] The following year the Royal Supremacy was instituted in a further series of acts of Parliament. Catherine of Aragon's status was officially downgraded to that of Princess Dowager. The new Act of Succession confirmed Henry's marriage to Anne and ensured the succession to their lawful male heirs, and failing male heirs it would pass to Elizabeth. In November 1534, the Reformation Parliament made King Henry Head of the Church in England, and the Act of Supremacy declared him to be ordained of God for the spiritual as well as the material welfare of his subjects. Thus Henry was invested with authority over the national church, now thoroughly independent of Rome. Under the Act of First Fruits and Tenths all clerics were required to pay the equivalent of a year's income, plus a further tenth of their yearly revenue, to the Crown.[20] A new treason bill became effective from 1 February the following year. Besides actual acts of violence against the king or the state, treason was now defined as any desire maliciously expressed, in 'words or in writing', to kill or harm the king, queen and heir, or to deprive them of their titles; it would also be treason to call the king a heretic, schismatic, tyrant, infidel or usurper.[21]

Although Henry was now prepared to welcome Lutheran ideas about the Christian's duty of obedience to his prince rather than to the papacy, the Royal Supremacy was not based on specifically Protestant principals. Nor was it even an adaptation of Luther's 'two kingdoms' (see p. 17). Having rebelled against Rome, Henry had not the smallest intention of restricting his authority to civil affairs, and submitting to his domestic clergy in spiritual things. Through the Supremacy, Henry *gained* power over the church, which he did not have before, and which he would never surrender. Articles of faith and points of doctrine, as well as clerical appointments, would from now on be determined ultimately by the king, not his divines. Henry kept his title of 'Defender of the Faith', and when he granted Archbishop Cranmer the authority to formally pronounce on his divorce, he proudly referred to 'our spiritual jurisdiction'. Henry may have recognised two kingdoms, the spiritual and the secular, but he would be prince and sovereign in both.[22]

Not everyone was able to accept the new order. Thomas More, Bishop John Fisher and a group of Carthusian monks were the most famous dissidents, who refused to confess Henry as Head of the Church, and they paid for it with their lives. It is possible that More and Fisher might have been allowed to wile away the rest of their days in the Tower, but the pope's decision to make Fisher a cardinal goaded Henry into bringing them to trial and the inevitable condemnation.[23] This apart, resistance was generally muted. Fear alone cannot explain this, because Henry's subjects were bold enough to make plain their affection for Catherine, while the feelings of most of them for Anne ranged from grudging acceptance to simmering hostility, as the king well knew. The mood of the country so long ago is bound to be difficult to gauge precisely, but it may be said fairly confidently that the English people were fonder of Catherine than the Renaissance papacy. The injustice done to her was keenly felt; the affront to Rome less so.

The Royal Supremacy was founded on the conviction that England was a sovereign, independent nation state in spiritual as well as civil affairs; and that supreme authority resided in the king, who was answerable to God alone. This was the divine will, Henry and his allies claimed, well attested by admittedly distant history. The man who did most to actually bring the Royal Supremacy into being was Thomas Cromwell, now the king's Principal Secretary and chief minister. But he was not the author of all the new ideas on English sovereignty. Before he was appointed to the king's council, Henry was already determined to divorce Catherine and marry Anne. Cromwell played little if any role in preparing the *Collectanea*, and claims of English independence from Rome had been heard before he even entered Wolsey's service. Nevertheless, he was an expert in harnessing the ideas of others and making first-rate use of them. Cromwell not only prepared the main legislation like the Appeals and the Supremacy Bills, he also steered them successfully through Parliament and onto the statute books. In doing so, he raised the standing of the monarchy to a level higher than it had ever been hitherto. Unlike his predecessors, Henry was prince of the church as well as the state.

Although the Royal Supremacy was believed to be the will of God, parliamentary statute was the means used to implement it on earth. It follows, therefore, that the stature of Parliament, as well as that of the monarchy, was likewise raised to unparalleled heights. Arguably the most momentous constitutional change in English history since the Norman Conquest had been brought about not by revolution, war or dictat, but through Parliament.

In the 1530s the prestige of both Crown and Parliament rose, and rose *together*, in tandem. The Crown did not gain power at the expense of Parliament, or vice versa. A unique equilibrium, created chiefly by Cromwell, was achieved that would last throughout the Tudor age, until coming under severe strain, and finally breaking apart, under the Stuarts.

Cromwell carried on in like manner throughout his life, strengthening and enriching the Crown, frequently at the expense of the clergy and the nobility, but at the same time always working through Parliament. He was a parliamentary statesman, not in the sense that he believed in, or even conceived of, parliamentary democracy as we now know it; but because whenever something that mattered needed doing, Cromwell drafted a bill and placed it before Parliament. Even though vested interests in one House or the other often frustrated his plans for economic and social reform, he never lost his faith in the institution or in the authority of statute. Once he even produced a bill to give legal sanction to royal proclamations – the Act of Proclamations, 1539. These proclamations, incidentally, were issued in support of existing statutes and to give added impetus to them where necessary; they were never meant to replace statutes, or smooth the way to tyranny by allowing arbitrary rule that bypassed Parliament.[24]

THOMAS CROMWELL AND THE PROTESTANT REFORMATION

There were two distinct aspects to the English Reformation. The first was the Royal Supremacy, discussed above. This, however, as noted already, was not a Protestant settlement, despite the role of Henry's Lutheran chief minister in establishing it. Henry did not throw off the Roman yoke because he was minded to become a Lutheran. He might be called a schismatic in the sense that he cut England off from Western Catholic Christendom; but apart from the matter of papal primacy, Henry was no destroyer of the medieval Catholic faith. In Henry's England some church devotions, like the cult of the saints and relics, would soon be watered down, and pilgrimages virtually abolished; but more fundamental dogmas like the Mass, transubstantiation (in doctrine though not in name) and clerical celibacy were retained. Above all, Luther's justification by faith alone never won favour with Henry. The only real spiritual authorities that Henry was willing to recognise were the church fathers.

Now Henry had three evangelical Thomases on his council, each holding a key office of state: these were Cromwell, Cranmer and Audley as Principal Secretary, Archbishop of Canterbury and Lord Chancellor respectively. During a recent visit to Germany, Cranmer had secretly married the niece of Andreas Osiander, the prominent Nuremberg divine, while Cromwell had effectively taken charge of the task of spreading the evangelical message throughout England. Head of the Church Henry may have been, but things were going on in the church that the king was only vaguely aware of.

Cromwell supported, encouraged and in some cases financed from his own money his growing band of evangelical protégées. Some, like Christopher Mont and Richard Taverner, he engaged in translating Lutheran works, such as Melanchthon's *Apology of the Augsburg Confession*, into English. Others like Robert Barnes concentrated on preaching, in the pulpit and the open air. Cromwell then persuaded Henry to appoint a number of evangelicals as bishops, including Hugh Latimer, Nicholas Shaxton, William Barlow and George Brown, though when he made his recommendations Cromwell wisely stressed their loyalty to the Royal Supremacy, not their Protestant faith.[25]

Cromwell also set about trying to interest Henry in the Lutherans. He began by introducing the king to the writings of Melanchthon, Luther's chief ally and one of the finest scholars in Europe. It was an astute move. Henry had still not entirely forgiven and forgotten his bruising encounter with Luther in the early 1520s; but he found the mild-mannered, deferential Melanchthon a much more attractive figure, especially when Philip dedicated his *Loci Communes* of 1535 to the king, with generous praise for Henry's love of learning and true Christian doctrine. Henry replied to Melanchthon's dedication with a personal letter signed 'Your friend, King Henry VIII' and a gift of 200 crowns. The *Loci* did not succeed in making a Lutheran out of Henry; but the king was sufficiently impressed and interested to want to parley with the Germans on theology, and to consider a religious and political alliance with them and the recently formed Schmalkaldic League, the alliance of Lutheran states.

The evangelical movement received a massive boost when Henry, in January 1535, appointed Cromwell Vice-Gerent in spirituals, specifically to organise a nationwide visitation of the monasteries. Cromwell's policy at this stage was to reform the monasteries from within rather than destroy them. To try and tug them away from medieval ways and beliefs, monks were required to confess the king's headship of the church, and certain traditional medieval customs like keeping relics were forbidden. Cromwell was responsible for recommending appointments in the religious houses, and whenever the opportunity arose he planted evangelical men and women loyal to the Royal Supremacy in the monasteries and nunneries. This reformation from within encouraged the spread of Lutheran ideas in the unlikeliest of places, and it enjoyed some success: monks loyal to Cromwell and in his service wrote to him confessing justification by faith with a fervour and conviction that Luther himself would have been proud of.

Then something happened which threatened briefly to derail the Reformation. Henry's infatuation for Anne Boleyn had faded, and once again a sonless marriage stirred up fears of divine disfavour. Anne's miscarriage on 29 January 1536 – the day Catherine of Aragon was buried – confirmed his forebodings, because by now he had found a new love in the quiet, meek

Lady Jane Seymour. Henry decided to put Anne away, just as he had done with Catherine. The pretext would be a marriage precontract that Anne was believed to have had with Henry Percy many years ago, before she became Henry's mistress. However, while his ministers were working on this point and on other constitutional aspects of the case, startling news was brought to Henry one day near the end of April: Anne, it was claimed, had a string of lovers, including gentlemen within the king's close circle. After a swift examination of key witnesses, Henry was convinced by what he heard. Whether he was right to be is one of the most disputed topics in Tudor history.[26]

In discussing Anne's guilt or innocence, the historian is faced with two virtually irresolvable problems. The first is that some of the relevant papers are now missing, so we do not have all the facts. Second, the point at issue is not the existence of evidence, but the interpretation of it.

Consider this, Anne to Henry Norris, one of her alleged lovers: 'If ought came to the king but good, you would look to have me.'[27] There is no doubt that Anne said these words – she admitted them, and others may have overheard them. The problem, 500 years on, lies in deciding exactly what they meant. On the basis of these and similar exchanges, Anne's prosecutors alleged that she and Norris were lovers. Others prefer the defence of Gilbert Burnet, one of the ablest of the older historians. Anne, according to Burnet, had been careless and indiscreet, and 'her carriage seemed too free' with certain gentlemen at court: but she was no adulteress. Her 'indiscretions' cost her her life because Henry now despised her.[28]

The reader will have to be judge and jury. The fall of Anne Boleyn, however, is fertile ground for credulous and excitable conspiracy theories, one of the plagues of the modern age; and so the reader might care to bear in mind that there is no reliable evidence whatsoever that any of the witnesses against Anne were tortured into making false confessions, or that the government framed her on trumped up charges to get rid of her. Something for sure had been going on in secret in Anne's circle; whether it was as bad as the indictment alleged, we may never know.

Cromwell quickly shrugged the drama off and carried on with the work of the Reformation. He now had the opportunity to draft articles of religion and accompanying injunctions, and he made skilful use of it, easing as much Lutheranism past Henry as he safely could without arousing the king's suspicion. The moderately Lutheran Ten Articles, strongly influenced by Melanchthon's *Loci* that had been dedicated to Henry, were binding on all clergy, and became required reading at church services, in schools and in the home. This way the 'new learning' reached the widest possible audience, the length and breadth of the land.[29]

But the path of reform is seldom an easy one. Soon after the Ten Articles were published, fierce opposition flared up in the northern parts, first in

Lincolnshire and then the larger rising commonly known as the Pilgrimage of Grace. Besides a list of economic grievances, the pilgrim-rebels complained bitterly about various reformist measures like the abolishing of holy days, the attacks on the saints and purgatory, the suppression of the smaller monasteries, and the appointments of evangelical bishops and ministers of state 'of low birth' – chiefly Cromwell, though also Cromwell's ally, Thomas Audley. However, because Henry had approved the reforms that the rebels opposed, the king saw the rising as a challenge to his own royal authority. Henry's response was cunning and ruthless. He first enticed the rebels with fair words to talk with him; and then, when government forces had gathered sufficient strength, he sent his chief military commander, the Duke of Norfolk, to crush them without mercy.[30]

The insurrection was soon over, and it left Cromwell unharmed, as powerful as ever at Henry's right hand. Henry's Supremacy in church and state was also intact. As if to celebrate the king's triumph over the rebels, the Bishop's Book declared that Christian kings and princes were divinely instituted to 'be as the chief heads and overlookers [sic] of the said priests and bishops, to cause them to administer their office and power committed unto them'. Henry then felt confident enough to enrich himself yet further at the expense of the old church, and so began the dissolution of all the monasteries, another huge task administered by Cromwell with his accustomed efficiency.[31]

Cromwell was an imaginative and ecumenical reformer. In the late 1530s relations between Wittenberg and Zürich, now under Henry Bullinger's pastoral guidance, were much better than they had been during Zwingli's lifetime. Hopes were high at one point that the Swiss might be persuaded to sign the Wittenberg Accord, a statement on the Eucharist prepared by Melanchthon and accepted by Luther and Martin Bucer, the Strasbourg reformer who had previously been close to Zwingli. Cromwell then authorised his own discreet contacts with the Swiss, knowing that if they were to sign the Accord, the satisfying result would be evangelical unity on the continent and the strengthening of the Schmalkaldic League, which Cromwell was trying to persuade Henry to join. Sadly for him, these hopes came to nothing.[32]

Perhaps Cromwell's proudest evangelical triumph was the English Bible. The spur to this may have been the loss of William Tyndale, who had been betrayed to the authorities in Brussels, with, it was alleged, the connivance of English bishops opposed to Cromwell. According to the Tudor historian, Edward Hall, Cromwell tried hard through his diplomatic contacts to secure Tyndale's release, but to no avail. Tyndale perished at the stake in October 1536, though as the custom was in the Low Countries, he was strangled before the fire was lit.[33] The following year, however, Cromwell persuaded Henry to approve in principle the placing of a Bible in all churches, for lay people as well as clergy to read. Already there were two English Bibles available, one by Miles Coverdale, the other the so-called 'Matthew Bible' by John Rogers. Both were trusted allies of Cromwell. But men in the English clergy hostile to Cromwell noted that Coverdale and Rogers had made extensive use of existing translations, including those of Luther and Tyndale; and perhaps to pre-empt any opposition this might provoke, Cromwell decided to produce a new version translated directly from the original languages. He entrusted the work to Coverdale. Grafton and Whitchurch were chosen to be the publishers. The new Bible – the Great Bible as it became known, chiefly due to its impressive size – would be produced at Paris, where printing was reckoned to be of the finest quality.

The project was not allowed to go ahead unchallenged. Though the French authorities had promised their cooperation, they soon came under relentless pressure from Cromwell's opponents at home and abroad, including Rome, to stop the work. Printing in France was abruptly halted one day. During the flurry of negotiations that followed, Cromwell managed to strike a deal with the French that would return not only printing equipment but also some confiscated Bibles to England. By the time of his death in summer 1540, Cromwell's cherished aim of providing every parish in the country with an English Bible was finally accomplished. This was also a posthumous victory for Tyndale, because the Great Bible was heavily indebted to him, and full of Tyndalian phrases. The English people could now read Tyndale, only slightly modified, free from the risk of a charge of heresy.[34]

Cromwell's role as England's premier reformer in the middle part of Henry's reign is well attested by his contemporaries, friend and foe alike. Yet strange to relate, it was in danger of going unrecognised until the late Sir Geoffrey Elton began to bring us back to the right paths. The Victorians had invented – this is the most charitable word that comes to mind – the idea of Cromwell as a secularist or an English Robespierre, a view that still persists in certain parts. For the record, therefore, it may be useful, particularly for students, to collate a sample of the testimonies from Cromwell's own generation who knew him best.

Cromwell was the 'principal author' of all the 'innovations in religion', according to the French ambassador, Charles de Marillac.[35] 'Wherever the king goes', says Chapuys, ambassador from Charles V, 'Cromwell, who accompanies him, goes around visiting the abbeys and convents in the neighbourhood, taking inventories of their lands and revenues, amply instructing the people in this new sect.'[36] Cromwell has 'done more than all others together' in the cause of the 'reformation of religion and the clergy', agreed Archbishop Cranmer, apparently content to be number two in the Reformation party.[37] Hugh Latimer thanked Cromwell that 'your lordship hath promoted many more honest men, since God promoted you, than hath many men done before your time, though in like authority with you'. Latimer's tribute ends:

'Blessed be the God of England that worketh all, whose instrument you be.'[38] Similar testimonies come from other evangelical bishops like William Barlow, Nicholas Shaxton and George Browne.[39] Opponents were under no illusions either; Cromwell was the chief hate-figure of the leaders and activists in the Pilgrimage of Grace.[40] Foreign reformers also knew who was directing the Reformation in England. Cromwell corresponded cordially with Luther and Melanchthon: Luther's letter of 9 April 1536 commended Cromwell's good-will 'in the cause of Christ', and prayed that the Lord would 'complete the good work begun in him' (Cromwell).[41]

Cromwell's influence with the king began to decline when Henry became disillusioned with the Lutherans. Several times Henry had invited Philip Melanchthon to England, but Elector John Frederick of Saxony repeatedly refused, on the grounds that such a visit was not necessary for Henry to decide whether he wanted to accept the Augsburg Confession and join the Schmalkaldic League. Then when a Lutheran delegation, though without Melanchthon, did eventually arrive in England in summer 1538, important differences soon emerged on private Masses and clerical celibacy: Henry was strongly for both, the Lutherans equally strongly against. Henry then enforced his own views in the Act of Six Articles, 1539. Nor was Henry ever won to justification by faith alone, and he failed even to understand the fine details of Lutheran theology.[42]

By the spring of 1540 Henry had had enough of Lutheranism. He was, moreover, unhappy with his new German bride, Anne of Cleves. Because she was related to Elector John Frederick of Saxony, this marriage had been arranged to give Henry a diplomatic link with the Germans which would not require him to make a formal commitment to their Augsburg Confession. It was Cromwell's idea, though he had the good sense to make sure that the final decision was Henry's. Cromwell had taken care to carry Henry along with him at every stage of the negotiations leading up to the signing of the marriage contract. The popular story that Cromwell lumbered the king with an unwanted wife by sending him misleadingly flattering reports and portraits of Anne, then paid for his deception with his life when Henry met her in the flesh and famously 'liked her not', is a piece of uninspired fiction. Cromwell's downfall was ensured when Henry fell madly in love with Catherine Howard, the nineteen-year-old niece of the Duke of Norfolk, always a potential rival to Cromwell despite protestations of loyalty and friendship. Now Henry wanted another divorce. He gave his ministers no specific royal command; he counted on their loyalty to gratify him and make the arrangements for him. Stephen Gardiner, Bishop of Winchester, Cromwell's chief enemy, was willing to do so; but Cromwell, whose responsibility the matter chiefly was, tried to save the Cleves marriage. He was also trying to revive the fortunes of the reformers that had sunk so depressingly low. So Henry, now infatuated with

Catherine, lent his ear to the whisperings of Cromwell's opponents; read-ily and encouragingly he listened to far-fetched claims and charges against him, including heresies against the Sacrament and conspiring armed rebellion, accusations which Henry later admitted were false.

Cromwell was condemned to die by an act of Parliament known as attain-der, but on the scaffold he had the last word. He denied the charges against him, and then he pledged to the assembled crowd that 'I die in the Catholic faith'. This he immediately followed up with a classic Lutheran confession and prayer, blasting the medieval teaching of merits and good works, trusting entirely in grace and the righteousness of Christ for salvation.

There are many who have been taken in by this apparently penitent profes-sion of the 'Catholic faith', imagining that Cromwell had caved in to pressure and recanted. Those who knew Cromwell knew better. Melanchthon heard of 'atrocious crimes' in England – Anne of Cleves was humiliatingly divorced and 'men of our opinion in religion were murdered … The English tyrant has slain Cromwell' (*Anglicus tyrannus Cromwellum interfecit*).[43]

It was part of the reformers' polemic to claim that, far from introducing new ideas, they were really restoring the ancient Christian truths that the popes and the medieval clergy had cast aside. In their disputes with the Romanists, reformers habitually declared their loyalty to the Nicene Creed and the Holy *Catholic and Apostolic* church, drawing a clear distinction between that and the medieval Roman church. In the Augsburg Confession itself, perhaps the foundation document of Protestantism, Melanchthon insisted that no other teaching could be found therein than that of the true, 'universal Catholic Church' (*ecclesia catholica*). He said the same in his later *Variata*: 'In doctrine and in ceremonies, nothing contrary to Scripture or the Catholic Church is received among us.' In other words, the reformers, not the papists, were the real, genuine, authentic Catholics. Thomas Cranmer would later take the same line in his writings on the Eucharist. Cromwell's 'Catholic faith' was just another example of that polemic (and a piece of roguishly ironic gallows humour). From his last words and prayer, it is about as plain as it can be that he died a Lutheran.[44]

Shocked though they were at Cromwell's fall, evangelicals remained true to the belief in passive Christian obedience in the face of injustice or adver-sity. At least, they did on the surface. Ancient classical writers like Aristotle and Cicero had endorsed tyrannicide; and when Melanchthon heard that Cromwell was dead, he slated Henry as the 'English Nero', and he called to mind words attributed to the Roman scholar Seneca (d. AD 65), formerly a tutor to Nero and later implicated in a plot to kill the emperor: 'No victim is more acceptable to the gods than the blood of a tyrant.' Philip wished that 'God might put this mind into some brave man'.[45] Maybe this was no more than a lapse in a moment of anger; besides appreciating Cromwell and his life's work, Melanchthon had held out high hopes for Henry, and what happened in summer 1540 left him bitterly disappointed. Nevertheless, it may be a fore-taste of what is to come later in this story, and an example of how an opinion, at first drawn entirely from theology, may be shaped and altered by events.

Thomas Cromwell, meanwhile, left England with a strong monarchy and a strong Parliament (and an economy in enviably good shape as well, though that is not the main subject here). Especially striking is the relationship between the two. 'Of our absolute power we be above the law', Henry had declared in 1520. But in 1543 he would say that 'we at no time stand so highly in our estate royal as in the time of Parliament, wherein we as head and you as members are conjoined and knit'. Elton ascribes Henry's change of empha-sis – from the king apparently alone to the king *in Parliament* – chiefly to the work of Cromwell in establishing the Royal Supremacy through parliamen-tary statute.[46] It may also be noted that because of the Supremacy, Henry was a more powerful king in 1543 than in 1520; nevertheless, in his own words, he was at his *most* powerful when 'conjoined and knit together' with Parliament. This was the singular effect of Cromwell's work – to raise the standing of Parliament and the Crown at the same time; neither institution had to yield power or influence to the other.

The second main aspect of Cromwell's legacy was the foundation he laid for the future Protestant England. In this he had the good fortune to be able to build on the labours of others, chiefly Tyndale. His chief continental influ-ences came from Luther and Melanchthon in Germany rather than the Swiss reformers. Significant, however, is not just what Cromwell did, but the manner of it. He was a realistic, pragmatic and flexible reformer. Everything was done constitutionally, and within, though at times only just within, the parameters allowed by Henry. Justification by faith alone went hand in hand with obedi-ence to the king. Cromwell could not claim that everything he ever did had the king's full knowledge and blessing; but he could rightly claim that he had never violated a specific command of the king, or an act of Parliament or a royal proclamation.

Cromwell's flexibility was best seen when the Act of Six Articles passed onto the statute books. The act was a severe blow for the reformers, yet Cromwell urged his supporters to comply with it. He hoped that Henry would soften in time and lighten the burden of the act, or even shelve it. Cromwell used all his ingenuity and ability to advance the Reformation, but he was determined to act with the king's consent. If he could not secure that consent, he would wait: and not only wait, but grin and bear with something very un-Lutheran. He would not rush in reckless haste to make a martyr of himself; he had no time for pointless heroics.

Cromwell had a near reverence for kingly rule and authority. One reason, certainly, was Romans 13, and Luther's teaching that the state as well as the church was a divine institution. Other reasons were more practical. Like all Henry's ministers, Cromwell had little choice but to give way to Henry; he was the king's servant, appointed to advise and attend on the king, not to rule over him. And after the Wars of the Roses and the endless feuding among the ambitious nobility of the previous century, the rise of a strong Tudor monarchy was seen as an assurance of stability and prosperity, a development that Cromwell did his utmost to encourage. He also felt a strong personal loyalty to Henry: as Wolsey's servant Cromwell stared ruin in the face after the cardinal's fall, but Henry appreciated his talents and raised him to the chief position on the council. A consequence of all this was that Luther's line on obedience to princes, which Tyndale had also followed, underwent a slight change in England. 'God must be obeyed rather than men' had become, in effect, 'My king, right or wrong'. The second is not entirely at odds with the first, because if the king was God's ordained ruler on earth, then obviously he was no *ordinary* man. And so the principle had become acceptable in England that even in a matter of conscience, like the infamous Six Articles, a subject should yield to his prince. This was neither Lutheran, nor Zwinglian nor Tyndalian; it was uniquely Cromwellian. A new pattern had been set for English Protestants for the remainder of Henry's reign, and for years after.

HENRY'S LAST YEARS

By the time of Cromwell's death, the Protestant seed had been planted in England and had begun to take root. Its growth was difficult and at times dangerous for as long as Henry lived, but if the religious climate of the king's last years was not conducive enough to allow it to flourish, neither was it harsh enough to smother it completely. The message was getting through: purgatory was a fake, Masses for the dead were useless, salvation was solely a gift of grace; and Bibles and evangelical literature were circulating discreetly. The genie was out of the bottle, and there was no putting it back in again.

As an example of the uncertainties of these years, in September 1541 Archbishop Lee of York was ordered to destroy all remaining shrines in the north. Then, two years later, restrictions on Bible reading came into force, partly in response to complaints from traditionalist clergy that the Great Bible contained translation errors. Also in 1543 the King's Book was published, and although Cranmer did his best for the evangelical cause, he could not alter Henry's determination to formally outlaw justification by faith alone; Cranmer then gave in as graciously as he could. On the other hand, evangelicals and their sympathisers could be found in prominent positions in the bishoprics, the universities, the court and the king's household. Prince Edward's tutors – John Cheke, Richard Cox and Roger Ascham – were all discreet evangelicals close to Cranmer, as well as first-class scholars. Henry must have realised this, though why he did not insist on a balance of men of the old faith and those of the new is not clear.[47]

The evangelical party was now led by Thomas Cranmer, who was, if possible, even more devoted than Cromwell to the principle of kingly authority in the spiritual as well as the civil sphere. Cranmer sorrowed for the church in the days of the apostles, when for their guidance 'there were no Christian princes … but only the consent of the Christian multitude among themselves'.[48] This is one reason why, evangelical though Cranmer was, he never lost the trust and love of the king. In the so-called 'Prebendaries' Plot' of 1543, his opponents, led by Stephen Gardiner, prepared a list of charges against the archbishop and then reported the matter to Henry, who affected to take them most seriously. Unknown to Gardiner, however, one evening Henry took a boat trip up the Thames, and arriving at Lambeth Palace he bid Cranmer come aboard. 'Ah, my chaplain, I have news for you', said the king mischievously. 'I know now who is the greatest heretic in Kent.' Henry produced the articles that were supposed to incriminate Cranmer, and directed Cranmer to conduct the investigations. But Cranmer's rivals were not finished yet, and soon they tried again. This time Henry gave his approval to the Privy Councillors to question Cranmer about alleged heresy, and even to commit him to the Tower if necessary. After this Henry sent for Cranmer and told him what the Council was about to do. Henry then gave him his ring. Next morning Cranmer appeared before the Council, and was solemnly informed that he was under arrest. Then, to the consternation of the Council, he calmly produced the king's ring. The distinguished but ashen-faced personages of the Council were summoned to Henry's presence to receive a stern royal rebuke. Cranmer had survived, and triumphed.[49]

The religion of Catherine Parr aroused no suspicion when she became Henry's sixth and last queen in July 1543. However, her devotional work *The Lamentation of a Sinner*, written soon afterwards, testifies to a deep conversion, though exactly when this happened is not clear. So Henry, having executed a Lutheran Vice-Gerent and ditched his Lutheran policy, had now unknowingly found himself a Lutheran wife. And how Luther would have loved the irony of the Gospel penetrating into the king's household, even into his bed. He would also have had warm praise for Catherine's *Lamentation*. Many years before, in 1519, Luther had written a pastoral meditation on Christ's Passion, and how the Christian should reflect upon it. Luther had no time for the sentimental contemplation that he had practised as a monk; instead Christians should believe in their hearts that Christ died for us, and learn God's love for the world in giving His Son. This is exactly what Catherine was doing in the *Lamentation*, twenty-five years later. It is rather unlikely that she had read Luther's *Meditation*, so the resemblance between the two works was a striking meeting of minds.[50]

Wisely, Catherine did not publish her work while Henry was alive. Mindful of the fate of some of her predecessors, even flirting with reform was a dangerous thing to do, especially after the publication of the King's Book. Yet Catherine became a discreet patroness of evangelicals and of learning, and it was not long before she roused the attention of that ever-watchful traditionalist hawk, Stephen Gardiner. John Foxe, the Elizabethan historian martyrologist, describes how she enjoyed discussing theology with Henry, but on one occasion she must have overstepped the mark, leaving Henry grumbling aloud at having a wife who presumed to teach him – the Defender of the Faith – on matters of religion. Gardiner took his cue to plant the suspicion of the queen's heresy in the king's mind, warning him 'how perilous a matter it is to cherish a serpent within his own bosom'. Gardiner then drew up articles against Catherine for heresy. Ominously, Henry signed them. The plan, drawn up with Henry's consent, was to search the rooms of the queen and her ladies, then take Catherine to the Tower. All the while, the unsuspecting queen carried on speaking her mind freely to the king, even suggesting a few more reforms to the church.

Then Henry told his physician, Dr Wendy, about the articles against Catherine, but commanded Wendy to tell no one else. Soon after this (still according to Foxe) the articles strangely 'fell from the bosom of one of the councillors', and were picked up by 'some godly person' and brought to the queen. She was terrified when she saw them, with Henry's signature on them. Henry came to see her and she appealed for mercy, promising to be unreservedly subject to him. 'But you are become a doctor, Kate, to instruct us', Henry admonished. Catherine denied it: she had merely sought to make conversation with him and humour him; she knew his interest in theology, and wished only to bring him some relief from his illnesses. 'And is it even so, sweetheart?' enquired Henry. 'Then perfect friends we are now again.' Next day Henry, Catherine and her ladies were walking in the garden when Thomas Wriothesley and an armed guard arrived to take the queen to the Tower. Wriothesely was only doing as he was bid, but Henry, now satisfied with his wife's confession, bellowed furiously at him, calling him 'Knave, beast and fool' and sent him slinking away.[51]

So Foxe's story goes, but this time Foxe is uncharacteristically vague on a key point. Though he was able to narrate exhaustively the charges and proceedings against the Protestant martyrs of Henry's and Mary's reign, he gives no details of the articles against Catherine. He relates private conversations between Catherine, the king and Gardiner that only an intimate confidant could have known about; then he tells us that the articles against her were deliberately misplaced and picked up by some 'godly person', whom he does not name, before being handed to the queen. So the charges were hardly a secret. Despite this, Foxe is unable to say what they were.

Henry's bizarre behaviour in the 'Prebendaries' Plot' and with Catherine, inexplicable in so many ways, has at least one common element. In both cases Henry gave the go-ahead to the conspirators, and then made fools of them when he skewered their plans. The workings of Henry's mind are seldom straightforward; and it is all too easy to see only a bloated, gouty old bully who enjoyed intimidating and humiliating his ministers, his subjects and even his wives. But although he could be cruel and tyrannical, in a strange way he could also be quite broad-minded on religion. He had his limits of course, with the papacy at one end of his tolerance spectrum and heresies against the Sacrament at the other; but within these limits his bishops frequently found themselves with considerable leeway and freedom. He let Cranmer argue strongly for justification by faith during the preparation of the King's Book; and before the Six Articles were passed, Catholics and reformers alike could argue for and against communion in one kind, confession, clerical marriage and private Masses. When the time came for a royal decision, however, Henry expected to be obeyed. Obedience, more than this or that doctrine, became the key to survival under Henry. No evangelical himself, he tolerated evangelicals in his kingdom, his household and on his council – provided they obeyed. Even heretics condemned to be burned were offered a pardon if they submitted to the king.

Church affairs were not Henry's sole concern in his last years. With Cromwell no longer around to restrain him, the king's yearning for military glory surged once more within him, and he was soon waging war against the Scots and also, in an alliance with Charles V, against France. Fired with zeal for his cause, Henry crossed the Channel with his armies and took to the field in person, leaving Catherine as Regent in England. In summer 1544 the English successfully besieged Boulogne. Unfortunately for Henry, as with his earlier foreign adventures in the 1520s, rivalries among the allies broke out, and he and Charles disagreed over tactics. To Henry's fury and embarrassment, Charles made a separate peace independently with Francis. Henry's position was now precarious because he was still at war with Scotland, and Francis was making provisional plans to aid the Scots and invade England. Henry, as determined to hold on to Boulogne as Francis was to retake it, tried to recruit mercenaries from the German Lutheran princes. The cost of his Franco-Scottish wars was severely aggravated by high inflation, compelling Henry to borrow from foreign money markets, debase the currency, re-mint coins and levy various taxes on his long-suffering subjects. Although his father had bequeathed him a financially sound legacy, which had been generously augmented by the revenue obtained by the Crown from the dissolution of the monasteries and other Cromwellian measures, Henry had plunged England into a financial crisis, and for little real tangible gain. Fortunately Francis's invasion plans came to nothing, and Henry was able to open peace talks without losing too much face. Eventually, after much hard bargaining, England and France concluded a peace treaty at Adres in June 1546.[52]

At home, periodic bouts of persecution continued to make life hazardous for reformers. Henry's unpredictability could seem (in retrospect if not at the time) almost comic. In 1546 he proscribed the Bibles of Tyndale and Coverdale, seemingly unaware that Cromwell's Great Bible, still standing proudly in every parish church in the land, was substantially the work of these two. Nevertheless, evangelicals held their ground, and could even take some encouragement. According to Foxe, at a banquet in August 1546 to celebrate the recently concluded peace with France, Henry talked openly of more church reforms, including the astonishing suggestion that he and Francis should agree to replace the Mass with a Protestant communion service. A week later Henry appeared at his most benign when he received a delegation from the Schmalkaldic League, the first such embassy since Cromwell's time, though this one came to discuss diplomatic affairs only, not theology.[53]

Then, at the end of 1546, reformers enjoyed a spectacular and unexpected double success when two of their most powerful foes, Gardiner and the Duke of Norfolk, fell from favour. Gardiner's customary discretion deserted him, and he offended Henry by unwisely involving himself in some obscure land dealings, for which he was struck off the list of councillors nominated by Henry to rule if Prince Edward came to the throne as a minor. Yet more dramatically, the Earl of Surrey, Norfolk's son, was executed for treason, and Norfolk sent to the Tower. Attainder against him was approved by Henry, but Norfolk was spared the axe because by this time Henry was seriously ill, and Sir Anthony Denny urged him to prepare for the end. Reflecting on his past, Henry spoke briefly of the mercy of Christ, which was 'yet able to pardon me all my sins, though they were greater than they be'. After a short sleep Henry awoke and called for Cranmer, who arrived in the early hours of 28 January 1547. By now the king was barely able to speak, so Cranmer asked for some sign that Henry trusted entirely in Christ for his salvation. Henry grasped Cranmer's hand as hard as a dying man could, and passed away.[54]

THE EDWARDIAN REFORMATION

Edward's accession allowed the evangelical party, waiting, surviving and biding its time in Henry's last years, to burst triumphantly into the open. Cranmer set the mood with his address at Edward's coronation: 'Your Majesty is God's Vice-Regent and Christ's vicar within your own dominions, and to see, with your predecessor Josiah, God truly worshipped, and idolatry destroyed, the tyranny of the Bishops of Rome banished from your subjects, and images removed.'[55] Soon pillars of medieval orthodoxy like transubstantiation, clerical celibacy and the sacrifice of the Mass, came tumbling down. The Act of Six Articles was repealed, and prominent bishops were bundled out of their palaces and dioceses. Some, like Gardiner of Winchester, were held in detention.

But the English Reformation had changed a little since Cromwell's time. No longer did it take after Luther and Melanchthon, for it began with something that Luther had firmly stamped on in Wittenberg twenty-five years before. A campaign against images in churches, far more sweeping than anything Cromwell had done or even tried to do, became official government policy, carried out ruthlessly and with little obvious attempt to win hearts and minds. A more significant change concerned the Eucharist, a subject which Cranmer and his closest confidant, Nicholas Ridley, had been studying closely. They were now convinced that Luther was mistaken about the 'real presence', and that the Zürich reformers were in the right: Christ was present spiritually in the Eucharist, but not substantially or corporally.[56]

The European evangelical movement was going its separate ways, and bridging the gap seemed ever more unlikely. On the one hand were the Lutheran churches of northern Germany and Scandinavia; on the other, the so-called 'Reformed' churches, the main ones being those of Zürich, Calvin's Geneva and now the England of Edward VI. The term 'Reformed' came to be used because these churches claimed that Luther – by holding on to images, the real presence and liturgical services – was not, despite his valiant efforts for the true faith, really reformed enough.

Another difference between the two evangelical groups concerned predestination, the doctrine chiefly linked with the great church father St Augustine, that the elect are predestined by divine decree. This implies that the *non*-elect must be damned by the same decree. It was Philip Melanchthon who prevented this doctrine from becoming an evangelical consensus. Melanchthon had been resisting it since the 1520s. Salvation, said Philip, is God's gracious offer to all mankind, and there is no hidden divine decree that arbitrarily calls some to blessing while consigning others to perdition. (Technically this is known as 'universal grace'.) Melanchthon was supported by his Lutheran colleagues, at first cautiously, eventually solidly. The Reformed, however, admittedly with varying degrees of intensity, followed the Augustinian line. Cranmer was a predestinarian, though the doctrine's most prominent advocate was that still emerging giant in Geneva, John Calvin. Nor did Calvin shy away from taking predestination to its unsparingly logical conclusion: that the sovereign God has decreed, probably before the foundation of the world, salvation for some and damnation for others, and His will is fixed and irresistible. A notable exception among the Reformed, however, was Henry Bullinger in Zürich, whose views were more akin to Melanchthon than to Calvin. The subject of predestination will reappear with a vengeance in this story in the section on the Puritans and the Stuart churches. It will be very controversial then; but it had its origin nearly fifty years before the Puritan movement, properly speaking, began.[57]

Cranmer was leading England on to Reformed ground, aided by like-minded evangelical luminaries from the continent. Peter Martyr, the refugee Italian, was appointed Regius Professor of Divinity at Oxford, while Martin Bucer from Strasbourg took the same post at Cambridge. Cranmer did not, however, close the door on contacts with Wittenberg; he still had a high regard for Melanchthon, and the feeling was mutual. More than once Cranmer tried to arrange a conference to discuss and hopefully resolve outstanding differences, but for various reasons this proved impracticable.

In 1549 Cranmer completed his first Prayer Book, a moderately Reformed work that made a few small concessions to those still attached to the old ways, like the use of traditional vestments, candles and a delicate commemoration for the dead. It was widely expected that these concessions would be temporary, and that a more stoutly Reformed Prayer Book would appear before long.[58] Nevertheless, a fair degree of ceremonial remained. So, too, did the episcopalian structure of the church, unlike continental Reformed circles. Thus the Edwardian Church was taking on a distinctive English form, assimilating continental influences but not entirely following Zürich or Geneva, at least not in its organisation and outward appearance.

In all things Cranmer was acting with the full backing of the new king. Edward was only twelve years old when the Prayer Book was published, but he was a highly intelligent boy receiving a princely education in the classics, arts, humanities and theology. He read his Bible keenly, and, somewhat unusually for a young man, he seemed very partial to a good sermon. His notebooks testify to a sound understanding and approval of the new learning in all its aspects, including the Reformed teaching of the Eucharist. In 1550, when John Hooper was about to be confirmed as the new Bishop of Gloucester, Edward noted a reference to the saints in the traditional oath, and, without consulting the elders who were present, he picked up his pen and majestically struck it out. In temperament, if not in faith, he was every inch his father's son.[59]

The Council of Regency appointed by Henry to rule while Edward was a minor was headed by Edward Seymour, Duke of Somerset as Lord Protector. He had been a military commander during Henry's Scottish wars of the 1540s, waged by the aging king after Cromwell's conciliatory approach to the Scots was cast aside. In Edward's reign Somerset renewed the war with his northern neighbour, but he combined this with appeals to the Scots to make church reforms of the kind that England had done, and he also held out the prospect of the two nations uniting and becoming 'Great Britain'. This is believed to be the first known use of the term. It was also the first time that an English Protestant statesman used armed force in pursuit of a policy in which religion – the advance of the Reformation – was one element. Somerset planned to garrison and thereby subdue Scotland, secure the marriage of Edward to the infant Scottish Queen Mary Stuart, and establish Edward as overlord of Scotland. In their resistance to the English the Scots were aided by their traditional allies the French, and Mary Stuart was moved out of Somerset's way to France. On the whole Somerset's Scottish policy was not a great success, though the garrisons did manage to keep the northern border well defended.[60]

Like most leading Edwardians, the Protector belonged to the Reformed rather than the Lutheran faith. Before long his government was acting against the old faith and its chief adherents by imposing restrictions on the Mass, preaching and printing. Stephen Gardiner, the most powerful voice of opposition, was confined to the Fleet, then released, then confined to his home, then locked up in the Tower after preaching a sermon in which he disobeyed directions given him by the government. Edmund Bonner of London, though more compliant, was deprived of his bishopric and imprisoned. The Council also tried to make Princess Mary conform, and a dispensation allowing her to hear Mass in private was intended mainly as a temporary, exceptional measure. The government was alert to the risk that Mary might become the focal point for Catholic resistance. No less important was the need to appease her cousin, the Emperor Charles V. Many Englishmen feared that Charles, following his victory over the Schmalkaldic League at Mühlberg in 1547, might seek to avenge his aunt, Catherine of Aragon, and attack England. So besides relaxing the pressure on Mary to some degree, Somerset and his Council tried to present England's religious changes in a deceptively moderate light during their dealings with Charles. This policy enjoyed some success. Instead of threatening to invade, Charles allowed the English to recruit mercenaries from his lands, and he closed his ports to ships that the French had used in the Anglo-Scottish war. An Anglo-Imperial treaty of 1543 covering various subjects, including trade, was ratified in summer 1549.[61]

On the home front not everything proceeded smoothly. Protests against reforms, and especially the compulsory removal of images from churches, intensified when the government decided to enforce the Prayer Book. Fears about new taxes worsened the problem, and risings broke out in Cornwall and Devon. Their main demands were that the church should stay as it was when Henry died, at least until Edward came of age. Rebels besieged Exeter, while unrest spread to Buckinghamshire and Oxfordshire before the rebels suffered a decisive defeat by government forces commanded by Lord Russell. This discontent, however, has to be balanced against popular demonstrations elsewhere in the country in favour of reform. So the debate on how well, or how grudgingly, the Edwardian Reformation was received by the English people continues to be an open one. Some welcomed it, others did not; but quantifying the support and opposition accurately is likely to remain an absorbing, if ultimately impossible, task for modern researchers.[62]

In Edward's reign, as in Henry's, church reform proceeded against a background of political intrigue and crisis. With his temperament as well as his policies, Somerset was upsetting his colleagues, including the powerful and ambitious John Dudley, Earl of Warwick, until now a close ally. The murky details of the plot against Somerset are difficult to unravel now, but only the outline is needed here. Warwick was probably the prime mover. In October 1549 Somerset, having heard of an imminent attack by Warwick and others, tried to move King Edward to Windsor castle. Somerset then surrendered, allowing Warwick to become Lord President of the Council. Fears that reform would be halted were unfounded; Warwick well knew Edward's evangelical convictions, and with an eye on his own future when Edward reached adulthood, Warwick made no effort to interfere with Cranmer's reforms. A reconciliation of sorts took place between Somerset and Warwick, and Somerset's daughter, Anne, married Warwick's son. But differences on policy soon re-emerged; for example, Warwick pursued an Anglo-French alliance, while Somerset favoured the Anglo-Imperial concord already reached with Charles V. More seriously, Somerset was suspected of aiming for power again. This time Warwick acted ruthlessly: Somerset was arrested for high treason and executed in February 1552. Warwick, now Duke of Northumberland, became the undisputed head of Edward's government.[63]

The affair was hardly an encouraging omen for Protestant government, when two men supposed to be of the same faith, and until just before the coup, similar political views, could fight to the death. Nevertheless, the replacement of Somerset with Northumberland produced little overall policy change. During the winter of 1551/2, Cranmer revised the Prayer Book, taking counsel again from Bucer and Martyr, though not always following it. More forcefully Reformed than the 1549 edition, it was presented to Parliament in April. The spiritual presence in the Eucharist was clarified and emphasised, while signs of the cross just before the Words of Institution, included in the previous edition, were taken out. Not a trace was to be found any more of intercession for the departed. Unlike Luther's liturgical reforms, Cranmer allowed only limited scope for sacred music. There is some evidence that Cranmer had in his mind yet further reforms that would bring England closer still to the Genevan order of service.[64]

But there were no plans to reduce the role or the authority of bishops. A good deal of church ceremonial also remained, and this was not to everyone's liking. The traditional custom of kneeling to receive communion ran into opposition from those who saw it as an unwanted remnant of popish idolatry: one sharp critic was the Scots reformer John Knox, now in England at Nothumberland's invitation. With unusual vigour Cranmer defended kneeling, and the Council supported him. Cranmer won this small but animated contest; but others around him were getting a little impatient with the measured pace of reform, pressing him to go further and faster. Such men were forerunners of the later Puritans.[65]

The following year the Forty-Two Articles were completed, detailing the doctrine of the Edwardian church (later to become, in Elizabeth's reign, the Thirty-Nine Articles). The Edwardian church seemed now to be consolidated on firm ground. Then evangelical hopes were suddenly and savagely dashed when Edward was struck by a fatal illness, believed to be pneumonia.

Edward had already been pondering the succession laws laid down in Henry's will. According to the law as it stood, if Edward died without an heir (which no one had seriously expected or feared until now) his half-sister Mary, the Catholic, would inherit the throne, followed by Elizabeth, the Protestant. In summer of 1553, aware that he was dying, the young king and his evangelical council feared, with good reason, that Mary would undo the Reformation and restore the Catholic faith. So a change to the succession laws was decided on. But rather than bypassing Mary and going directly to Elizabeth, the plan was to disinherit both sisters, the Catholic and the Protestant, and chose instead Lady Jane Grey. Jane, the eldest granddaughter of Henry VIII's younger sister Mary, was married to one of Northumberland's sons, Guilford. Like Edward, Jane was a dedicated Reformed Protestant, and four days after Edward's death on 6 July the authorities in London proclaimed her queen. Mary protested strongly to the Council, resting her claim to succession on the authority of King Henry's will. The Council replied that she was illegitimate and 'unheritable' (sic), and she should be 'quiet and obedient, as you ought'.[66]

According to Foxe, Jane was about Edward's age, but 'in learning and knowledge of the tongues … superior', comparable 'to the university men, which have taken many degrees of schools'.[67] This was praise indeed, bearing in mind that nothing had been spared to give Edward the best possible education worthy of a Tudor prince. It seemed at first that Jane would be accepted at home and abroad. For political reasons the Catholic King Henri II of France, though a notorious persecutor of evangelicals in his own kingdom, was alarmed at the thought of Catholic Mary on the English throne because she was the cousin of the Emperor Charles V, chief European rival of the French king. So Henri was willing to overlook Jane's Protestantism and welcome her instead. Charles himself was diplomatic; he assured Northumberland that he had always wished to see Mary marry in England, and even if she became queen he would not press her to 'make alterations as to religion and customs'. He urged that the matter be settled 'not by force and violence, but by the authority of Parliament'. Imperial ambassadors reported that Mary's prospects looked 'well nigh impossible' without the assistance of a large military force, which Charles was unwilling to offer; as late as 11 July they were saying that no popular demonstrations for her had taken place. Some seemed resigned to the evangelical *fait accompli*. So secure did Jane appear, if only fleetingly, that leading modern writers on Tudor England are calling Mary's accession a *coup d'état*.[68]

But Northumberland and his Council played into Mary's hands by making two fateful blunders. According to the ambassador, Northumberland had a plan to 'seize' Mary as soon as Edward died; but if so, the plan failed. He also failed to convince the English people of the legitimacy of the revised succession law by which Jane was made queen. Mary took full advantage of Northumberland's clumsiness. She gave her would-be captors the slip, and soon she was moving among the network of friends and contacts in East Anglia that she and her closely knit household had forged during her brother's reign, rallying support from the influential gentry. She sensed, moreover, that many Protestants were decidedly uneasy about the hurried alterations to King Henry's will. Though there is little doubt that Edward had consented to the scheme – he may have been the prime mover – the whole affair looked suspiciously like a coup by Northumberland, never a much loved man, to seize the Crown for his family. These suspicions were fuelled when a rumour was started that Edward had been poisoned.

Mary was now actively seeking support from Protestants as well as Catholics, and getting it. According to Foxe, sympathetic Suffolk gentry petitioned her not to alter Edward's Settlement, and Mary promised 'no innovations' in religion (Foxe's words). Again to quote Foxe, 'she was being guarded with the power of the Gospellers'. Mary had completely outmanoeuvred Northumberland; from Catholic and Protestant alike, popular support swelled rapidly and swept her decisively to the throne. On 19 July 1553 she was proclaimed queen in London. Northumberland and some of his closest allies, though not Cranmer, were tried for treason and found guilty. Northumberland then renounced the Protestant religion and received Mass, but his conversion failed to save his life, and he was executed in August, confessing the Catholic faith on the scaffold. So an undistinguished career came to its end. Jane, queen of England for less than a fortnight, remained for the time being confined in the Tower with her father.[69]

MARY: STRUGGLE FOR SURVIVAL

For much of her adult life the new queen had been a reluctant conformist (under Henry) or a dissident (under Edward). More loyal to her mother than to her father during Henry's first divorce, she naturally despised the settlement that invalidated the Aragon marriage and pronounced her illegitimate.

Rickmansworth Library
Kiosk 1

11/02/2020 13:56

Customer ID: ******2753

Payment method: Cash
Type: Payment
Requested Amount: £0.75

Tendered Amount: £2.00
Paid Amount: £0.75
Change Given: £1.25

Thank you for using Hertfordshire Libraries
Enquiries / Renewals go to
www.hertfordshire.gov.uk/libraries
or call 0300 123 4049

Her submission to the Royal Supremacy was an unpleasant necessity, made only after an assurance that it was acceptable to Charles V; because on her, as his ambassador put it, depended the 'tranquillity of this kingdom and the reform of the many great disorders and abuses by which it is troubled'.[70]

Her relationship with Anne Boleyn had been understandably a bad one, though relations with Thomas Cromwell and Catherine Parr were quite cordial. Developments in Edward's reign strengthened rather than weakened her religious allegiance. In 1547, Catholic ambassadors approvingly reported her devoutness in saying four Masses a day. Mary remained a thorn in Edward's side, ever more insistent on her rights to hear the otherwise forbidden Mass. She defended herself shrewdly; she hid her loyalties to Rome, and always maintained that she was merely carrying on with the form of services authorised in the church of King Henry's day, which, she said, ought to stay in force at least so long as Edward was a minor. Edward was exasperated with his sister's obstinacy, though Mary could always count on his government's need to maintain good relations with Charles to ensure her safety and independence.[71]

When she became queen, Mary received some unexpected advice from overseas well-wishers. On religion, Charles urged her to be cautious and make no sweeping changes. As early as 9 September 1553, however, his ambassador noted, a little anxiously, that Mary was resolved to restore the papal church, even though in most parishes in England 'services are sung and consecration is made after the fashion of the new religion'. He remarked on the 'difficulties that she has met in restoring the Mass'. The question of papal authority is 'odious, not in this kingdom alone, but in several parts of Europe': so much so that his Venetian colleague warned Mary 'not to be too fervent a Papist'. This advice Mary ignored.[72]

In January 1554 Mary faced the first real test to her authority. She rejected an appeal from Parliament to marry within the realm; she was determined to marry King Philip of Spain, son of Charles V. The Privy Council accepted Mary's decision. Then an ambitious conspiracy led by Thomas Wyatt, son of the poet of the same name, was hatched to marry Princess Elizabeth to Edward Courtenay, Earl of Devon, and make Elizabeth queen. Elizabeth had no knowledge of this. Wyatt mustered a sizeable but generally unimpressive force and set off to London from Rochester. The citizens of the capital remained loyal, and Wyatt and his motley crowd were quickly defeated. Most English Protestants held fast to the traditional evangelical line that princes, even of the opposing religion, should not be resisted or rebelled against. (After the Devon disturbances in Edward's reign, Cranmer had called civil war the 'greatest scourge that can be'.)[73]

Wyatt's rising was a miserable failure: he was quickly put on trial and executed. So were Jane Grey and Lord Guilford Dudley, even though they were only observers and not accomplices. No evidence was found, then or since, to incriminate Elizabeth. The government came through it all entirely unscathed. Mary would face stiffer opposition in Parliament than she did from Wyatt. The landed gentry doughtily opposed schemes to disinherit Elizabeth. By a series of deft political manoeuvrings they also made sure that they held on to church lands acquired under Henry and Edward following the dissolution of the monasteries. Any hopes the clergy had of recovering their property were thwarted by Parliament.

Closing her eyes and ears to the disquiet in the country over the prospect of a foreign king, Mary married Philip in summer 1554. She then set about rolling back the Edwardian Reformation. The Royal Supremacy was repealed and the nation reunited with Rome. Papal authority was restored, and Cardinal Reginald Pole returned from exile as papal legate. Medieval heresy laws were reactivated. Churches were adorned with images, sacred artwork, candles and crucifixes once more. Revised homilies and catechisms were prepared. Plans were drawn up to restore the monasteries, and nearly 2,000 married priests were ordered to put their wives away and live celibate. England had become a Catholic country once again.[74]

But the core issue had changed since Luther's discovery of justification by faith alone over thirty years before. The chief heresy in Mary's England was not justification by faith, or the primacy of Scripture, or even whether the pope was Christ's vicar on earth. Whilst Roman orthodoxy was expected on all points, in the disputes at the major Oxford trials of Cranmer, Latimer and Ridley, and in scores of lesser trials up and down the country, one issue dominated all others – the Mass, and specifically the doctrine of transubstantiation.[75]

But why was this? The answer lies partly in Mary's papal legate and principal churchman. Reginald Pole was the son of Margaret, Countess of Salisbury, and grandson of the Duke of Clarence, younger brother of Edward IV. Relations between Pole and King Henry broke down in the 1530s when Pole refused to accept the Boleyn marriage and the Royal Supremacy. Pole left England and went to Europe, where he became part of an Italian-based movement known as the *spirituali*. Though loyal to the medieval church, the *spirituali* sympathised with Luther on one point at least: they agreed with him that salvation is not achieved by works, vows or monasticism, but on simple faith in Christ (though the 'faith' of the *spirituali* would be found and nurtured only within the Roman Church and the Seven Sacraments). The *spirituali* drew considerable support, especially in Italy, but also aroused strong opposition. The movement faced a crisis in January 1547 when the Council of Trent passed a decree on justification, which, though it did not receive papal ratification in Pole's lifetime, forcefully rejected Luther and the *spirituali* as well. It left Pole a deeply disappointed man, though by the time of Mary's accession he had reconciled himself to Trent. If, however, justification had been the chief controversy in Mary's reign, it would have been all too easy for

English Protestants to seriously embarrass Pole by recalling his past to mind, especially as many in Rome still viewed him with suspicion for his *spirituali* connections.[76]

If taken in isolation, and slightly out of context, the sermons of certain Marian loyalists could sound almost Lutheran. No less a figure than Thomas Watson, Bishop of Lincoln, reminded his flock that 'the sum ground of all our faith, which is, that we believe to be saved only by the merits of our Saviour Christ', whose atoning death was a 'sufficient price and ransom for the sins of all': the faithful attended Mass to show how 'we put our singular and only trust of grace and salvation in Christ our Lord, for the merits of His death and passion, and not for the worthiness of any good work that we have done or can do'. Not everyone in Mary's England preached like this, but Watson is witness to the remarkable degree of fluidity on the theme of salvation in the medieval and Marian church.[77]

The issue of papal primacy – whether the pope was Christ's vicar, head of the universal church and St Peter's rightful heir – was also a difficult one for Mary. Papal authority was restored, but not with any evident relish. As Diarmaid MacCulloch put it, it was 'not a winning theme'.[78] As noted already, the English gentry were extremely loath to give up the lands and property they now enjoyed following the dissolution of the monasteries in Henry's days; they were prepared to make a formal act of submission to the pope and receive his pardon, but markedly less willing to offer Rome any fruits worthy of repentance. Besides, Protestant dissidents could always appeal to the precedent of King Henry of blessed memory, who had rebelled against Rome and made himself Head of the Church. The official line of Mary's government was that Henry had been deceived by evil-minded councillors: but no one really believed this.[79]

These subjects, therefore, were potential embarrassments for the government. The Mass, by contrast, had long since been the centre of popular religious devotion in England. It was also the chief casualty of the Edwardian Reformation. Cranmer had condemned the sacrifice of the Mass, rejected the real presence of Christ on the altar, and banished the adoration of the Host. The restoration of the Mass in its past form, therefore, became emblematic of the restoration of the old religion ruptured under Edward.[80]

Mary's personal devotion to the Mass was fuelled by her antipathy to two men: Thomas Cranmer and Nicholas Ridley. It is reliably claimed that Cranmer was spared a treason trial for the part he played in transferring the succession to Jane Grey only because Mary was determined to see him face a fiercer trial for heresy.[81] Mary had her reasons to hate Cranmer. He was the man who, when Henry's divorce negotiations were deadlocked, had revived the king's spirits with the idea of consulting Europe's universities about the validity of her mother's marriage. Cranmer later formally pronounced that marriage void and Mary a bastard. He was especially close to Anne Boleyn, the usurper queen in Mary's eyes. And it was Cranmer who had led England, under Edward, to a Reformed position on the Eucharist.

The man who first persuaded Cranmer to rethink his Eucharistic outlook was Nicholas Ridley. He had a singularly unpleasant encounter with Mary in Edward's time. He paid her a visit one day, and once the opening greetings were over he offered to preach before her the coming Sunday. This request she sharply refused, and spoke 'many bitter words against the form of religion then established'. Ridley bid her an icy farewell. Later he was furious with himself for forgetting to shake the dust off his feet in disgust when he left her. Then, during Jane Grey's brief reign, Ridley delivered a forceful public preaching at Paul's Cross, urging the people to support Jane and reject Mary because she was illegitimate, and 'would bring in foreign power to reign over them'.[82]

To destroy the Edwardian experiment and its leaders like Cranmer and Ridley, and to cleanse the land, Mary launched a relentless assault on heresy that condemned nearly 300 people to death by fire. The martyrdoms were chronicled, painstakingly and devoutly, by John Foxe in his *Acts and Monuments*, a work that would soon become second only to the Bible in the hearts of English Protestants. A good Calvinist, Foxe was hardly an entirely unbiased observer, but he was a brilliant historian with a gift for compelling narrative, and support for the overall picture he gives of heroic endurance can be found among his bitterest opponents. Soon after the burnings began, Bishop Gardiner of Winchester, Foxe's most notorious *bête noire*, wanted them stopped. He had no sympathy with heretics, but he along with others could see how counterproductive they were. Protestant dissidents were not frightened into submission as the authorities had hoped. The more fires blazed, the bolder they became.

Many things sustained them in their hour of trial. One was the English Bible. If our revisionists may write romantically about churchgoers loyal to the old faith hiding their images from the official iconoclasts under Edward, it is not too fanciful to imagine people secretly reading their Bibles and their Prayer Books under Mary. Hard evidence of secret activity is inevitably difficult to find, but even before Mary's reign began, the Bible in English, to quote David Daniell, 'had seeped into many parts of national life'. Thomas More once claimed that two-thirds of English people could read. More may, of course, have been exaggerating in order to frighten the ruling classes and magnify the danger to the existing order of Bible reading. His estimate could also be weighted in favour of London and his own circle, not taking sufficient account of the remoter parts of England where educational standards were generally lower. A lot depends, too, on how literacy is defined, and whether by 'read' More meant the ability to read *Utopia*, or a few verses from the Bible, or just enough to sign your own name. Whatever he really meant, the likelihood is that more Tudor people than we realise had at least some reading ability, and that this had improved during the twenty years since More died. Yet, as Foxe records, even the illiterate were listening in large numbers to passages from Scripture read aloud, and committing them to memory.[83]

Mary and Pole had badly underestimated the power of the written Word, now in the English tongue and in the hands of the people. Tyndale, Cromwell and Cranmer could be got rid of at the scaffold or at the stake, but their works lived on to defy and eventually defeat the queen. The persecution revealed the underlying strength of the new faith. It also furnished the English language with some of the most famous of all last words; of Latimer to Ridley at the stake: 'Be of good cheer Master Ridley, and play the man. For we shall today light such a candle to the true faith of Christ that I trust, by God's grace, it will never be put out in England.' The government's attempt to humiliate as well as burn Cranmer appeared to be succeeding when he bowed to extreme psychological pressure and recanted, only to fail disastrously when he renounced his recantation to a large audience and died a Protestant. The government was mortified by the bravery of condemned heretics, many of them upstanding Tudor citizens in all other respects. So great was the admiration they aroused in the onlookers as they went to their deaths that Cardinal Pole, no less, had to warn people in his sermons not to be deceived, because what appeared to be courage was really a 'devilish pertinacity'.[84]

The nation was not convinced. People could read the signs of the times aright. Mary was forced to suffer the same misery that had once plagued her mother and her former enemy, Anne Boleyn – she had no heir. To add to her wretchedness, her lawful successor, according to King Henry's will, was Anne's Protestant daughter, Elizabeth. This will was the same document to which Mary had appealed in order to uphold her own rights as queen instead of Jane. It had made Mary's Counter-Reformation possible. It was now about to ensure its swift undoing.

In a report of the Venetian ambassador to the Venetian senate in May 1557, Mary's envy and hatred of Elizabeth are laid bare. 'What disquiets her [Mary] most of all is to see the eyes and hearts of the nation already fixed on this lady [Elizabeth] as successor to the crown, from despair of descent from the queen.' Mary's hatred was fanned by the well-known fact that Elizabeth was 'averse to the present religion'. She had been born, bred and educated a Protestant; and although she was 'living catholically', everyone could see that she was only pretending, and in truth 'more than ever' attached to the Protestant faith. Mary's bitterness, the ambassador continued, was aggravated by the goodwill her husband, King Philip, was showing to Elizabeth. He was the one who had dissuaded Mary from sending her sister into exile. Without Philip to restrain her, Mary, 'for any trifling cause would gladly have inflicted every sort of punishment upon her'.[85]

The ambassador then gave his assessment of the state of affairs in England: 'Externally and in appearance the Catholic religion seems day by day to increase.' Monasteries were being rebuilt, images brought back in churches, the ancient rites restored and heresies suppressed. But: 'These things are done either from fear or to deceive, some persons, by appearing Catholic, wishing to ingratiate themselves with the queen … in general they make a great show and cause the matter to appear much more than it really is, it being known on the other hand that the public mind is more than ever irritated, though they dare not show it …'. Apart from 'a few pious Catholics … none of whom are under 35 years of age, all the rest make this show of recantation, yet do not effectively resume the Catholic faith, and on the first opportunity would be more than ever ready and determined to return to the unrestrained life previously led by them … in short to be free from all the external acts enjoined to Catholics'. (He means freedom from prescribed fasting and confessions, and the liberty of all, including clergy, to marry.) The Protestant faith – the ambassador called it a schism – 'took deep root' in Edward's time. Nevertheless, such is the authority of the Crown that the English will do whatever the prince tells them; 'they would do the like by the Mohammedan or Jewish creed' if the king commanded it. Many, however, were worried about losing the church property they had bought in the previous reigns, and the Catholic religion will be in greater danger still should Elizabeth succeed. 'Nothing could render her more popular … through the restitution to herself and to the crown of all those resources … of which the queen has deprived it.' At the very least Elizabeth will 'withdraw obedience to the pope, were it solely for the sake of not seeing money go out of the kingdom for the despatch of its bishoprics, nor is it to be told how great a grievance that is to everybody'.[86]

The Reformation in England was a 'failure', says one of our revisionists, positively.[87] According to this ambassador, the failure was the attempt to overturn the Reformation. Mary tried desperately hard, but the goodwill she had enjoyed at the start of her reign had vanished. What nowadays would be called 'public opinion' had swung against her. One important factor, again according to the ambassador, was that the gentry and the nobility were afraid that Mary might override parliamentary opposition, and let Rome reclaim the church lands that they had bought or inherited from their fathers. This hardly points to a deep, inward spiritual yearning for the core of Protestant faith. It may well be that the wealthier classes prized the chiefly external benefits of Protestantism, like owing property that once belonged to the clergy, more than the nuanced theology of Luther or Calvin. Even so, it shows a regime beset by troubles. Unquenchable moral opposition of the martyrs; greed and self interest of the gentry and nobility; public disillusionment with Mary and her foreign husband: and all this was just the beginning of her woes.

No longer was it a question of whether Elizabeth would be crowned queen, but when. The thought of this, and the affection the people had for her Protestant sister, tormented Mary. To quote an ambassador again: 'the greater part of England is opposed to the queen, most hostile to King Philip and his dependents, and much inclined towards the Lady Elizabeth'.[88] Pope Paul IV, meanwhile, had vindictively revoked Cardinal Pole's legateship; and in spite of all his efforts to restore the Catholic religion in England, Pole was summoned to Rome to answer charges of heresy dating back to his former *spirituali* days. After an entire life of faithfulness to Rome, amid many dangers, Mary now had to defy the pope to protect Pole. She did so with characteristic Tudor vigour. Yet her reign carried on disintegrating around her. King Philip was at war with France, Rome was on the side of the French, and in a humiliating military defeat at the hands of England's ancient enemy, Mary lost Calais to France. She was dying a more lingering, agonising death than her martyrs. In late summer 1558, she thought she was pregnant. Nobody else believed it, and they were proved right; it was not a child in her womb, but a cancer in her stomach. On 17 November 1558, she and Pole died within hours of each other. The English Counter-Reformation was over, and the reign of Elizabeth had dawned.[89]

3

ELIZABETH, 1558–1603

THE PRINCESS

Before Elizabeth was three years old, in the early months of 1536, her mother was rejected by the king, arrested, tried and condemned to death for adultery. Some kind, sympathetic adult had to explain the tragedy to her: it may have been Kate Ashley, her governess and confidante, or possibly Catherine Parr, Henry's last wife. Relations between Catherine and Elizabeth were warm and agreeable. In December 1544, aged twelve, Elizabeth wrote to her stepmother telling her that she had translated a devotional work entitled the *Mirror or Glass of the Sinful Soul*, showing how the soul 'can do nothing good except by the grace of God, through which she hopes to be saved'. Elizabeth and Catherine must have been close: in 1544 it was indiscreetly brave to put such thoughts on paper, because justification by faith alone had been condemned in the King's Book of the previous year. Elizabeth probably owed her early evangelical education to Catherine. Major Lutheran works like the Augsburg Confession and the *Apology* were still available in evangelical circles. However, the queen may also have counselled her fearless young stepdaughter to be chary about such matters while her unpredictable father reigned.[1]

Elizabeth had something that may be described as charisma, personality or, nowadays, 'star quality'. Even in Edward's reign, when her prospects of becoming England's sovereign were remote, astute foreign observers like the Venetian ambassador already sensed future greatness: 'Her figure and face are very handsome', he wrote, 'and such an air of dignified majesty pervades all her actions that no one can fail to suppose that she is a queen.' She had received a royal, classical education befitting any heir to the throne; the ambassador said she was a fine scholar in Latin and Greek, fluent also in French, Italian and Spanish. Roger Ascham was her tutor from 1548–50, and besides her gift for languages Ascham praised her skills in music, art and the humanities: she had read Cicero, Titus Livius, her Greek New Testament, Isocrates and Sophocles. For her theological education she studied Philip Melanchthon's *Loci Communes*, in Ascham's view 'best suited, after the Holy Scriptures, to teach her the foundations of religion, together with elegant language and sound doctrine'. The results were impressive. She was bubbling over with evangelical enthusiasm according to John Hooper, Bishop of Gloucester, and she enjoyed lively conversation and debates. She was, Hooper went on, 'inflamed with the same zeal for the religion of Christ' as Edward; and with her admirable knowledge of Latin and Greek she could defend it 'by the most happy talent, so that she encounters few adversaries whom she does not overcome'.[2] The curious notion of some modern historians that Elizabeth was a Tudor secularist, wanting in spiritual conviction and depth, would have baffled her contemporaries.

The influence of Catherine and Melanchthon are the best pointers available to Elizabeth's religious outlook. Catherine had died in 1548, before the full range of Edwardian reforms had been put into operation. In the context of the Edwardian Reformation, she had been an old-style evangelical, nurtured more on Luther and Melanchthon than Zwingli and Calvin. With this stepmother to guide her, Elizabeth would have had little time for transubstantiation or the sacrifice of the Mass, but she might also have been disquieted about the denial of the real presence that became the orthodoxy under Edward. Nor is she likely to have welcomed the enforced removal of images from churches; it was well known that she appreciated the beauty of holiness while worshipping, retaining candles, a crucifix and tasteful images in her private chapel. When, in his dying days, Edward altered the succession to ensure the survival of his Reformed Church, it can hardly be coincidence that he passed over Elizabeth as well as Mary, and his choice lighted on Jane Grey. Unlike Elizabeth, Jane had embraced the Reformed Eucharistic teaching as ardently as Edward or Cranmer. During Jane's brief reign, moreover, Elizabeth was publicly branded a bastard, and not by wily Winchester or some predictable foe, but by that pillar of Edward's reign, Nicholas Ridley.[3]

It would be an exaggeration to say that all this made Elizabeth an outsider or a dissident during the Edwardian Reformation. However, she was not right at the heart of it either. Consequently, she was less motivated than a Cranmer or Ridley to want to die for it. She was, so to speak, lagging a bit behind mainstream evangelical opinion in England. When she became queen her settlement would be a modified, slightly more conservative version of Edward's, and all her adult life she firmly resisted attempts to carry on down the Reformed road, as Edward had planned to do.

This point may help to understand more generously her conformism under Mary, and it is astonishing how *un*generously the subject is often treated. Most of us have not even the vaguest idea what life must be like under threat of persecution, or the uneasy reflections swirling around in Elizabeth's mind. The queen's sister she may have been, but she was in grave danger almost from the start of Mary's reign, before the heresy laws were reinstated and the burnings began. Mary's refusal to conform under Edward carried little risk of death or serious punishment, but Elizabeth under Mary had no such security. Bishop Gardiner, Mary's Lord Chancellor, and Simon Renard, the emperor's ambassador, both feared that Elizabeth was a threat to Mary; and after Wyatt's revolt, even though no evidence could be brought against her, they were pressing the queen to put her on trial for her life. She was confined in the Tower in spring 1554, and imprisoned for nearly a year after that at Woodstock, before being returned to Hampton Court and living under the watchful eye of Mary's advisers.[4]

There Elizabeth conformed, though not from the heart, and neither because her faith was fragile. She was following a tradition. The obligatory attendance at Mass was indeed objectionable to Protestants; but evangelicals under Henry, like Cromwell, Cranmer and Catherine Parr, had all attended Mass, and it did their faith no harm. Thomas Cromwell in particular had set the example for a pragmatic and occasionally pliable style of Protestantism. A great opportunist, who would push the evangelical cause forward wherever and whenever he could, Cromwell also knew when to give way. He was a master of the art of making the best of things, even in, or especially in, uncertain and testing times. As seen already, when Henry was determined to enforce his Six Articles, including clerical celibacy, private Masses and transubstantiation (in doctrine though not in name), Cromwell realised that resistance was hopeless. So he advised his supporters to wait patiently, to swallow these bitter pills for a while, trusting in better times to come. Not all would agree with his counsel on principle here, but it is surely possible to see the influence he had on the course of the Reformation in England. Evangelicals who grew up while he was in power learned how to survive in dangerous times, many of them safely negotiating Henry's last years, and Mary's reign as well.[5]

Alec Ryrie has described a 'culture of recantation' prevailing under Henry. It was a culture in which evangelicals who overstepped the mark and got into trouble would, as if by instinct, invariably look for a way out rather than go forward towards a glorious death. There were exceptions like Hitton, Frith and Bilney, but some of Mary's most notable martyrs – men like Cranmer, Latimer and Rowland Taylor – had climbed down gracefully under Henry.[6] This mindset might also be called a culture of deference to the king as God's ordinance on earth, which Cromwell had done so much to instil. Even in spiritual things, deference had become the better part of valour. Such was the climate in which the English evangelical movement was formed and developed, so it is not surprising if the same spirit lived on under Mary. What is unique about the Marian persecution is not the number of Protestants who conformed, for they were part of a tradition dating back to Henry (probably further back still, to the pre-Reformation days of Lollardy). The really unique feature was the number of people, high and low, resolutely determined *not* to conform, to endure death by fire rather than submit. The new mood is well illustrated by Cranmer. Under Henry, Cranmer had yielded to the Six Articles and the King's Book; nevertheless, in September 1553 he publicly rebutted a rumour that he had now accepted the Roman Mass. He followed up this defiance with a forthright critique of the Mass, as if challenging the authorities to arrest him.[7]

To make these points is not to deny the obvious. Anyone facing the prospect of a terrible death is likely to waver or shrink back momentarily, and can readily be forgiven for doing so. It seems, however, far too conveniently easy, especially for those of us who have never had to face such agonising dilemmas, to say that Elizabeth and others conformed simply due to lack of resolve, or because their faith was found wanting when put to the test.

Allowance must also be made for calculation and strategy. Elizabeth was next in line to the throne should Mary die childless, which was looking ever more likely. After Elizabeth, the Catholic Mary Queen of Scots was the heir apparent: Mary was the granddaughter of Margaret Tudor, Henry VIII's sister, and many Catholics felt that Mary's title was superior to Elizabeth's because Henry's marriage to Anne Boleyn had been declared invalid. Elizabeth knew, therefore, that on her all Protestant hopes depended. So why throw them all away? Why put all the good work of Tyndale, Cromwell, Cranmer and many more in jeopardy? Why not do as Cromwell had done, and live with the Mass for a short while, hoping for a better tomorrow? The same reasoning may explain the conformity of her closest friends and advisers, like William Cecil and Matthew Parker, her future Principal Secretary and Archbishop of Canterbury respectively.

These men, like Elizabeth, have been labelled 'Nicodemites', after the secret disciple in John's Gospel (John 3:2; 7:50; 19:39); but it is presuming too much to take it for granted that a 'Nicodemite' is routinely uncommitted or lukewarm. John Calvin may have thought so when he spoke dismissively of those who hide their faith in times of trouble and persecution, and it is a measure of Calvin's huge influence that moderns invariably use the word in this derisory sense, as if Calvin's opinion is the only one that matters. But the usefulness and even the desirability of a secret disciple had not gone unappreciated. Before Calvin, Luther commended 'good, pious Nicodemus' who, while hiding his true beliefs, was doing God good service when he thwarted the plan of the Pharisees to arrest Jesus (John 7:51). So it often is, said Luther, when enemies threaten the church: God makes a fool of them and 'puts a Nicodemus in their midst … to foil the plots of powerful rulers and angry lordlings'. In the Old Testament Hushai performed a similar service as a well-placed spy acting for King David (2 Samuel 17:1–16).[8] In some Reformist circles, therefore, though admittedly not all, the Nicodemite, far from being a symbol of a weak or vacillating spirit, was an effective, acceptable and even honourable aspect of evangelical strategy. That most consummate Protestant operator, Thomas Cromwell, would certainly have approved. Those of a like spirit under Mary probably had no idea that future generations would sneer at them for it.

Besides, if God could ordain a ruler who turned out to be displeasing to Him, He could also frustrate that ruler's ungodly designs; and it is providentially ironic how Mary's husband, Philip of Spain, became Elizabeth's protector. Mary Queen of Scots was now living at the French court and engaged to Francis, son of King Henri II. Should she ever become queen of England, an alliance would inevitably be formed between England and France, and France was Spain's chief rival on the continent. To prevent this, Philip decided he would overlook Elizabeth's Protestantism for the time being, and he became her benefactor. It was thanks chiefly to him that Elizabeth was spared banishment, or worse. This was a favour she never forgot; she would gratefully refer to it more than once in later years.[9]

Philip's realpolitik shows how religious differences, impassioned though they could be, could also be waived when it suited a prince to do so. Philip was the son of the Holy Roman Emperor, a man scarcely less responsible than the pope to defend the faith and doctrine of the medieval church. Nevertheless, here he was putting his religious vocation aside in the interests of statecraft. Foxe describes Elizabeth's preservation under Mary as miraculous. Moderns may not approve of the miraculous, so maybe we should say it was extremely and unforeseeably fortuitous. No one could have dreamed that the survival of the future Protestant Queen of England, the English Deborah, would depend so much on the good offices of His Most Catholic Majesty, the King of Spain.

THE QUEEN AND HER SETTLEMENT

After Mary's death, the new queen entered London in January 1559 to joyful popular acclaim. The lavish ceremony that greeted her was organised by Richard Hilles and Richard Grafton, former supporters of Cromwell, who had kept their heads down and successfully outlived Mary's reign. Everyone knew that changes to the national church were imminent. Elizabeth was England's first adult Protestant sovereign, blessed with some of the ablest advisers of the Tudor age in men like William Cecil, Nicholas Bacon and Matthew Parker: and she acted swiftly.[10]

Elizabeth threw aside all that Mary had done and reinstated the Edwardian Protestant Reformation, though with small alterations. She preferred the title of Supreme Governor to Supreme Head of the Church, a title her successors have used ever since. She was adamant that her priests were to be properly clad in traditional clerical clothing during services. Following her first Convocation in 1563, the Forty-Two Articles of Edward's reign were slightly revised and slimmed down to the Thirty-Nine Articles of Elizabeth's, the foundation confession of the Church of England. The most interesting change concerned the Eucharist. Here the carefully edited articles, and the subtle rephrasing in the Prayer Book, whilst not spelling out the real presence as strongly as the Lutheran Confessions had done, nevertheless held out the prospect of it 'to those who wished to find it', as Diarmaid MacCulloch aptly put it. Elizabeth had watered down the Reformed language and doctrine of Edward's time, a fact that did not pass unnoticed among her clergy; and many of them were disappointed.[11]

Elizabeth preferred Luther and Melanchthon, and especially Melanchthon, to the increasingly influential John Calvin. She told a Spanish diplomat that she would like a church settlement based on the Lutheran Augsburg Confession or, if that were not possible, 'something else like it'. As events turned out she did not take the Confession, though at one point observers thought she would do. But with a slightly revised Prayer Book and set of Articles, she did produce something very like it. The outcome in the end was uniquely *her* settlement, not an exact replica of something else.[12]

The new order reflected the personality and beliefs of the queen. If anyone doubts whether Elizabeth was a classic evangelical, they should read the Thirty-Nine Articles and the Prayer Book, and they will see that it is all impeccably Protestant. Cecil, Parker, Grindal and others could never have railroaded the queen into accepting something she did not believe in from the heart. Tudor kings and queens did not sleepwalk while major changes were made in church and state. Nor does her fondness for candles and sacred artwork in her private chapel make Elizabeth a closet Catholic or 'Nicodemite' (in entirely the wrong sense of the word). Candles, images and the crucifix were disapproved of in Zürich and Geneva; but all over northern Germany and Scandinavia, Protestants of the Lutheran variety found nothing irreconcilable between justification by faith alone and the beauty of holiness. The priest or pastor made the sign of the cross when reciting the Words of Institution and the baptismal formula; congregations bowed at the name of Jesus and knelt to receive communion; while images or paintings of Mary, Jesus and various Biblical settings were normal ornamentations inside churches.

Herein, however, lay a problem: because the chief overseas influence on English Protestantism as a whole, if not on the queen personally, was now John Calvin, not Luther or Melanchthon, many Englishmen were hoping that the queen would continue from where Edward left off, and bring England closer into line with Geneva and Zürich. They were unhappy about the revised wording on the Eucharist in the Prayer Book and the Articles, and shocked when they heard about the crucifix and candles in her private chapel. This was not the Genevan way. Elizabeth and her clergy did not share *precisely* the same spiritual outlook, a fact which would soon lead to tension: this will be discussed later in this chapter.

Meanwhile, and fortunately for Elizabeth, intricate theological differences between Wittenberg and Geneva mattered mainly to clergy and academics, and less to her loyal parishioners. Despite the difficulties, therefore, the new settlement was a huge success. Without a drop of blood being spilt she had completely transformed the church of her sister. Any disquiet, whether by defeated Catholics on one side or disappointed Calvinists on the other, was expressed constitutionally in Parliament or in private gatherings. To the north a revolution had broken out in Scotland, while France and the Low Countries were in the throes of religious turmoil; but England in the early years of Elizabeth was an enviably peaceful and stable land.

Her success, however, may raise questions about the spiritual depth of the Tudor people if they could apparently be switched, like some electronic gadget, from a state of devout Protestantism under Edward, to devout Catholicism under Mary, then back again under Elizabeth. Did they simply believe, unthinkingly, whatever their superiors told them to believe? The answer is probably more subtle than this.

Some years ago it was commonplace to see the Reformation as a struggle between a dynamic, emerging religious cum cultural movement on the one hand, and a powerful but morally decrepit medieval church on the other, with the 'new learning' eventually victorious, despite fierce but ultimately impotent attempts to hold back the irreversible tide. It may be better to see it as a contest between *two* vigorous theologies, the outcome of which was tantalisingly uncertain in England before Elizabeth's reign began. As C.S. Lewis pithily put it, looking at it through the eyes of the ordinary Tudor citizen, the Reformation was a 'quarrel among his Betters'; and in the sixteenth century the common man was supposed to do more or less what his Betters told him to do.[13] It was, of course, the same throughout Europe. But Luther in Saxony and Calvin in Geneva had each prevailed in his own patch, and they fought their battles, using the pen and not the sword, with Romanist opponents in someone else's territory. In England the protagonists lived together: Tyndale and More, Cromwell and Gardiner, Cranmer and Pole, Mary and Elizabeth. As a result the balance tilted first one way and then the other. Not necessarily superiority of argument, but constitutional propriety, like the succession law, and the accident of royal births (or lack of them), gave each party in turn its temporary ascendancy. The twists and turns of these years must have left ordinary men and women, apart from the committed few on either side, not indifferent exactly, but confused and sorely in need of guidance. Mary, fatally for her, had lost their trust, as the ambassador said, and this trust had transferred to Elizabeth (see p. 70), a lady of striking personality and charisma, and greatly loved. One likely reason, therefore, why the people so readily accepted her settlement was, simply, that it was *hers*; they were showing their trust and goodwill. It was not an overwhelming popular demand for justification by faith alone that swept Elizabeth to the throne; nevertheless, the success of her Reformation would never have been achieved without a willing and supportive populace, receptive to the new faith if not yet wholeheartedly wedded to it.

A LESS DEFERENTIAL PROTESTANTISM

In 1555 the Emperor Charles V abdicated, leaving his brother, King Ferdinand, to take charge of negotiations with the Lutherans at the forthcoming *Reichstag*. The result was the Peace of Augsburg, which accepted, though with some reluctance, the religious division in imperial Germany. On the principle of *cuis regio eius religio*, each prince was free to determine the religion of his own state, whether Catholic or Lutheran. Calvinists were not technically covered by the agreement.[14] Though not universally welcomed, the Peace of Augsburg nevertheless reflected a growing realisation that disagreements over religion since the Reformation need not be made the cause of armed conflict. In a similar vein we have already seen princes prepared to overlook doctrinal disputes in favour of dynastic considerations: Catholic Henri II of France was at war with Catholic Mary of England and Catholic Philip of Spain, who was playing court to Protestant Elizabeth, because he preferred to see her on the English throne rather than Catholic Mary Queen of Scots and her French husband.

The accidental death of Henri II in 1559, mortally wounded during a joust, left France without an adult heir. Henri's attitude to his Protestant subjects had been much the same as Mary's; but during the infancy of Francis II and Charles IX, the formidable queen mother, Catherine de Medici, was cautiously thinking over the sort of pragmatic ideas that led to the Peace of Augsburg. In July 1561 the French organised a national colloquy attended by Catholics, Calvinists and so-called *moyenneurs*, those willing to seek common ground, even compromise, for the sake of civil peace. The Calvinist delegation was led by Calvin's deputy, Theodore de Bèze (anglicised from now on as Beza). The Calvinists were offered a few limited concessions, but nothing substantial on core subjects like transubstantiation. Political leaders, Catherine among them, wondered whether the Augsburg Confession might be serviceable as a basis for negotiations; but this was rejected by both Beza and the Catholics. Catherine then arranged a conference to try and reach agreement on the Eucharist, which rather predictably failed. With forlorn hopes of concord gone, Catherine and her allies considered what they called a civil tolerance, effectively an acceptance of two religions in one kingdom. No one actually liked the idea of two churches and two confessions in France, but to Catherine and others it seemed, at least for the time being, the lesser of two evils; better by far than civil war.[15]

Such attitudes, however, whether based on genuine pragmatism or cold realpolitik, were far from universal. Running alongside them was a new Protestant militancy, rising into the open as a result of the unremitting persecution of Protestant dissidents in France and the Netherlands, as well as in Mary's England. The seed of the church is the blood of the martyrs, runs the old adage, but repression as a weapon of the state is liable to backfire unpredictably. To be sure of success, it must be carried out with the utter ruthlessness of a Stalin or a Hitler, which few sixteenth-century rulers could match, otherwise it may succeed only in stiffening the resolve of its targets. It may test, purge and refine; but it can also radicalise and harden, and this is what it was doing in the British Isles and on the continent. In the middle of the sixteenth century the early evangelical consensus, on the unconditional rejection of rebellion, began to give way. Romans 13, the text that required obedience to princes, was undergoing a reinterpretation.

It is reliably believed that St Paul's epistle to the Romans was written during the early part of Nero's reign, when the Roman Empire, though unchristian, had not yet become a persecuting anti-Christian power. The persecutions instigated by Nero himself, and carried on by his successors, were still in the future. This left open the question of whether 'the powers that be', to whom obedience was due, meant the power existing when Paul wrote, or, alternatively, all the powers that are, have been and ever will be, no matter what their character. In the early stages of the Reformation, the tendency was to take it in a virtually absolute sense. Now, however, attitudes were changing. In the opinion of some, 'the powers that be' would have to be godly, or at least not excessively ungodly, if they were to qualify for the unfailing obedience of all their subjects.

Anthony Gilbey, Master of Arts at Christ's College, Cambridge, a Marian exile, radically departed from tradition when he denounced Henry VIII as a persecutor and a 'lecherous monster'. Another Marian exile was John Ponet, former Bishop of Winchester in Edward's reign, now living in Strasbourg, where he wrote *A Short Treatise of Politic Power*. Ponet accepted that kings were ordained of God; but they were ordained to rule justly. If, therefore, a king becomes a tyrant, he forfeits his God-given authority to rule. If Parliament, or a similar institution, proved unable to restrain such a tyrant, then Ponet suggested that some godly individual or group may be inspired to do so. Christopher Goodman, a like-minded man, published a work entitled *How superior powers ought to be obeyed* in Geneva in summer 1558. Like Ponet and Gilbey, Goodman claimed that godly people had the right and even the duty to overthrow a wicked king or queen.[16]

Goodman was a friend of John Knox, the brilliant and formidable Scots reformer. Knox had lived in England in Edward's reign, and then, like most leading foreign evangelicals, he was forced into exile when Mary became queen. Unlike most English men and women who died at the stake, Knox had no qualms about attacking Mary personally. He would fearlessly say the sort of thing that few Protestants had hitherto dared to think. For example: 'had she, I say, and such as now be of her pestilent counsel, been sent to hell before these days, then should not their iniquity and cruelty so manifestly have appeared to the world'. Knox had not forgotten Romans 13 and the command to obey the powers that be. When, however, princes 'commit against His glory … He hath commanded no obedience, but rather He hath approved, yea, and greatly rewarded such as have opposed themselves to their ungodly commandments and blind rage'. Knox's unbending logic led him to this conclusion: 'it had been the duty of the nobility, judges, rulers *and people* of England, not only to have resisted and againstanded [sic] Mary, that Jezebel, whom they call their queen, but to have punished her to the death, with all the sort of her idolatrous priests' (italics mine).[17]

Knox was a man with strong views on what the role of women should be – or rather should *not* be – in the government and public life. He remains magnificently famous for his *First Blast of the Trumpet against the Monstrous Regiment of Women*, a work directed chiefly at Mary Tudor and Mary Queen of Scots, though unhappily published in England just in time to coincide with the accession of Elizabeth, the one on whom English Protestant hopes depended. Elizabeth was livid when she heard of this salvo against the capabilities of her sex and her calling as queen. Just as alarming to her was the fact that in her neighbouring northern kingdom, Knox and others had now openly abandoned the principle of unreserved opposition to rebellion.

Friends of Knox testify to his warmth and personal kind-heartedness. He could, though, be severe on those who strayed from the straight and narrow path, and with English 'Nicodemite' Protestants who had conformed under Mary he was even less sympathetic than Calvin had been to those who did likewise in France and Italy. Like an Old Testament prophet who feared no man's reputation, Knox magisterially took to task no less a figure than William Cecil, Elizabeth's Principal Secretary:

For to the suppressing of Christ's true Evangel, to the erecting of idolatry, and to the shedding of the blood of God's most dear children, have you, by

silence, consented and subscribed. This your most horrible defection from
the truth known, and once professed, hath God to this day mercifully spared.

Knox remained wholly unfazed at the furore his *First Blast* had caused. He
seemed almost unable to understand why it should have given any offence at
all. He calmly suggested that Elizabeth should admit that he had been right to
condemn the government of women as a general principle; and in return he
would concede that she, like the Biblical Deborah, was a divinely permitted
exception. This was meant as a peace offering.[18]

Though Knox had formerly supported Luther on Romans 13, he was
now stressing the distinction between a ruler and the office he held. Like
all reformers, Knox had great respect for the office; but if a ruler abused
that office, the obedience of his subjects was no longer called for. Resisting
a king who turns tyrant was not the same thing as resisting the *office* of a
king. Godly resistance, for Knox, had become a Christian responsibility. To
this Goodman agreed, and he revised his understanding of Acts 5:29 ('God
must be obeyed rather than men'). According to the traditional evangelical
view – indeed the traditional orthodox Christian view – this text was a sort
of last resort, when a prince commanded something contrary to conscience.
In that case the Christian might not be able to obey; but neither should the
Christian resist with violence, and he should patiently endure the displeasure
of the prince if he could not placate it. Goodman, however, turned this text
into a duty of resistance. Like Knox, Goodman agreed that the civil power
was ordained of God; but it was ordained to do good not evil, so a ruler who
enforces evil has lost his right to obedience. He who resists such a tyrant is
obeying God, not men.[19]

So Knox and Goodman did not merely *justify* resistance to bad rulers; they
endorsed it as a duty. They even claimed that it would be sinful *not* to resist
tyrants. Such opinions, naturally, were causing consternation in high places.
Elizabeth's mild-mannered Archbishop of Canterbury, Matthew Parker, was
shocked to learn that books by these two were circulating in London; he
feared only anarchy if 'such principles be spread into men's heads'.[20]

Goodman and Knox had departed not only from Luther, Tyndale, Cromwell
and Cranmer, but also from Calvin, now the dominant force in Reformed
Protestantism. Calvin continued to stress that the citizen was under a divine
command to be submissive to the civil power, 'even if we lived under Turks,
tyrants or deadly enemies of the Gospel'. Rebellion he condemned unequiv-
ocally. Only if the government commanded idolatry or forbade true religion
could the Christian invoke Acts 5:29 in its traditional sense and disobey. Even
so, such disobedience must be without violence or sedition. (To this counsel his fellow countrymen did not listen, as the story of the French Wars of
Religion horribly proves.)[21]

Calvin did, however, add two points which revolutionary and innovatory spirits might have found more attractive than he intended. The first is a passage from the *Institutes* headed 'when God intervenes, it is sometimes by unwitting agents'. Here Calvin ventures further than Luther or the early English reformers. Sometimes, says Calvin, God 'raises up open avengers from among His servants, and arms them with His command to punish the wicked government and deliver His people, oppressed in unjust ways, from miserable calamity'. Calvin cites Moses delivering the children of Israel from the tyranny of Pharaoh; and such servants acted 'by God's lawful calling'.

In the second, also from the *Institutes*, Calvin envisaged a society so constituted that a body such as magistracy exists to protect the people against the tyranny of an aberrant ruler; for example the ephors in Sparta, or the tribunes in ancient Rome, and 'perhaps, as things now are, such power as the three estates exercise in every realm when they hold their chief assemblies'. Calvin did not command *them* to suffer a tyrant: they may, and indeed should, fulfil their constitutional obligation, resist the tyrant and protect the 'lowly common folk'. Calvin does not call for the tyrant to be removed or destroyed, just resisted.[22]

It is important not to misinterpret Calvin here, or to take his words out of context. He did not elaborate on the finer details of his argument, but he was certainly not advocating insurrection or even a mass protest movement, and he shared Luther's patrician distaste of popular agitation. On the first point, he did not mean that any man jack in Christendom with a grievance or a cause could claim to be Moses; examples like Moses are rare and chiefly historical. Calvin was doing no more than putting the finishing touches to his thesis on civil government, and including a special exception that St Augustine had once used. Augustine also opposed tyrannicide; but added that when Samson destroyed himself and his enemies 'this can only be excused on the ground that the Spirit ... secretly ordered him to do so'.[23] As with Calvin and Moses, Augustine was not making Samson a pattern for the church. Taken as a whole, therefore, Calvin's position is quite intellectually understandable. Unfortunately, in times of trouble, strife and heightened tension, including such an exception at all risks distorting the entire argument. It gives radical spirits something they can latch on to. What is to stop anyone claiming, as Thomas Müntzer did in Germany, a divine commission, given by revelation, to destroy a godless ruler? How can it be proved, beyond all possible doubt, that what someone says is a revelation is not a revelation, just a fancy or a dream?

Regarding Calvin's second point, what he meant was this: if a king had to be restrained, then only those institutions lawfully entitled to do so should proceed against him, and then only by constitutionally defined means. It seems reasonable enough, even wise. Still, it is not difficult to see how this could be used by more excitable spirits. Calvin quoted the estates of France as an example of a body organised to defend the rights and liberties of the people. What role, therefore, could the English House of Commons, a similarly constituted assembly, claim for itself if it feared that kingly rule was becoming tyrannical, or popish?

So John Calvin, the prince of the Reformed Churches, the dominant influence on English Protestantism in the middle and late sixteenth century, could be accommodated, if only just, to radical views by those with a mind to do so, especially after his death in 1564 when he was no longer around to clarify his meaning. He may not have meant to, but he had left a dangerous door ajar.

Having made the point about the rise in militancy, it must now be stressed that, in Elizabeth's early years as queen, the views of Goodman and Knox were held by only a small minority of Englishmen. Nevertheless, the fact that such views had been heard at all indicates a significant hardening. The divine right of kings was not denied, but no longer was it quite as absolute as it had been. And whether readers agree with Goodman and Knox or not, it is surely impossible not to see some force in their logic. For how long could people be expected to believe that a state which persecuted the people of God was an ordinance of God?

There are also signs of Knox's influence on a few of the accompanying notes to the Geneva Bible, produced by Genevan scholars in the late 1550s with the help of English members of the Geneva congregation, among them Anthony Gilbey. This was a work of impressive scholarly and literary merit. (Goodman and Gilbey were first-class scholars, whatever interpretation is put on their opinions.) The Geneva Bible included helpful notes to clarify the meaning of the text, and more cross-referencing from one text to another than in previous English Bibles. It also included doctrinal notes, which are mainly Calvinist, though agreeing with the Thirty-Nine Articles. Occasionally, however, a touch of the new militancy is discernible. The story of David sparing his persecutor, Saul, because he was the anointed king had hitherto served as a command for obedience even to unjust rulers; but according to the notes in the Geneva Bible this was David's 'private cause' only. Jehu then comes in for fulsome praise for slaying the murderous Jezebel by throwing her out of her palace window – a 'spectacle and example of God's judgements to all tyrants' (1 Samuel 16:9, 2 Kings 9:30–3). The fact that Jehu was acting in his capacity as the commissioned and lawful king, and not as a private individual, is not emphasised by the commentators. A small point perhaps, but it is impossible to imagine Thomas Cromwell or Cranmer approving this edition had either of them been editing it. Nevertheless, between 1560 and 1649 nearly 150 editions of the Geneva Bible, roughly half a million copies, were published and avidly read in both England and Scotland.[24]

And dramatic events in Scotland were now demanding the attention of Elizabeth and her government. Mary, Queen Regent of Scotland, had been showing unusual indulgence to the Protestant nobility in the hope of winning their support for the marriage of her daughter, the future Mary Queen of Scots, to the Dauphin of France. She enjoyed some success with her conciliatory policy, but in 1559 she abruptly abandoned it and forbad any form of communion other than the Mass. The Protestants defied her. Knox, now back in Scotland, was in Perth preaching with accustomed fervour against idolatry and popery. When a Catholic priest punched a supporter of Knox who had tried to prevent him saying Mass, the Protestants started a spate of iconoclasm in churches and the friaries, though under Knox's direction they did show commendable restraint in dealing with the friars personally. There was no lynching, though the friars were required to hand over their wealth to the poor. Nevertheless, the troubles at Perth were tantamount to rebellion, and Regent Mary ordered French soldiers under her command to crush it. Knox now handled his cause with some skill. He persuaded the Protestant nobility that what had happened was not an uprising that threatened the security of the state or the Queen Regent personally; rather it was a necessary defence of the true Protestant religion. A compromise agreement offering pardon to the rebels if they left Perth soon broke down. Knox continued his preaching, and in St Andrews, with the full support of the Provost and the council, churches and monasteries were stripped of images and adornments.[25]

Forces loyal to Knox, known as the Congregation, generally avoided pitched battles with government troops by making temporary truces, which both sides knew would not last. For a while they were able to frustrate the government. Despite some successes, however, Knox realised that his loyalists were not on their own strong enough to resist and defeat the Scottish government, which was backed by France. So he looked to England for help. He had little time for what he called that 'bastard religion' in England, with its 'mingle mangle' of ceremonies and liturgies; but besides being a fiery preacher he possessed an astute political mind. He realised that Elizabeth, unlike her father, had no desire to rule over Scotland, and that she was more than content to remain queen of England. He also knew that whatever her personal views were about him, Elizabeth would readily see the advantage of driving the French out of Scotland, and having an ally rather than an ancient enemy on her northern border. Elizabeth, therefore, could hardly refuse to help; nor would she demand any English control over Scotland as a price for that help. Negotiations that followed were difficult, but Regent Mary's reliance on France played into the hands of the Congregation, because it was able to accuse her of submitting Scotland to foreign rule. In October 1559, a motion on behalf of 'the nobility and commons of the Protestants of the Church of Scotland' pronounced her deposed. A 'Great Council of Scotland' was established in its place. Thanks to Cecil's diplomatic skills, it consisted mainly of notables more amenable to Elizabeth than Knox.[26]

On 6 July 1560, the Treaty of Edinburgh was agreed, and the French were required to withdraw all troops from Scotland. The Scottish Parliament then established Protestantism on the Geneva model as the state religion. The strength of Protestantism in Scotland was astonishing, and how to account for it is still a matter for some debate, especially as Knox had been out of Scotland for much of 1550s. A key factor was the commitment of a few dedicated but highly influential people to the new teaching, now being consummately harnessed by Knox. What is most significant for this story, however, as well as the sixteenth- and seventeenth-century history of the British Isles, is that in Scotland, quite unlike England, the Reformation was established following a revolt against the lawfully constituted ruler. As revolutions go it was neither particularly violent nor bloody – about twenty Protestant and two Catholic deaths compared with hundreds in England – and it could claim a great deal of popular support and even justification. But it was a revolution nonetheless.[27]

Worse was soon to follow for advocates of divine right. Following the death of Regent Mary, her daughter, Mary Queen of Scots, still a Catholic and now a widow following the loss of her French husband, reigned over what was now a Protestant state. Despite this the English ambassador, Randolph, reported that the Scots were generally well disposed towards Mary, 'saving John Knox, that thundereth out of the pulpit'.[28] But it was not the thundering of Knox that destroyed the unhappy queen. When she married Henry Stuart, Lord Darnley, her Protestant subjects murmured uneasily, and began to wonder what a Catholic king might have in store for them and their new religion. At first Darnley tried to be conciliatory, and he went to listen to a sermon of Knox (which went on so long that Darnley had to miss his dinner in order to go out hawking that afternoon before darkness fell). In fact, the issue was soon to resolve itself without Knoxian resistance, because Mary's marriage was a disaster. A string of misfortunes began when Darnley led a group of assassins to murder Mary's secretary, David Riccio, for reasons never fully understood and still debated. Then Mary, even though she had issued royal orders to punish adultery among her subjects, took a lover called James Hepburn, earl of Bothwell, a married man and a nominal Protestant. In February 1567 her husband, now king of Scotland, was murdered. Mary's connivance in the deed was widely believed in, though never proved beyond all doubt. Mary then went to live with Bothwell until he could settle his divorce; then she married him. Mary had succeeded in shocking Catholic Europe and Scots of all persuasions, and she was taken prisoner by her own nobility. No respecter of persons, Knox demanded that Mary, queen though she was, be put on trial for murder and adultery. Angry crowds chanted 'burn the whore' as she was led captive through the streets in Edinburgh. Humiliated and disgraced by her own people in her capital city, Mary was forced to abdicate.[29]

In England Elizabeth, though not blind to Mary's faults, was nevertheless horrified at the Scots rebellion. In a rage she threatened to invade Scotland if Mary were executed. Back came the reply that if English troops entered Scotland, Mary would be put to death immediately, and Scottish lords would seek the help of France. (This may have been a bluff; nevertheless, it was an effective one.) Elizabeth's empathy for Mary as a sister queen, however, was not reciprocated. To most of her English subjects it was bafflingly misplaced, especially when Mary arrived as an unwanted refugee in England. Eventually, nearly twenty years later, Mary was caught up in a plot to kill her royal hostess. Elizabeth's formidable minister of state, Francis Walsingham, intercepted incriminating letters from Mary via a messenger, supposed to be part of the plot but actually one of Walsingham's well-placed spies. Yet even now Elizabeth was loath to consent to the death of an anointed queen, however guilty, and at Cecil's suggestion Mary's execution warrant was despatched to her gaoler without Elizabeth's formal consent.

Somewhat against her will, Elizabeth was also drawn into the conflicts raging in the Netherlands and France. The Dutch lived under Spanish rule, and troubles broke out in 1562. The reasons were many and varied. They included the savage persecution of Protestant heretics, fears that King Philip was about to intensify the Inquisition, burdensomely high taxes, and the nationalist resentment that Spanish rule had provoked among the local nobility. In the Netherlands, as in England and Scotland, Lutheranism was being eclipsed by a more robust brand of Reformed Protestantism. As so often in these conflicts, outbreaks of iconoclasm became a distinct feature of resistance. The rising was answered ruthlessly by the Duke of Alva in 1567, though the rebellion was renewed five years later. Elizabeth was eventually persuaded to help the Dutch as part of her overall policy of containing Spanish power, but she had little love or sympathy for rioters and image breakers. Their cause, she said, 'had neither reason, virtue nor religion, the only aim being liberty against God and Princes'.[30]

In France, meanwhile, Catherine de Medici's pragmatism failed to halt the slide into religious war. L'édit de Saint-Maur of September 1568 suppressed Huguenot liberty of worship, and though in theory liberty of conscience was not entirely forbidden, many Protestant ministers were required to leave the country. As elsewhere in Europe, the Huguenots were becoming radicalised. Among them the 'Knoxian' view gained ground, that princes who denied the true religion and resorted to persecution had set themselves against God, and had effectively forfeited their right to rule and to the obedience of their subjects. Elizabeth did help the Huguenots at various stages of the French wars, but seldom did she do so wholeheartedly. Once she vented her exasperation on Cecil, who was more supportive towards them: 'I want to get clear of this', she rapped in a council meeting, 'and not involve myself any longer with you and your brothers in Christ.'[31]

Elizabeth's horror of rebellion, even if the cause may have had some excuse, may be ascribed to a princely aversion to the rule of the common man, and also to her Lutheran (or Philippist) upbringing. But she could also draw on her own personal experience. She survived Mary's reign and became queen, not by resisting Mary or by stirring up the people against her, but simply by waiting on Providence (and a bit of prudent conforming). But waiting patiently, and suffering patiently if need be, was the way of the first generation of reformers, and most of them had now passed on. A new generation had arisen, ready if called upon to fight for the cause. To Elizabeth it was shocking, deeply disturbing and it boded ill for the future. This rebellious spirit, she recalled, had begun in Germany with the Peasants' War, then spread to France, Scotland and Flanders, and 'perhaps some day it will happen here'.[32]

THE PURITANS

In Edward's reign, John Hooper had described Elizabeth as a young lady full of evangelical enthusiasm and zeal. This had been tempered by five years of uncertainty, anxiety and the disagreeable necessity of having to conform under Mary. All her erudition and learning, and her celebrated fluency in languages, was of little practical use while Mary reigned: it all had to be suppressed. The ability to sparkle in conversations and debates suddenly counted for nothing. The woman who had come through the shadow of death, and who now sat on the throne of England, was more mature and reserved than the one that Hooper knew. She had painfully learned the limitations of mere knowledge. From now on the emphasis would be on stability, tranquillity and good order. The matriarch of the Church of England was determined to avoid religious discord in her realm or her church. She was flexible and ecumenical, usually prepared to give way on inessentials for the sake of peace and quiet. She detested the bickering and wrangling over sacred subjects like the Eucharist, now bedevilling the Reformation. But she did not want a soulless outward conformity and nothing more. A great deal of time and thought had gone into vetting the articles of the church, the new Prayer Book, and all other ecclesiastical arrangements, until she was entirely satisfied with them. What she desired above all else was to give her people that precious, priceless gift of stability and peace. Harmony and blandness are different things.[33]

The faithful were not expected to show too much initiative or zeal. Some of them, however, had rather a lot of zeal, and too much love of innovation for the queen's taste. Shortly after her settlement had been established, Archbishop Parker was vexed by the disobedience of some ministers to the queen's order requiring them to wear the appropriate clerical garb. Normally a mild, scholarly man, Parker called them 'silly recusants … I would wish them out of the ministry, as mere ignorant and vain heads'.[34] This may seem a trivial point, but it reflected an undercurrent of dissatisfaction with the Elizabethan Settlement. Many of her Protestant subjects, forced into exile during Mary's reign, had tasted life in continental Reformed churches like Calvin's Geneva, and they returned home to find the English church grievously wanting by comparison. What rankled was the fact that too many features of her church seemed far too 'popish': besides the matter of vestments, examples included kneeling at communion, making the sign of the cross at baptism and other ceremonial aspects of the services. The gradual formation of a movement (for want of a better word) was taking place that would come to be known as Puritan. The more devout among them were also known as 'the godly', the 'saints' and even 'the elect'.

The Puritans emerged from within Reformed Protestantism, without ever coming to dominate it. Nothing comparable was to be found in the Lutheran Church until the Pietist movement more than a century later. The primary concern of the early Puritans was not the closing down of alehouses, brothels, theatres and other dens of iniquity, as happened during the later republic: what the Elizabethan Puritans wanted was a more thorough, root and branch reform of the church. For the godly, it was not enough for the church to *be* reformed in the faith and doctrine set out in its confessional articles; it also had to *look* reformed. And if it didn't look reformed, then it couldn't be *properly* reformed. Most items and customs reminiscent of the old religion – vestments, a crucifix, candles, images, altar tables and organs, kneeling – were suspect and should be discarded.

The Puritans were also convinced that the established church was far too lax in ministering the sacraments to all and sundry, regardless of their moral state. Puritans felt that only true, pious Christians should receive communion, even though the Prayer Book did allow ministers to refuse communion if necessary. (This was done occasionally, but only in exceptional cases.) Puritan ministers also complained of a widespread ignorance of the basics of the Christian faith amongst the laity, a scandal they blamed on a negligent priesthood. The godly may have had a point here. 'Few come into a church on the Sabbath day', sighed the Elizabethan Bishop Pilkington in England; 'but the alehouse is ever full'.[35]

Another point of contention was that the Prayer Book failed to grant preaching its rightful, principal role in church services. Elizabeth's Settlement provided for readings from the Bible and authorised homilies. But Puritans preferred to have the Word expounded in a sermon; it was not enough that passages of Scripture be merely read to the people. The primacy of preaching and the enthusiasm for sermons became hallmarks of Puritanism. It is recorded that one godly minister preached every day of the week, and four times on Sundays, for twenty years. The preacher, according to Sir Edward Dering, a Puritan minister and accomplished scholar, was the one 'by whom the people do believe'. Godly parishioners, if they were dissatisfied with the local state church minister, did not hesitate to go to a neighbouring parish in the hope of hearing a preacher more to their liking. One reason why Puritans disliked liturgy and ceremonial in church services was that it distracted people from the message of the sermon. Puritans sang with fervour, but they tended not to favour congregational responses or prayers. As a rule Puritan parishes did follow the Prayer Book, as they were legally bound to do, and only in exceptional cases was the Geneva Book used in defiance. Puritan ministers, however, would discreetly adapt the Prayer Book when they felt it was safe to do so, by leaving out objectionable requirements like kneeling and making the sign of the cross.[36]

By all accounts Puritans were sincere, usually well-educated people; they understood Protestant doctrine well, and were diligent in doing good works in their communities. A Puritan was no respecter of persons. They preached fearlessly to all classes, and they did not flatter the nobility. They were also capable of over-earnestness and a certain want of tact, which, despite undeniably good intentions, may have grated with their fellow countrymen. Here is one of them writing to a Kentish dignitary, reproving him for ungodliness:

> Though I know that our Saviour Christ hath given us a straight charge not to cast precious stones before swine, nor to give that which is holy to the dogs, yet I see so many examples of his unspeakable mercies that I know not any swine so wallowing in the mire, nor any dog so returning to his vomit, of whom I have not some hope that he may be a pure and clean creature in Israel. This maketh me bold with a good conscience to write unto your honour …

If the recipient, Lord Abergavenny, had read any further, he would have found himself likened to 'an enemy of the cross of Christ, whose belly is his god, whose end is destruction …'.[37]

Many state churchgoers, according to the godly, were nowhere near devout enough. George Gifford described how, in his view, religion was ordinarily received: 'Let the preacher speak ever so plain, although they sit and look him in the face, yet if ye enquire of them so soon as they be out at the church doors, ye shall easily perceive that … it went in at one ear and out at the other.'[38]

Again, the godly may have had a point. The Supreme Governor of the Church of England expected her people to dutifully turn up on Sundays, listen to a sermon or a homily, receive the Sacrament, follow the order of service in the Prayer Book, rising, kneeling, sitting, making the sign of the cross, reciting prayers and the ancient Creeds when they were bid. When the service was over they would go away and be good citizens. The sheep were to be cared for, not to care for themselves; neither were they expected to have to do too much thinking for themselves. Bishops and priests were charged with feeding and shepherding the flock, and they were not supposed to wrangle or argue with one another over points of doctrine. Stability, tranquillity and uniformity were the honourable aims. Nevertheless, it *could* all lead to a state of spiritual drowsiness. So were the godly simply injecting a bit of much-needed life and vitality into a stodgy, formalised church and a semi-vegetative laity?

Yes and no. How, for example, could the godly be so sure that the Word was having so little effect? They had to judge from the outward appearance: it did not look as though it was bearing much fruit; not enough people seemed as eager for sermons as the godly; people in the pews appeared unresponsive and undemonstrative when the Word was preached to them; and so on. Such fears were not new; ever since Luther reformers had despairingly wondered whether their labours were producing any real results. The first reformers, however, took refuge in the words of the Creed: I *believe* in the holy Catholic and apostolic church. That church is a spiritual gathering of the faithful, and because it is impossible to see into the heart, it is also impossible to know the true spiritual state of the heart. Outward enthusiasm may be transient and shallow, even deceptive. Early reformers believed as an act of faith that the church would grow through the ministry of the Word and the Sacrament, even though appearances may often be discouraging. The godly had faith too; but they liked to see as well, and if they could not see the true church with their own eyes, they feared it wasn't there. Puritanism was a preaching and seeing Christianity.[39]

But the godly were not always looking for good fruits in others. As one writer has aptly said, 'Puritans were constantly taking their own spiritual temperatures'.[40] This led to a renewed interest in the moral law of the Old Testament, and to something that became known as 'Covenant theology', according to which God demands a moral code from His people. Covenant theology was derived from the Zürich reformers, Zwingli and his successor Henry Bullinger, though not from Luther and Melanchthon in Wittenberg. The Puritans were using, and slightly adapting, Covenant theology as an assurance of their elect status. Almost to a man Puritans were predestinarian, and to satisfy themselves that they really did belong to the elect, they looked for signs or proofs of election in their own hearts and lives. They examined themselves rigorously, to check whether their sorrow for sin ran deep enough, that their good works were good enough, that they prayed, read the Bible and attended sermons devoutly enough.[41]

This moral temperature taking is, ironically, just the sort of thing that Luther used to do when he was a monk and before he became a reformer. It is what he and Melanchthon had spent so much time since then urging believers not to do. Put simply, the dilemma is this: How do I know that I, a fallen and sinful man, am saved? Or as Job of old said: How can a man be just with God? (Job 25:4.). According to the German reformers, assurance of salvation was found in believing the promise of salvation for all who believe (John 3:16 etc.). Puritans did not openly deny this. But the more predestination was pushed into the centre of Protestant theology, the greater the danger that one question would arise to nag at the mind, namely this: If the list of the elect and the damned had already been drawn up in some secret decree before all time, how could anyone be sure that that promise applied to him? Such certainty was impossible – unless infallible signs that identify the elect were known to exist. This is what was exercising the minds of the godly. They were not necessarily more extreme or fanatical than their neighbours, they were simply thinking the doctrine of predestination through to its logical conclusion and working out its implications. The danger, however, is that this kind of self-examination could easily lead to self-absorption, and ideas of personal righteousness – exactly the opposite of the Reformation principles.

Lest it be thought that I exaggerate the difference between the Puritans and the early Reformation, the following is paraphrased from the work that Elizabeth knew well, Philip Melanchthon's *Loci Communes*, 1535. It may help to see the godly through Elizabeth's eyes, and explain her hostility to them.

> The certainty of salvation comes only by listening to the Gospel and the promise of forgiveness for Christ's sake. Only the Gospel can free the conscience from doubt, and the Gospel excludes all our worthiness and merit. Only this way can the conscience be at rest. Otherwise the conscience cannot stand before God's law. True believers know they are never without sin, so the law of God can only terrify the mind. If we consider our own worthiness, then only doubt and anxiety will remain, because no true conscience will claim to be guiltless. So let us hold to the promise of the Gospel, which is universal, and reject all these 'pernicious imaginations regarding predestination'; for God gave His Son that 'whosoever believes may be saved' (John 3:16; Galations 3:22).[42]

If, as is quite likely, Elizabeth had also seen Melanchthon's classic commentary on Romans, she would have read the same views expressed yet more strongly: This promise of the Gospel is for all, and it should not be obscured by speculations about predestination: such 'false and impious thoughts … slander and corrupt' the divine promises; to indulge in disputes about election is nothing else than to 'doubt the promise, to cast aside the Gospel and accuse God of falsehood'.[43]

Because this is what Elizabeth had been nurtured on, excessive godly pre-occupation with predestination could only have raised her suspicions, even alarm. This was nothing less than another Gospel. It was based not on a divine promise revealed to all in the written Word, but on a secret divine decree that had to be learned experimentally by self-examination, and, ironically, by good works. Whilst it is true that many early reformers – Melanchthon perhaps more than most – were exercised about righteous living, they never imagined a Christian's conduct to be reliable proof, or even a sure guide, to his saved or elect status.

Church government was another subject that had become unexpectedly controversial. The background to this may be traced here briefly.

Luther was prepared to respect the existence and ecclesiastical role of bishops, including the episcopal structure, provided they allowed him to preach the Gospel (and keep his wife). This offer was made just before the diet of Augsburg in 1530, and it came with a touch of typically Lutheran bite. 'We will do you bishops no harm', he assured them; 'we are more use than all your scholars and the pope's … more godly heretics you have never had, nor will ever find'. If Rome agreed, Melanchthon would have acknowledged the pope as chief pastor of the western church.[44]

Some of our text books claim that Luther frequently contradicts himself on church government, because in his writings he can be found putting forward different ideas in different places and occasionally changing his mind. But this is flexibility, not indecision or contradiction. For Luther, no one form of church government was obligatory as an article of faith, so a little experimentation is to be expected. It was chiefly a practical matter; there was no divine law for one system or another. Existing medieval arrangements were fine, provided they allowed the Gospel.[45]

In this respect Elizabeth's church bore a closer resemblance to those in Germany and Scandinavia than in Geneva, because Calvin took a slightly different line. Calvin was willing to allow for what was suitable to the times, and he seemed content to accept bishops as lawful in England and elsewhere. He preferred, however, to organise the Geneva church on what he felt was a more Scriptural basis. Calvin's thought is based primarily on Ephesians 4 and the gifts of apostles, prophets, evangelists, pastors and teachers for the building and edification of the church. The first three categories, he argued, were not intended to be permanent; but pastors and teachers would always be needed.[46] Calvin's recommendation for church government comprised four ministries: pastors to preach and minister the sacraments, doctors to teach doctrine, elders to deal with church discipline, and deacons to take care of the poor and other Christian social duties. The system allowed for overlap;

a pastor may also be an elder, and a doctor a pastor. Calvin never put the Genevan magistracy under the authority of the church, though he did try and forge a close relationship between the two.[47]

After Calvin's death, his successors in Geneva, led by Beza, argued that this Presbyterian system, as it came to be known, was the form of church government that had a Scriptural mandate, and consequently it behoved true Christian churches to follow it. Church government, therefore, was no longer purely a practical matter. It was turning into an article of faith. It also contained an element of danger. Beza's doctrine, if rigorously applied in England, threatened to make bishops redundant. Moreover, although it did not deny the authority of the sovereign, it did not easily harmonise with an episcopal church with the king or queen as her Supreme Governor. To those jealous of the Royal Supremacy in church and state, Presbyterianism was seen as a challenge to the existing order. Feelings were equally antagonistic on the other side. Beza had a low opinion of the English church, a view shared by his godly allies in England. Not every English Puritan was a Presbyterian, and some of those who were may not have been as ardently committed as Beza. But although Puritan leaders, like Thomas Cartwright and John Travers, accepted that a defective church government did not threaten the salvation of souls, they also stressed that an unreformed church risked serious spiritual decay, and worse still, an outbreak of divine anger.[48]

Cartwright, who had visited Geneva, was now Lady Margaret Professor of Divinity at Cambridge University. During the spring of 1570 he delivered a series of lectures on church government, and although the full text of these lectures has been lost, it is known that they caused considerable controversy. Now facing expulsion, Cartwright sought temporary refuge in Geneva once more, where he was accorded an honourable welcome. But one man's departure could not stamp out the new teaching, and more and more young men were emerging from English universities, where they had been taught that the organisation of the national church was more Papist than Protestant, and seriously flawed.[49] 'If only', sighed the Puritan Thomas Wood, 'they had at the beginning sought a full reformation according to God's Word, and an utter abolishing of all Papists' dregs': in Edward's time they 'went forward as knowledge increaseth ... but now having greater light we go most shamefully backward'. More radical Puritans were now denying that Elizabeth's bishops were part of the true church: according to John Udall they 'are in league with hell and have made a covenant with death'.[50]

Most Puritans claimed that no fundamental doctrinal gap separated them from the established church, and some modern historians seem willing to take this at face value. But the Puritans *would* say that, because few of them were rash enough to brazenly accuse Elizabeth's church of being doctrinally false. If, however, they really believed in the four-fold system of church government, as a doctrine and an article of faith, when the Elizabethan Settlement did not, then there *was* a clear difference in doctrine. To illustrate how serious a crisis was developing, Archbishop Parker gloomily noted in 1573 how fast Puritan ideas were spreading: 'and but that we [bishops] have our whole trust in God, in her Majesty, and in two or three of her council, I see it will be no dwelling for us in England'. Parker had reason to be concerned. John Field, admittedly one of the most radical of all Puritans, called Elizabeth's Settlement 'far worse than that of popery, if worse may be'. Even Cartwright could speak of 'heaps of our people', who, though not papists, nevertheless remained in 'an utter ignorance of the truth'. He meant non-Puritan churchgoers, even though they went to their parish church every Sunday. This is not the sort of language people use about minor, purely cosmetic differences.[51]

Church discipline, said Cartwright, is 'the order which God hath left, as well to make the doctrine of the church most effectual and to give ... a sharper edge unto the preaching of the Word'. This discipline was a 'part of the Gospel'.[52] Cartwright discussed Christ's Headship of the church, and how the church should be 'governed according to the form and policy which He hath prescribed' (a quote from Calvin). But Christ had not prescribed an epis-copal church government, so 'this form of policy which is by archbishops, and such bishops as we have, is not the means to knit us one to another in unity under the dominion of Christ'. So Elizabeth's Settlement was not conducive to the spiritual unity of the church. Cartwright was now implicitly making church unity dependent, in one degree or another, on the right kind of church government, and in doing so he was standing the early Reformation on its head. The Augsburg Confession and the *Loci* expressly denied this: 'For the true unity of the church it is enough to agree concerning the teaching of the Gospel and the administration of the Sacraments ... It is not necessary for the unity of the church that traditions be the same.'[53]

It may be objected that I have brought in the names and works of Luther and Melanchthon more than is warranted in a discussion of mid-sixteenth-century England. They are relevant because on the throne was a queen who learned her theology by reading them, and especially Melanchthon, and she preferred them to Calvin and Beza. Elizabeth was a child of the early Reformation. The godly regarded that as something flawed and imperfect, which had to be put right before England could finally cross the Jordan into the Promised Land. But Elizabeth was entirely satisfied with it, and saw nothing at all imper-fect in it. In her eyes the Puritans were trying to undermine, even undo her settlement, not bring it to perfection; and again it must be stressed that it was *her* settlement, whatever continental influences may be discerned in it, so any challenge to it could be seen as a challenge to the queen personally.

It may also be claimed that doctrinal differences between the Puritans and the 'orthodox' Elizabethans should not be exaggerated. Some modern

writers have said as much. But contemporary evidence reveals a view somewhat less blasé than this. Passions really were rising. The Earl of Leicester,
believed to hold Puritan sympathies himself, confessed that 'I found no more
hate or displeasure almost between Papist and Protestant than is now in many
places between many of our own religion'.[54]

There was another disquieting fact about the godly from Elizabeth's point
of view. Although most of them were peaceable folk and upright citizens, their
doctrinal agenda had much in common with her bête noire John Knox. John
Udall was bitterly frustrated by the failure to establish a Puritan settlement,
and he warned, enigmatically though ominously, that 'if it come in by that
means which will make all your hearts ache, blame yourselves'. Cartwright
approved a work by Dudley Fenner, which, like Knox and Goodman, supported the right of magistrates to oppose and remove a tyrant. Of course,
neither Fenner nor Cartwright nor Udall had Elizabeth in mind, and by no
means were all Puritans radical men. Nevertheless, the gap between some
leading Puritans and Knox was a narrow one.[55]

By now Puritans were making deep inroads into the universities, especially Cambridge, though Oxford also had godly graduates and tutors. Like
more traditional reformers, they encouraged Bible study based on the Greek
and Hebrew texts, using all available humanist tools of rhetoric and logic in
order to seek out the true meaning. They also adopted a practice first used
in Zwingli's Zürich known as 'prophesyings'. A little less charismatic than
the title suggests, these were meetings designed to cultivate techniques in
Scriptural exegesis, mostly using the Geneva Bible, and to develop preaching
skills in front of lay people as well as academics. Many were well attended.
When Elizabeth heard of these developments, however, she reacted with
anger and ordered her Archbishop Grindal, who had succeeded Parker, to put
a stop to them. She was more than content with priests who could 'read the
Scriptures and homilies well unto the people'. As always, she valued stability
above innovation and godly enthusiasm.[56]

Grindal was embarrassed by the queen's order because he had some sympathy with the 'prophesyings'. He also understood that the preaching ministry
stood in need of improvement. He searched the Scriptures, the fathers and
more recent authorities to reinforce his case that prophesyings ought to be
allowed to continue, at least under the watchful supervision of bishops, who
would make sure that nothing radical or subversive was going on. To Elizabeth
he confessed that he would be acting against his conscience if he suppressed
them as she had commanded. 'Bear with me I beseech you, Madam', he
implored, 'if I choose rather to offend your earthly majesty than to offend
the heavenly majesty of God'. But Madam would suffer no beseeching, and
Grindal was unceremoniously bundled out of office and placed under house
arrest. Elizabeth replaced him with John Whitgift, a man more after her own

heart, who acted quickly against the Puritans and the prophesyings. Whitgift's theological position was essentially Calvinism with bishops. He issued three articles to be binding on all clergy: Elizabeth's authority under God alone, in church and state, was sacrosanct; the Prayer Book was the only book to be used in church services; and the Thirty-Nine Articles were a statement of faith fully in accordance with Scripture. The Puritans accepted the first and the third of these. The second, with all its 'popish' ceremonial, was a stumbling block to many of them.[57]

Then in the long running 'Admonition controversy' between Whitgift and Cartwright, Whitgift was uncompromising with the godly. Scripture, insisted Whitgift with Elizabeth's blessing, does not command one form of church government. He quoted from the New Testament to show the variety of practice in the early church, when all Christians preached and baptised; it was only when the church became established that a regular ministry was instituted. That ministry was a worthy Christian tradition, and a Christian queen had every right to appoint bishops to oversee the welfare of the church. This should be accepted by all true and loyal subjects.[58]

Whitgift attacked two 'false principles and rotten pillars' in Cartwright's work. The first was Cartwright's demand for a Presbyterian system of church government, because that was the one authorised in the times of the apostles: here Cartwright was simply wrong, because the apostles had done no such thing; the Presbyterian system was no more divinely approved than any other. Cartwright's second 'rotten pillar' was his view that, as a matter of principle, none of the ceremonial used in the Roman Church should be permitted in the Church of England. Again Whitgift disagreed: the Church of England is entirely free to use comely ceremony and liturgy if her leaders and her queen wish to do so; nothing is wrong with that.[59]

Whitgift had no truck with Puritan professions of loyalty to Elizabeth, and how thankful they were to have her as their queen, and that they wished only to carry on the good work of reform to bring it to perfection. For Whitgift, this was all godly humbug:

> Neither the authority of the prince, the ministry, the government of the church, the administration of the sacraments, the ceremonies, the discipline, the form or matter of public prayers, nor almost anything else can please you; and, howsoever now in words you confess that you are most deeply bound unto Her Majesty, etc., yet both in tongue and in deed divers of you declare that your meaning is nothing less. For why do you then so unorderly, so undoubtedly, so spitefully, publicly and privately, in word and in writing, deface her proceedings, slander her government, deprave the reformation that she hath made, with sects and schisms divide the realm, set dissension among the people, make the papists more stubborn, drive back

those that were well-nigh persuaded, thrust a misliking of the state into the hearts of many protestants, encourage her adversaries, separate her faithful subjects one from another, and greatly disquiet herself?[60]

Cartwright had been looking admiringly on the more reformed churches of Scotland and France; they were 'examples before your eyes, to encourage you to go forward to a thorough and speedy reformation … to altogether remove whole antichrist, both head and body, and branch, and perfectly plant the purity of the Word …'. Whitgift was unimpressed. 'England is not bound to the example either of France or Scotland', he retorted patriotically. 'I would they both were (if it pleased God), touching religion, in that state and condition that England is.'[61]

Even the Prayer Book had now come under godly fire. A widely read Puritan work had called it 'an imperfect book, culled and picked out of the popish dunghill, the mass book, full of abominations; for some, and many of the contents therein, be such as are against the Word of God'. Whitgift was furious. Had not the Marian martyrs 'sealed this book with their blood', he demanded? Cartwright admitted that the martyrs were 'excellent personages'; but 'their knowledge was in part', and 'although they brought many things to our light', they had been 'sent out in the morning ere ever the sun of the Gospel was risen so high'. Cartwright added – and here he had a point – that some of Mary's martyrs *were* dissatisfied with the Prayer Book, and wished that Cranmer had reformed the church more radically.[62]

Elizabeth was aghast at the discontent in the church. What worried her most of all was the revolutionary potential, as she saw it, in Puritanism. It was a dangerous new development, even if, as yet, only a few of her godly subjects shared the ideas of Knox and Goodman. Nor did all her bishops seem as stoutly loyal as Whitgift, so she took them to task for their failure to curb the Puritans. 'You suffer many ministers to preach what they list, and to minister the sacraments according to their own fancies, some one way, some another, to the breach of unity: yea, and some of them so curious in searching matters above their capacity as they preach they know not what.' Such men, she demanded, should preach 'all one truth … or be compelled to read homilies … for there is more learning in one of those than in twenty of some of their sermons'. (This suggests that what she disapproved of was not preaching exactly, but specifically the sort of *Puritan* preaching that she feared would be the result of the prophesyings.) To an ambassador she spoke about a letter she had received from an unnamed correspondent abroad, who feared that the papists would prevail in England because the Protestants dislike their queen. 'And indeed they do', she added, 'for I have heard that some of them of late have said that I was of no religion … both these [papists and Puritans] join together in one opinion against me, for neither of them would have me to be queen of England.'[63]

The Puritan party, meanwhile, argued its case in the Parliamentary session of 1586, seeking to adopt the Geneva liturgy. Elizabeth then ordered the Commons to meddle no more in church affairs. Members listened glumly as the Speaker told them: 'Specially you are commanded by her Majesty to take heed that none care be given or time afforded the wearisome solicitations of those that commonly be called Puritans, wherewithal the late parliaments have been exceedingly importuned.' Yet despite this royal intervention the debates continued, and Peter Wentworth, one of the most outspoken Presbyterians, suffered a spell in the Tower. Through it all Elizabeth remained immovable; there would be no further reforms to her church settlement. Puritan demands, the Commons were told, were 'prejudicial to the religion established, to her crown, to her government, and to her subjects'.[64]

Not for the first time in her life, King Philip of Spain came to the queen's aid in an unexpected way. Following the defeat of the Armada in summer 1588, the godly joined in the national celebrations and thanksgivings; but this great victory may have actually harmed their cause. For years they had been warning that failure to complete the godly reformation was risking divine anger; but the crushing defeat suffered by the forces of His Most Catholic Majesty the King of Spain, one of the mightiest princes in Europe, seemed unassailable evidence of divine favour, not displeasure, on Elizabeth and all her doings.

Whether by coincidence or not, after 1588 Puritanism suffered a sequence of unfortunate reversals. This was the year that the Earl of Leicester died, and he had been the councillor most sympathetic to them. Another high placed sympathiser, Sir Francis Walsingham, died in 1590. By now the government now enforcing a series of severe anti-Puritan measures, as a result of which prominent Puritans were removed from the ministry and even jailed. John Udall was sentenced to death for seditious language, though later pardoned. Further orders were issued by the government to enforce obedience. Cartwright was committed to the Fleet, and High Commission and Star Chamber proceedings were instituted. The most damaging charge was that Puritans denied the queen's authority in the church. This was potentially treasonable, though convictions for treason were rare, and many persons arrested were released sooner or later. Then disastrously for the Puritan mainstream, two of their radical brethren on the fringe, Edmund Copinger and Henry Arthington, announced to a startled audience in London's Cheapside that they had received a revelation from heaven; and they followed this up by proclaiming a simpleton called William Hackett as Messiah and king. To the government this was a horrendous outbreak of fanatical excess, shockingly reminiscent of the days of Thomas Müntzer. Puritanism was badly tainted by the Hackett affair, and now close to becoming a proscribed religion.[65]

In the face of the queen's anger, the godly could either defy her or submit. Most chose to draw back from confrontation, and wait in the hope of better times. A few decided they had no choice but to leave the established church, and consequently the Separatist movement began to take shape.

The origin of the Separatists may be traced to the underground churches in Mary's reign, particularly the London congregation, though there were very few of these. Separatism in Elizabeth's time grew steadily, led by John Greenwood, a former priest, and Henry Barrow, a country gent with a legal background. Both men denounced Elizabeth's church as apostate for reasons that by now will be familiar: it permitted mixed congregations of godly and ungodly; its church government failed to conform to apostolic ways; and its liturgy was full of 'popish' ceremonial. Separatists were accused of civil disobedience, but they denied any seditious intent. Nevertheless, Barrow and Greenwood were executed in 1593, convicted under the anti-papist act of 1581, which made it a capital offence to seek or contend for the overthrow of the church and the Royal Supremacy. Not all Puritans became Separatists; many rejected Separatism on principle, though they sympathised with those who felt they could no longer conform. But the gap between unhappy Puritans still in the state church, and those separating from it, was a small one; while prospects for keeping the church united in the bonds of peace were bleak.[66]

THE ANGLICANS

'He that goeth about to persuade a multitude that they are not so well governed as they ought to be, shall never want attentive and favourable hearers.' So began the *Laws of Ecclesiastical Polity* by Richard Hooker, an Oxford don and supporter of Whitgift, a man who, in the view of many since, was the father of what has become known as Anglicanism.[67]

The *Laws* are a series of contemplative reflections on the relationship between faith and reason, Scripture and tradition. The reader does not have to wait long to find the Calvinist and Puritan stress on the unfathomable will of God coming under critical scrutiny: 'God worketh nothing without cause', says Hooker. God does all things not just because He wills to do them; He always has a reason, though that reason may be, and often is, unknown to us. 'He worketh all things according to the *counsel* of His own will, not just to His own will.' Nature itself 'is nothing else but God's instrument'.[68]

Hooker was the most eloquent opponent of Puritanism after Whitgift. Soon he turned his attention to the frequently heard contention of the godly that Scripture 'must be the rule to direct in all things'. Hooker's counter arguments were not those of a modern liberal quarrelling with a 'fundamentalist'.

Nowhere does Hooker fault the godly for taking the Bible too literally: on the Creation, the Incarnation and the Resurrection he took it just as literally as they did. Hooker treated the book of Genesis as a historical narrative: besides the Creation and Cain's murder of his brother he also quotes it in the *Laws* to prove 'how quickly sundry arts mechanical were found out, in the very prime of the world' (Genesis 4.20–2). All things needful for salvation can be found in Scripture, Hooker assures us. There are, however, many other things, such as the arts, sciences and civil affairs, not covered in Scripture; and here natural reason and good sense are quite adequate. Reason is God-given and it is perfectly competent to judge; and it is wrong to despise all human authority in such matters. Scripture, when rightly used and not taken out of context, is 'most invincible', and 'in strength and value exceedeth all'. Man can learn much from nature, but he will not learn the way of salvation there; for that he must look to Scripture, in which 'every sentence thereof is perfect, and wanteth nothing requisite unto that purpose for which God delivered the same'. But if nothing may be done except what Scripture expressly says, then parents do wrong when they tell their children to go to sleep; and (heaven forbid) servants 'shall stand still, till they have their errand warranted unto them by Scripture'.[69]

Hooker was leading on to the controversial issue of the day: whether the Presbyterian system of church government was commanded in Scripture. Hooker denied this, and he accused Puritans of despising the learning, wisdom and reason that come from experience and tradition. Yet in the *Laws* he never fails to stress the primacy of Scripture. 'We do not add reason as a supplement of any maim or defect therein, but as a necessary instrument', to help in a right understanding of sacred texts. 'Theology, what is it but the science of things divine? What science can be attained unto without the help of natural discourse and reason?' Reason in things divine, however, is unprofitable without the 'aid and assistance of God's blessed Spirit'. But God's Spirit may 'aid and direct men in finding out by the light of reason what laws are expedient to be made for the guiding of His Church, over and besides them that are in Scripture'. Though this must have raised Puritan eyebrows, it was comfortably within the boundaries of classic Protestantism. Melanchthon was saying much the same sort of thing seventy years before during troubles with religious radicals in Germany, who, unlike English Puritans, almost boasted of their lack of learning as if ignorance was a virtue, and who claimed a special insight through divine revelations.[70]

But back to Hooker: on church government, to disregard Scripture would be 'profane, impious and irreligious'; nevertheless, 'a number of things there are for which the Scripture hath not provided any law, but left them to the careful discretion of the church'. As a result, 'what kind of ordinances would be most for that good of the church … all this must by reason be found out'.

Hooker commended Whitgift, who had made a clear distinction between divine truths necessary for salvation, and 'matters of ecclesiastical polity'. The first were 'fully and plainly taught in Holy Scripture'; the second were not, and did not need to be. The first were 'not capable of any diminution or augmentation at all by men; the other apt to admit both'.[71]

Like Whitgift, Hooker defended, even praised, the rites and ceremonies used in the church that the godly disliked. The aim of religious ceremonial is edification, to move the heart and mind to 'reverence, devotion, attention and due regard' to spiritual things. It was foolish to say that everything that looked popish should, on principle, be abolished. 'Contraries are cured by their contraries', Thomas Cartwright had said; and 'Christianity and Antichristianity, the Gospel and Popery, be contraries; therefore Antichristianity must be cured, not by itself, but by that which is contrary unto it'. Not quite, says Hooker wittily. 'He that will take away extreme heat by setting the body in extremity of cold shall undoubtedly remove the disease, but together with it the diseased too.' Even Geneva, Hooker goes on, retains some popish customs, such as godfathers and godmothers in baptism, and the use of wafer cakes in communion. These are neither commanded nor forbidden in Scripture. 'These things the godly there can digest. Wherefore should not the godly here learn to do the like?' Hooker quotes an ancient authority approvingly: 'Where the faith of the holy church is one, a difference in customs of the church doth no harm.' Not for the first time, the *Laws* cites Calvin against the godly, who, for a time at least, was happy to leave it 'free unto all churches to receive each their own custom'. Difference and variety may be a good thing; otherwise it will be thought that 'religion is tied to outward ceremonies'.[72]

A little more provocatively now, Hooker defines the 'visible church' as that which professed one Lord, one Faith, and one Baptism. This would make the Roman church (just) part of the visible church, and it was certain to rattle the godly.[73]

At this point the *Laws* begins to branch off, slightly though discernibly, not just from Puritanism, but also from mainstream English Protestantism. Hooker was a lover of sacred art and beauty. Exalted worship reflects the majesty of God, and this applies to church buildings and decor. He would not despise congregations who genuinely lacked the means to beautify their churches; but 'the majesty and holiness of the place where God is worshipped … serveth as a sensible help to stir up devotion, and in that respect no doubt bettereth even our holiest and best actions in this kind'. As the Psalmist King David said: 'O worship the Lord in the beauty of holiness.'[74]

There is no defect in Scripture, says Hooker, 'but that any man, *what place or calling soever he hold in the church*' will find 'needful instruction unto any good work which God requireth' (italics mine).[75] In part this is Hooker letting it be known that he is just as devoted to Scripture as the godly; but it is also a rebuff to the Puritan insistence that the preacher and preaching have a special, virtually indispensable, place in expounding Scripture. Hooker commends preaching, but he commends public and private readings of Scripture as well: the Word of God is power unto salvation, and 'not only by being delivered unto men in Sermons'. Pace the godly, 'sermons are not the only preaching which doth save souls'. Hooker accepts that sermons are 'as keys to the kingdom of heaven'; nevertheless, the 'bare reading' of Scripture, with the aid of the Spirit of God, is able to 'convert, to edify, to save'. Reading may even be preferable: for a passage of Scripture is 'properly the Word of God', while a sermon on Scripture is likely to be influenced by the 'wit of man', which is why they 'oftentimes taste too much of that corrupt fountain from which they come'. (To godly ears this was near sacrilege.) Hooker wonders whether the Puritan love of sermons may be unduly influenced by the personality of the preacher: 'his virtue, his gesture, his countenance, his zeal, the motion of his body, and the inflection of his voice'. In other words, a rousing sermon may be good fun, exciting and entertaining; whether it is also the pure, unadulterated Word of God is another matter. With a plain Scripture text, or a well-prepared homily, there is no doubt.[76]

Hooker then exalts prayer – public more than private. He sees the ordained minister not just as a preacher, but as a leader in public prayer, even an intercessor for the congregation. The very act of ordination is a 'seal', that God will 'effect the thing whereto He ordained it, in blessing His people and accepting the prayers which His servant offereth up unto God for them'. So ordination is not solely – no longer, perhaps, even primarily – to preach to the people; there is 'this other part of his function', to lead the public prayers of the church. Hooker commends Rome for recognising public prayer as a 'duty entire in itself'; and the English church does well to do likewise, 'both morning and evening whether sermons may be had or no'. Almost satirically Hooker derides 'this form of theirs' (the Puritan form) as 'No sermon, no service'. Hooker will have none of it.[77]

An exquisite section follows on music, the art with the power to reach and stir 'that very part of man which is most divine'; it is a 'thing which delighteth all ages … as seasonable in grief as in joy'. He defends at length the church liturgy; but the prayer 'for mercy upon all men' troubles him, because it raised the thorny issue of predestination. It is not clear (at least not clear to me) whether Hooker was confused, unable to make up his mind, or simply wary of upsetting orthodox Calvinists like Whitgift. Redemption is 'for all', he says in one place; but in the next sentence 'we know there are vessels of wrath to whom God will never extend mercy'. A little further on God has a 'general inclination' to save all men; but, because not all men are saved, maybe He also has 'a more private occasioned will which determineth the contrary'.[78] This is the problem with predestination: it is one of those issues where it is better to be either wholly for or wholly against. The only alternative is theological waffle, albeit lofty waffle. Calvinists and Puritans at least had consistency on their side; Hooker did not. His cautious – dare we say timid – approach to predestination, a doctrine he obviously did not like, is a little surprising given the fact that Elizabeth was known to be unenthusiastic about it. Also, according to one contemporary witness, Philip Melanchthon and Henry Bullinger were the continental divines most valued by preachers in Elizabeth's days; yet whereas Melanchthon had taken the axe to the root of the predestinarian tree seventy years before, Hooker does no more than chip away at the branches.[79] Nevertheless, in England Hooker was unconventional for his time; and however cautious he may have been on this point, it is another example of him moving away, albeit slowly and hesitantly, from what had been standard English Protestantism since the days of King Edward and Thomas Cranmer.

Hooker's lofty view of divine worship naturally embraced the Sacraments. These are neither mere signs nor ancillaries to preaching; they are 'powerful instruments of God to eternal life'. In these 'heavenly ceremonies' are imparted 'the vital or saving grace of Christ unto all that are capable thereof'. Nearer to Melanchthon and Calvin than Luther or Zwingli, Hooker sees the essence of the Eucharist as being in the 'real participation of Christ and of life in His Body and Blood by means of this Sacrament'. On the contentious issue of the real presence, Hooker wishes that men would 'give themselves to meditate with silence what we have by the Sacrament and less to dispute of the manner how'. The apostles never quarrelled among themselves over this. 'Curious and intricate speculations do hinder, they abate, they quench such enflamed notions of delight and joy as should be raised by divine blessings.'[80]

Hopefully this summary of the *Laws* has not gone on too long, but it is necessary to give a broad introduction to the Anglicans because they have an important part to play in this story. On the use of natural reason in matters like church government, and in other things not directly commanded by Scripture, Hooker differed little from major reformers from Luther to Whitgift. His esteem of church liturgy and comely ceremonial, his praise of sacred music, would have sounded rather unremarkable in Lutheran Germany and Scandinavia. On predestination he was nowhere near as radical as Melanchthon had already been a generation before Hooker was born. This may explain why Hooker has never made much impact outside England. In late Elizabethan England, however, Hooker really was unique, and his *Laws* a watershed in the development of the English Church. He did more than just lend his voice to Whitgift against Puritans. If Cranmer and Whitgift defended the liturgical and the ceremonial, Hooker exalted it. They (like the Puritans) were predestinarians; Hooker was not, at least not to the same degree. Puritanism was a 'sermon centred' Christianity; Hooker would raise public reading of Scripture, public prayer, the Sacraments and the liturgy, to the level of the sermon, if not beyond.

Perhaps there is something inevitable about this. Justification by faith alone, as Luther taught it, had been virtually unheard of in the Western Church for nearly 1,000 years. During the early stages of the Reformation, therefore, it was natural, even essential, that preaching should have the primary role. The message simply had to be told forth and explained in detail. By Hooker's time, there must have been very few people who did not know what justification by faith meant. It was heard from the pulpit, in school, from parents, from catechisms, week after week, even day by day. So sooner or later the sermon would, as it were, come under pressure to adapt, and maybe begin to lose the chief place it formerly and necessarily had. It was never in any danger of being abolished, but perhaps it had ceased to be quite as uniquely indispensable as before. Not everyone would appreciate going to church and listening to a preacher, a man whose livelihood was paid by the state, saying in different words the same thing that could be read in dozens of familiar catechisms: they might at least expect some variety. A renewed interest in other aspects of the Christian life, therefore, was not altogether surprising. Hooker was the catalyst for this development in England, and he directed the affections of like-minded people towards the Sacraments, liturgy and prayer.

With reformers since Luther, the highest art in theology, so to speak, was to believe and rightly understand divine truths, and be able to express them eloquently. Hooker did not despise this. What he wished to do was reclaim the sort of devotional piety traditionally associated with pre-Reformation times, and integrate it into the Elizabethan church. Like all original minds, Hooker goes backwards and forwards at the same time. On church government, in the context of the Reformation as a whole, he was really fairly orthodox, because he did little more than defend the existing Elizabethan order, just as Whitgift had done before him. But in his re-evaluation of the Sacraments and the liturgy, Hooker moved on from Elizabethan orthodoxy, though without critically undermining it. He was both orthodox and an innovator, and in both respects opposed to the Puritans.

Another feature unique to Hooker is worth noting briefly. When we call Thomas Cromwell Lutheran, and Cranmer Reformed, these are the nearest continental fits, not exact fits. (There are very few exact fits in the English Reformation.) As seen in Chapter 2, the Royal Supremacy was an English development, quite different from any idea or doctrine derived from Wittenberg, Zürich or Geneva; while the Edwardian church under Cranmer retained more of the ceremonial than Zwingli, Bullinger or Calvin had done. With Hooker, however, it is difficult to spot even a nearest fit. His appreciation of liturgy and sacred music is more like Luther than Calvin; but on the Eucharist he is closer to Calvin (though closer still to Tyndale); then he departs from Calvin on predestination without becoming fully Philippist. A new kind of Christianity was now coming into being, the Anglican kind, and it was finding favour in the highest places in the land.[81]

It is not known for certain whether Elizabeth read the *Laws*, but had she done so she might have found the language there agreeable. Her own attitude to sermons, for example, was notoriously less than enthusiastic, and she had no qualms about attending services in her private chapel that included communion, prayer and liturgy but not a sermon. She would fondly quote a distant ancestor, Henry III: 'that he had much rather put up with a humble devout petition to God himself, than hear the finest harangues about him from the lips of others'. One day, while listening with mounting impatience to a particularly long-winded court preacher, she ordered an attendant to signal him to stop. When Alexander Nowell was rash enough to censure the use of the cross in church services – a pious devotion beloved by Elizabeth – she interrupted him with a regal: 'Leave that; it has nothing to do with your subject.' The experience left the unfortunate Nowell 'utterly dismayed', according to Archbishop Parker, but the lesson was well, if painfully, learned. Preachers got the message, and sermons delivered in the presence of the queen were thereafter satisfyingly briefer than normal, as well as free, for the most part, from contentious subjects. Whenever Parker received lists of candidates for court preaching, he took care to weed out those unlikely to please the queen.[82]

Elizabeth's preachers faced a problem, simple and humbling. What could *they* teach *her*? She had learned her theology by reading Melanchthon, the finest scholar of the Reformation; she knew her Greek New Testament as well as any trained clergyman; she had closely supervised, edited and finally authorised the Thirty-Nine Articles and the revisions to the Prayer Book. What need had she of lectures or sermons? And who was qualified to offer guidance or instruction in the unfathomable ways of Providence to a princess who had been branded illegitimate by her father, struck out of the succession in her brother's reign, fearful of her life in her sister's, yet had survived all this to become Queen of England and Supreme Governor of the Church? To endure and prevail in trials as testing as these is far more demanding than learning from text books. She was one of those laymen, like Melanchthon in Germany and Thomas Cromwell before her, whose understanding of theology, doctrinal and practical, was at least as good as, probably better than, that of the most formally trained divines. Preaching to someone like this is a bit like playing a piece of music to Johann Sebastian Bach: no matter how skilled the performer may be, he will never match the accomplishment of the listener.

A sermon would need to be well above average to impress this lady. Dry, correct theology would simply not do, and it is small wonder that more and more she turned to sacred music and the beauty of holiness to enrich her spiritual life. She was quoted as saying that she never wanted to 'make windows into men's souls', and it hardly mattered to her that many of her finest court and sacred composers, like Tallis and Byrd, belonged to the now proscribed Catholic faith. Had she lived longer, the nascent Anglicanism of Hooker might well have received a formal royal commendation.

Another distinguished new Anglican was Sir Robert Cecil, the queen's most powerful minister in the closing years of her reign. An art lover and collector, Cecil was the chief patron of the arts of his day. Like the queen, he discreetly enjoyed services in his private chapel that included images, candles, sacred art and sacred music. His devotional reverence for the Eucharist matched Hooker's. Cecil saw nothing irreconcilable between this and the classic Protestantism of the Elizabethan Settlement and the Thirty-Nine Articles. His chaplain was Richard Neile, another Anglican, soon to be consecrated a bishop. More will be heard of Neile and his like-minded friends later in the reign of James.[83]

Whitgift and Hooker were not the only leading divines to counter the Puritan movement. A few supporters of the archbishop, who were eagerly following the debates, latched on to the fact that the office of a bishop dated from the time of the apostles (1 Timothy 3:1–7; Titus 1:5–9). In 1587, John Bridges was saying that because the episcopal office was established by the apostles, it must be an office instituted of God, and more than just a worthy church custom. To which the Puritan Walter Travers noted, with satisfaction, that Bridges was beginning to see the light at last: he was admitting that church government was, after all, a doctrinal subject taught in Scripture.

But Travers may have been unprepared for what followed. Writers in the 1590s, like Thomas Bilson, Richard Bancroft and Hadrian Savaria, took the ideas of Bridges to new levels. In the early church, they said, all clergy preached and ministered the Sacrament; but the 'power of the keys and the right to impose hands' had been entrusted only to select men like Timothy and Titus. Further, though the word 'bishop' was originally one and the same as pastor or elder, gradually over time it came to be used to describe such senior men in the church. Bishops, therefore, as they are now known, could claim apostolic succession. So episcopacy, concluded Savaria, was 'the form of government which was ordained of God, and delivered of the apostles and confirmed of the fathers'. This left the godly hoist with their own petard: Scripture did indeed lay down a specific form of church government, but it was the episcopal system, not the Presbyterian one. A few episcopalians, as if eager to outdo the godly in zeal, condemned the abolishing of bishops as a sin on a par with the Arian denial of Christ's Deity. They also insisted that the Christian prince was a divine institution, though derived more from the Old Testament than the New (Deuteronomy 17:14–20, David, Solomon etc.). In practice, the prince would be expected to exercise authority in the church through the bishops rather than directly by dictat.[84]

The principle now being formulated, of episcopacy by divine law (*jure divino*), was not endorsed by Elizabeth, or Whitgift, or Cecil or Hooker. Nor was it laid down in the Thirty-Nine Articles.[85] It got no official approval until the reign of Charles I and Archbishop Laud. Already, however, it was a sign of the times and of things to come. The divide between Anglicans and Puritans was becoming irreparable. The Puritan party, meanwhile, badly weakened though it was during Elizabeth's last years, had not been destroyed, and nor were godly hopes and ideas driven out of men's hearts.

TUDOR TWILIGHT

In view of previous sections on the revolutionaries and the godly, or the *un*godly as Elizabeth might have called them, a reminder may be timely that her reign did not consist solely of domestic agitation. This was an age bristling with ideas on all sorts of political, religious and cultural themes. Nor did she spend all her time restraining enthusiastic innovators. The larger part of the country was loyal and content. It is, however, the nature of history that controversialists grab more attention than less demonstrative people.

Apart from the Puritans, the other party most opposed to her Settlement were the Jesuits. The papal bull, *Regnans in Excelsis*, issued in 1570 and proclaiming Elizabeth excommunicated, put her Catholic subjects in an unpleasant quandary. They probably perceived that the queen, mindful of her own unhappy days in Mary's reign, was loath to have any of her obedient subjects 'molested by any inquisition or examination of their consciences in causes of religion', as she put it.[86] There is no reason to doubt the genuineness of these words, or that a large number of Catholics would have preferred to live quietly and loyally while secretly practising the old faith and causing no trouble. Many still sought to do so. Others, inspired by the Jesuits, dreamed of the re-conversion of England, and were prepared to die for it. A series of strong measures against papists as well as Puritans were then enforced. Many priests were jailed or executed for treason, which made the closing years of Elizabeth's reign seem more repressive than she intended.

Yet the Puritans and the Jesuits were the only groups that constituted a grave challenge to Elizabeth. Danger threatened briefly in the north during 1569–70 following the unwanted arrival of Mary Queen of Scots in England, when the Duke of Norfolk, angry at Elizabeth's refusal to let him marry Mary, absented himself from court without leave. It was suspected, quite rightly, that a rising was being planned. His northern allies, the Earls of Northumberland and Westmoreland, had even fixed a date, 6 October. But Norfolk's nerve failed him, and he returned to London and submitted to the queen. Northumberland and Westmoreland received a royal summons to London, which they defied. Urged on by zealous supporters, they celebrated Mass at Durham cathedral and set off on an expedition to release Mary. Then for reasons not too clear, the rebels lost heart, perhaps because the support they drew fell short of expectations. The rebellion petered out, the leaders submitted and the law exacted its revenge on the guilty in the normal manner.[87]

Elizabeth's parliaments could be lively and demanding, but they remained loyal. At times they badgered her to name a successor, and she would tell them to mind their own business, or fob them off with sweet reassurances, promising that she would act only in the very best interest of her realm and her people, and consider the matter afresh when the time was right. She feared rivalry would break out if a succession list was drawn up. The Privy Council was just as concerned as the Commons about the succession, but whenever it raised the subject it met with a similar response. More than once she gave the Commons a slap on the wrist for meddling with her church settlement, which most members accepted meekly and made little fuss about. There was nothing like an official opposition, or a Parliamentary party pitted against a Royalist one. There was no political crisis serious enough to threaten the peace of the realm. Nor had the power of Parliament increased appreciably since the days of Henry VIII and Thomas Cromwell. When Peter Wentworth argued for unrestricted free speech on any matter, and that the prince had no right to forbid it, he was despatched to the Tower, and few voices were raised in protest.[88]

The issue that caused most frustration in her closing years concerned the monopolies. This touched on the cherished royal prerogative, because a monopoly was a royal grant to an individual giving him and his company exclusive rights to trade in certain goods. It was a privilege that could all too easily be abused. When pressed to make changes and to liberalise trade, Elizabeth's first reaction was to stall; but her parliaments of 1597 and 1601 were uncommonly persistent in urging that grievances should be listened to and redressed. The queen then staged the most captivating climb-down in constitutional history. She was surprised, she said, and much displeased to hear that certain monopolists may have abused their privileged position. She would review the situation immediately. Some were revoked; in other cases people were allowed to seek recompense through the courts. This was Elizabeth's 'golden speech', in which she assured them that 'though you have had and may have many mightier and wiser princes sitting on this seat, yet you never had nor shall have any that will love you better'. Then she bid all the members kiss her hand. The Commons were completely overcome, and with lumps in the throat they filed past her for the last time.[89]

It has frequently been said that no other sovereign, or era, in English history has aroused a more lasting fascination. No apology need be offered for repeating a truth, even though modern historians, making fault-finding a virtue, indulge themselves by clipping Gloriana's proud wings from a safe distance. There is much talk nowadays, especially among our revisionists, of Elizabethan myth-making, as if the glory of the age was made up by adoring and impressionable admirers. It is a curious perspective on the reign that gave so much: the successful establishment of a church settlement that has endured for nearly 500 years and spread throughout almost the whole world; genuine political giants like the Cecils; evergreen stories of the Armada and the adventures of Drake and Hawkins; artists of the calibre of Tallis, Byrd, Dowland, Shakespeare, Marlowe, Sidney, Spenser and many more lesser-known names that would, in any other age, stand out as figures of exceptional talent. These are not myths. They are all blessedly real events in the lifetime of a real queen. Personal faults and failings there may have been, for no one is free from blemish; but a few carping voices will never succeed in denying her greatness. In the words of the finest dramatist of her reign, they will harm her no more than 'sparrows eagles, or the hare the lion'.[90]

4

JAMES, 1603–25

THE THEOLOGIAN KING

In the days of Elizabeth the Puritans had waged a struggle to reform her church according to their liking. Officially they had lost the contest, and Elizabethan orthodoxy had prevailed. Yet the issue was still smouldering, though silently and covertly, when the great queen died in March 1603. Soon it would flare up again; and in the reigns of her two Stuart successors, this struggle would run alongside another one just as dangerous, this time between the Crown and the liberties of Parliament.

James VI of Scotland and I of England was a descendant of Margaret Tudor, sister of Henry VIII. Margaret had married James IV of Scotland, and their son was James V. His daughter, Mary Queen of Scots, was the mother of the James of our story. His Tudor ancestry made him the most likely successor to the childless Elizabeth, even though she had, admittedly ever so unwillingly, executed his mother when James was only a young man.[1]

Tradition has handed down the most unflattering testimonies of James. He was said to be a timorous man, with large, rolling eyes that made embarrassed visitors shy away from him and take their leave as soon as protocol would permit. Whenever he walked he would ceaselessly fiddle with his codpiece. He was slovenly in manner and appearance, with a thick Scots accent that few of his English subjects could understand. Despite a wife and children, it was frowningly reported that he showed inordinate affection to young men who benefited significantly and undeservedly from his patronage. Henry IV of France allegedly called James the 'wisest fool in Christendom'. It is not clear whether this remark, if indeed it was ever made, was intended dismissively, or, if all men are fools, as an ironic back-hand compliment.[2]

But these are not the only opinions that have survived. The Venetian ambassador, reporting to the Venetian senate, described James as by nature 'placid, averse from cruelty, a lover of justice'. The king regularly went to chapel and had no desire for war, though his preference for peace and stability over military exploits, a feature he shared with his predecessor, 'little pleases many of his subjects'. James, however, 'does not caress the people, nor make them that good cheer that the late queen did, whereby she won their loves'. James shows 'no taste for them, but rather contempt and dislike'; as a result he is in turn 'despised and hated'.[3]

Modern historians, who frequently prefer pulling famous names from the past off their pedestal, have gone into reverse with James. Many side with the ambassador, taking a much more favourable view of him. He is now regarded as a competent king of Scotland, intelligent, canny, astute, and a man of peace not war. Nevertheless, he was puzzlingly short on what moderns might call 'image', and far less effective than Elizabeth at winning the people's love and trust. James seemed strangely loath to capitalise on the goodwill that his English subjects accorded him at his accession and coronation. He particularly resented having to put in an appearance in front of large numbers of people. 'God's wounds!' he growled one day, on being told that a sizable crowd had gathered eagerly expecting to see his royal person: 'I will pull down my breeches and they shall also see my arse.' In our days, if a man like James entered public life, he would be inundated with letters from public relations consultants offering their services to improve his image.[4]

James was fortunate in that he could count on the services of a first minister of the highest calibre in Robert Cecil whose political skills ensured a smooth transition from one monarch and one dynasty to another; and also, in Francis Bacon, one of the finest intellects of the age. The new king was not short of sound advice when he arrived in London, and the bickering in the church ensured he would need it.

Bacon was no great admirer of the Presbyterian system, but like Robert Cecil, he was opposed to harsh persecution of the godly and the silencing of talented preachers. Insightful in things spiritual as in most other things, Bacon argued the case for freedom among all shades of Protestantism. 'It is good', he believed, that 'we return unto the ancient bonds of unity in the Church of God, which was, one faith, one baptism; and not one hierarchy, one discipline.' In the essentials of the faith, Bacon endorsed the words of Jesus: 'he that is not with us is against us'. However, 'in things indifferent and but of circumstance', Bacon took liberty to adapt the Gospel to: 'he that is not against us is with us'.[5]

English Puritans were still smarting from the wounds delivered by Elizabeth, but they held high hopes of James, who had been raised and educated by godly tutors in Calvinist Scotland. Many may have recalled that he had written to Elizabeth, over ten years before interceding for Cartwright and Udall when they were held in detention. A Millenary Petition – essentially a petition to reform the church along moderately Puritan lines – was accordingly presented to him on his accession. James obligingly arranged a conference at Hampton Court to hear and join in the debates. In the event, little came of it. Pragmatist that he was, James did allow some limited reforms; he permitted the prophesyings that Elizabeth had forbidden, and that were now less controversially re-classified as 'exercises'. But the Puritans were soon to discover that his real intention was to consolidate and strengthen the existing church, both in doctrine and organisation. To dissent and nonconformity, James was implacably opposed.[6]

Though James had hardly known John Knox personally – he was only a child when Knox died – James could not stand the memory of the man. In fact, James had little reason to have any love for Puritans. He had been tutored by George Buchanan, a fine scholar but a ferocious disciplinarian, and a supporter of the duty of godly subjects to resist wicked kings or tyrants. James recalled how he had been 'persecuted' by Puritans as a child and a young man in Scotland, though he did not seem to be entirely cowed by his harsh upbringing. Once in 1585, when only nineteen, he told a hectoring cleric, James Gibson, that 'I will not give a turd for thy preaching'.[7]

Presbyterianism, James was reported to have said at the time of the Millenary Petition, 'as well agreeth with a monarchy as God and the devil'. Looking at the issue through the king's eyes the reader may see his point, forcefully though it was made. A fellow countryman of the king's, James Melville, once explained that there were two kingdoms in Scotland: 'there is Christ Jesus the king, and His kingdom is the Kirk, whose subject King James VI is, and of whose kingdom not a king, nor a lord, nor a head, *but a member* (italics mine).[8] Strictly speaking, therefore, the Presbyterian system, unlike the one in England, did not recognise the king as Head of the Church (though some alternative place of distinction could no doubt be found for him). In that sense, it could be seen as a challenge to the Royal Supremacy. Yet there is an irony in this. As noted in the previous chapter, not every Puritan was a Presbyterian; and Puritanism under James was more concerned about the general level of godliness in society and the 'popish' ceremonial in church services than a wholesale overhaul of church government along Genevan lines. Presbyterianism had gone into decline, or at least into the background. The king and his ministers either did not appreciate this, or more likely they suspected that Presbyterianism was merely slumbering.[9]

During the Hampton Court conference James spoke scathingly in private about the godly. 'We have kept such a revel with the Puritans here these last two days as was never heard the like', he confided to a trusted ally; 'they fled me so from argument to argument without ever answering me directly'. James told another friend he had been given 'a book of theirs as may well convert infidels, but it shall never convert me'. The conference was barely over before plans were laid to enforce conformity and curb Puritanism more than ever.[10]

Canons approved by Convocation in 1604 required all ministers to confess that the Prayer Book was entirely in accordance with Scripture. A few of the godly petitioned the king, hoping he would exempt them, or have the statement modified. James listened to them frostily and unsympathetically. Then Richard Bancroft, a long-standing opponent of Puritans, was consecrated archbishop in December 1604. In no time Bancroft demanded that all clergy accept the canons in three particular respects: they should confess the king's supremacy; they should admit that the Prayer Book was in accordance with Scripture; and likewise the Thirty-Nine Articles.

The godly were now under intense pressure. They accepted the first and third readily enough, but they baulked at the second. Many held out, even when James supported Bancroft's uncompromising stance. In February 1605 James was handed a petition pleading for ministers who had not subscribed, but it included an unfortunately worded clause suggesting that if he did not hear them understandingly, many of his people would be deeply unhappy. To James this seemed a veiled threat, and he directed the council to proceed against them. Robert Cecil was generally loath to deal severely with the godly, but on this point he had little choice but to back James and Bancroft. 'Religious men of moderate spirits may be borne with', Cecil confided to a friend: yet 'such are the turbulent humours of some that dream of nothing but a new hierarchy directly opposed to the state of a monarchy', which could only 'nourish schism in the church and commonwealth'. Cecil feared 'schisms in habit as well as in opinion'; and that 'unity in belief can not be preserved unless it is to be found in worship'. The godly were now in danger of losing that sympathy in high places that they had enjoyed in Elizabeth's reign from men like Leicester and Walsingham. Even Cecil, for all his moderation, feared that the course the Puritans were taking 'is no safe way in such a monarchy as this'; and that these men, 'by this singularity of theirs in things approved to be indifferent by so many reverend fathers of the church … do daily minister cause of scandal in the Church of England'.[11]

S.R. Gardiner, whilst admitting Cecil's considerable abilities as a minister of the Crown, reckoned he was also too unadventurous, too much stuck in the mould of the previous reign. Resisting change, however, can be just as bold as yielding to it, and Cecil's point is worth noting, whether it is agreed with or not. He admitted that there were things indifferent in the church, and by this he meant the subjects that vexed the godly, like the liturgy, church government and ceremonies. But it was not the difference of opinion that concerned Cecil. His criticism of the Puritans was that, if they had their way, they would tolerate *no* difference of opinion; for their views they claimed a divine mandate. Cecil was indeed being traditional, if traditional means Elizabethan – but for a reason. The Puritans were seen in government circles as potentially, if not yet actually, seditious. Elizabeth had kept them in order, and the new king was determined to do likewise.

In fact, there was much about James that the godly may not have realised when they welcomed him to the English throne. Somewhat uncharacteristically for a Scotsman, James admired events and the state of affairs in England. In Elizabeth's reign, shortly after his intercession for Cartwright, James had reflected on how the Reformation in Scotland was 'extraordinarily wrought by God, wherein many things were inordinately done by a popular tumult and rebellion'; and he regretted that reform had not proceeded 'from the Prince's ordour [sic], as it did in our neighbour country of England, as likewise in Denmark, and sundry parts of Germany'.[12] Even then, as King of Scotland, he appreciated the Elizabethan church so much that he tried to make the Scots Kirk a bit more like it. 'For the space of six years before my coming to England', he would say, 'I laboured nothing so much as to depress their party [the Puritans] and re-erect bishops again.' He had been successful in persuading the Kirk to accept bishops once more, having promised that they would be neither Anglican nor papist, and adding the sweetener that they would be the answer to the long-held wish of the Scots clergy for direct representation in Parliament. He had also sought to increase the practical power of the bishops by restoring their revenues. Some time after this these bishops received new powers with the creation of courts of high commission. Subtly and steadily James was trying to freeze out the Presbyterian system, to reintroduce the espiscopal structure under royal authority, and make the Presbyterian assemblies effectively redundant by transferring their role to a body similar to Convocation in England. This step by step Anglicanising continued when, as King of England as well as Scotland, he introduced into the Kirk hitherto rejected devotional practices, like kneeling at communion. In 1616 his orders for the refurbishment of the royal chapel in Holyrood Palace included an organ, images and paintings of the Twelve Apostles. But here he went too far, and even loyal Scottish bishops respectfully suggested that he should 'stay the affixing of these portraits'. James was disappointed, but he had the good sense to know when not to enforce his royal authority. The portraits were not affixed; nevertheless, at Holyrood during the king's visit in 1617, the liturgy was gently reformed on Anglican lines. James seemed content with his modest reforms, and he never tried to make them compulsory throughout the Kirk. Nor did he try heavy-handedly to absorb the Kirk into the Church of England.[13]

He also took care not to treat English Puritans too repressively. He dealt astutely with all comers – Calvinists, Puritans and the ever more influential Anglicans, like Lancelot Andrewes. In a calculated balancing act he allowed preachers of various shades to preach before him. He appreciated sermons more than Elizabeth, and sometimes he asked for copies to be printed for him to read during leisure moments. After a sermon he would engage the preacher in conversation and invite him to dine at the royal table. He also auditioned promising young preachers. On one point, though, James did agree with Elizabeth – he liked sermons to be brief and to the point.[14]

The preacher James came to admire more than most was Andrewes. The king was impressed with his learning and fine oratory, though he tactfully did not throw himself wholeheartedly behind the Anglicanism of Andrewes. But detached observers had no doubts where the king's real sympathies lay. According to the Venetian ambassador in London, James was, right from the beginning of his reign, nervous about the Puritans and their growing influence in Parliament and the country following Elizabeth's death, and particularly the view of some of them that the king should not have the authority to veto parliamentary legisla-tion. As early as February 1605, in a report to the Venetian senate, the ambassador dwelt on the king's 'violent hatred' for the Puritans, which he concealed partly out of prudent statecraft, and partly because of their renewed strength. Two years later the ambassador described England as a land of three religions: 'the Roman Catholic and Apostolic, the Protestant and the Puritan'; and James belonged to the second, to the church of Elizabeth that he inherited.[15]

Besides the Puritans, English Catholics had also welcomed James to England. James's personal preference, like that of Elizabeth, was to let law-abiding Catholics live in peace. The infamous Gunpowder Plot, discovered in November 1605, understandably caused a sensation, but a brief one. Cecil's efficient intelligence service had penetrated this Stuart terrorist cell as the plot ripened, and the ring leaders were easily rounded up. Many Catholics were as horrified by it as their Protestant neighbours were. James took the trouble to appeal for calm; he urged the people that there be no backlash against Catholics, most of whom he called his 'good and faithful subjects'. Supported by Cecil, the king tried to win over the loyal Catholics. He was reluctant to strictly enforce the recusancy laws that required Anglican confor-mity, and which were admittedly rather severe on paper. Aware that treating Catholics roughly would invite reprisals abroad, James vowed he would never be the one to teach foreign papist rulers 'the way to plague the Protestants in their dominions'. On this last point James was not just putting the Commons off with blandishments, and he could point to similar conciliatory measures by other European princes. The Peace of Augsburg of 1555 was still holding in German lands. The Edict of Nantes of 1598 allowed freedom of worship in most of France for Catholic and Protestant alike, effectively ending over thirty years of intermittent but bitter conflict; and it cannot have gone unnoticed by James that this policy of toleration was substantially the work of the French King, Henri IV, who had to impose his royal will over an initially hostile assembly and legislature. Then in 1609 Mathias – King of Bohemia and Hungary and subsequently emperor – granted similar concessions to his Bohemian Protestant subjects.[16]

But if James meant no ill to Catholics, his fears of Puritanism stuck with him throughout his life. Like Elizabeth before him, he preferred papists to Puritans. To quote the ambassador again, they were 'a sect he loathes more than he does the Catholics, because it more than any other destroys the authority of the crown'; James was planning, step by step, to use episcopal authority to check, and if possible, crush the godly.[17]

HIS EARLY PARLIAMENTS

In 1604 the House of Commons welcomed James loyally and cordially. Certain members then respectfully let it be known that they had graciously restrained themselves in Elizabeth's last years 'in regard to her sex and age', because they hoped for 'freer times' to come. The Commons, like the Puritans, were expecting good things from James.[18]

Yet the Commons, like the Puritans, had much to learn. For a start, James was much more pro-Spanish in foreign policy than they were. When a French agent of Henri IV approached Cecil, hoping for English aid in a plot involving the Moors against King Philip III of Spain, James would hear none of it, and he told Philip what was afoot. The agent was arrested, tortured and executed in 1605.[19]

The views of James on the royal prerogative and the Crown's relationship with Parliament would also cause unease. A king, according to James, may be judged 'only by God, to whom only he must give account'; while Parliament was 'nothing else but the head court of the king and his vassals', which has no power to make any law 'without his sceptre be to it, for giving it the force of a law'. A good king, James conceded, 'will frame all his actions to be according to the law; yet he is not bound thereto but of his good will, and for good example to his subjects'.[20]

Whilst it had been true for centuries that without the Royal Assent no bill could become law, James seems, nevertheless, almost to be suggesting that Parliament was beholden to royal goodwill. Contrast Henry VIII, who made this announcement just before elections in May 1536 for the forthcoming Parliament:

> Such matters of most high importance have chanced for the preservation of
> our honour, the establishment of our succession in the Crown of this realm
> … have been to us and to all the lords of our Council thought necessary
> to be discussed and determined in our High Court of Parliament to be
> assembled for that purpose.

The 'matters of most high importance' included the fall of Anne Boleyn and
the need for a new Succession Act in favour of Queen Jane Seymour. To
debate and decide on these matters, Parliament was necessary. Henry did not,
of course, expect Parliament to oppose him. Nevertheless, he felt bound to
call Parliament, and act in concert with it. Even if the statement had been
drafted by his minister, Thomas Cromwell, Henry would never have made it
if he had not agreed with the tenor of it. The esteem for Parliament shown by
Henry personally, not just by Cromwell, is not found in James.[21]

James was no tyrant, and he resolved to exercise his absolute God-given
sovereign right to rule for the benefit of his country and his people; but even
a benevolent kind of despotism was not exactly what the Commons had been
hoping for. The king's early parliaments were neither rebellious nor especially
demanding, though James was disappointed when mutual Anglo-Scottish
dislike and distrust defeated his hopes for a formal Act of Union between
England and Scotland. One of his problems as his reign unfolded was finance.
Income from royal estates had consistently fallen since the days of Henry VIII,
mainly due to substantial selling of Crown lands during the Tudor age. Other
sources of Crown revenue included customs and feudal rights, but these were
not adequate to compensate. More and more James was compelled to borrow
from the City of London. Matters were not helped by the fact that James was
far more extravagant in his lifestyle than Elizabeth. As a result, the new king
was beginning to seriously strain the nation's finances.

In the Bates Case of 1606, Judge Baron Fleming upheld the right of the
Crown to levy impositions (import duty) by royal prerogative as well as by
common law. Some observers were concerned that this ruling could be a
threat to the rights of Parliament, because historically kings of England
needed Parliament in order to raise tax. It prompted suggestions among MPs
that Parliament should be called annually, not just when the king decided
he needed it. James was annoyed; he sent a sharp note to the Commons telling them they had no right to meddle with his royal prerogative. This only
stiffened the spirit of independence in the Commons. A petition was drafted
defending the 'ancient and fundamental liberty' of Parliament in discussing 'all
matters concerning them and their possessions, goods and rights whatsoever'.
One angry member said openly that he wished the king 'would be pleased to
live of his own'. As for the king's favourites at court, it was 'unfit and dishon-
ourable that those should waste the treasure of the state who take no pains to

live of their own, but spend all in excess and riot, depending wholly upon the bounty of the prince'. James, said Gardiner, had 'flung his money away till he was forced to apply for help to the House of Commons', and he found the Commons in no mood to pour good money after bad.[22]

The valiant but ultimately unsuccessful efforts of Robert Cecil to provide a lasting solution to the finances of the Crown drew forth angry words from James. He was irritated with Cecil for persevering doggedly with a parliamentary solution. The king ordered the minister to seek the 'next best means how to help my state, since ye see there is no more trust to be laid upon this rotten reed of Egypt, for your greatest error hath been that ye ever expected to draw honey out of gall'. Cecil, a statesman with a Tudor constitutional mindset, knew that Parliament was not an institution that could be bypassed as James was suggesting. 'That place', he faithfully reminded the king, 'hath ever been the only foundation of supply to those princes whose necessities have been beyond the cares and endeavours of private men.' Cecil knew there would be trouble if James showed contempt for Parliament. 'The storm comes before it breaks', he warned his master. Not long after this, in May 1612, Robert Cecil passed away, leaving the way open for a new generation of men to serve as councillors to the new Stuart kings.[23]

In 1614 the Crown was still badly short of cash, despite the revenues received from yet more sales of land, and awards of knighthoods and baronetcies in return for a fee. James decided to summon Parliament again; but the government's barely concealed attempt to ensure the election of pliable, supportive candidates was thwarted in many places. Even in London, a well-known Puritan named Fuller overcame official disapproval to win the vote. Nevertheless, James's opening address started well. He cited three reasons for the new assembly: to strengthen the national religion in the face of the increasing threat of popery at home and abroad; to confirm the succession to his grandson should Prince Charles die without an heir; and to raise money.

Members were full of goodwill regarding the first two. It was the third that proved controversial, especially when the subject of impositions, to which the Commons was opposed, came up in debates. Tempers flared when, in the Lords, Bishop Neile attacked the Commons for daring to meddle in such matters, implicitly questioning their loyalty to the Royal Supremacy. The Commons were furious; they resolved to appeal to the king and suspend all further parliamentary business. Sir Edwyn Sandys, one of its more thoughtful members, urged his colleagues not to do this; besides embarrassing James needlessly and causing a breach with the Lords, any action against Neile could easily in future be used against the right of free speech in either House. This argument won the Commons over: there was no appeal to the king, but no more business with the Lords either. James then rebuked the Commons, reminding them that it did not lie in their power to dissolve or stop the normal working of Parliament. Eventually Neile, under pressure from fellow peers anxious for a settlement, made a partial climbdown; he pleaded he had been misunderstood, and he never meant to besmirch the Commons or doubt their loyalty. The Commons were not satisfied and tried to press charges against the bishop. James now decided that he had had more than enough with a Parliament that had neither granted him any money nor passed any bills for Royal Assent, and he dissolved it. The 'Addled Parliament', as it came to be known, was hardly a major constitutional crisis, but the tetchiness on display had done nothing to foster harmony between the king and the Lower House.[24]

Having failed to secure a satisfactory solution to his funding crisis from Parliament, James appealed directly to the country. In September, November and into the following year (1615), a batch of official letters was sent out to the counties and boroughs inviting a donation. Though many recipients did oblige, a surprising number declined, even though many gentry were legally tenants of the Crown. Frequently the king's representatives met with the same reply: if the Crown needed money, surely the right thing to do was to call Parliament. This was more than just a stalling tactic, or a natural distaste for parting with money. Normally loyal Englishmen felt that going behind Parliament's back was simply not the right thing to do.

James was bitterly frustrated. Dissatisfaction with the king's methods was also rising worryingly. 'Nothing seems wanting to cause an upheaval except suitable leaders', wrote the Venetian ambassador. James was showing 'increasing abhorrence ... for the toils and cares involved in government'. To escape from them he 'lives almost entirely in the country, accompanied by a few of his favourites'.[25]

Disagreements, tensions and now even a strong mutual dislike between the king and his people – a dangerous mix of grievances virtually unknown in Tudor times – had begun to set in.

IRELAND AND THE PLANTATIONS

The Protestant Reformation in Ireland had begun with Thomas Cromwell, who secured the appointment of evangelicals as Irish missionary bishops. One of these was George Browne, Archbishop of Dublin, whose debut sermon there was encouragingly well received, according to one who heard it. Another was Richard Nangle, a Professor of Theology and an Irish speaker, sent out to be Bishop of Clonfert in the west of Ireland, and who was soon arousing opposition, which means that his message was being listened to by the natives. Nangle was harassed not only by the local established clergy, but also by powerful local magnates, who, though not necessarily good Catholics, were jealous of their independence, and resented any outside interference whether from Dublin, Rome or London. Nangle was forced to return to Dublin in 1538, but four years later he was granted a rectory in Kilmacduagh, near Gort in Galway. Not much else is known about Nangle, but his ministry seems to have borne good fruit, because in 1586 Sir Richard Bingham, governor of Connacht, told Walsingham, Elizabeth's minister, that the people of Galway were, most of them, 'very well affected in religion … and more given to embrace the doctrines of the Gospel generally than any people in Ireland'.[26]

This success, however, was something exceptional and short lived. Following Cromwell's fall English policy in Ireland, though never dormant, had suffered from a marked lack of drive and imagination.

The problem was not the legitimacy of English rule there, because after an unsuccessful rising against Henry VII in 1487, the papacy had directed the Irish clergy to be subject to the king. Henry VIII, in his closing years, then took English overlordship a stage further and made himself King of Ireland, and appointed Anthony St Leger as Lord Deputy. Mary was determined to hold on to her second kingdom, and largely because of her loyalty to Rome, the Pope was persuaded to recognise Henry's *fait accompli*.[27]

By now the Prayer Book had been introduced for use in the official, Protestant Church of Ireland. The problem was that the clergy in the newly established church were not especially impressive. Few had a university education, most did no more than read from homilies rather than preach, and in practice the Prayer Book was used very patchily. Queen Mary's reign and her church policy were welcomed, and in Elizabeth's time foreign Catholic powers, notably Spain, were quick to capitalise on the preference of the Irish for the old faith. Jesuit missionaries and seminary priests were soon active in Ireland as well as in England. In the face of this resurgent, dynamic Counter Reformation, the Church of Ireland clergy, most of them at best only half Protestant, fell away in droves, taking many of the people with them. In 1595 Bishop Lyon, serving in Munster in the dioceses of Cork, Cloyne and Ross, complained that 'within these two years … where I have seen a thousand or more at church or sermon, I now have not five'. Even in Galway the people were flocking back to the old faith. English sovereignty in Ireland was threatened and nearly finished by a nationalist rising in the late 1590s, which Elizabeth's government took nine costly years to defeat.[28]

When James succeeded Elizabeth, the late queen's Irish war was at last over and won, thanks chiefly to her commander and Lord Deputy, Charles Mountjoy. Following his victory, Mountjoy asked to be relieved of his post and to return home. His request was granted, and in 1604 he was replaced by Sir Arthur Chichester, who had fought against the Armada, and served under Drake in the Indies and under Mountjoy in Ireland. Chichester was one of the few Englishmen who saw real beneficial opportunities in Ireland; he called it folly to be seeking colonies across the Atlantic in Virginia and the West Indies when Ireland lay neglected and undeveloped.[29]

Chichester then issued various proclamations for the pacification of Ireland. The Irish people, he declared, were the king's subjects, and the king would 'defend them and theirs from the injuries, oppressions and unlawful exactions of the chief lords'; they are the 'free, natural subjects of His majesty, and are not to be reputed or called the natives, or natural followers of any other lord or chieftain'. One problem for Chichester was that his apparent goodwill towards the ordinary people could undermine the authority and influence of the Irish chieftains who had led the resistance to Elizabeth. Chichester then turned his attention to law and order generally, and to resolving disputes regarding ownership of land and the rights of the lords, gentry and tenants. Impartial justice, he reckoned, could not, at least not yet, be entrusted to the Irish because they were far too susceptible to bribes and intimidation. One solution that occurred to him was to encourage more English and Scots to settle in Ireland, particularly in Ulster.[30]

Law and order was not Chichester's only concern. The inhabitants of Ireland comprised three main groups. The first was the native Irish, who had lived there for centuries. The second was the so-called 'Old English', immigrants from England since the days before the Reformation. Both groups were mainly Catholic. Protestant settlers since the Reformation formed a third, smaller group. So the Protestant government in London was now confronted with a problem: whether to tolerate Catholicism on a virtually nationwide scale in Ireland, and if not, how it could enforce the Protestant faith on a defiantly Catholic populace. Naturally this subject aroused much discussion and debate. On hearing a rumour that James was minded to toleration, the Archbishop of Dublin and the Bishop of Meath protested strongly. This appeared to have the desired effect, and on 4 July 1605 James issued a proclamation enforcing church attendance and banishing Catholic priests, though this seemingly hard line was modified by a set of royal injunctions issued the following year. James, Cecil and Mountjoy were anxious to create a Protestant Ireland if that were still possible, but they did not believe in coercion on principle. They had no time for the idea of Sir Parr Lane, a Munster settler who urged that religion must be 'squared by the word', and 'maintained by the sword'. Among the lines penned by this would-be poet were these:[31]

> Win faith by law, and rather lead than draw,
> And where need is, bestow the lash of law.

Chichester did not support this either, and he was now ready to carry out the king's wishes. He realised, he told the Irish, that he could not force anyone's conscience; but as the king's deputy he simply wanted the people to spend one hour a week in a church listening to a sermon in obedience to the king. Predictably, not many Irish complied. Serious trouble was avoided, partly because the penalties against recusancy in Ireland were generally too mild to provoke any, though the threat of even a fairly affordable fine was hardly the ideal way to commend the new faith to the people.[32]

The Dublin government continued to insist that the king enjoyed the sovereign right to order his subjects to attend church, though it admitted that he could not 'compel the heart'. Chichester insisted that 'I have dealt as tenderly as I might' in enforcing the king's proclamation, but he was beginning to wonder whether he would have to give up on the adults and concentrate his efforts on converting the youth and the children. 'I am not violent', he maintained, with justification, and he did not wish to proceed with ill-judged zeal 'like a Puritan in this kind'. The outcome of all this was rather inconclusive – a directive to attend church that was rarely obeyed, very half-heartedly enforced, and sometimes not enforced at all. Because many local officials such as magistrates and sheriffs were Catholic themselves, fines that should have been imposed were frequently either waived or not collected. Chichester then took a series of practical measures to promote the Protestant faith without antagonising opponents of it. He took an active interest in clerical appointments, and was anxious to improve the quality and calibre of ministers and preachers. He supported the translation of the Prayer Book into Irish and organised its distribution throughout the country.[33]

The deputy then returned to law and order and less controversial reforms of the justice system. He toured Ulster and the north, hearing and arbitrating on land disputes; he encouraged the richer gentry to support schools, and he tried in various ways to improve the administration of the country. The chief justice, Sir James Ley, was pleasantly surprised by the welcome he received during a circuit around County Wicklow, and the apparent willingness of the people to accept a more developed legal system. A lasting satisfactory settlement of the nation was still a long way off, but prospects were encouraging, at least for a short period. In the aftermath of the Irish war, there was little sign of the dreadful times soon to come.[34]

In 1607, rather than submit to English rule and a steady decline in their influence, the Earls of Tyrone and Tyrconnell, the most prominent northern Irish chieftains, left their ancestral homes and went into exile. Chichester then made a proposal. The earls' lands, he suggested, should become the property of the Crown, and be divided among the local people for cultivation. The land that remained unoccupied *after* this division should be given to those who had done their king good service; and also to English and Scots settlers, who would in return build a castle on that land that would serve as a garrison. This would, at a stroke, create a landowning Irish class, and moreover provide for the defence of the country. If his proposal were not accepted, Chichester feared the only solution would be to expel the natives from much of the north. His ideas were well received by the king.[35]

The government now began legal moves to convict the earls of treason in their absence in order to complete the acquisition of their lands. Chichester then had to deal with a distraction, a minor and unsuccessful rising. This he quickly put down. But political instability, allied to the danger of further risings, forced the government to proceed more urgently with its policy of colonisation, and commissioners were appointed to make detailed plans. These commissioners, however, did not support Chichester's idea to divide the lands of the exiled earls among the Irish people *first*, and then allocate what remained to the colonists. Mindful of the recent rising and fearful of something similar in the future, the commissioners wanted to make sure that the natives were not living together in large blocks in an easily defensible area. They feared, too, that colonists living in small, scattered communities among the Irish would be vulnerable to attack, and that it would be better to put them in larger groups where they would enjoy safety in numbers. Therefore, to quote Gardiner, the commissioners looked at the map of Ulster 'as if it had been a white sheet of paper', and worked out a plan to settle natives and colonists in the safest, most convenient way from the government's point of view. This revised plan meant that many native Irish would have to be moved from their homes to lands reserved for them by the government.[36]

Eventually the commissioners' view prevailed over Chichester's earlier proposal. In the distribution of land, the colonists rather than the Irish were given priority. Thus the so-called Plantation of Ulster began in real earnest. Over the next twenty to thirty years, scores of Irish were displaced as Anglo-Scots settlers arrived. A series of political, social and religious measures followed, more for the benefit of the settlers than the native people. The official Church of Ireland was increasingly composed of Calvinists and those with Puritan sympathies: Austin Woolrych has called it the 'colonial class at prayer'. Its articles – the Irish Articles – were formulated in 1615, based on the Elizabethan Thirty-Nine Articles, but modified to include, among other things, a strong and uncompromising line on predestination.[37]

Despite the unfairness in the way the plantation policy was managed, Ireland enjoyed increasing prosperity in the reign of James. There is evidence, too, of intermarriage among the different communities, and of settler and native people living side by side seemingly agreeably. Nor did all the new arrivals from England and Scotland turn out to be zealous Puritans. Some were more practical than idealistic, more interested in cultivating their land and making a return on it than evangelising or 'anglicising' the natives. Although bishops and clergymen tended to see the Church of Ireland as a godly company living amid heathens, like Israel of old surrounded by pagan nations, these settlers needed the natives as farm labourers, workmen, tenants, even as customers, so it was not in their interest to be oppressive. Others have made the point that no one in 1625 foresaw the disaster that would overwhelm the land in the next reign.[38] Still, no amount of material prosperity could sufficiently compensate for the sense of humiliation that subjected or displaced people are bound to feel. What might have happened had Chichester had his way on the subject of land allocation is one of the great 'what ifs' of Anglo-Irish history.

MORE PROBLEMS IN THE CHURCH

'Let not the church nor churchmen be disgraced in your charges, nor Papists nor Puritans countenanced: countenance and encourage the good churchmen.' So spoke James to the Star Chamber in 1616.[39]

The following year James left London to visit Scotland. On his way back in August he passed through Lancashire. There he was presented with a petition to allow lawful recreations on Sunday, which local magistrates, going beyond the parameters laid down by statute, had forbidden. James agreed at once. Piping, dancing, archery, maypoles and other innocent pleasures, though not bull-baiting or bear-baiting, were to be allowed after church services. Following this so-called 'Book of Sports' affair, Sabbatarianism became, perhaps not altogether accurately, inextricably associated with Puritanism.[40]

The issue had its origins in the previous reign. In a series of royal injunctions, Elizabeth had required her people to spend holy days hearing the Word of God, receiving communion, catechising and engaging in other spiritual pursuits, though the caveat in the similar Edwardian homilies remained in force – there should be no needless or superstitious avoidance of normal and necessary work, as if such abstinence held some special moral merit. Elizabeth required Sunday observance on the grounds that it was an agreeable Christian tradition, a day which should be set aside for spiritual things. It was not claimed that the Sunday was a divinely appointed day. But the regulation of Sunday activities and the penalties for transgressions were never finally resolved, and debates on the subject continued. It was not long before others wanted to go a stage further than the official line. Thomas Cartwright had argued that the Mosaic judicial code, which called for the death penalty for Sabbath breakers, was permanent and binding on the church: this was roundly rejected by Archbishop Whitgift.[41]

From around 1617, a new group began to emerge known as the Saturday Sabbatarians, or alternatively Judaizing Christians, keepers of the Jewish law. It was not a large movement, and it was said that 'their opinions made His majesty exceeding merry on one Sunday dinner'. Nevertheless, James felt sufficiently concerned to warn his people not to listen to 'that private spirit …

which our Puritans glory in; for then a little fiery zeal will make thee turn Separatist, and then proceed to something worse'.[42]

The Separatist churches that had come to the king's attention were slowly beginning to be a feature of English church life. One of their prominent leaders was Henry Jacob. He was a Puritan clergyman, back in England after a short continental exile, and he had recently founded a Separate godly gathering. For some time Jacob had supported a congregational organisation of the church which would be free from the jurisdiction of bishops, though he took care to avow his loyalty to the king. Jacob churches began developing, admittedly on a small scale at this stage, into a rival to the established parish church, even though Jacob claimed to recognise the parish churches as true churches. They were no threat to the government, and they wanted little more than to be left alone and worship as they pleased. But the very principle of Separatism was something alien, and, from the point of view of the authorities, suspect and highly unwelcome.[43]

Still, it was something of a relief to Puritans to hear that James opposed the teachings of the Dutch theologian, Jacob Arminius. Like Richard Hooker before him, Arminius had cautiously challenged Calvinist orthodoxy on predestination. Again like Hooker, he could not bring himself to deny predestination completely, so he took refuge in the thought of the infallibility of divine foreknowledge: this meant that God foresaw, rather than predestined, the elect and the non-elect. His opponents replied that foreknowledge and predestination are two different things. However, the details of the controversy can be passed over here as Nicholas Tyacke and others have covered them thoroughly. James confirmed his orthodoxy by appointing George Abbot, a good, solid Calvinist as Archbishop of Canterbury on the death of Bancroft. Nevertheless, in spite of his formal approval of the condemnation of Arminius at the synod of Dort, there were soon signs that James was modifying his view, if only slightly. He made no objection when Lancelot Andrewes preached in his presence and took a swipe at those who imagined they have inscrutable divine decrees 'at their fingers' ends, and can tell you the number and the order of them just with 1, 2, 3, 4, 5'. During the king's latter years, clergymen sympathetic to Arminius advanced to the bishops' bench: Richard Neile to Durham in 1617, Andrewes to Winchester the following year, and George Montaigne to London in 1621.[44]

As the reign of James wore on, therefore, the godly were getting ever more estranged and frustrated, while the reaction against Calvinism and Puritanism was growing. These quarrels spilled over into parish life. Staunch Puritans pitied the spiritually vegetative condition of the average state church member, as they saw it. The 'country fellow', said John Earle, a seventeenth-century writer, 'goes to church in his best clothes and sits there with his neighbours, where he is capable only of two prayers, for rain or fair weather'. The godly

THOMAS CROMWELL.

Lord Privy Seal, Vicar General & Lord Chamberlian.
Created Earl of Essex 17. Ap. 13. H. 8. Beheaded 28 Iuly. 1540.

1. Thomas Cromwell. (Courtesy of Ipswich School archive)

2. Oliver Cromwell, from a painting by an unknown artist. (Author's Collection)

ANNO ·ÆTATIS· ·SVÆ ·XLIX·

3. Henry VIII by Hans Holbein. (Author's Collection)

Non secus vnda mari paulatim accrescit et alta
Neptuni frontem supereminet, vt sua tandem
Vis ruit, et pelago labens deuoluitur imo ;
Quam tua te VOLSEDE tumens euexit honoris
Aura, et sublimen super-eebuit ardua regis ;
Culmina, sed tandem conuerso CARDINE rerum,
In scopulos, rigidasq; extrusa est gloria syrtes.
Terra olim corpus, tumuit, iam corpore tellus.

4. Portrait engraving of Cardinal Wolsey. (The History Press Archive)

5. Edward, Prince of Wales. (Author's Collection)

IANA GRAYA

Regia stirps tristi cinxi diademate crines
Regna sed omnipotens hinc meliora dea

6. (*Above left*) Thomas Cranmer by Gerlach Flicke. (THP Archive)

7. (*Above right*) Lady Jane Grey. (THP Archive)

8. Portrait engraving of Mary, Queen of England. (THP Archive)

The burning of M. Iohn Rogers, vicar of Saint Pulchers, and Reader of Paules in London.

The description of Doctour Cranmer, howe he was plucked downe from the stage, by Friers and Papists, for the true Confession of his Faith.

The burning of the Archbishop of Canturbury, Doctor Thomas Cranmer, in the Towne-ditch at Oxford, with his hand first thrust into the fire, as here it is described before.

9. The burning of John Rogers, 4 February 1555, the first of Mary's martyrs. (THP Archive)

10. The martyrdom of Archbishop Cranmer, 21 March 1556. (THP Archive)

11. Seal of the Exchequer in the reign of Elizabeth I. (THP Archive)

12. Great Seal of Elizabeth I. (THP Archive)

13. Portrait of Sir Walter Raleigh. (THP Archive)

Clemens et Regni moderatrix iusta Britāni
Hāc forma insigni conspicienda nitet.

Tristia dum gentes circùm omnes bella fatigant,
Caesáq; erroris toto grassantur in orbe.
An. Dni   pace beas longa, Vera et pietate Britannos:
Iusticia moderans miti sapienter habenas.   1579
Chara domi, celebrisq; foris, longauaq; regnū
Hic teneas, regno tandem fruitura perenni.

14. Frontispiece to Saxton's maps of England, from the engraving by Augustine Ryther, 1579.
(Author's Collection)

15. Mary Queen of Scots, the 'Brocas' picture. (THP Archive)

16. Portrait engraving of Robert Cecil. He warned King James that the 'storm comes before it breaks'. (THP Archive)

CORONO

EXHILER

ELIZA, TRIVMPHANS

Gulielmus Rogerius sculp. Lº. 1589.

17. 'Eliza Triumphans', from the engraving by William Rogers, 1589. (Author's Collection)

18. James I & VI and Anne of Denmark. (THP Archive)

19. Prince Henry of Wales, eldest son of James and Anne. He died of typhoid in 1612 aged eighteen, leaving his less gifted brother Charles (the future Charles I) as heir to the throne. (THP Archive)

20. Portrait engraving of Francis Bacon. (THP Archive)

21. Charles I and Henrietta Maria. (THP Archive)

22. Print of a Van Dyck painting of Charles I, reproduced by Hollar at the time of the king's execution in 1649. (THP Archive)

23. Charles I, from the engraving by William Hole, 1625. (Author's Collection)

24. (*Above*) 'The Sovereign of the Seas' from the engraving by John Payne, 1637. (Author's Collection)

25. John Hampden, from Nugent's *Life of Hampden*. (Author's Collection)

yours Oliver Cromwell.

26. (*Above left*) John Pym, from a miniature by Samuel Cooper. (Author's Collection)

27. (*Above right*) Oliver Cromwell, from a miniature by Samuel Cooper, in the Baptist College at Bristol. (Author's Collection)

28. Statue of Oliver Cromwell, by Thorneycroft, erected at Westminster in 1899. (Author's Collection)

29. John Milton, from an engraving by Faithorne. (Author's Collection)

30. Charles II in middle age. (THP Archive)

31. Coronation of Charles II in Westminster Abbey. (THP Archive)

Cambridge divine, Richard Kilby, appealed to laid-back state churchgoers to rouse themselves and show more zeal: 'Is not this your religion', he demanded reproachfully, 'to say your prayers, to hear service without any special stirring of your heart?' Kilby would have gone down well in Preston, where a certain Lawrence Clarkson loved nothing more than to listen to godly ministers 'thunder against superstition, and sharply reprove sin and prophaning the Lord's Day'; sermons like this made 'tears run down my cheeks for joy'. Ranged against the Clarksons and the Kilbies were the likes of Mistress Susan Kent, a feisty young Wiltshire lady, in turns bored stiff and irritated by the conscientiousness of her Puritan minister. When he starts his 'bibble babble that I am weary to hear', she told a neighbour, 'I can then sit down in my seat and take a good nap'. She missed her old parson, who 'never did dislike games and dancing', but she could not stand his godly replacement – 'a plague or pox on him'.[45]

Tensions between the godly and the not so godly were simmering up and down the country, and there was no doubt where the king's sympathies lay. In 1619 James Cathkin, a Scottish bookseller living in England, excused his absence from church at Christmas on the grounds that 'holy days have been cast out of our Kirk', because it was deemed by the elders and ministers 'superstitious to keep them'. When James heard this he was furious: 'The devil take you away, both soul and body', he roared. 'For you are none of my religion … Ye are worse than Turks and Jews … Farts on you and the session of your Kirk.'[46]

JAMES'S LATER PARLIAMENTS

James had successfully negotiated the marriage of his daughter Elizabeth to the Calvinist Elector Frederick of the Palatinate in 1613. He was also thinking about a Spanish Catholic match for Prince Charles. A Calvinist son-in-law and a Catholic daughter-in-law may neatly sum up James's foreign policy. It was ecumenical and peace-making, carried on in the hope that his neighbours would admire it and copy it, promoting peace rather than war. Like most Protestant princes, James did not support Frederick's subsequent rash and disastrous defiance of the Emperor Ferdinand II, which ignited the terrible European conflagration of the Thirty Years War. Only after Ferdinand's early military successes, when the danger of imperial domination in Europe alarmed Catholic and Protestant nations alike, did the conflict widen, dragging in the French alongside Protestant kings. Ferdinand's ruthless determination to roll back the progress of Protestantism in his territories, and throughout Europe if he could, had been underestimated at first.[47]

But many of James's subjects were dismayed when the king did not support Frederick with arms, especially after the crushing victory of the imperial forces at White Mountain in October 1620. They also had serious misgivings about the proposed Spanish marriage for Prince Charles. When Frederick was driven from his lands, the English war party gathered strength. James was sufficiently strong-willed to resist pressure to commit his kingdoms to a continental war that he feared was in the interest of neither Britain nor Protestantism in general, but he had great difficulty in convincing Parliament and the country that such discretion was the better part of valour. Nor was he the kind of king to tolerate dissent from his subjects, and he issued a proclamation forbidding people to speak on affairs of the state. This provoked much resentment, and it was under the shadow of the European war that the first session of James's third parliament opened in January 1621.[48]

Nevertheless, Parliament began well for the king when the Commons dropped an idea to grant members immunity from imprisonment for rash words spoken during debates. James was then voted two subsidies. Proposals to enforce the Sabbath more strictly than the king's Declaration of Sports quickly fizzled out when a message was received saying that the king might be displeased. The House, however, was not entirely obliging, and it started inquiring into certain grievances, such as patents of monopoly, which James had granted to his royal favourites. When James was pressed to increase the penalties on Catholic recusants, he declined cannily and diplomatically. If he persecuted English Catholics, he replied, how could he appeal to Catholic powers on the continent to show mercy to their Protestant subjects? 'I hold that we ought not to force the conscience of any one', he told Parliament; but if only 'our church tried as hard to inculcate the true way as the Jesuits, Puritans and others try to pervert it, so many would not go astray'.[49]

On 28 May, while the Commons was busily debating various measures, the king decided to adjourn Parliament, for reasons not entirely clear. The Commons were disappointed, and they urged the Lords to support them in a bid to persuade the king to change his mind. When this failed, muffled complaints could be heard in the chamber. Towards the end of the first session, on 4 June, Sir John Perrot voiced the thoughts of many in a speech lamenting the misfortunes of Protestants in Bohemia and Germany: he urged the Commons to issue a declaration stating that if James's peacemaking efforts failed, they would be ready to risk life and property for the defence of true religion. The Commons agreed, and a declaration was prepared in record time. James was annoyed when he first heard of the declaration; but when he read the expressions of loyalty to himself as well as to the Protestant faith contained in it, his canny nature came to the fore, and he directed that it should be translated into all the main European languages to show the continental powers the fidelity of his people. A possible crisis had been averted. The Commons and the merchant classes had further good news in July, when a royal proclamation revoked eighteen monopolies and promised a review of many more.[50]

The second session of this parliament resumed on 20 November, with the House still in a largely anti-Spanish mood. It went less well for the king than had the first. A notable speech by John Pym in the Commons, though very deferential to James personally, revealed much hostility to Spain and papists everywhere. Like many, Pym was appalled at the prospect of a Spanish Catholic bride for Prince Charles. Again James tried to forbid Parliament from meddling with high affairs of state. This royal rebuff might have been accepted in sullen silence, because Parliament had provoked royal anger before with uncalled-for remarks about proposed dynastic marriages. Mary Tudor's marriage to King Philip of Spain had caused much disquiet, and so had Elizabeth's much talked about Anjou match, though this eventually came to nothing. James, however, did not handle his parliaments as skilfully as the Tudors had done. Exasperated by the tendency of the Commons to question his policies, he reasserted his right to 'punish any man's dismeanours [sic] in Parliament, as well during their sitting as after'. Now it was the turn of the Commons to be offended. James replied that if he had to consult Parliament on foreign policy, how could he negotiate properly with foreign princes and their ambassadors? How could they ever trust his word? James then raised the stakes when he told MPs that they owed their Parliamentary privileges to the gracious will of past kings, not to any 'undoubted right and inheritance'. This the MPs could not take: they were sure that their liberties *were* their inheritance. One member feared that the king's word would 'strike the affection and soul of every member of this House'. In the heated debates that followed he was shown to be right.[51]

Williams, the Lord Keeper, trying to calm troubled waters, came up with a compromise. Privileges of the House, he suggested, were *originally* due to the favour of kings, but that favour having been granted, they were now part of the inheritance of Parliament. James, still angry at Parliament's intrusiveness into foreign policy as he saw it, was loath to accept this peace offering. He suspected that Parliament would only take advantage of it, and in no time they would be calling their privileges an inheritance without acknowledging the favour of past kings who had granted them. He stressed, however, that he had no desire to limit 'any lawful privileges that ever that House enjoyed in our predecessors' times'. The Commons then made a protestation. It declared that 'the liberties, franchises, privileges and jurisdiction of Parliament are the ancient and undoubted birthright and inheritance of the subjects of England'. Furthermore, affairs of church and state as well as lawmaking 'are proper subjects and matter of counsel and debate in Parliament'; and during those debates 'every member of the House hath, and of right ought to have, freedom of speech ...'. But the protestation was not laid before the king. Members were anxious to defend their rights, but they did not want a confrontation with the Crown. It was simply entered into the Commons Journals.[52]

Gardiner argues that neither James nor the Commons were entirely technically right on this point, though the historian's sympathies lay with Parliament, which he believed was right in spirit if not in the letter. Even in the reigns of Richard II and Henry IV, Parliament had claimed the right to monitor and control the king's finances and even his choice of ministers.[53] None of this, however, lessens the significance of the quarrel between James and his Parliament. The proceedings in the Commons left James fuming, and he ordered the Journals of the House to be brought to him. With his council and judges looking on, he tore out the offending page. Urged on by Gondomar, the Spanish ambassador, James decided he should punish certain members for their outspokenness. Three were sent to the Tower, and Pym was detained in his London home, effectively under house arrest. James then dissolved Parliament on 28 December.[54] Thus James's third Parliament ended acrimoniously, just like the first two, only this time worse. No Tudor monarch had had such an unhappy record with the representatives of the nation.

With his troublesome Commons dispersed, James pursued his foreign and diplomatic policy unhindered. Possibly because he had taken to reading Richard Hooker, he seemed ever more ecumenical in his outlook. He had distant dreams of a reunion of Christendom. He even made cautious approaches to Rome, and seemed prepared to consider the idea of recognising the pope as Chief Pastor or Patriarch of the Western Church. He wrote to the pope in September 1622, addressing him as 'Your Holiness', seeking the pope's support to end the 'calamitous discords and bloodshed' on the continent; he urged the pontiff to 'be pleased together with us to put your hand to so pious a work'. Nothing of note came from these overtures; what is really significant is that a Protestant king made them at all.[55]

In summer the following year, Prince Charles paid a visit to Spain in an attempt to woo the infanta, taking the Duke of Buckingham with him. There Charles slightly spoiled the romantic journey when he offended Spanish protocol, and the lady herself, by climbing over a wall in her private garden to surprise her. After lengthy but eventually fruitless negotiations, Charles and Buckingham returned to England, with the prince neither married nor even engaged, and as disillusioned with the idea of a Spanish marriage as most of the country. Embittered by the experience, both he and Buckingham became enthusiastic supporters of the war policy against Spain. By now James was reluctantly abandoning his hope that by marrying Charles to the infanta he might help bring peace to Europe, and also, by means of a generous Spanish dowry, ease his debt problems. He invited Parliament to tender its candid advice. This would be his last Parliament, and the session began in February 1624.[56]

The Commons, hostile as ever to Spain, were no more sympathetic to James's hopes of peacemaking than they were last time they met. Many were clamouring for a war by sea to plunder Spanish treasure, and this time they had Prince Charles and Buckingham on their side. James stalled, and he managed to pacify the martial spirit among his subjects, only to see it turn on his ministers. In May the Commons succeeded in impeaching Lionel Cranfield, the Lord Treasurer, on a corruption charge, with evidence less than entirely convincing. To the king's disgust, Charles and Buckingham had joined the Commons against Cranfield. Prophetically, James called Buckingham a fool for 'making a rod with which you will be scourged yourself', and he warned his son and heir that 'you will live to have your bellyful of impeachments'.[57]

James did accept a Monopoly Act, under which the Crown could grant monopolies to corporations but no longer to individuals, but he was critical of other bills presented to him for assent. One would have required stricter enforcement of the Sabbath, prompting James to demand why there should be 'no recreation to the poor men that labour hard all the week long, to ease themselves on the Sunday'. He blocked another measure to punish recusants more severely. He then scolded the House for the impeachment of Cranfield, and told members that in future they should not criticise his ministers without his authority and unless he deemed it justified. Finally, to the dismay of the House, he accused them of acting in bad faith over a subsidy bill. There was no impulsive dissolution this time, but on 29 May James prorogued Parliament until November.[58]

Tensions over foreign policy persisted. James did not want to abandon completely his hopes of a Spanish alliance until he was sure he could secure an Anglo-French one to replace it. His abiding fear was that an all Protestant coalition against the emperor and Spain would be seen as a purely religious war, which would serve no purpose except to compel all other Catholic princes to take the Spanish side. Instead, James hoped to divide Catholic Europe by encouraging Catholic nations like France and Venice, both disturbed by the growing power of Spain and the emperor, to forge an anti-Spanish, anti-imperialist alliance with the Protestant powers of Sweden, Britain and Germany. Persevering in this policy, despite the misgivings of the Commons, James succeeded in arranging a marriage treaty with France, whereby Charles would marry Henrietta Maria, sister of the French King Louis XIII. During the negotiations for the marriage, James, under strong pressure from Charles and Buckingham, agreed to relax the recusancy laws, and grant his Catholic subjects effectively toleration and liberty of conscience. The desire to keep this concession a secret from the prying eyes of the Commons may have been the reason why the House, due to reconvene on 2 November, was prorogued once more until 26 February: the official reason (really the excuse) was that London in November was unhealthy and prone to disease.[59]

The marriage treaty was ratified in December, by which time the old king's health had seriously deteriorated. Prince Charles, the heir to the throne, signed a private promise to the French, not officially part of the treaty, but a written promise nonetheless. 'On the faith and word of a prince, both for the present and in the future', it ran, 'I will promise to all the Roman Catholic subjects of the crown of Great Britain the utmost liberty and franchise in everything regarding their religion', provided only that they 'render the obedience which, as good and true subjects, they owe to their king'. Secret government orders were then issued to the courts not to proceed with any further charges against Catholics, and the Lord Keeper was directed to set free all imprisoned Catholics. Fines might still be imposed if new charges were brought by a magistrate unaware of this aspect of the agreement, but this was intended only to mislead the people into thinking that some action was still being taken: any such fines would be secretly refunded. To make the deception yet more convincing, a public order was issued banishing priests currently in prison; but neither Parliament nor the country were told that, under the new Anglo-French accord, there was nothing to stop them coming back again if and when they wanted to do so. Three months after the conclusion of the treaty, in March 1625, James was dead, and the prince who had made these secret promises became King of England, Ireland and Scotland.[60]

RÉSUMÉ

Because this chapter has concentrated on the difficulties he faced, perhaps it should be stressed that the reign of King James was, on the whole, fairly successful. Disputes and controversies were at least kept within manageable bounds. Modern minds may be more sympathetic than some in times past to a king who, though not blessed with the natural charm of Henry VIII, Elizabeth and Charles II, sought peace rather than war, even when many of his people, including many in the Commons, were urging it; and who preferred to treat loyal Catholic subjects with leniency rather than repression. When he was dead, people missed him, and remembered him with more affection than when he lived. This king, to quote the seventeenth-century writer Sir Anthony Weldon, 'lived in peace, died in peace, and left all his kingdoms in a peaceable condition'.[61]

He also, however, left potentially dangerous underlying problems unresolved. His parliaments, though rebellion was far from their minds, were more restive and awkward than in Elizabeth's day; while James seemed more than once to show markedly less respect than the Tudor monarchs to the indispensable role and liberties of Parliament in English constitutional life. James admired the English Reformation for the reason that it had been directed from above rather than by radical commoners like John Knox, which in one sense is true; but he seems not to have fully appreciated the fact that all along the English Crown had acted in and through Parliament. The Reformation, politically and spiritually, was established by statute in the reigns of Henry and Edward. When Mary undid it, she undid it through Parliament, and when Elizabeth re-established it on a permanent basis, she did so through Parliament. For better or worse, in good times or in bad, whatever the individual's own standpoint, Parliament was central to English constitutional and also spiritual life.

In view of his antipathy towards the Commons, it is hardly surprising that the vexed question of the rights of free speech for members while sitting and debating had not been settled. Nor, despite James's best efforts, could Parliament and the nation be convinced that a papist queen for his son and heir would help secure the Protestant faith in Britain and on the continent. The Irish policy, though unlikely to provoke a hostile rising in the king's lifetime, was, to put it at its mildest, insensitive and unfair towards the inhabitants. Meanwhile, the Puritan movement was strong, the Separatist movement was growing, and the emerging Anglican party was gaining influence in high places; and none of the differences that had caused these factions to emerge had been resolved or looked likely to be. If anything, the gap between them was widening, and the attitude of the antagonists hardening. Though James cannot be blamed for the ruinous reign about to follow, insightful minds were nervous and looking ahead with foreboding. 'There is a storm coming towards our church', said the Bishop of Exeter mournfully in 1622.[62]

Despite the goodwill of the nation towards him, Charles's first parliament, which first met in June, did not proceed agreeably. Most members, blissfully ignorant of the pledge Charles had made to the French, were determined that the recusancy laws against Catholics ought to be enforced, even strengthened. Then Charles, though supposed to be a supporter of war against Spain, declined in his opening speech to spell out exactly what his war policy would cost, or even what his precise plans were. Because the Commons was sympathetic in principle to helping foreign Protestants against the Catholic forces, Charles was offered a subsidy, but it was a mere tenth of the amount that Charles really needed had he been in earnest. King and Commons were not on the same wavelength. The Commons was expecting a naval war to plunder Spanish ships, which, it fondly hoped, would cost little and yield a great deal; but following the French marriage treaty, Charles and Buckingham were thinking of a land campaign as well.[3]

The first parliament then looked as though it would peter out. Charles decided he would end it on the apparently considerate grounds that London was afflicted by plague, and many members were anxious to leave for the safety of the shires. But before all the members had left, Sir John Coke, put up to it by Buckingham, let the sixty or so members still in London know something of the true costs of war, though no attempt was made to convince them of the necessity of a major continental campaign by land as well as by sea. Coke did not ask the remaining members to grant the money, only to express their willingness and goodwill. The depleted Commons, however, were not prepared to bind their departed fellow members. This embarrassment was ended on 11 July when the House was informed that the king wished to adjourn the sitting and to convene again at Oxford on 1 August.[4]

So the first parliament, despite the initial goodwill towards the king, ended unpromisingly. Charles did not have enough money to finance a war, he had not taken the Commons into his confidence, and he had withheld relevant facts until most members had gone home. The superficial allure of war and glory appealed to king and Commons alike, but most MPs were in the dark about the strategic plans and financial details, if indeed there were any. As if this were not enough, the Commons had pressed for the enforcement of recusancy laws against Catholics, which the king had promised the French he would revoke. Torn between the Commons and the French, Charles decided he would pursue the penal laws as the Commons wished. This may have been a sweetener to induce them to be more generous with money, but it provoked bitter complaints from Henrietta Maria and French ambassadors over breach of trust. Now Charles felt obliged to sweeten them too, and officials hinted that although the laws would be applied to satisfy the Commons, sentences might not be actually carried out. Within a few short months of his accession Charles had got himself into a shoddy constitutional pickle, the like of which was unknown in Tudor times. This was not the way that national government was conducted in the days of Henry VIII and Thomas Cromwell, or Elizabeth and the Cecils.[5]

When Parliament reconvened at Oxford, it started badly for the king. Sir Edward Giles drew attention to a pardon that had been granted to a Jesuit, and he wanted to know why. Sir John Eliot declared, with solemn though unknowing irony, that he could not imagine the king authorising this pardon in view of the promise he had made to enforce the penal laws against papists. Ministers of the Crown could only stall; and it boded ill for the king's hopes that Parliament would grant him more money.[6]

Three days later Charles appeared in person. In a very brief speech he reminded the House that it too had supported war against Spain. He concentrated entirely on the general needs of the navy, and left it to his ministers and servants to deal with the details. Sir John Coke then gave as upbeat a statement as he could on affairs in Europe. Denmark was now in the war on the Protestant side. The German princes were more confident. The French king, also opposed to Spanish expansionism, was at peace with his Huguenots subjects. Coke, however, still failed to specify an actual sum of money, and his vagueness left the Commons puzzled and faintly suspicious. Sir Francis Seymour said that he had lost confidence in the king's ministers. Sir Robert Phelips was bolder still. He recalled the parliament of 1624, when three petitions had been made: first, that the prince should wed a Protestant; second, England should aid the Dutch; third, true religion should be preserved. He invited the House to consider the state of the nation now. He doubted whether the terms of the French marriage were any better than the defunct Spanish one. Like Seymour, Phelips feared that 'there wanted good advice' around the king. But he went further, and appealed to members to learn the lessons of history, and to reflect that 'when kings are persuaded to do what they should not, subjects have often been transported to do what they ought not'. Without clarifying this enigmatic comment, Phelips concluded that the Commons should deal with internal affairs of state, and not support policies and plans that were neither fully understood nor properly explained.[7]

During the debates that followed, Buckingham was the minister increasingly feeling the heat. Buckingham decided he would invoke the spectre of popery and give the Commons all it had asked for. The laws against Catholics, he assured them, would be prosecuted in full. (Horrified French envoys were privately promised that these laws would only be temporary.) Buckingham then gave a vigorous defence of his conduct and policy. His speech received a mixed reception in the Commons. It was unfortunate for him that news was just arriving of renewed attacks on English ships and sailors by pirates, despite Buckingham's earlier boast that he would make the seas safe. These tidings tilted the balance against the minister. Sensing danger, Charles decided to dissolve Parliament.[8]

However, because the question of funding remained unresolved, Charles realised that he would have to call another parliament fairly soon. Hoping to secure a more compliant assembly than the previous one, a commission was issued in November to set in motion the recusancy laws against Catholics. Charles also calculated that if he made awkward men like Seymour and Phelips sheriffs, they would not be able to stand for election. By such means one of the king's supporters was confidently looking forward to an altogether more satisfying parliamentary session – an 'inestimable harmony of agreement between the King and his people'. But good fortune was not on the government's side. About this time the nation learned that a much trumpeted expedition to attack Cadiz in September had failed dismally. It was a further damaging blow to the prestige of Buckingham, chief organiser of the botched venture, who had hoped it would win him fame and popularity.[9]

Charles's second parliament opened in February 1626. Sir John Eliot, previously a supporter of Buckingham, had been shocked at the sight of wretched, destitute and half-starved sailors returning from the fiasco of Cadiz. He forcefully called for a Parliamentary inquiry into such past failings before any promises could be made for future supplies. Demands of this kind were unheard of in the days of Henry VIII and Elizabeth. Maybe the Commons of Tudor times would not have dared. More to the point, with ministers of the calibre of Thomas Cromwell and the Cecils around the monarch, the need would not have arisen.[10]

The Commons then asked what advice individual councillors had tendered to the king regarding the subsidies granted in the 1624 parliament. When this request was rather predictably declined, the Commons did not press the point. The crunch came when the Commons was asked to provide money without any unseemly probing or questioning. The Commons resented this, and vented its frustration out on Buckingham. Cadiz, the failure to deal with piracy, his alleged appropriation of Crown lands for himself and his friends, were all laid against him. Charles stood loyally by his beleaguered minister, but the Commons persisted, and the king became increasingly convinced that herein lay a challenge to his royal authority as well as to Buckingham's place on the council. Charles then addressed Parliament directly and magisterially: 'Remember', he admonished them, that 'Parliaments are altogether in my power for their calling, sitting and dissolution; therefore, as I find the fruits of them good or evil, they are to continue or not to be'.[11]

Undeterred, the Commons pressed on with charges against Buckingham with a view to his possible impeachment. This ancient judicial process had fallen into disuse in the fifteenth century, but it had been revived in the reign of James to get rid of Lord Chancellor Bacon and Lord Treasurer Cranfield. Buckingham, ironically, had been one of the main accusers of Cranfield; now he was reaping what he had sown. Then one morning during the current session the Commons was alarmed to discover that two of its most vocal members, Eliot and Digges, each of whom had said things displeasing to the king, were missing. Enquiries quickly revealed that both men had been sent to the Tower. The Commons was outraged. 'We are all resolved to have them out again', wrote one member to a friend, 'or we will proceed to no business.' They were soon released, though Eliot had to remain in custody until his house had been searched for incriminating evidence: in the event nothing was found there. Charles, determined to hear no ill word spoken of his favourite minister, then dissolved Parliament.[12]

So Charles had rid himself of another bothersome assembly. He was convinced that his efforts to reign and rule worthily were being frustrated by a few determined but unrepresentative troublemakers, and that he enjoyed widespread support in the country at large. So he tried to raise money by means of a 'free gift' (my quotes), and when that failed, a forced loan. As the name suggests, this was a loan to the Crown where the lender has little choice. In purely financial terms the loan was somewhat more successful than the 'gift', but even its limited success came at an embarrassing price. The Chief Justice was asked to declare the loan legal, but to the dismay of the king he said he could not do so.[13]

Meanwhile, for reasons complicated but mainly trivial, England's relations with France were deteriorating just as those between France and Spain were showing signs of improvement. Charles and Buckingham then decided on a pre-emptive strike against France. The target would be the offshore Ile de Rhé, and Buckingham would take command. Confidence soared when the French and their newfound Spanish allies did not immediately appear to give battle. A government poet, with more zeal than perception, elevated Charles above Edward III and Elizabeth in England's hall of military fame:

I saw third Edward stain my flood
By Sluys with slaughtered Frenchman's blood:
  And from Eliza's feet
I saw the vanquished Spaniards fly.
But twas a greater mastery,
  No foe at all to meet;
When they, without their ruin or dispute,
Confess thy reign as sweet as absolute.

Unhappily for Buckingham, the foe was wisely waiting and biding his time. The English attack on Rhé was a complete failure which used up most of the forced loan. It left Charles with little alternative but to recall Parliament again. It met in March 1628.[14]

In his opening speech the king made it plain that he expected Parliament to cooperate, to help him, to do what he asked and provide more funds. Otherwise, he hinted he would have to employ other means. But the Commons was in no mood to be browbeaten, and Edward Coke sought to introduce a bill against imprisonment without trial. Eliot invoked ancient laws and liberties, and castigated the popish sympathisers in the church. (These included Archbishop William Laud and his party, to be discussed in the next section.) Another complained bitterly about mismanagement of funds, extra-Parliamentary taxes and infringement of liberties, though he was careful to absolve the king personally: he put the blame, though indirectly, on the Crown's ministers.[15]

The Commons then moved on to more specific matters. Coke introduced his Bill of Rights, which would have made it unlawful to impose any tax without the consent of Parliament, or to imprison any subject without trial. During debates on the Bill of Rights, Sir Walter Erle declared that 'the subject hath suffered more in the violation of the ancient liberties within these few years than in the three hundred before'. In committee Sir Nathaniel Rich likened the king to a debtor whose mantra was: 'I owe you nothing, but pray trust me.' I trust the king, avowed another, but 'we cannot take his trust but in a Parliamentary way'. John Pym, now emerging as a major force in the Commons, was vigorously championing the historic rights of Parliament. Like Erle, Pym looked way past the previous Tudor age, and invoked the rights of the English people in and since Saxon times, which had survived the Norman Conquest and all else since. 'There are plain footsteps of those laws in the government of the Saxons', declared Pym, and they were 'of that vigour and force as to overlive the Conquest'.[16]

Eventually the Bill of Rights was modified into a Petition of Right, the reason being that whereas a bill could be vetoed by the king, a petition was more likely to receive a favourable answer. One clause in the Petition appealed to Parliamentary precedent in the reign of Edward III, and urged 'that no man hereafter be compelled to make or yield any gift, loan, benevolence, tax or such like charge, without common consent by Act of Parliament'. When Charles, jealous of his royal prerogative, gave an uncertain, evasive initial reply, the Commons drew up a remonstrance listing two major complaints: government mismanagement and popish innovations in the church. At last Charles accepted the Petition and five subsidies offered with it, though the total sum was still nothing like what he really wanted. To the king's intense annoyance, however, the Commons did not abandon its remonstrance.[17]

The Commons also went into committee regarding tonnage and poundage (duties on imports and exports). Since the days of Henry VI, tonnage and poundage had been granted by Parliament virtually unconditionally to a new king for as long as he reigned. The purpose was to protect the seas. In one of Charles's previous parliaments, however, Sir Walter Erle noted that English ships had recently been attacked by pirates off the Scilly Isles, and that even the Channel was not entirely safe. Erle proposed that, pending investigations, tonnage and poundage should be granted on a year by year basis. The Lords did not pass this bill, but the renewed interest in the subject raised the king's suspicions.[18]

Charles announced that he would, once again, prorogue Parliament. The Commons' next move was to draw up a second remonstrance, more daring than the first. It included the statement that 'the receiving of tonnage and poundage, and other impositions not granted by Parliament, is a breach of the fundamental liberties of this kingdom, and contrary to your Majesty's answer to the Petition of Right'. The Commons, therefore, 'do most humbly beseech your majesty to forbear any further receiving the same; and not to take it in ill part from those of your Majesty's loving subjects who shall refuse to make payment of any charge without warrant of law demanded'. Charles replied that 'I owe an account of my actions but to God alone'. He then curtly prorogued Parliament to 20 October.[19]

Whether tonnage and poundage really was included in the Petition of Right is a debateable constitutional point. Charles was adamant that it was not. Technically the king was in the right, according to Gardiner, who argued that the appeal of the Commons to the Petition in the second remonstrance was a 'daring attempt to take up new ground'. The wording of the Petition was 'that no man hereafter be compelled to make or yield any gift, loan, benevolence, *tax, or such like charge* without common consent by Act of Parliament'. All depends, therefore, on how the italics (mine) were understood. However, Gardiner also argued that even if the Commons was 'formally in the wrong', it was nevertheless acting in the national interest given the king's well-known penchant for trying to bypass Parliament when it suited him. This is a matter probably best left to constitutional experts. The main lesson for our story is that the distrust between King and Commons was growing daily.[20]

More grief and vexation awaited the king when, in August 1628, Buckingham was stabbed to death on his way to a meeting with the Venetian ambassador. The killer was John Felton, who had served under Buckingham at Rhé. A promotion which he expected had been denied him, and like many other soldiers and sailors he had not received wages due to him. Reports of the remonstrance turned his hatred of Buckingham into murder. Charles and his confidantes were horrified; but on the streets of London the news was greeted with rejoicing, and Felton was toasted in taverns and ale houses before being hanged at Tyburn.[21]

When Parliament resumed in January 1629, the question of tonnage and poundage soon came to the forefront again. The Commons had encouraged merchants to withhold payment to the king's tax collectors, even though those who followed this advice were threatened with imprisonment by government officials. Charles then made a conciliatory gesture: he conceded that tonnage and poundage was not his by right, but claimed it was a matter of necessity for normal expenses of royal government. This was quite well received by the Commons. It is just possible that this vexed question might have been amicably resolved but for the deep distrust between King and Commons, exacerbated by the fact that Charles had recently authorised a highly slanted printing of the Petition of Right.[22]

Meanwhile, a feisty controversy was brewing in the church. In a typically bold speech, Eliot voiced grave concern at the appointments of men like William Laud, Richard Neile and Richard Montagu as bishops: these so-called 'Arminians', according to Eliot, were a danger to the true religion of England. Eliot and those who agreed with him were now raising the question of who should define exactly what the true religion was – Convocation or Parliament. Convocation was dominated by bishops, and bishops were appointed by the king, who was aghast at the idea that Parliament should discuss church matters let alone arbitrate on them. In the church, therefore, as well as in affairs of state, a contest was unfolding in which the authority of the king would be pitted against the authority of Parliament, and specifically against the increasingly demanding Commons. Lying behind this was the aversion of the Commons to the new bishops who now enjoyed the king's favour.[23]

With the Commons clamouring for action against Catholics and Arminians, as well as his ministers and general government incompetence, Charles decided on an adjournment. The Commons reassembled on 2 March, only to be told by the Speaker, Sir John Finch, that the king had ordered a further adjournment to the 10th. When Finch put the motion, which the government expected would be a formality, cries of 'No!' resounded all around the House. Eliot then rose to his feet. Finch told him that he had a command from the king to leave the chair if any member tried to speak out of turn. As Finch made to rise, two members, Denzil Holles and Benjamin Valentine, forcibly held him down. 'God's wounds!' thundered Holles. 'You shall sit till we please to rise.' Eliot, asserting parliamentary sovereignty with customary boldness, declared that the House held the right to adjourn itself, but that a declaration regarding the church must be read first. Another member agreed; the Commons, he cried, should not be 'turned off like scattered sheep as we were at the end of the last session'. Forced to decide between King and Commons, the Speaker opted for the king, and refused to read the declaration. Then Eliot rehearsed the grievances regarding the church and arbitrary government, though as ever he blamed the king's ministers rather than the king personally. Heated debates in the Commons followed: then a knock-ing was heard at the door. The king had sent for the mace. Sir Peter Heyman threatened the Speaker with 'some mark of punishment to be set upon you by the House'. There was more knocking at the door, this time from Black Rod with a message from the king. A guard was about to force the door open. Holles then hastily read out a resolution. It condemned anyone who supported popery, Arminianism and extra-Parliamentary levies as a 'capital enemy to this Kingdom and Commonwealth'. Anyone who had paid tonnage and poundage duties not granted by Parliament was 'a betrayer of the liber-ties of England'. The House had stood its ground; with its honour intact it adjourned itself and the members left.[24]

Immediately after this scene, Charles formally dissolved Parliament. In his exasperation he derided the protests of the Commons as things 'hatched out of the passionate brains of a few particular persons'. Nine such particular persons, including Eliot, were committed to prison. When questioned in the Tower, Eliot refused to answer, 'because I hold that it is against the privilege of the House of Parliament to speak of anything that was done in the House'. After a great deal of legal wrangling over the exact nature of their offences in law, King's Bench sentenced Eliot and two of his allies to heavy fines and imprisonment at the king's pleasure or until they made a formal confession to the general charge of conduct endangering the peace of the realm. Still in confinement, Eliot died of consumption in November 1632.[25]

Meanwhile, the so-called Personal Rule had begun, the eleven-year rule of Charles I from 1629–1640 without a parliament. But now it is necessary to digress to the church, and specifically to these 'Arminians' and alleged popish sympathisers who had aroused the ire of Eliot and many of the Commons. Some call them High Churchmen, others Arminian, yet others Anglo-Catholic. For the sake of convenience they will be referred to here as Laudians, after the most influential of them.

THE LAUDIANS AND THE DEFORMATION

On a visit to Scotland in 1633, Archbishop Laud was shocked by the spartan interior of many Scottish churches, now stripped of sacred art and adorn-ments, and he was told that these were the changes made at the Reformation. In that case, he replied, it would be better described as a *Deformation*. He did not mean that Scotland or England should have remained forever part of the Roman church, but he was deeply unhappy with the form Protestantism had taken in Britain. He was determined to do something about it.[26]

William Laud and his party emerged from the anti-Puritan movement begun by Richard Hooker. Around 1617, when King James was enticing a

cautious Kirk to gently reform itself along Anglican lines, Laud was re-intro-
ducing the works of the fathers, the councils and even the medieval schoolmen
into the theology curriculum at Oxford University, despite fierce opposition
from the Calvinist party there. Reformers as a whole had few objections to
reading the fathers, at least up to the time of St Augustine, but almost to a man
they despised the medieval theologians; hence the antagonism of the Oxford
Calvinists. As if to deliberately wind up the godly, Laud recommended that
the fathers could profitably be read before turning to Calvin.[27]

Laud detested Calvinist predestination, a doctrine dear to Puritan hearts. He
set in motion stiff measures to stifle and suppress predestinarian preachers and
supporters.[28] This inflamed the godly party. One of them, Thomas Salisbury,
injudiciously warned of impending divine wrath against Laudianism, hinting
with little subtlety that it might take the form of a rebellion. The authorities
began proceedings against him; but they did so through the king's commissioners rather than through an open trial before a jury, which suggests that
they were unsure whether normal legal methods would produce the required
result. For this reason, the right of trial according to due processes of the
law was another demand included in the Petition of Right. Fears grew that
Charles's government was becoming a threat to civil liberties. Salisbury cited
the ancient Spartans prepared to 'sacrifice themselves in so good a cause as
the liberty of their country'. Prophetic and provocative, he called England a
'commonwealth'.[29]

Laud was a man with a mixed reputation, who combined personal kindness
to the poor with severity on matters of ecclesiastical discipline. Under James,
and more so under Charles, he advanced impressively, becoming Bishop
of London in 1628 and Archbishop of Canterbury in 1633, two days after
Abbott's death. As archbishop, Laud tried to extend his authority to Oxford
and Cambridge universities as well as the parishes. He wanted to impose conformity to Anglican rites and ceremonies on foreign Protestant churches in
England, and also on English communities abroad, such as Holland, where
services were generally conducted along Presbyterian lines. Similar plans were
drawn up for English settlers in the American colonies until the outbreak of
civil war intervened and put a stop to them.[30]

As archbishop, Laud refused the offer of a cardinal's hat. The significance
of this is not the refusal, but the fact that the offer was made in the first
place. No one in Rome would have dreamed of such an idea for Parker,
Whitgift or Abbott. Also revealing is the reason Laud gave for declining.
'Something dwells within me', he explained, 'which will not suffer me to
accept that till Rome be other than it is.' His predecessors might have been
a bit more forthright.[31]

During the years of the Personal Rule, Laudian changes continued
apace. Since Elizabeth's day, Puritan ministers and parishes had been able to

discreetly adapt the Prayer Book as it pleased them, and mostly they got away with it; but such low profile non-compliance was now threatened by Laud's determination to compel liturgical uniformity. Ceremonies, he insisted, were not merely edifying and useful for decorum in churches (though many Puritans denied even that); Laud now appealed to the Old Testament for a divine mandate for the ceremonial in the church of God.[32]

Laud had a great sense of propriety, besides a fondness for regulation. He disapproved of people bringing their pet dogs to church, a long-standing custom in England, because it seemed to him to lower the spiritual tone of services. This went down badly with dog lovers everywhere. Another of his early innovations, this one supported by Charles, was a requirement to move the communion table from the nave of the church to the east end, and to have it surrounded by rails. Kneeling at the altar rail to receive communion was to be made compulsory. This was resented by the godly because it seemed popish.[33]

The question of images in churches was now resurfacing. Bishop Richard Montagu, another Laudian, argued that images should be permitted so long as they were not abused or falsely worshipped. Elizabeth and James would not have minded this; but it riled the godly, who, like Zwingli, Cranmer and Calvin before them, were convinced that images in churches violated the second commandment. They also seemed to be causing confusion. Before taking her seat in the pew, Emily Browne of St Edmund's liked to bow before one of the church windows on which was engraved a depiction of the Deity. A concerned Puritan asked why she did so. 'I do it to my Lord God', she replied. But where is He, persisted the godly man. 'In the window, is He not?' the good lady replied.[34]

More significantly, Laud and his party were making episcopacy a distinct order in the Christian ministry. No longer was episcopacy just the most admirable or suitable form of church government, based on tradition and custom (this had been the consensus from Thomas Cromwell to Cranmer, Elizabeth, Whitgift, even Hooker). According to the Laudians, episcopacy was a divine institution, therefore a divine law (*jure divino*). This idea had been heard before from men like Bridges and Savaria in the last years of Elizabeth (see pp. 108–9). Then, however, it was the opinion of a few; now it was a Laudian orthodoxy. It was a departure not just from Puritanism, but also from the Reformation mainstream. Laud's new thinking – new in a Protestant sense – ensured that he and the Puritans were now at loggerheads over something more far-reaching than style or ceremonial. A damaging dispute was looming over which form of church government had a divine command, and was thus binding on the church. Was it episcopacy, or the Presbyterian system, supported by many of the godly? (And even those Puritans not fully committed to Presbyterianism still opposed Laud on this point.)[35]

Laud was encouraging the belief in the transmission of apostolic grace in episcopal ordination. Put more simply, this meant that bishops were a sort of spiritual conduit, not just to the *times* of the apostles, but also to the *grace* that the apostles were blessed with. One of Laud's supporters, John Yates, quoted Cardinal Bellarmine approvingly, saying that 'there can be no visible church where there is no visible succession from the chairs of the apostles'. All this ran counter to standard Protestant teaching – that apostolic succession simply meant continuing in the same faith as the apostles, which could be done, if necessary, without bishops.[36]

Bishops, it may be observed, had enjoyed mixed fortunes since the Reformation. With Luther they were acceptable though not obligatory, rather like images in churches. Calvin would have tolerated them, but he preferred the Presbyterian model; Beza and the Puritans would have swept them unceremoniously away. They staged a partial recovery thanks to the efforts of Hooker and Andrewes before finally, under Laud, attaining the lofty dignity of a divine institution.

Nostalgia for the pre-Reformation past was another feature of Laudianism. When repairs were necessary to St Paul's Cathedral, Laud called on the people to give generously, and to rouse their spirits he invoked a devotional bygone age. 'Remember former times', he appealed, 'when religion was in life, the world in love with it, with what alacrity works of this kind were performed, no cost spared, nothing too good, no thing too much for God and His church ...'. John Swan was sorry to see that 'religion hath nowadays lost much of that bright beauty, which in ages heretofore she was known to have'. Even the monastic estate was praised by John Normanton for its piety and good works. The same Normanton, Fellow of Caius, commended Thomas Aquinas, the prominent medieval theologian who had been the target of sustained polemical attack from Luther, Calvin and all mainstream reformers.[37]

The Laudians were not unalloyed admirers of the medieval church – there were criticisms of it too – but a feeling grew among them that much piety, spirituality and beauty of holiness had been lost since the Reformation. This may have been the case in England in the reign of Edward VI; however, it was not true of the Reformation everywhere. On a visit to Sweden the English writer, Bulstrode Whitelocke, reported how in the churches there he saw 'many pictures of saints and other images ... a high altar with a rich carpet of velvet embroidered in gold, and a stately crucifix upon it ... and none could see a difference between this and the Papists' churches'.[38] In fact, there was some talk of rapport, even union, between the churches of England and Sweden in the 1630s which Laud neither opposed nor advocated; but nothing came of it. Laudians occasionally used Luther for tactical purposes, to show that images in church were not intrinsically anti-evangelical. Luther thus came in useful as a convenient big stick with which to bash the godly. This apart, the Laudians seem to have had little affection for him. Lutheran dogma on the Eucharist was particularly unappealing, and Laud found the bitterness of much Lutheran polemic deeply distasteful. 'Hardly have I seen more gall drop from any man's pen', he noted censoriously after reading an exceptionally barbed anti-Calvin tirade penned by the chaplain to the Elector of Saxony. One Christopher Potter loftily dismissed the 'jarrs and divisions' between Lutherans and Calvinists as of no consequence to the Church of England, 'which followeth none but Christ'.[39]

Laudian dissatisfaction, therefore, was not limited to Calvinism or even to Puritanism; it extended to the Reformation as a whole. Laudian divines were now saying that the Roman Church held the fundamentals of the faith. Laud and Bishop White reproved Romanists for worshipping images, though others like Montagu were less critical. Transubstantiation was still rejected, though opposition was moderating. Some, including Laud, saw it as nothing worse than an unacceptable way of defining the real presence in the Eucharist. This was one of the most sensitive subjects of all, because seventeenth-century Puritans had not forgotten the 300 Protestants burned under Mary Tudor for denying transubstantiation. The Laudian Bishop Forbes of Edinburgh defended the adoration of the Host, though he wisely stopped short of calling for its reintroduction into the Church of England. Laud opposed the invocation of the saints; Montagu, milder as ever, preferred to call this a mistake. Opposition to the Roman Catholic doctrine on salvation had seemed unanimous up until now, but even here signs of softening could be detected. When William Covell argued that the difference between Rome and the Church of England was more a misunderstanding than an irreparable breach, Laud neither endorsed him nor condemned him. Forbes disliked the expression 'faith alone justifies', because it implied that good works had no value or usefulness. Papal infallibility was conveniently dismissed by some Laudians as a mere fancy of the Jesuits.[40]

Though Laudians rejected Rome's jurisdictional claims of papal primacy, and though they criticised the Council of Trent for its lack of canonical authority, they could express their opposition to Trent in unusually mild terms. Montagu even cited Trent approvingly on justification and freewill. 'Where is the vast difference', he wanted to know, between Trent and the Protestant Confessions that 'these clamorous promoters [Puritans] imagine': Puritans do little but 'brawle at the shadow of their own fancies'.[41]

Readers may feel the difference is rather obvious. Here is Article 11 of the Thirty-Nine:[42]

We are accounted righteous before God only for the merit of our Lord and Saviour Jesus Christ, by faith, and not for our own works or deservings:

Wherefore, that we are justified by faith only, is a most wholesome doctrine, and very full of comfort.

Here is Trent:[43]

If anyone says that by faith alone the impious is justified … and that it is not in any way necessary that he be prepared and disposed by the movement of his own will, let him be anathema.

Assuming that Montagu had actually read the Thirty-Nine Articles and the decrees of Trent, then either he was just teasing the godly, or else indulging in the sort of nimble theological contention beloved of certain schoolmen.[44]

Not surprisingly, Montagu had been challenged over his views on justification, faith and good works, though by skilful use of words he and his supporters avoided disciplinary action. Nor was Montagu the only one to take a charitable view of Trent. 'As evil as things were carried out in the Trident Council', declared Bishop Buckeridge, 'it is hard to demonstrate that the Trident Council hath erred in any article of faith which is fundamental.' By contrast Philip Melanchthon, the mildest of Protestant reformers, in his last major work condemned Trent as full of gross errors, contrary to the very foundations of true apostolic Christianity. Puritan fears of a re-Catholisation of England, therefore, were by no means entirely unfounded, and they were increased yet more by the knowledge that the Catholic queen's chapel in Somerset House was open to all and well attended.[45] This theological disputing, incidentally, was no longer confined to the universities, colleges and the world of academia. Though this may have been the case in Elizabeth's time when the Puritan movement was in its infancy, in the reigns of James and Charles, as others have shown, these controversies, particularly over predestination, were frequently fought out in public, dividing priests, lecturers and parishes, with even laymen joining in.[46]

Charles, meanwhile, had asked the pope to grant English Catholics permission to take the oath of allegiance to him, and in December 1634 Gregorio Panzani arrived from Rome to discuss the affairs of Catholics in England. Charles delegated his secretary, Sir Francis Windebank, a man well known for his hostility to Puritans, to meet the papal emissary. Panzani was an artful fellow. He recommended to his authorities at Rome that gifts of sacred pictures and flowers might be sent not only to Charles's ministers, but also to their wives, in the hope that 'we shall gain not only the men, but their wives and daughters as well'. When Windebank suggested that only Jesuits and Puritans stood in the way of a union between the English church and Rome, Panzani replied that the Jesuits could be packed off somewhere to make that blessed event easier. No commitments were forthcoming from either Charles or Laud, but Panzani enjoyed a favourable reception at the English court, and he listened appreciatively to gushing compliments on the spiritual beauty of the old faith that aroused such hostility among the godly. 'When will such splendour be restored to our church?' sighed Edward Martin, a Laudian, when his eyes alighted on a picture of an ancient saint in Jesus College while guiding Panzani around Cambridge.[47]

The possibility of sending an English agent to Rome, mainly on the queen's behalf, was now discussed. Montagu then told Panzani that several bishops, including Laud and many of the lesser clergy, now broadly agreed with most Roman dogmas, and consequently the way was clear for serious discussions on church unity to begin. Panzani was pleased to hear this, but he suggested that it might be better to wait for proposals from the king or one of his senior ministers. Montagu promised he would speak with Laud. In their enthusiasm Montagu, Windebank and others fancied a sort of negotiated reunion, with the papacy so delighted to receive England back into the fold that generous concessions would be offered. Montagu even dreamed of the day when English episcopal orders would be acknowledged in Rome. At this point even Panzani felt that he ought to dampen down the fervour just a little. He knew, if Montagu did not, that the only reunion acceptable to Rome was one on Rome's terms. The Puritans knew this too; so the more cosying up to Rome that went on in court, the more suspicious and infuriated the Puritans became.

In fact, Montagu was probably exaggerating the Roman Catholic leanings of the other bishops. Laud did not meet Panzani personally on his visit, and Charles was not going to humble himself before the pope. Laud saw the Church of England, not the Church of Rome, as the ideal church. Because Laudians believed in the essential equality of bishops, they could not accept the pope's spiritual primacy, though they might have accepted a Roman patriarchate. Nevertheless, a mediating role seemed attractive: Peter Heylyn, a preacher to King Charles, declared that it was due to the Providence of God that the Church of England, 'depending on neither party, might in succeeding times be a judge between them, as more inclinable to compose than expose their quarrels'.[48]

So what was driving Archbishop Laud? In his own words he would say:

Since I came into this place, I laboured nothing more than that the *external public worship* of God – too much slighted in most parts of this kingdom – might be preserved, and that with as much decency and uniformity as might be; being still of the opinion that *unity cannot long continue in the church where uniformity is shut out* at the church door. And I evidently saw that the public neglect of God's service in the outward face of it, and the nasty lying of many places dedicated to that service, had almost cast a damp upon the *true and inward* worship of God. [Italics mine.][49]

This Laudian uniformity, his deep longing, his whole life's work, was exactly what his Puritan detractors despised so bitterly. Even the ceremonial of the Edwardian and Elizabethan Prayer Book was too much for most of them. They wanted less and less of it all. Yet the very thing that the Puritan would gladly have dumped was, for Laud, essential to the well being, the unity and inward spiritual worship in the church. With Laud, to quote Gardiner, 'it was not the heart which was to pour itself out in definite forms, but the forms which were to train and discipline the heart'.[50]

Laud was convinced that there was something too individual about Protestantism, too obsessed with man's direct relationship with God at the expense of the life, liturgy and worship of the church. Laud would have the soul reared, cared for, educated, guided and directed by the church. To quote Gardiner again: 'From the cradle to the grave man's life was to be surrounded with a succession of ecclesiastical acts influencing his soul through the gates of the senses.'[51]

The Laudian ethos, as Gardiner well said, 'might be regarded as holding a middle place between Rome and Calvinism; but it might also be regarded as a feeble copy of Rome'.[52] This is exactly how it looked to the godly. In Elizabeth's day the Puritans complained that the church was not reformed enough. They could now complain that the church of Laud would be barely reformed at all, at best a pale imitation of Rome.

Here, too, is a big difference between Laud and the early Reformation. For Luther, and for Elizabeth, though not for the Calvinist or the Puritan, the external worship with its liturgy and ceremonial is good, edifying and desirable: but never essential. Luther's one thing needful was the Gospel believed from the heart. Inward renewal has to come first, otherwise ceremonies and liturgy, however attractive they may be to the senses, are of little real spiritual value. Not so with Laud. In this sense Laudianism struck not just at Puritanism, not even at Calvinism; it was a parting of the ways from the Reformation as a whole. Laud could always invoke Elizabeth's love of good order; but she never claimed she had a divine mandate for church ceremonial, or for bishops.

Over 100 years before Laud, Philip Melanchthon, in a work which Luther felt was worthy to be canonised, declared with all the joyous confidence of the new convert who has just seen the light that even the Sacraments were not absolutely essential for the believer. Baptism and the Lord's Supper do not save; they are testimonies and seals of the divine will; believe the Gospel and you will be justified without the sign; the Sacraments are signs given to confirm and strengthen faith. 'I cannot explain', Melanchthon went on, 'the nature and power of faith satisfactorily in mere words. Those who have known the power of sin, whose consciences have been struck by the knowledge of sin, take delight in it.' Melanchthon was not, of course, recommending Christians to do without the Sacraments; he was merely making the point that even they do not compare to the gift of saving faith, and this is not the language or the spirit of men like Laud. More typical of them is Montagu, addressing Charles in 1636 as the king raised up for 'bringing back, renewing, restoring, repairing, protecting and preserving the ancient rites, the ceremonies of our forefathers, the apostolic and ecclesiastical traditions'.[53]

Rites, ceremonies, traditions – this is what was stirring the soul of Richard Montagu, not the liberating, redeeming power of saving faith. But to the Puritan, these rites reeked only of popery, and threatened the undoing of all godly hopes.

One of the luxuries of reading church history, however, is that there are two ways of looking at almost everything, including the Laudian-Puritan dispute. One sees Puritanism as a deeply personal faith, forthright, vibrant, filled with conviction, which despises showy human ceremonies and the rule of ecclesiastical stuffed shirts like Laud: its core was the soul's direct link with the divine. From the Puritan viewpoint, Laud looks flabby, starchy, pompous, regimented, innovative only in a thoroughly unwelcome popish direction. On the other hand, many Stuart people found Puritanism aggressive, strident, noisy, over-demanding, over-bearing, intrusive and divisive, a disturbance to civil and spiritual peace. Laud, for all his fussiness and orderliness, offered stability, calm and quiet. Lovers of art and beauty would appreciate his church services. Neither would he burden the faithful with a surfeit of sermons and catechisms, nor seek to prevent harmless pleasures on the Lord's Day. Whether Laudianism or Puritanism was a welcome development is entirely a subjective matter which no amount of research will ever settle: let the reader be judge.

But there was little sign of brotherly love between them. Poor Laud became the target for some wickedly pungent satire and lampooning in engravings, woodcuts, pamphlets and cartoons. After issuing some church canons, he was depicted triggering a military canon that backfired in his face. Elsewhere he was at the helm of a ship steering it straight towards the mouth of hell; in bed vomiting up canons and anti-Puritan Star Chamber orders; locked in a cage with the queen's papist confessor, Father Phillips. 'Never man hath had so many scandalous abuses cast upon him', the harassed prelate sighed. His allies on the Bishops' Bench got similar treatment, often portrayed as hideous beasts or pests. Nor has the unfortunate archbishop fared much better from some modern historians: he was the 'greatest calamity ever visited upon the Church of England' (Patrick Collinson); the 'enemy of all things evangelical … the powerful and bigoted reactionary' (David Daniell). The satire was not all one way, however, and plays poking fun of the godly were frequently staged in front of appreciative audiences. One who found them highly amusing was the king.[54]

So was Laud a Protestant, in any real sense of the word? He always insisted that he was loyal to the Thirty-Nine Articles, a classic Protestant Reformation document, and the historian is bound to take him at his word. But the Puritans also professed loyalty to the same articles. Unfortunately, these articles could not bring unity. The controversy over church government, for example, had arisen *since* the Thirty-Nine, not over it. The same is true of other arguable areas, like predestination. The only way round this difficulty was to read the articles, or the ones in contention, in a Laudian or a Puritan fashion.

On predestination, for example, Article 17 of the Thirty-Nine is carefully designed to avoid strife. The language follows Ephesians 1 very closely: the elect are called by grace and 'obey the calling'; they are chosen 'in Christ'. Nothing is said about the godless or predetermined damnation. So Montagu may have had a point when he cited this article *against* the godly. Nevertheless, it could be argued that Calvinist predestination can be *inferred* from Article 17 simply by taking it to its logical conclusion: for if the elect are 'called', then surely it follows that the non-elect are *not* called. Both sides could, therefore, claim allegiance to the Thirty-Nine Articles while disagreeing bitterly with each other.[55]

The same applies to the Eucharist and the real presence. 'The altar', says Laud, 'is the greatest place of God's residence upon earth … yea, greater than the pulpit, for there 'tis *Hoc est corpus meum* [This is my Body], but in the pulpit 'tis at most but *Hoc est verbum meum* [This is my word].'[56]

Here Laud was delivering a two-pronged attack on the godly. The Puritan believed in the primacy of the sermon, but Laud would shift Christianity's centre of gravity from the sermon to the Sacrament and the accompanying ceremonial. (Also intriguing is Laud's 'at most', another dig at the godly: *sometimes* the Word of God is heard in a sermon, but not always.) More seriously, this was an indirect but unmistakable attack on classic Reformed, Calvinist theology. Whatever gloss he may have subsequently put on what he said, the words clearly refer to the real presence of Christ *on the altar*, which Puritans, following Calvin, all rejected. Although Laud had always distanced himself from transubstantiation, to godly ears he must have sounded uncomfortably close to it.

So which side was faithful to the Thirty-Nine Articles, Laud or the godly? Both could claim to be, depending on how the articles are understood. The classic Reformed and Calvinist doctrine of the Eucharist was that because Christ has ascended into heaven, there can be no real, substantial or corporal presence in the Sacrament. This had appeared in the Edwardian Forty-Two Articles, but Elizabeth did not like it, and it is not in the Thirty-Nine. Article 28 is worded discreetly: 'The body of Christ is given, taken and eaten in the Supper only after a heavenly and spiritual manner, but the means whereby the body of Christ is received and eaten in the Supper is faith.' The words 'faith' and 'spiritual' have Calvinist undertones; but when allowance is made for what was deleted, the door is left open for an objective presence of some sort. This is how it had been understood in Elizabeth's day, especially as the queen had also restored the wording of the 1549 edition of the Prayer Book, much to the disappointment of her Calvinist clergy.[57]

So for those minded to be contentious, the exact meaning of Article 28, like that of Article 17, is open to interpretation and arguable. When deciding on the final wording of the articles, Elizabeth and her advisers had been flexible, willing to recognise the element of mystery and the indefinable in sacred subjects. One unlooked-for consequence was that a later generation of Puritans and Laudians could insist that each of their opposing doctrines agreed with the formulas of the church because, as Gardiner perceptively noted, they were busily applying their own interpretations to the formulas.[58] It could not be otherwise. Neither party had properly existed when the Thirty-Nine were composed, but both parties, adversaries though they were, felt obliged to claim the Thirty-Nine as their own, so to speak, or at least take care not to transgress them flagrantly.

Unfortunately for the Puritans, they lived under a disadvantage in this respect. A declaration of the king had made the bishops, his own appointees, the authorised interpreters of the Articles. As Conrad Russell said, effectively this made the Laudians the official interpreters of the doctrine of the Church of England.[59]

CHARLES AND THE CHURCH

'Cherish no man more than a good pastor; hate no man more than a proud Puritan.' These words Charles had read from his father in the late king's *Basilikon Doran*, and he took them to heart.[60]

In 1622, three years before his accession, the Venetian ambassador reported that Charles 'opposes the Puritans vehemently', though Catholics 'generally hope well of him'. In those days Charles appreciated divines like Hooker and especially Lancelot Andrewes. It was Andrewes who turned the then Prince Charles away from the roughly orthodox Protestantism of James and in the direction of Laudianism.[61]

When he became king in 1625, Charles made Richard Montagu his chaplain. The king then authorised Laud to draw up a list of clergy, clearly identifying with an 'O' or a 'P' (orthodox or Puritan) those fit for advancement – the Os – and those to be rejected – the Ps. Two years later Archbishop Abbott, a Calvinist in the tradition of Whitgift, was shunted aside because he declined to give the forced loan the official sanction of the church. For legal and ecclesiastical reasons Abbott could not be formally deprived; nevertheless, control of ecclesiastical courts and other official duties were now in the hands of a commission headed by Laud. Charles lost little time in delivering a further kingly rebuff to the godly by making Montagu Bishop of Chichester. Like his royal master, the Duke of Buckingham was also a friend of the Laudians. When the future Charles II was born in May 1630, Laud baptised him and composed a devout prayer for him, while Puritans glumly wondered among themselves what the future might hold for the Church of England.[62]

Charles was now a leading – we might say a militant – advocate of episcopacy. Even more than his father he was convinced that Presbyterianism was inherently subversive. Because contemporary Calvinists rejected episcopacy, Charles feared that none could 'with a safe conscience' take communion with them. For similar reasons, the Laudian Viscount Scudamore refused to receive communion with French Protestants. Church government had now become a fundamental issue, an issue of Christian fellowship. It was not some over-zealous divine that made it so, but the king and Head of the Church himself.[63]

Divisions over episcopacy and Calvinism were aggravated by renewed disputes over the Sabbath and traditional parish customs. Somerset wakes were feasts held to honour the saints after whom local churches were named. Celebrations, however, could get out of hand and too frisky for the liking of the godly, and a Puritan delegation persuaded Chief Justice Richardson to issue an order banning them. Laud then intervened to reinstate the wakes, and Charles supported him, blaming the Puritan Sabbatarians for interference and unauthorised zeal.[64]

Laud was not a man known for his merry spirits. Once he laid on a sumptuous feast after a graduation day at Oxford, followed by plays and other entertainments and a round of congratulatory speech making. According to his biographer, however, Laud treated the occasion as an 'arduous but necessary ordeal', and when it was at last over, 'a nuisance safely disposed of'. Laud then ordered a stocktake of the cutlery and other articles, and he took the trouble to record that two spoons were missing.[65] It was once said of the Puritans that they opposed bear-baiting, not because it gave pain to the bear, but because it gave pleasure to the spectators. In similar fashion Laud seems to have disapproved of the ban on wakes, not because he was especially fond of such amusements himself, but simply because he could not stand Puritans.

Laud also, in 1633 when Parliament was safely dissolved, persuaded Charles to re-issue the Book of Sports, this time with an amendment to protect wakes from Puritans, who were predictably appalled. Charles then commissioned Bishop Francis White to write on the subject. White's *Treatise of the Sabbath* appeared in 1635, dedicated to Laud. It was good, said White, to set aside a convenient time for the worship of God. The observance of the Lord's Day is a church tradition, and Christians are under a general obligation to obey their leaders in church and state on such matters. But for Christians, unlike the

Jews, there is no moral *law* for setting aside one day in seven, so moderate pas-times are permissible any day of the week, including Sunday. The Sabbath laws of the Old Testament are not binding on the church, and there is no divine command to make Sunday the Christian Sabbath. Probably more by coinci-dence than anything else, White was remarkably similar to Luther. However, he provoked a hostile reaction from the godly in England; he fuelled the hos-tility between Laudians and Puritans, leaving the godly more alienated than ever from the church leaders.[66]

Nor were these tensions eased when some English Catholics, watch-ing developments keenly, found they had some common ground with the Laudians, at least in a mutual distaste of the godly. Many of these Catholics hated the Jesuits almost as much as Laud hated the Puritans. They hoped not only for friendlier relations with Laud's party, but also that Charles might appoint a Catholic bishop to minister to his flock, who would in turn prom-ise loyalty to the king. Many Catholics later held responsible positions in the army on the king's side during the Civil War.[67]

Catholics, however, did not abandon their religion in droves to convert to Laud, and it is not difficult to see why. Laudianism was, if anything, an encouragement to them to hold fast, to persevere in the old faith; because if conformity to 'the church' was so necessary for spiritual welfare, as Laud argued, why must it be the church of Charles and Laud? Why not the Roman church that had stood for centuries? With the king and the archbishop appar-ently looking in that direction, Catholics and Puritans alike were able to see, though with widely conflicting emotions, the *possibility* of England returning to Rome. This prospect heartened the Catholics and maddened the godly in roughly equal measure.[68]

By now some Puritans had had more than they could stomach, and they set out to seek a new, more congenial spiritual life on the continent or in the American colonies. Those who stayed in England had the option of joining the growing number of Separatist and Independent churches; and this was an important development because from these churches would arise the most effective leaders of the future New Model Army.

Their blueprint was the Jacob church, begun in the reign of King James (see p. 128). Jacob and his followers believed in the headship of Christ not just over the church universal, but also over each individual, Independent church. In so doing they were introducing a third form of church govern-ment – Independency – different from both Presbyterianism and episcopacy. Independents were congregations 'of visible, holy Christians', as they would say, though what motivated them was zeal for godliness rather than con-ceit. These were gatherings of saints whose faith was real and demonstrable, unlike those who went to church and simply sat in the pews and listened. Their pastors were maintained by voluntary collections not by tithes; but any adult male member of the church might take on the role of expounding the Scriptures in the congregation as and when he felt led to. Some Separatist-Independents were imprisoned in the early 1630s, but government repression predictably did little except harden them. Others made the hazardous ocean crossing to New England, about as far away from the long arm of Laud as it was possible to be.

At home, internal divisions did as much as Laud's strictures to hinder their progress. One point in dispute was how much communion they should have with the state church. Some, partly to comply with the law, continued to have their children baptised in the parish church, while others were unhappy with even limited contacts. Some believed that those who left the state church to join them ought to be baptised again, others did not. By 1638 a Baptist congregation in London, under the leadership of John Spilsbury, was regularly practising 'believer's baptism'. Baptist communities increased, but divisions among them persisted: some favoured baptism by immersion, others by sprinkling, though the first was more generally preferred.[69]

An insight into the beliefs and mindset of the Separatists is revealed in the notes of one of their members, William Kiffin, who converted in 1632. He and his companions were wont to meet at five in the morning for prayer, and to relate 'what experience we had received from the Lord'. Later they would read from the Scriptures, and 'speak from it what pleased God to enable us'. These were not formal church services with a structured liturgy, just gatherings of the godly, often from more than one parish. Of others it was said that, even when discussing affairs of the world like buying and selling, they 'would speak very heavenly'. This was just the sort of unauthorised religious spontaneity, individualism and independence that rankled with Laudian clerics like John Browning. He spoke for many of his party when he recommended liturgical prayer as a 'means of salvation', and he attacked the 'frantic humour of our times' by which men prayed as they felt led or motivated: this was 'false, deceitful and dangerous ... repugnant to all reason, religion and Christian practice'.[70]

Kiffin was one of the growing number of people termed 'quasi-separatists' by one historian who has researched them closely (Murray Tolmie): godly people who met together without entirely forsaking the state church. Many became full Separatists, though by no means all. A robust country gentleman joined one of these quasi-Separatist gatherings at Ely: his name was Oliver Cromwell. A little later a young John Bunyan would be attending another at Bedford.[71]

Puritanism was on the rise, the Venetian ambassador reported, despite the king's attempts to repress it. There were many, he went on, living in fear of what the future might bring, because some day 'this pest may be the one which will ultimately disturb the repose of this kingdom'.[72]

Towards Civil War

Despite appearances, and despite the suspicions of many of his subjects, there is little real evidence that Charles was considering a formal reunion with Rome. Nevertheless, the church reforms of the king and his archbishop, besides antagonising the Puritan party inside and outside Parliament, were also sure to change the spirit and character of the church, perhaps even some of its written articles of faith. However, by remodelling the church he inherited, and by imposing his own unique stamp on it, was Charles not simply following Tudor precedent? This is what Henry did, and then Edward, or rather Cranmer on Edward's behalf, and with the young king's fulsome approval. Then Mary did it according to her own pleasure, followed by Elizabeth according to her quite different pleasure. It had almost become a Tudor tradition. Then James broke with tradition: he was the first prince encountered in this story who sought to consolidate rather than alter the church settlement that he inherited. In one sense, therefore, Charles merely reverted to the familiar policy of the Tudors. So why did Charles fail so badly where the Tudors succeeded so well?

One key factor is that relations between the king and Parliament had never sunk as low as they had under Charles. A more immediate point is that the Tudors reigned and ruled over England, and ever since the days of Henry VIII and Thomas Cromwell, the King of England was Head of the Church. But Charles was King of Scotland as well, where Presbyterianism was more powerful than it was in England, and Presbyterianism did not recognise the king's spiritual headship in the English way (see p. 115). As James had realised, the Kirk had to be coaxed on ecclesiastical subjects, not dictated to. The Scots, moreover, were less deferential than the English to the principle of the authority and divine right of kings. To Elizabeth's horror they had overthrown Mary Queen of Scots and established the Reformation by a revolution, albeit one of history's least bloody revolutions; and they endorsed more boldly than even the most aggressive English Puritans the right to depose unworthy kings. South of the border the godly were discontented, but they were not mobilising for war. Ever since Wyatt's rising against Mary Tudor fizzled out dismally, most Englishmen simply grumbled, complained, huffed and puffed, or put up with what they did not like as cheerfully as they could. One Scotsman, Robert Baillie, spoke dismissively of the 'obsequiousness and almost superstitious devotion of that nation towards their prince'.[73] A few Englishmen may have talked in secret about the right of resistance, but the Scots had actually used it; and it was Charles's attempt to impose his church policy on the Scots that ignited the Great Civil War in his three kingdoms.

Charles had been crowned at Scotland in 1633, where he had received a warm and affectionate welcome. This, unfortunately, he quickly forfeited by the tactlessly elaborate religious ceremonial. The Calvinist Scots were aghast at the sight of the altar, rich clerical vestments, candles, the crucifix and bishops kneeling devoutly before it. They had thrown away these 'popish' customs in the days of John Knox. Another provocation occurred in December 1634 when the Lord Chancellor of Scotland, the Earl of Kinnoul, died, and Charles appointed the Archbishop of St Andrews to replace him. Other bishops supportive of Charles and Laud soon found their way on to the Privy Council. Promoting bishops to positions of civil authority rankled with the Scots even more than it did with the English, especially the Scots nobility and the political and legal classes, who saw bishops as a threat to their privileges. In fact, the largely Presbyterian Scots did not particularly want bishops at all, not even in pulpits and dioceses, never mind in places of power. They had tolerated them in small quantities mainly out of deference to James. Despite this, Charles was already thinking of further reforms that were bound to cause more unease, including the compulsory use of the English Prayer Book in Scotland.[74]

If the policy was bad the timing was worse, because Charles proceeded against Scotland with an unhappy England behind him. Besides Laud and tonnage and poundage, Ship Money was another grievance. This was a rate imposed on ports and coastal towns, as part of the Crown's emergency powers, to protect the country from invasion by sea. However, when Charles wanted to impose the levy on inland towns as well, John Hampden and others objected on the grounds that the king was trying to raise taxes without winning the necessary agreement from Parliament. Ship Money was being levied to provide an impressive fleet to protect English shipping and trade, and to defend England from danger. Few doubted that the build-up of the navy was in the national interest: what worried a growing number of people was the method used. It deliberately bypassed Parliament, and it appeared to breach the spirit if not the letter of the Petition of Right.[75]

With Ship Money, as with tonnage and poundage, the issue at stake was the rule of law. In June 1636, a certain Richard Chambers was sentenced to a fine and imprisonment for not paying tonnage and poundage charges, and he appealed to the Court of the King's Bench. His appeal was curtly dismissed. Justice Berkeley held that 'there was a rule of law and a rule of government, and that many things which might not be done by the rule of law might be done by the rule of government'. As Gardiner says, this was tantamount to a judicial ruling that Charles was bound by no law.[76]

Also in June, Secretary Coke applied Berkeley's neo-absolutist theme to all areas of church and state during a speech in Oxford. It was, he said,

an axiom and fundamental rule of government that all our laws and statutes are the king's laws ... all courts of law or equity are properly the king's courts: all justice therein administered, be it civil or martial, is the king's justice ... all corporations, societies, nay counties, provinces and depending kingdoms have all their jurisdictions and governments established by him for public good to be changed or dissolved.[77]

To many Parliamentarians, this sounded like a declaration of arbitrary, despotic government, and it is not hard to see why. But what is the essential difference between Coke and Thomas Cromwell, who, a century earlier, put his rival Stephen Gardiner, Bishop of Winchester, on the spot by demanding: 'Is not that that pleaseth the king a law?'[78] Set the words of Cromwell and Coke side by side, and the concept of kingly divine right seems hardly to have changed since the days of the Tudors. What has changed, however, and changed almost out of recognition, is the way the concept is understood and carried out in practice. The Tudors were great constitutionalists, and no one epitomised this mindset more than Thomas Cromwell. Never did he try to exclude or override Parliament, even when it frustrated his proposals for economic and social reforms, as it frequently did. He would flatter it, cajole it and some-times manipulate it; and he had no qualms about interfering with elections to secure the success of candidates favourable to Henry. But he never showed contempt for it, or pretended he or the government could do without it; he never treated it as something not wholly integral to the English state and constitution. Everything Cromwell tried to do he did through Parliament: the Royal Supremacy itself was established through parliamentary statute. 'That which pleaseth the king' may well have been law in abstract principle; but before it became an established, documented and enforceable law, it would have to be sealed by parliamentary statute.

Cromwell was also a genius at persuading Parliament to grant Henry gen-erous subsidies even when the country was not at war, and he went about this delicate task in exactly the opposite way from Charles's ministers. Cromwell always presented the facts before Parliament: he told them exactly how much money was needed, why it was needed and where it would go; then he appealed to the loyalty of Parliament to the king. It worked, every time.[79]

In the 1530s, a recognisable unity had existed between Parliament and the king. Granted it was an unequal union, between the king's majesty and a gathering of the king's subjects. Nevertheless, it was still a unity. As Henry VIII himself had put it, 'we no time stand so highly in our estate royal as in the time of Parliament, wherein we as head and you as members are conjoined and knit'. One hundred years on, so it seemed to a growing number of the English people, the government of England consisted of Charles, his senior Laudian bishops and his hand-picked council, backed up by a subservient judiciary, with Parliament shunted contemptuously to the sidelines.[80]

The third writ of Ship Money issued in October 1636 roused such resent-ment that even Henry Danvers, Earl of Danby, a long time loyal servant of the Crown far removed from militancy, appealed to the king to abandon extra-parliamentary levies and summon a new parliament. The Earl of Warwick offered Charles similar advice, though more bluntly. Warwick boldly told the king that his method of government was not the same as that of Elizabeth and James, and that many of his loyal subjects were afraid their liberties were being taken from them.[81]

Charles paid no heed to either of them. The collection of Ship Money proceeded apace in early 1637, with the endorsement of a majority of the judiciary. Resentment of such extra-parliamentary taxes was now almost universal. They seemed to strike at the very legitimacy of Parliament and the principle of taxation by parliamentary consent. (Soon even five of twelve judges nominated by the king would raise their heads above the parapet and speak out against it.) Meanwhile, more anti-government feeling showed itself when three of the most outspoken Puritans – William Prynne, Henry Burton and John Bastwick – were sentenced by the Star Chamber court to fines, the pillory, loss of ears and imprisonment for attacking Laudian reforms with their admittedly inflammatory writings. Prynne had suffered unpleasant punishment three years earlier, but this time he and his friends drew much sympathy from the watching crowds as sentences were unsparingly carried out. To try and stifle Puritan critiques of the government, severe restrictions were imposed on printing.[82]

Charles has troubled the nation, wrote the Venetian ambassador, 'about the two great causes of religion and the diminution of the liberty of the people'; the king will be 'very fortunate if he does not fall into some great upheaval'. The people were 'disaffected to such a pitch that if they had leaders, which they have not, it would be impossible to disquiet them'. It has reached the stage where the Puritans 'abominate the rites observed in the churches of the Protestants hardly less than the Mass itself'.[83]

With England restless and resentful, Charles made a fateful decision. He enforced the English canons, liturgy, episcopal church government, and a slightly revised version of the Prayer Book on his Calvinist subjects in Scotland. His manner lacked all the finesse and subtlety that James had used to gently usher in mild Anglican reforms to some Scottish services (see pp. 117–18). Little if any attempt was made to consult the Scots or win their consent. A few amenable bishops got involved, which only made bishops less loved than ever both north and south of the border. It would be hard to imagine a more disastrous policy for the northern kingdom, nor one more needless. Most Englishmen and women who loved their Prayer Book had no desire to force it on the Scots if the Scots did not want to use it, and most Scots were content to put up with Laudianism provided it stayed in England. Neither kingdom hungered for a religious conflict. Yet it was a king of Scottish royal stock who antagonised and completely misjudged the mood of his native people.

Fierce resistance to the royal order began immediately. At St Giles church in Edinburgh in July 1637, the dean began to read from the Prayer Book. Almost at once his hesitant voice was drowned out by the uproar from his congregation. When the bishop rose to speak, a woman hurled a stool at him. When magistrates ordered the church to be cleared, more violence was wreaked on the church building, especially the windows. The bishop was pelted with stones as he hastily made an undignified escape; he was probably lucky to get out alive. Disturbances spread alarmingly; but Charles, typically, could see them only as an entirely unforgivable act of disobedience to his authority. He gave an order to enforce the new regulations and punish rioters. But passions were rising, and even Scots who disliked mob violence strongly sympathised with the protests. 'The whole people thinks popery at the doors', wrote Robert Baille, an anxious chaplain fearing desperately for the future.[84]

South of the border the government's problems mounted. In November 1637 the trial began of John Hampden for his refusal to pay Ship Money. Crown lawyers argued that sheer necessity was sufficient justification for the king to levy tax without calling Parliament. This necessity was exaggerated, countered Hampden's lawyer, Holborne, who astutely pointed out that the writ for Ship Money failed to mention any danger to the realm. Besides, he went on, 'by the fundamental laws of England the king cannot, out of Parliament, charge the subject – no, not for the common good unless in special cases'; not even for the 'ordinary defence of the kingdom unavoidably in danger to be lost'. Bankes, the attorney-general, replied that the court had no right to subject to scrutiny the circumstances under which the king should or should not take such a decision. The king's power to act was 'innate in the person of an absolute king and in the persons of the kings of England; so inherent in the king that it is not in any ways derived from the people, but reserved to the king when positive laws first began'.[85] So the government's case came down to this: the king could do as he pleased and he must be obeyed, pure and simple.

In February 1638, the Scottish Lord Treasurer , Traquair, loyally but fearlessly told Charles to his face that the Prayer Book would have to be withdrawn from Scotland, otherwise an army of 40,000 men would be needed to enforce the king's writ. Charles sent Traquair back to Edinburgh with a proclamation: the order regarding the Prayer Book must stand. Charles promised to graciously pardon those who had disobeyed him so far, provided they ended their disobedience at once. Any more disobedience might count as treason.[86]

The Scots assembly replied by setting up the National Covenant, which promptly defied the king by rejecting both the canons and the Prayer Book. The Covenant then appealed to the Assembly and to Parliament in support of their religion, thus reigniting the Crown versus Parliament controversy already in full swing in England, though so far less violently. Almost the entire Scottish nation was united. 'In my judgement', wrote Traquair, 'it shall be as easy to establish the Missal in this kingdom as the Service Book.' Still Charles seemed unruffled by all the commotion; he simply insisted that the Covenant be revoked. When it was not, the king began making preparations to invade Scotland.[87]

Again the timing was as ill-fated as the policy, because in England in June the judges delivered their verdict on the Hampden trial. Justice Berkeley was the most outspoken for the Crown. He ruled that 'the law knows no such king-yoking policy' as Holborne had maintained. On the contrary, 'the law is of itself an old a trusty servant of the king's; it is his instrument and means which he useth to govern his people by'. Sir George Croke dissented vigorously. Bypassing Parliament to raise money was unlawful, he said, and it was no excuse to plead necessity, because Parliament could always be summoned quickly if danger threatened the realm. Finch, Chief Justice of the Common Pleas, admitted that constitutional checks and balances to supreme authority were useful and even necessary, but he argued that the king had the right to set these aside in times of need. 'Acts of Parliament to take away his royal power in the defence of the kingdom are void', he held. Clarendon later recalled that Finch's verdict 'made Ship Money much more abhorred and formidable than all the commandments by the council table and all the distresses taken by the sheriffs of England'. Finch's view, however, prevailed. Judgment was given by a majority of seven to five against Hampden, and Charles lost no time in enforcing the collection of Ship Money.[88]

With discontent now simmering dangerously, the lofty mind of John Milton was warring against the church of Charles and Laud. In his *Lycidas* Milton depicts St Peter casting reproach on the worthless Laudian hirelings:

> Enow of such as for their bellies' sake
> Creep and intrude, and climb into the fold!

The apostle Peter, the 'pilot of the Galilean lake', the one thrice commissioned to tend the flock of Christ, sorrows to see that 'the hungry sheep look up and are not fed'. Prophetically Milton saw,

> That two-handed engine at the door
> Stands ready to smite once and smite no more.

This menacing 'engine' has triggered a good deal of debate. Gardiner reckons the 'idea of the axe laid to the root of the tree seems most natural'. Others have suggested the two-edged sword of Revelation 1:16. Perhaps the warning of Revelation 3:20, delivered to the lukewarm and self-satisfied Laodicean church, may be relevant – 'Behold, I stand at the door'. If the exact meaning escapes us the thrust of the message is clear: judgement is about to fall on the church of Laud unless it repents.[89]

In December (1638) the Scottish Assembly in Glasgow formally abolished episcopacy as well as the Prayer Book and the offending cannons. The Presbyterian form of church government was re-established. The assembly ratified the principle laid down in the Covenant that even the king had no right to tamper with the established Protestant religion of the Scottish nation. The Scottish Assembly had now asserted its right to determine and uphold the state religion even, if necessary, against the king. The lesson was not lost on the House of Commons and the Puritan party south of the border.[90]

In the early months of 1639, Charles was raising an army to deal with the rebellious Scots. The First Bishops' War, so called because of the controversy over episcopacy, was a messy, inconclusive affair. The City of London refused to grant the king a loan; revenues from Ship Money were not enough to compensate, and were in any case running out; a truce at Berwick in June solved nothing substantial; and Charles, urged on by his chief minister Wentworth, remained determined to subdue the land of his birth that had defied him. Wentworth recommended summoning Parliament, but chiefly as an experiment, so that, in Secretary Windebank's words, Charles 'might leave his people without excuse'; and if this parliament failed to oblige the king with the necessary support and funding, Charles would be fully justified in using 'extraordinary means rather than, by the peevishness of some few factious spirits, to suffer his state and government to be lost'.[91]

Parliament met in April, 1640. The next month Charles dissolved it; hence its unimposing epitaph, the 'Short Parliament'. The threat of invasion from Scotland had not intimidated the Commons into submission. Harbottle Grimston, member for Colchester, complained about invasions of a different kind, on the liberties of Parliament and the nation. John Pym made a two-hour speech in which he likened the powers of Parliament to 'the body politic as the rational faculties of the soul to a man'; he also attacked Laud's 'new ceremonies and observances which had put upon the churches a shape and face of popery'. Pym reviewed political grievances like tonnage and poundage, Ship Money and the eleven years without a parliament. Throughout he spoke with restraint, choosing his words with care, and he was warmly applauded in the House. Worse still for Charles, it was plain that the English Commons had little keenness for war with the northern neighbour. An early dissolution was inevitable when Charles heard to his horror that a petition was to be drafted urging him to make peace with the Scots.[92]

Parliament was dissolved, but Convocation – the assembly of the clergy – remained, and in May it agreed a subsidy and passed a new set of ecclesiastical canons. Though the language of these canons was reasonable and moderate, their effect was largely to endorse the Laudian love of ceremonial unity that was the cause of so much friction up and down the land. One of the canons declared that the 'most high and sacred order of kings is of divine right'; it invoked the words of St Paul, that all who resisted the king resisted the ordinance of God (Romans 13:1). Ever since Luther this had been the reformers' stock answer in the face of political agitation; but now it was wearing a bit thin. It only irritated the Commons and the Puritans even more.[93]

The Second Bishops' War began in August 1640, when the Scots, having decided on attack as the best means of defence, drew up plans to invade England. With Newcastle vulnerable before them, the threat loomed that the Scots Covenanters would cut off the supply of coal to the rest of England. Once again Charles turned to the City of London for a loan; once again the City dragged its feet. The king's ministers, Strafford and Cottington, were equally unsuccessful in persuading the Spanish and the French to lend money in return for English aid on the continent. The only offer of money and men came from Rome, but it came at an extortionate price – Charles would have to return to the Catholic faith.[94]

Meanwhile, the Scots army crossed the border, and after meeting only derisory resistance it occupied Newcastle with embarrassing ease. In September the Covenanters took control of Edinburgh Castle. There was no option now for Charles but to call another parliament. A truce with the Scots was agreed at Ripon, one of its provisions being that it would cost the English £850 a day for the privilege of having a Scottish force on English soil. The leading northern gentry were to pay the first month's instalment, with future payments to be determined by Parliament.[95]

The eventful Long Parliament met on 3 November 1640. Impeachment proceedings soon began against Strafford and Finch, while the judges who had supported Finch against Hampden were severely censured. Parliamentary unanimity prevailed until the Root and Branch petition was drawn up calling for the entire abolition of bishops, which exposed divisions in the Commons. Church government was one of the thorniest issues. Not all Puritans were demanding a full Presbyterian system for the national church, and some would have accepted a more limited episcopacy; but most members agreed that bishops had abused their power, and that if episcopacy was not to be abolished outright, it ought to be reformed by Parliament. Action soon began against Laud, described by Grimston as the 'root and ground of all our miseries'. He and his fellow bishops were accused of suppressing the true Reformed religion, while tolerating, even encouraging, popery and Arminianism. Concerns were voiced regarding the Irish army, a largely Catholic militia raised by Strafford when he was Lord Lieutenant of Ireland. Strafford, now the king's chief minister, was still technically its general, and many feared he would use it to browbeat Parliament into submission. The Commons demanded that the army be disbanded. Suspicions of popery in high places were fuelled when

Charles, after the intercession of the queen, pardoned a Catholic priest condemned to death under Elizabethan laws; this infuriated the Commons, while the City shelved its plans to offer a loan. Debates began on a bill for annual parliaments, with Oliver Cromwell one of its strongest supporters. This gradually evolved into the Triennial Act, fixing a maximum of three years between parliaments. None of this was on the king's agenda for Parliament.[96]

Heated debates continued through spring 1641. In May, and to forestall any plans the king may have had for its dissolution, a bill was approved which laid down that the present Parliament could only be dissolved by Parliament itself. More demands were made for the abolition of bishops. The Protestation Oath was composed: all who signed it pledged their loyalty to the king, but they pledged also to defend the 'true reformed Protestant Religion against all popery and popish innovations', and the 'power and privileges of Parliament, the lawful rights and liberties of the subjects'. Thus the Protestant cause and the cause of Parliament were yoked together.[97]

Then an alleged army plot was uncovered. Devised by some of the king's supporters, it included an idea to bring the army to London to intimidate Parliament. The Commons put out a statement saying that anyone involved in such action, 'without special order of His majesty, with the advice and consent of both Houses of Parliament … shall be accounted and taken for enemies to King and State'. Reports of French forces mustering to aid Charles and Henrietta Maria revived suspicions of a popish plot, possibly connived at by the queen. Rumours of a French fleet in the Channel caused panic in London on 8 May. Four days later the trial of Strafford reached its climax, with the minister's execution before a crowd estimated at 200,000. He had been condemned by attainder, a somewhat arbitrary law enforcement method that had existed since 1459, under which a person could be condemned by Act of Parliament without a formal trial.[98]

Strafford felt the full force of the anger of the Commons against the king's eleven years' personal rule without Parliament. It was charged that he did 'subvert the fundamental laws and government of the realms of England and Ireland … and introduce an arbitrary and tyrannical government against law'; and that he sought to 'subvert the rights of parliaments and the ancient course of parliamentary proceedings', which the Commons alleged was treason. It was widely suspected that he had plans to enlist Irish forces to help suppress Parliamentary opposition in England. Pym had led the attack on the minister. Pym defined the relationship between the Crown and its people, represented in Parliament, in language that no Tudor would have objected to: 'The King and his people are obliged to one another in the nearest relations. He is a father, and a child is called in law *pars patris* [literally: part of the father]. He is the husband of the Commonwealth; they have the same interest; they are inseparable in their condition …' Strafford's treason, it was alleged, was that he had contrived to break this unity. The attainder was passed; and at last the king, pressed by peers, the council and judges, and fearing mob violence against the queen, yielded to the clamour for Strafford's head. The fall of Strafford was as much a humiliation for Charles as a victory for Pym. Under Henry VIII, ministers fell when they lost the king's favour; but Strafford was destroyed by the power of an outraged Parliament, despite the king's devotion to him and his desperate yet impotent attempts to save him.[99]

Divisions continued in Parliament over whether bishops should be reformed or abolished. A bill to exclude bishops from the Lords was rejected in the Upper House, which then set up a committee of its own to enquire into church reforms. Bishops were causing endless and heated debates, though supporters and opponents differed more in the fervour of their opinions than in the opinions themselves. Viscount Falkland wittily noted that 'they who hated the bishops hated them worse than the devil; they who loved them did not love them so well as their dinner'. Then on 22 June Charles seemed to make a concession when he reluctantly accepted the tonnage and poundage bill, which denied the king's right to levy money except through Parliament. Two days later Pym presented Ten Propositions: two of the most significant were a plea to Charles to replace 'evil counsellors' with those 'as the Parliament may have cause to confide in', and the demand for the removal of papists from the court and the queen's circle. The Lords supported most of the Propositions, demurring only over matters affecting the queen. Such parliamentary solidarity disappointed Charles, who hoped he could exploit divisions between the Houses.[100]

Charles tried to ignore the Propositions. Instead he made another concession by giving his assent to a bill abolishing Ship Money. He also set off to Scotland, despite being urged by the Commons not to go. The official reason for his visit was the need to ratify the Anglo-Scots treaty that had at last been completed; but many in England feared that he might seek the aid of the Scots, and the English army still in the north, to restore his authority over Parliament by force.[101] When, however, the Scots army camped in England returned home, such fears seemed unduly alarmist, and the mood in England began to swing slowly in the king's favour. Charles was heartened by signs of division between the Commons and the Scots, and he was doing his utmost to woo the Scots. When he crossed the border he even attended Presbyterian sermons and listened with self-enforced devoutness. At the same time, and in utmost secrecy, he sent messengers to Ireland to canvass support from Protestant Royalists and also Catholic Irish.[102]

At this point the Commons seemed to overreach itself. In September it pressed vigorously ahead with proposals to overturn Laudian church policies: these proposals included the removal of 'all crucifixes, scandalous pictures of one or more persons of the Trinity, and all images of the Virgin Mary', plus tapers and candlesticks, and an order to stop all bowing at the name of Jesus. 'All dancing or other sports either before or after divine service' were to be 'forborne and restrained' on Sunday. Outside the Commons this was not everywhere well received. Then when further changes were proposed to the Prayer Book, rifts in Parliament, not only between Lords and Commons but also in the Commons itself, opened up once more. In a now depleted House, Sir John Culpepper spoke up for the Prayer Book, and despite opposition to it, or at least parts of it, led by Oliver Cromwell, Culpepper carried the day with a majority of eighteen. Before the differences could be completely resolved, Parliament adjourned.[103]

Charles, meanwhile, carried on dangling the prospect of concessions before the eyes of the Scots, and he did so with some accomplishment until a plot known as the 'Incident' was uncovered. Some Scots Royalists had planned to seize leading Covenanters, and the complicity of the king was widely believed despite official denials. The 'Incident' reawakened suspicions of the king's motives north and south of the border, and any hopes Charles might have had of military support from Scotland now vanished.[104]

In October, about the same time as the unfortunate Incident in Scotland, disaster engulfed the king's third kingdom – Ireland. The Irish rebellion may initially have been fairly limited in its aims. The 'Old English' – pre-Reformation settlers, many still Catholic – generally professed loyalty to Charles. Many native Irish did likewise, but they had their grievances, mainly over the denial of their rights and liberties, and the recent colonisation by Anglo-Scots settlers. The Irish wanted Ireland to be a broadly independent kingdom with its own Parliament, loyal to the Crown perhaps, but not subservient to the Commons. Naturally they also sought freedom of worship, Catholic worship. But the simmering bitterness among the native Irish against the recent colonisation and the unfair allocation of land quickly boiled over, and reports of the slaughter of thousands of English settlers soon reached the shocked House of Commons. The most reliable estimates suggest around 12,000 were massacred or perished through hunger and cold. Charles declared that he would raise an army to punish the rebels; but such were the fears of popery, and so deep the mistrust between king and Commons, many suspected that his real aim was to use the army against Parliament.[105]

In November Pym and his allies completed the Grand Remonstrance, a statement of by now familiar grievances. Partly because the Commons recognised the comparative strength of the Royalist-episcopalian party in the Lords, the Remonstrance was effectively a direct appeal from the Commons to the nation. It blamed papists, bishops and evil councillors for 'the pernicious design of subverting the fundamental laws and principles of government, upon which the religion and justice of the kingdom … were firmly established'. Another demand was for parliamentary control of royal appointments, a hugely controversial point and for many a step too far. Some MPs spoke vigorously against it, fearing that Pym was too radical. During debates more harrowing news arrived from Ireland of the plight of the settlers and the cruelty of the natives. This, and continuing fears of a popish plot, may have helped Pym secure the passing of the Remonstrance by 159 votes to 148 in the early hours of 23 November, after over twelve hours' intense debating.[106]

Charles, meanwhile, had returned south, having made certain concessions to the Scots similar to those that Pym and his party were calling for in England. On 25 November the king entered London to a warm and charitable welcome from a large crowd. He promised them he would uphold the Protestant religion as it had been established in the times of Elizabeth and his father, 'if need be, to the hazard of my life and all that is dear to me'.[107] If Charles had spoken thus from the heart a few years earlier, he might have struck a pleasing chord with his people; for there were many among them who hoped to see their king steering a middle course between Laudianism and Puritanism, faithful to the Elizabethan Settlement. In November 1641, unfortunately, even the king's most loyal supporters would have struggled to take this pledge on trust had they weighed it carefully: for this was the same king who had advanced Laud and endorsed almost everything he had done. It also proved, if proof were needed, that Charles was only feigning when he appeared to show deference to Presbyterianism during his recent visit to Scotland.

The king's words convinced neither Puritans nor Parliamentarians. On 1 December the Grand Remonstrance was presented to him. Via the Militia Bill, Pym's party now sought control of the army as well as the church. Rumours were rife that Parliamentary leaders would be tried for treason. But Pym was gaining support among the City of London, a crucial ally due to its financial clout. Opinion in the City swung further towards the Commons when elections to the Common Council on 21 December produced results endorsing Pym. Charles then dismissed the Remonstrance; and he restated his loyalty to episcopacy and the Church of England, which, though it annoyed the Commons, was appreciated by some peers in the Lords. The mood in London grew feverish amid fears that Charles, egged on by the queen, was considering afresh whether to grant toleration to Irish Catholics and use the Irish army as a lever against the Commons. Nor were the citizens of London ignorant of the political drama unfolding, and agitation spread to the streets. Quite a different crowd from the one that had recently cheered the returning king rushed into Westminster Hall one day crying 'No bishops' and 'No popish lords', before being chased off by armed officers. Another mob smashed up the organ at Westminster Abbey. The king's supporters and a goodly number of peers were dismayed when many in the Commons openly sympathised with the rioters and refused to condemn them. The Lords began to debate a motion that Parliament was, under such circumstances, no longer truly free. It was defeated by a tiny majority of four.[108]

But just when divisions between Lords and Commons were opening up again, Charles played right into the hands of the more aggressive Commons. Because of the recent disturbances, some bishops, fearing for their lives, had stayed away from the Lords. These bishops then unwisely supported a protest to the king. This asked him to declare all Parliamentary business during their absence, including the vote on the freedom of Parliament, null and void. There is some evidence, though it is not conclusive, that this scheme went ahead with the connivance of the king and those around him. Exactly what he hoped to gain is not clear, but the sympathy that he had in the Lords quickly frittered away. Royalist Lords now united with the Commons in confirming the liberty of Parliament, and when Pym moved for the impeachment of these bishops, the Lords raised no objection.[109]

'I never saw the court so full of gentleman', noted a witness of these troubled times. 'Everyone comes hither with their swords.' The Royal guard was strengthened and 'a company of soldiers put into the Abbey for the defence of it'. Most citizens 'shut up their shops, and all gentlemen provide themselves with arms'; it is 'a wonder there is no more blood yet spilt'. The observer was in no doubt that 'if the king do not comply with the Commons in all things they desire, a civil war must ensue'.[110]

Charles and Pym were now suspecting each other of armed action, either a crackdown from the king or a coup by Pym. About the last straw for the king was an ugly rumour that impeachment proceedings would be brought against the queen, a rumour Pym did little to suppress. Charles decided he had to act against five prominent Parliamentarians – Pym, Hampden, Holles, Haselrig and Strode. They would be charged with sedition. At the last moment a sixth name was added, Lord Mandeville. The king's plan was to go to the House in person with an armed guard to arrest them. Alas for Charles, fates had conspired against him; he could now do nothing aright. Somehow his plan leaked out. One report has Charles hesitating fatally at the last moment, and the queen urging him on to 'pull these rogues out by the ears'. Eventually Charles arrived at the House in the afternoon of 4 January, by which time these rogues had escaped in a barge. The king made a short speech, then he looked around him in vain. 'I see all the birds are flown', he confessed wearily. The king was humbled in his capital city, in the presence of the elected representatives of the nation.[111]

King and Commons were now virtually at war. Hoping for foreign aid, Charles tried to secure Hull, where a sizeable military arsenal was stored, by appointing the Earl of Newcastle as governor of the city. Anticipating the king's move, Parliament ordered Sir John Hotham to take control of Hull. On 5 February the Lords, under pressure from the Commons and outside, passed the Bishop's Exclusion Bill which they had previously opposed. Charles, perhaps hoping he could yet exploit divisions in Parliament on church reforms, made some concessions; but his opponents guessed he was merely stalling, at least until the queen and the Crown jewels were safely out of the country. On 23 February she set sail from Dover. From the cliffs, Charles watched the ship till it was out of sight. To try and prevent the king making war, the Lords then gave its support to the Militia Bill, to bring the defence of the realm under Parliament's control. More conciliatory than the Commons, the Lords may have intended this to be no more than a temporary curb on royal power, but the king could see it only as another attack on his authority and divine right.[112]

One of the few subjects on which the quarrelling English could reach a consensus was Ireland. Anglo-Scots forces under Harcourt, Grenville and Monck had now arrived in Ireland to put down the rebellion. In February Lords and Commons, episcopalians and Puritans united behind a proposal for a massive confiscation of Irish lands for the benefit of Anglo-Scots merchants and speculators. To this the king readily agreed. Vengeance against the Irish had begun, with no mercy shown and seldom any prisoners taken. 'We put some fourscore men to the sword', wrote one officer when Trim was retaken; 'but, like valiant knights errant, we gave quarter and liberty to all the women'. The women at Trim were lucky; it had become the norm to slaughter them and the children along with the men.[113]

Back in England, loyalist forces were rallying round the king. The so-called Kentish petition upheld the established church, the Prayer Book liturgy and episcopal government, though pointedly it did not endorse episcopacy as a divine law; it also voiced growing fears of religious radicalism. Parliament did nothing to calm these fears when it threatened the petition's leaders with arrest. Charles, meanwhile, set off for the north. On 19 March he entered York, but he found little passion for war there; instead a general if forlorn desire for reconciliation awaited him. Next month, still mindful of the need to secure an eastern port to receive supplies from Denmark or elsewhere in Europe, Charles set out for Hull, now under Hotham's control. Acting under Parliament's orders, Hotham refused to admit the King of England to the city. 'Actual war is levied upon us', said Charles, furious and humiliated; he then issued a call to arms in Yorkshire to guard his person. On 1 June Parliament issued Nineteen Propositions demanding parliamentary approval in areas traditionally the prerogative of the Crown: these included nominations to the king's council, the principal offices of state, the army and judiciary; and the education and marriages of the king's children. The Propositions also required acceptance of the Militia Bill and the Petition of Right, and effective prosecution of the recusancy laws. It was tantamount to a demand for Parliamentary rather than royal sovereignty of the kingdom. And it was a measure of how far apart the two sides were, that one member of the committee that drew up the Propositions described them as the very least that Parliament could now accept. They have, he said, 'been brought down to the lowest degree of moderation and respect'; they were the 'only means which is left' to secure agreement between king and Parliament.[114]

On 17 June Newcastle was secured for the king by a small squadron of Royalists. Parliament retaliated by sending troops to Leicestershire, where another Royalist force was gathering. Parliament then wrested control of the fleet from the king. With king and Parliament raising arms and money for war throughout the country, people groaned and trembled at the thought of the misery in store for them. 'They promised us all should be well if my Lord Strafford's head was off', a northern lady wrote to a friend; yet 'since then there is nothing better'. She and those around her felt 'like so many frightened people … if I hear but a door creak, I take it to be a drum'.[115]

Radical Parliamentarians were challenging the principle of the divine right of kings as never before. 'Power is originally inherent in the people', wrote Henry Parker, and in the present confusion Parliament should be obeyed rather than the king. In the parishes of eastern England, altar rails, surplices and hoods were torn down and set alight by zealous armed men, with equally zealous citizens joining in: among them was a redoubtable group of women known as the 'holy wives'. The Prayer Book, that cherished emblem of the Edwardian and Elizabethan Reformation, was ripped up and burned. On 18 August the Commons declared that all who gave armed assistance to the king were traitors. Four days later Charles raised his standard at Nottingham. 'It is strange to note', reflected the lawyer and writer, Bulstrode Whitelocke, 'how we have insensibly slid into this beginning of a civil war, by one unexpected incident after another … which hath brought us thus far, and we scarce know how.'[116]

6

CIVIL WAR, 1642–49

The Reluctant Fighters

In the reign of King Charles the original Reformation, begun in England by William Tyndale and Thomas Cromwell, later established by Elizabeth, looked as though it would bifurcate. Loyal Elizabethans had not disappeared, but they found themselves squeezed on either side by Laudians and Puritans. Ironically, these two hostile groups shared one thing in common: they both, in their different ways and for different reasons, found the Reformation somewhat unsatisfactory. It had been too thorough for the Laudians, but not thorough enough for the Puritans.

So what had become of those who remained loyal to the spirit, letter and tenor of the Elizabethan church, and who followed neither Laud nor the Puritan party? As a rule less demonstrative people leave fewer traces of their existence. Recent researches, however, have unearthed petitions during these troubled times by a significant band of men and women who loved the Prayer Book, and looked back with affection and nostalgia to the days of Elizabeth and James. These people were unhappy not only with Laud and his allies, like Montagu, but also with their present king. They were prepared to accept the apostolic origin of bishops, but they did not embrace the Laudian principle of bishops by divine law. Nor did they rise to the bait when zealous Puritans attacked the Prayer Book as something composed by 'imps of hell'. They resisted the temptation to claim divine inspiration for it, and deleted from one of their petitions the words in an early draft that it was 'penned by inspiration of the Holy Ghost'. They rejected Puritan charges that their church was only half reformed, and to Separatism they were utterly opposed. Men like Joseph Hall, Bishop of Exeter, were increasingly worried by the polarisation in the church and the antagonism between Laudians and Puritans. Like many, he perceived a spiritual decline since the better times of Elizabeth and James. Such people were now faced with an agonising choice as the nation slid towards a war they did not want. Most of them, though with little enthusiasm and many misgivings, would take the king's side.[1]

Supporters of the king and Parliament did not divide conveniently along social or geographical lines. Royalists supported Charles because of fear of radicals in Parliament, the church and the country; while Parliament resisted the king in order to defend its privileges and because of fears of encroaching popery. But many people were committed to neither side, and, mindful no doubt of the terrible ravages on the continent during the Thirty Years War, were determined to do all they could to avoid conflict at home. To quote Clarendon, 'the number of these who desired to sit still was greater than of those who desired to engage in either party'. In over twenty counties neutrality pacts were agreed, in which local gentry, whatever their views on Laud, Pym or Parliament, would raise a militia to preserve peace rather than enlist under the banner of either the Crown or Parliament. These neutrals were forced to choose only when unwanted commissions from the king or Parliament were handed to them, or when they were confronted by men in arms representing one side or the other. Many empathised with Sir Edward Dering, who longed for a 'composing third way'. But no such option lay in sight, and eventually Dering obeyed a summons from the king's army, going 'out of my own house and from my own county the most unwilling man that ever went'.[2]

Some neutrals may have been motivated by cowardice, fear, or the love of an easy life: but not all. For many, the choice lay between the devil and the deep blue sea, like Sir Edmund Verney, Knight Marshal, and a man of similar spirit to Dering. On most points Verney had opposed Laud and the bishops, and supported Parliament in its recent tussles with Charles. 'I do not like the quarrel', he confessed; 'I do heartily wish that the king would yield and consent' to the wishes of Parliament. Yet Verney, in the hour of trial, could not 'do so base a thing as to forsake' his king; even though 'I have no reverence for bishops, for whom this quarrel subsists'. To his brother Ralph, who had joined the Parliamentary forces, Edward wrote with deep sorrow: 'I, who so dearly love and esteem you, should be bound in consequence – because in duty to the king – to be your enemy… I beseech you consider that Majesty is sacred. God saith, "Touch not mine anointed"… I shall pray for peace with all my heart.'[3]

Horror of rebellion was etched on the national consciousness. In one of the earliest skirmishes of the war a Parliamentary officer was mortally wounded. As he lay dying he begged God's pardon for his great sin in taking arms against his rightful king. A fellow officer, William Waller, confessed 'that great God who is the searcher of my heart knows with what a sad sense I go upon this service, and with what a perfect hatred I detest this war …'.[4]

Thomas Fuller had been a member of Convocation in 1640–41. He had opposed Laud, but he also had deep reservations about the Puritans. 'The sword', said Fuller, 'has two edges but never an eye.' Essentially this was the same sentiment as Luther over a hundred years before – whatever the justice of this or that cause, 'when Mr Mob breaks loose he cannot tell the wicked from the good; he just lays about him at random'. Fuller was a typical Elizabethan, a child of the early Reformation; unlike the godly he never imagined that it lay in the power or remit of man to create a state of moral perfection, or perfect government in either church or society. 'I speak not to dishearten men from endeavouring a perfect reformation', he pleaded, 'but to keep them from being disheartened when they see the same cannot be exactly observed.' With sighs and deep misgivings, Fuller took the king's side.[5]

William Chillingworth, another reluctant Royalist, was taken prisoner after the surrender of Arundel castle. A Parliamentary officer took the opportunity to argue strenuously for the justness of Parliament's cause. Chillingworth agreed that his captor spoke much that was true. But, he added, 'war was not the way of Jesus Christ'.[6]

So widespread was the unpopularity of the war that almost immediately after it had begun a peace party emerged, and it included Denzil Holles, one of the five members Charles had tried and failed to seize. Unfortunately, it was badly organised, with fuzzy aims and little realistic idea about what the terms of peace should be. The House of Lords proposed talks with the king. Under pressure from the City of London and the country at large, the Commons seemed inclined to agree, especially when early Royalist military successes in Yorkshire and the South-West raised fears of a quick, outright victory for the king and the consequent loss of parliamentary privileges. The would-be peacemakers, however, failed to agree among themselves on anything substantial. Some wanted peace at almost any price, others would accept peace and a monarchical settlement only after Charles had been defeated. Faltering attempts at negotiations soon petered out, with neither king nor Commons prepared to make any real compromise. The confusion and hesitancy of the peace party were easily exploited by hardier men, who, at the end of January 1643, pushed through a bill that would abolish episcopacy, making peace with the king and his allies more distant than ever.[7]

Besides, by spring 1643 the prospects for the Parliamentary forces had improved. Oliver Cromwell was earning a reputation as a formidable local commander in the field. His maxim – 'trust in God and keep your powder dry' – appealed to his soldiers, many of whom were godly Puritans willing to fight for the good cause, and with none of the scruples of Dering, Verney or the peace party. By April Colonel Cromwell had cleared most of the eastern counties of Royalist resistance, and next month just outside Grantham he scattered a Royalist force twice the size of his own.[8]

The battle lines were now being more recognisably drawn. For the king's most devoted supporters, the issue was simple: rebellion was wrong, rebels deserved to be punished, and not much more needed to be said. On the composition of the opposition, a detailed account was given by Richard Baxter, an army chaplain:

> Not that the matter of bishops or no bishops was the main thing (for thousands that wished for good bishops were on Parliament's side) … But the generality of people throughout the land (I say not all or every one) who were then called puritans, precisians, religious persons, that used to talk of God, and heaven, and Scripture, and holiness, and to follow sermons, and read books of devotion, and pray in their families … I say, the main body of this sort of men, both preachers and people, adhered to the Parliament.[9]

A godly militancy was spreading through the ranks of the Parliamentary forces. Parliament had already issued an ordinance against stage plays on the grounds that they were wholly unsuitable to the times. Whereas soldiers on both sides plundered and looted abundantly, Parliamentary armies, and not just those under Oliver Cromwell's command, systematically vandalised and desecrated churches, smashing organs, images and communion rails. At Worcester, the font and other sacred parts of the cathedral were ritually turned into a public convenience. In St Mary's at Cambridge, with Oliver present, a copy of the Prayer Book was ceremonially ripped to shreds. When a clergyman was conducting a choir service at Ely, Oliver, with armed soldiers at his side, bid him 'leave off your fooling and come down'; he then emptied the church of its terrified worshippers. John Stalham recalled in Essex, and doubtless the same happened in many other places besides, the 'casting out of ceremonies and service books as a menstruous cloth'. In April 1643 the Commons directed the Lord Mayor of London to ensure strict observance of the Sabbath. Next month Parliament ordered the burning of the offensive *Declaration of Sports*. The following year the Assembly of Divines required 'a holy cessation or resting all day, from all unnecessary labour, and an abstaining not only from all sports and pastimes, but also from all worldly goods and thoughts'.[10]

On 5 June 1643 Parliament heard what many members had suspected – Charles had established direct contacts with rebel Irish Catholics. The fledgling peace party, or what was left of it, was now destroyed. Partly because of this, and partly because Royalists had enjoyed marginally the better of the fighting in the early stages of the war, Parliament resumed negotiations with the Scots. The Scots took this opportunity to press Parliament's representatives to make further reforms to the English church along Presbyterian lines, and in August 1643 the Solemn League and Covenant was signed in Edinburgh. It vowed to defend the 'reformed religion in the Church of Scotland', and looked forward to the 'reformation of religion' in England and Ireland; it condemned popery and the episcopalian system, though it proclaimed loyalty to the king's 'person and authority'. Despite some resistance in England to Presbyterianism, the League was subsequently ratified after debates and minor amendments. The Commons then forged ahead with orders to utterly purge all church buildings of popish superstitions such as crucifixes, crosses, candles and images, and to destroy all altars. To all this the timid Lords gave its support.[11]

In early spring 1644 a lone voice was heard crying in the wilderness. Henry Robinson wrote a tract appealing for virtually complete liberty of conscience. For this blessing, Robinson admitted, a price might have to be paid: false religion would fare just as well, and perhaps better, than the true one, while the number of troublesome sects would swell unpleasantly. This, he felt, was a price worth paying, because truth surrounded by falsehood 'appears still more glorious, and wins others to the love thereof'. But practically nobody listened to Robinson. Parliament did not even take the trouble to condemn his book. Instead it went ahead with enforcing the Covenant; all Englishmen over eighteen were to take it, and any who refused were to be reported to Parliament.[12]

The Parliamentary party, however, was not entirely united. Oliver Cromwell described the battle of Marston Moor of July 1644 as an 'absolute victory obtained by the Lord's blessing upon the godly party principally'. Typical of Oliver's 'godly party' was a young officer Oliver knew, who died after being struck with cannon shot at the height of battle. Before he passed away he spoke of one thing that troubled him. It was not some secret vice, or unconfessed sin, or a longing to be reconciled with a friend or neighbour he had wronged; rather it was the fact that God was about to take him away too early in life, so that he could be 'no more the executioner of His enemies'. Oliver called him a 'precious young man, fit for God … a glorious saint in heaven'. He urged his dead comrade's father: 'Let this drink up your sorrow … Let this public mercy to the Church of God make you to forget your private sorrow.'[13]

This was the spirit of Oliver and his men, and it was not the same as the spirit of Oliver's superiors. Shortly after the same battle, the three leading Parliamentary generals – Manchester, Leven and Fairfax – all declared their support for a Presbyterian Church; but they also suggested that it was time to think afresh about a settlement with the king. This provoked an ill-concealed spat between Oliver and Manchester. Oliver had little love for Scots Presbyterianism; he would, he said, 'as soon draw my sword against them as against any in the king's army'. He would have preferred none but godly Independents in his ranks, though he was pragmatic enough not to insist absolutely on this, and to recruit all the support available to him. And whereas Manchester never stopped hoping for a settlement with the king, Oliver was relentlessly determined on all-out victory. When Donnington Castle was contested, Manchester worried and fretted: 'If we beat the king ninety and nine times, yet he is king still … but if the king beat us once we shall all be hanged.' To which Oliver replied: 'My Lord, if it be so, why did we take up arms at first?' Disagreements between Presbyterians and Independents, which had dragged out debates in the Commons on church reform, were now coming to the fore in the army as well.[14]

There was, however, one enemy against whom they could close ranks and unite, at least for a short time. Archbishop Laud, the Puritans' *bête noire*, now seventy-one years old, was on trial for his life. One of his most vocal prosecutors was his former adversary, William Prynne. The charge against Laud was treason: not against the king, of course, but because he had tried to subvert the true religion of the country. Ironically, as Gardiner well noted, the accusers and the accused were actually doing the same thing, though in different directions: Laud had tried to impose one form of church government – episcopacy by divine law – while the Commons had now decided on Presbyterianism. Also, both sides wanted changes to church ceremonial: but whereas Laud would richly add to it, the Commons were determined to sweep much of it away, including the Prayer Book. The Puritan-led Commons argued in justification that whereas Laud had been innovating to undo the Reformation, they wanted to continue the good work begun by others, and bring the hitherto incomplete Reformation to perfection, or something like it.[15]

To its embarrassment, however, the Commons realised that Laud could not be convicted under the existing Treason Act. As with Strafford, therefore, they resorted to attainder. The Commons added a new dimension to the crime of treason by insisting that any crimes deemed treasonable by Parliament were treasonable in *fact*, to which a slightly reluctant Lords caved in under pressure. Now condemned to suffer the fate of traitors, the former archbishop lodged a request that he may be allowed to die quickly by the axe, and not endure the ghastly ordeal of hanging, disembowelling and quartering. The Lords were eager to grant this, but so bitter was the hatred of Laud in the Lower House that the request was rejected without a division. The Commons did relent later, though they were adamant that Laud should be accompanied to the scaffold by two Puritan ministers rather than others of his own choosing.[16]

January 1645 was a sombre month for the episcopal party. As if to rub in its victory over Laud, a special committee was working on how best to implement Presbyterian reforms, and also, if necessary, to modify the Thirty-Nine Articles. On the 4th, following sustained Commons pressure, the Lords yielded to the demand to formally replace the Prayer Book with a Directory of Worship more Presbyterian in character. Six days later Laud was beheaded. Among his last words were the wish that 'it may be remembered I have always lived in the Protestant religion established in England, and in that I come now to die'.[17]

Legally at least, the Prayer Book was banished, and it seemed the final defeat for Laud. Yet before long the Directory was causing almost as much friction as the work it replaced. Laudians derided it, Independents found it too half- hearted, and even the Prayer Book's most vociferous critics had to grudgingly admit that Cranmer's work still enjoyed an enduring appeal among the people. Some of the Directory's stalwarts were undeterred by its mixed reception: William Prynne rejoiced in the prospect of a new form of ecclesiastical rule; but John Lilburne, who, like Prynne, had suffered under Laud for his outspoken Puritanism, was almost as opposed to Presbyterianism as he was to episcopacy. With his considerable fire and energy, Lilburne joined the chorus calling for complete freedom of conscience and worship. Lilburne and those like him were not opposed in principle to a state church; but it would be a 'greater snare than the Common Prayer' to compel all to pay tithes to finance it. This was an open and provocative attack on Presbyterianism. Lilburne was an Independent. He was also a lieutenant-colonel in the Eastern Association, to which Oliver Cromwell belonged.[18]

Charles was not slow to notice the divisions between his opponents. Apparently encouraged by them he promised his wife that 'I will neither quit episcopacy nor that sword which God hath given into my hands'. Even during exploratory peace talks at Uxbridge, Charles assured the queen and his closest confidants that he would never trust or 'put myself in the reverence of perfidious rebels'. And to the king that was all they ever were – 'arrant rebels, and their end must be damnation, ruin and infamy except they repented …'. Charles also received heartening news from his ally north of the border, the Earl of Montrose. Flushed with a string of victories in Scotland, Montrose promised the king that 'I doubt not before the end of this summer I shall be able to come to your Majesty's assistance with a brave army, which … will make the rebels in England as well as in Scotland feel the just rewards of rebellion'.[19]

In June, however, Charles suffered a crushing defeat at the battle of Naseby. To add to his misfortunes, many of his files and letters were seized and carried off to Parliament, where they were read aloud to the discomfort of his remaining supporters. No longer was there the slightest doubt that Charles had authorised the raising of troops from Ireland and elsewhere to help him deal with his rebellious English subjects. Yet in the midst of it all he remained unbowed. 'Let my condition be never so low', he vowed. 'I resolve, by the grace of God, never to yield up this church to the government of Papists, Presbyterians or Independents.'[20]

Others were ready to be more flexible. Some of the king's allies were urging him to make peace, while some of his opponents had not given up hope of the same. To Prince Rupert before the siege of Bristol in September, Fairfax proclaimed his loyalty to Charles; even now Fairfax put all the blame for the nation's ills on evil councillors who had misled the king. Fairfax gave his reasons and justification for fighting:

> To maintain the rights of the crown and kingdom jointly, a principal part whereof is that the king in supreme acts is not to be advised by men of whom the law takes no notice, but by his Parliament, the great council of the kingdom, in whom – as much as man is capable of – he hears all his people, as it were, at once advising him, and in which multitude of counsellors is his safety and his people's interest …[21]

But after Bristol fell, a different chord was struck by Oliver Cromwell: 'All this is none other than the work of God.' It was the joy of the victors 'that they are instruments of God's glory and their country's good … Presbyterians, Independents, all had here the same spirit of faith and prayer … pity it is it should be otherwise anywhere'. Oliver gave a new interpretation to Romans 13: 'God hath put the sword into Parliament's hand, for the terror of evil doers, and the praise of them that do well. If any plead exemption from that he knows not the Gospel.' As Gardiner noted when comparing the words of Oliver and Fairfax: 'In one is already to be discerned the future Lord Protector; in the other, the man who, more than any single person except Monck, brought about the Restoration.'[22]

That, however, lay still in the future. For now Charles was holding out; he faithfully promised the queen that he would never give up the Church of England, 'with which I will not part under any condition whatsoever'. Presbyterianism rankled with him even more than Independency. 'The nature of Presbyterian government', according to Charles, 'is to steal or force the crown from the king's head; for their chief maxim is … that all kings must submit to Christ's kingdom, of which they are the sole governors, the king having but a single and no negative voice in their assemblies.' To yield to them would be to 'go against my conscience and ruin my crown'. Charles did not waver even when he left Oxford, the Royalist headquarters, in May 1646 to surrender to the Scots at Newark. Next month Oxford surrendered to Parliament, and the period known as the First Civil War was brought to an end.[23]

THE GODLY DIVIDED

If the fighting had ceased, the debating and arguing had not. A settlement of the nation was not remotely in sight. No progress had been made in the controversy over the rights of the Crown and Parliament. For the moment, however, church affairs were uppermost in the minds of the parties. The City of London was now strongly Presbyterian, partly because wealthy merchants were looking forward eagerly to the prospect of becoming lay elders in the national church, and the prestige such honour would bring them. Others, meanwhile, were asking themselves whether a Presbyterian Church really would be preferable to an episcopalian one, and how they could be sure that the new elders, responsible for ecclesiastical discipline, would be an improvement on the bishops of old. In the Commons as well as in the army, the Independents were gaining strength.[24]

Independency had become a sort of third force in English life; it did not need the Royal Supremacy, though it could have recognised some nominal royal headship in the country as a whole. It also rendered the Presbyterian system of church government redundant. Independents opposed the Solemn League and Covenant, and petitioned Parliament not to enforce it against those who in conscience could not sign it. Independents were not all revolutionary, and some of their pastors held reputable positions such as lecturers in the established church. Unlike the Presbyterians, theirs were congregations of 'visible saints' that criss-crossed parish boundaries, whereas Presbyterians believed in a national church organised by region. Like many Puritans, Independents agreed that only the obviously godly should be admitted to communion; but whereas the Presbyterians wanted to keep the less godly within the visible church, Independents effectively excluded them from church membership, though they did not let up in their efforts to convert them. Independents admitted new members only after hearing them describe their conversion to the satisfaction of church leaders. William Carter, a leading Independent, liked to cite Revelation 17:4 – 'Babylon the Great, the mother of harlots' – with a novel twist: Rome, he said, is the great mother harlot, but 'all the parish congregations of England are the daughters, which are harlots'. Whether he was typical of Independents is not clear. Most Independents were willing to cooperate with other Puritans for the reformation of the church nationally provided the Independent principle was accepted, and that Independent congregations might exist alongside the parish church. They were well represented in the victorious New Model Army. One who had little time for them, however, was the Leveller, William Walwyn, whose verdict on them was scathing: 'all men going in their several ways of serving God', full of 'vain thoughts that they are in a way well pleasing to God'. Walwyn was especially scornful of claims to be led by the Spirit – 'these ecstasies, as they call them distempers'; but ask them for a 'demonstration of the Spirit, they can give you none'. He compared them to 'the man in Peter's chair, trusting in their own virtue and infallibility'. Walwyn was so disillusioned with national and Independent churches alike that he doubted whether such a thing as an authoritative church or ministry could ever exist on earth.[25]

Independency, however, had not travelled well north of the border, and the king was being pressed by the Commons and the Scots to accept Presbyterianism. By June 1646 the Parliamentary ordinances for establishing a Presbyterian system were at last completed, after many long months of negotiation and debate. To this Charles was implacably opposed. What appalled him most was 'not the change of government which is chiefly aimed at – though that were too much – but it is by that pretext to take away the dependency of the church from the crown; which, let me tell you, I hold to be of equal consequence to that of the military, for people are governed by pulpits more than the sword in times of peace'. Presbyterianism in place of episcopacy would be a change 'no less and worse than if popery were brought in, for we should have neither lawful priests, nor sacraments duly administered, nor God publicly served, but according to the foolish fancy of every idle parson; but we should have the doctrine against kings fiercelier [sic] set up than amongst the Jesuits'.[26]

This was Charles speaking from the heart to his beloved wife. To the king, a true Laudian, episcopacy was sacrosanct. Its overthrow would be the ruin of the church, and a threat to the very foundation of the monarchy, the state and the Stuart dynasty. From this conviction, Charles would never depart.

He could, however, be diplomatic and artful. Indeed he had little choice, so he pretended to be willing to make concessions to Parliament over church government, though his real motive was to spin out negotiations and buy time until support arrived from abroad. He clung to the hope that divisions between Parliament and the army, and between Presbyterians and Independents in Parliament itself, would work in his favour. After Naseby, therefore, though he was effectively in the custody of those who had fought and defeated him, the king's fortunes paradoxically appeared to be rising, especially when English and Scottish Presbyterians could not agree over the extent of authority that the elders of the new national church should have. The English generally preferred more lay control than was the custom in Scotland.

Parliament and the Scots, Presbyterians and Independents were now vying with each other for the privilege of negotiating directly with the king in order to reach an acceptable national settlement. They either did not know, or maybe they preferred to ignore, the fact that Charles had vowed as a matter of conscience never to give up episcopacy. Nevertheless, one idea being considered, originally floated by Charles to play for time, was a Presbyterian arrangement for a trial period of three years. After the three years, the king hoped, fresh elections would return a more Royalist Parliament; bishops would then be brought back in triumph, and Presbyterianism thrown aside.[27]

Parliament was under intense pressure to find a solution to the nation's difficulties, and it took the bait. Dissatisfaction over high taxation was widespread and Parliament had to find money somehow, so to the delight of Royalists plans were drawn up in the House to disband the army. As if prepared to ride roughshod over the army's sensitivities, it was proposed that no member of the House should hold a position of military command, a motion apparently directed chiefly against Oliver Cromwell. Another motion that all officers should accept the system of church government decided by Parliament was carried by a majority of 136:108.[28]

Soldiers of all ranks, many of them Independents, were furious. These were the men who had fought and won Parliament's wars, yet their only reward was ingratitude and contempt. The pay of foot soldiers was now four months overdue, and that of the horse and dragoons nearly a year in arrears. From ordinary soldiers and from officers, Parliament was bombarded with petitions to redress grievances: and besides arrears of pay these included provisions for widows and orphans of soldiers killed in war, and indemnity from prosecution for acts committed during the fighting. But instead of promising to review these grievances, the Parliamentary majority condemned the soldiers as troublesome agitators and 'enemies of the state and disturbers of the peace'. Almost as an act of spite, a proposal was put forward to channel available funds elsewhere. Parliament, in Gardiner's view 'as lacking in imagination as Charles himself', was antagonising the army's high command. Henry Ireton, Oliver's son-in-law, forcefully defended the petitions in the House, and only the intervention of calmer heads prevented a duel between him and the Parliamentary leader, Denzil Holles.[29]

Negotiations between Parliament and the army dragged on through the spring. When, in mid-May, Parliament apparently satisfied itself that the king's offer to concede Presbyterianism for three years was a basis for negotiations, the Commons pushed ahead with its plans for disbanding the army. The army now feared an alliance of Parliament and the Scots against it. The army decided it would wrest the initiative. On 2 June Cornet Joyce, a junior officer under Fairfax's command, advanced with a band of soldiers to seize the king from Parliamentary control. It did not greatly matter to Charles whether he was in the custody of Parliament or the army, so long as he could set the one against the other, but he asked Joyce what authority he had to 'secure my person'. When Joyce stammered and evaded, the king persisted. 'Have you nothing from Sir Thomas Fairfax, your general, to do what you do?' Eventually Joyce pointed out his commission – 'it is behind me'. Behind him was a detachment of soldiers of the New Model Army. Charles then displayed that calm, debonair wit so characteristic of him in moments of crisis. It was, he agreed, 'as fair a commission, and as well written, as I have seen a commission written in my life'. With the king's consent, Joyce escorted him to

Newmarket. The king was now in the hands of the armed forces of the kingdom, not of its Parliament.[30]

The army was determined not to disband until its grievances were met. On 15 June *A Declaration of the Army*, probably drafted by Ireton, though with Oliver Cromwell's full approval, effectively established the New Model Army as a political force. It called for parliamentary reform and the removal of members who had abused their privileges. It affirmed the right of the people, 'if they have made an ill choice one time to mend it in another'. It demanded fixed-term parliaments, the right to petition Parliament, the publication of national accounts, and liberty of conscience. Flexing its muscles yet more adventurously, the army levelled charges against eleven MPs for abuse of power and other evils, including the attempt to enlist help from outside England to renew the war. Fairfax, one of the most moderate army leaders, refused a Parliamentary order to withdraw forty miles from London. Before long, army militancy and pressure from colleagues forced the eleven members to ask for leave of absence from the House to try and diffuse the growing tension.[31]

While relations between the army and Parliament were bad and worsening, relations between the army and the king were, at least on the surface, unexpectedly cordial. The king was well treated and allowed to receive visitors. He was also allowed to keep his chosen chaplains, which meant that in private services he could enjoy the beloved Prayer Book, even though Parliament had set it aside in favour of the Directory of Worship. Oliver Cromwell personally gave an order to the king's guards that if they received any instruction from Parliament to dismiss the king's chaplains, it should be rejected. It is small wonder that Charles felt more like an arbitrator than a prisoner. Ireton seems to have gauged the king's mood, and one day he reminded Charles: 'Sir, you have an intention to be the arbitrator between the Parliament and us; and we mean to be it between your Majesty and the Parliament.' On 4 July Charles met Oliver personally, and although no official record of that meeting has survived, it was believed by witnesses to have been an agreeable encounter, and the army continued to hope for some understanding with the king.[32]

In August Henry Ireton, on behalf of the army leaders, drew up the Heads of Proposals. Its main provisions were for biennial parliaments; reform of parliamentary representation, so that the number of members for one county would be directly related to the rates that county was required to bear; and Parliamentary control of the army and navy. Royalists would be barred from the next two parliaments, and not allowed to hold public office for five years unless Parliament gave its specific consent. A Council of State would be created to negotiate with overseas powers, and, subject always to Parliament's approval, to make war or peace. This Council, which would effectively replace the Privy Council, was to be composed of persons 'now to be agreed on', suggesting that, unlike the Privy Council, the king might not have had com-

plete control over nominations. Though the Proposals do not specifically say
so, it reads as though Parliament was to have at least some say in nominations
to the Council. The Proposals did not demand the permanent abolition of
bishops, but bishops were to forfeit 'all coercive power, authority and jurisdiction'. All previous acts or directives 'enjoining' the Prayer Book were to be
revoked. (This word 'enjoining' may be significant: Ireton seemed to be leaving open the possibility that the Prayer Book might be permitted, provided its
use was not made compulsory.) Acts imposing penalties for non-attendance
at church, 'or for meetings elsewhere for prayer or other religious duties,
exercises or ordinances' were to be repealed. This would effectively sanction
independency, though the word itself does not appear. Finally, a general Act of
Oblivion would grant a sweeping absolution for all acts of war.[33]

Because the army had won the war, the Heads of Proposals was a generous
offer. The king would be restored to the throne, the survival of the monarchy
was assured, and Ireton, though a man of strong Puritan views, had been more
conciliatory than the House of Commons on controversial topics like episcopacy and the Prayer Book. In the opinion of many historians, Charles missed
a golden chance when he refused the offer. There were two main reasons why
he did so. Firstly, he was opposed to anything that might weaken his royal
prerogative. It was traditionally the right of the Crown to appoint the chief
councillors of state, and to make treaties with foreign princes, and Charles
was not prepared to surrender that right, or even part of it, to Parliament.
Secondly, the section in the Proposals on bishops, reasonable though it may
seem in the circumstances, was impossible for Charles. Never could he agree
to bishops losing real, effective spiritual authority. To a Laudian like the king,
bishops were channels of divine grace, not just senior pastors or figureheads.
The army leaders must have known this; they must also have known how
hostile Charles was in principle to Independency. This king would never want
his throne back at any price. It was his nature to keep hoping, persevering, and
if need be prevaricating, until he was finally restored to nothing less than the
full kingly authority that he was convinced belonged to him by divine right.
Besides, with his opponents weakened by internal disagreements, the king
felt he could drive a hard bargain. So when the Proposals were formally put
to him, Charles surprised both the army and his own advisers by confidently
telling them that he was the king, and without him they could do nothing.
Prisoner though he was, he remained sure that before long even the victorious army would be ready to 'accept more equal terms'.[34]

Meanwhile, ill feeling continued between the Commons and the army,
which in August occupied London. A radical spirit was also at work in the
army, decidedly unlike the recent conciliatory attitude of Ireton and Oliver
in their dealings with the king. Richard Baxter was alarmed to hear soldiers
championing 'liberty of conscience, as they called it', where 'every man might

not only hold but preach and do in matters of religion what he pleased'. These men 'took the king for a tyrant and an enemy', and 'were resolved to take down not only bishops, liturgy and ceremonies, but all that did withstand their way'. For the time being, however, this radicalism was kept firmly in check, and army leaders persevered with Charles in spite of his rebuff over the Heads of Proposals.[35]

All in authority knew that the nation now desperately craved for peace. Charles also knew that no one of influence at this stage envisaged a peace settlement without him; so he stalled and waited for divisions between the army and Parliament, Independents and Presbyterians, English and Scots to widen further. It may have been politically astute: whether it was statesman-like is another matter.

The Independents, meanwhile, were strengthening their position in Parliament. Oliver was keenly aware of the risk that the Scots might invade England on behalf of the king and the Presbyterians.

By the end of September, a small Republican party was emerging. Because Oliver did not support it, he was suspected of cosying up to Charles in the hope of favours or rewards after a settlement. As Charles continued to stall and drag his royal feet during talks, Oliver and Ireton were increasingly seen as at best ineffective, and at worst guilty of intriguing with the king. Radical minds were slowly beginning to think about an entirely new political order. As yet, Oliver did not belong to them. In a long speech in Parliament he insisted that his aim, and the army's aim, had all along been to preserve the monarchy and not destroy it. If more of this speech had survived we might be able to understand better the logic of why it was necessary to fight the king on the battlefield in order to preserve the monarchy. However, charges of dissimulation and hypocrisy levelled against Oliver miss the point. So deeply ingrained was veneration for the monarchy that even men like Oliver, Ireton and Fairfax had convinced themselves that the king had been misled by evil councillors into seeking to undermine Parliament and the Protestant religion; and so the war had to be fought to save not only Parliament and the church, but the king as well. Nevertheless, it is hardly surprising that suspicions of Oliver's motives were spreading, even among the army.[36]

Oliver defended himself boldly in debates with fellow officers, many more radical than he. Oliver insisted that the Council of the Army should not be 'wedded and glued to forms of government'. Nevertheless, he conceded the point that 'the foundation and *supremacy* is in the people' (italics mine), and that government should be exercised in practice by the people's Parliamentary representatives. It is probable, to quote Gardiner, that Oliver did not realise that with this 'doctrine of popular sovereignty he had broken with the king for ever'.[37] Oliver's words are radically at odds with the accepted wisdom of his times. The Tudors would not have denied that the king, God's anointed though he was, still had to rule with the *consent* of the people, otherwise he would have to rule by tyranny, and thereby risk inciting rebellion and plunging the country into civil war. But there is a huge difference between the *consent* of the people and the *supremacy* of the people, a principle utterly alien not only to Charles but also to his royal predecessors, and indeed the great majority of Tudor and Stuart people.

Almost as if he was aware of such talk, Charles began making plans to escape from the army's custody. The Scots offered to help him, and then to restore him to the throne if he would accept their proposals for church government. Somehow news of this offer leaked out, and the guard was strengthened. Militancy in the army, hitherto restrained by Oliver and Ireton, was now near boiling point. The time had come, said Captain Allen, to 'take away the negative voice of the king and Lords'. After a prayer meeting, 'diverse godly people' agreed with him. Though Oliver was still calling for moderation, Lieutenant Colonel Jubbes wanted Parliament purged of members opposed to the army, and he called on the army to declare the king 'guilty of all the bloodshed' of the war, though he stopped short of demanding the king's death. Major Goffe announced that he had heard 'a voice from heaven … that we have sinned against the Lord in tampering with *His* enemies' (italics mine). Still Oliver urged restraint. Like Goffe, he too believed in the possibility of revelations from above, but he reminded his fiery colleagues of the words of St Paul to 'let the others judge' on such things (1 Corinthians 14:29). While the army leaders were trying to calm the tempers of those below them, the Scots wrote to the Speaker of the Lords proposing the return of the king to London. Members were aghast at the idea. They feared that the sight of the king in the capital city would draw forth a wave of popular support that would restore him immediately to all the power he once had, with unhappy consequences for everyone who had opposed him. On 9 November Charles was told by confidants that radicals in the army sought his life. Two days later Colonel Thomas Harrison called for the prosecution of Charles as the 'man of blood'. Again Oliver resisted. That evening Charles made good his carefully planned escape with his close allies, and stole away to the relative safety of Carisbrooke Castle on the Isle of Wight.[38]

Complex negotiations continued through intermediaries, between Charles and the Scots, Charles and Parliament, Charles and the army, and also between the Scots, Parliament and the army. Parliament was preparing four propositions for the king, later to be known as the Four Bills. The first would give Parliament control over the militia for twenty years; the second and third rejected the king's declarations against Parliament; the fourth granted Parliament the right to adjourn itself. When the king heard this he decided he would prefer an accommodation with the Scots. Though they were pressing him to accept Presbyterianism, unlike Parliament or the army they were not asking him to surrender control of the militia, or to do anything that gravely weakened his royal prerogative. On 26 December, therefore, Charles signed the so-called Engagement with the Scots. The Presbyterian system would be imposed in England for three years, and during this period an assembly of divines would meet to consider what the future, lasting church settlement should be. Charles also agreed to suppress the sects, including Independents. In return the Scots supported the king's demand for a personal treaty in London. Should this be resisted, the Scots would issue a declaration supporting the king's right to control the armed forces of sea and land, his royal veto of parliamentary legislation, and his right to make appointments to the Privy Council. This declaration would be backed by force if necessary. It is almost needless to add that the king's heart was not in the Engagement. Although he had agreed to suppress the sects, only a month earlier he had hinted to Parliament that he would support some toleration. The Engagement and the Scots alliance was nothing more than another royal holding operation.[39]

Unfortunately, his manoeuvring was uniting the army against him. Practically no officer now imagined that a settlement with the king would ever be possible. To the army's disquiet, however, support for the king appeared to be reviving among the war-weary English people. On Christmas Day, 1647, many citizens gave vent to their irritation with Parliament's heavy-handed attempts to curb traditional festivities. 'Up with King Charles and down with Parliament', shouted a crowd in Canterbury. Churches in London, which had until recently seemed favourable to Parliament, blatantly used the Prayer Book and were decorated with rosemary and bay. Pamphlets poured forth from the Royalist presses attacking Parliamentarians and army leaders, especially Oliver, and lavishing praise on the king. Parliament was at a loss how to respond to the crisis. After hurried consultations it tried to ride it out. Because the king refused to accept the Four Bills, Parliament passed a Vote of No Addresses in January 1648, declaring that no further proposals or applications would be made to Charles.[40]

It was one thing to say that negotiations with the king were over, but quite another to decide where to go from here. Parliament and the army were thick with ideas on a new government and a new constitution, but no consensus looked like emerging. Some wanted the king impeached; one or two even speculated about a trial. Others, possibly including Oliver, thought of replacing him with his son and heir, the Prince of Wales, a highly unlikely scheme given the fact that the heir would hardly usurp his father's throne. A few voices called for a republic. To the exasperation of one of them, Edmund Ludlow, Oliver and his fellow officers 'kept themselves in the clouds, and would not declare their judgements either for a monarchical, aristocratical or democratical government, maintaining that any might be good in themselves, or for us, according as Providence should direct'. When pressed to be precise,

Oliver agreed the 'desirableness' of a republic 'but not the feasibleness'. This only fuelled suspicions that he was dissembling.[41]

On 11 February Parliament did itself few favours with the people by issuing an ordinance against stage plays, which demanded the destruction of seats and boxes, whipping for actors and fines for spectators. In March unrest spread through the New Model Army regiments in Wales. On 27 March, bonfires and celebrations on the streets of London marked the anniversary of Charles's accession. Pro-Royalist feeling was rising everywhere. When a leading republican MP, Henry Marten, proposed the deposing of the king, the City called for his restoration. Pro-Royalist rioters in London, though dispersed by the army, enjoyed the scarcely concealed sympathy of many more law-abiding citizens. All of this left the army leaders with a stark choice: either they had to submit to the popular mood, or defy it.[42]

Public opinion, of course, is notoriously fickle. Within living memory, London had seen demonstrations in support of Parliament and against the king's extra-Parliamentary taxation. The recent outbreak of Royalist sentiment may have been due as much to exasperation with Parliament and the army as love for Charles Stuart, and a desire for stability and peace and an end to conflict. Nevertheless, the advantage seemed now to lie with Charles. Parliament's problems worsened in April when Irish Royalists and Confederates in league with the Scots declared for the king. Once again the Scots urged Parliament to open negotiations with Charles, to establish Presbyterianism in England, and to suppress the Prayer Book and sects alike. On 25 April news reached Parliament that the Scots were raising an army to invade England. More disturbances were reported in Wales – noisy demonstrations in favour of the king and risings against the army led by Colonel Poyer. The situation there was now critical, so Fairfax and the Council of War decided to send Oliver to bring it under control.[43]

This was a time of much soul-searching among army leaders. At a meeting on 29 April, Oliver urged his fellow officers to examine themselves, and consider 'if any iniquity could be found in them', so that they might 'remove the cause of such sad rebukes' that they were suffering, with little obvious sign of relief. These were men who interpreted success and setback as signs of divine favour and anger respectively; but never, of course, could they admit that the slump in their fortunes was a divine judgement on them for taking up arms against the king in the first place. Instead they listened intently to a sermon by Major Goffe, who convinced them that the army had sinned by persevering in vain to reach an agreement with the king, a man who, as events since the soldiers captured him had proved, never had the slightest intention of accepting any of the terms offered to him. One of the officers later described how, with tears of repentance in their eyes, they resolved to do their duty, 'to go out and fight against those potent enemies'; and when the victory was won they would 'call Charles Stuart, that man of blood, to an account for the blood he had shed, and the mischief he had done to his utmost against the Lord's cause and people in these poor nations'.[44]

So the men of the New Model Army went out again to fight. Oliver headed for South Wales to suppress the risings there. On his way he rallied his troops, recalling how he had 'oftentimes ventured his life with them and they with him against the common enemy of this kingdom'. None of his soldiers could have been under any illusions that by the 'common enemy' he meant the king. No longer was Oliver the voice of moderation in the army. By July he had overcome all opposition in Wales. In August he smashed the invading Scottish force at Preston. Patchy outbreaks of resistance to the army, and accompanying demonstrations of loyalty to the king in Kent and Essex, were dealt with by Fairfax and other officers. To men like Oliver Cromwell these stunning successes, evoking the glory days of Marston Moor and Naseby, could be explained in only one way – the Lord was with them once more. 'Surely sir', wrote Oliver to the Speaker after Preston, 'this is nothing but the hand of God.'[45]

The Ways of Providence?

The army's successes in the field did not put an end to negotiations between the king and Parliament. Though still effectively a prisoner on the Isle of Wight, Charles had not given up trying to exploit the differences between his adversaries. He was now involved in complicated discussions about a treaty that would accept Presbyterianism for three years, after which a limited form of episcopacy would be permitted; he also offered Parliament control over the armed forces for twenty years and responsibility for the settlement of Ireland. Charles was, of course, only playing with his opponents. 'To deal freely with you', he confided to a close ally, 'the great concession I made this day – the Church, militia and Ireland – was made merely in order to effect my escape.' Unaware of this, though suspicious as always of the king's motives, the Commons drove a hard bargain and rejected the king's offer, even though the Lords were seeking a compromise. The queen, meanwhile, was doing her utmost to attract support from the continent, especially after the Treaty of Westphalia, signed on 14 October, brought the Thirty Years War to an end. Royalists in Ireland might also be persuaded to come to the aid of the king.[46]

But as Parliament continued to press its demands, and as Charles continued dissembling, cries for justice were heard louder than ever from the army. Oliver had not yet returned to London following his victory at Preston, but Ireton drew up his Remonstrance of the Army calling for the trial of the king, because negotiating with him had proved fruitless. Like many in the army,

Ireton no longer had qualms about blaming the king for being the 'grand author of our troubles'. Yet when Ireton laid his Remonstrance before the Council of the Army in November, he ran into unexpected opposition from Fairfax and others. The army went into debate over constitutional and political points. After much discussion it renewed an offer to the king, fairly similar to the earlier Heads of Proposals.[47]

But the army had also received intelligence about the king's plans to escape once more, so on 17 November Ireton and three fellow officers wrote to Hammond, Governor of the Isle of Wight, ordering him to 'see to the securing of that person'. The same day Charles rejected the army's final proposals. Ireton then overcame the resistance of Fairfax, and his Remonstrance, only slightly modified, was presented to the Commons on 20 November. The thought of the king on trial was deeply disturbing to many members, while others were offended with the army for interfering in constitutional affairs and making suggestions for electoral reform. Now it was the turn of the Commons to procrastinate. It postponed a decision for seven days. To the army's mounting exasperation, the Commons also continued negotiations on the finer points of the proposed treaty with the king. Charles was spinning the talks out as usual: he could never agree to abolish episcopacy, but he said he would consider its temporary suspension, and when it was restored, some limitations on the role and authority of bishops. (This was really no more than a straw for Parliament to cling on to, and to prevent the talks collapsing prematurely.) On 27 November the Commons procrastinated again by putting off the debate on the Remonstrance till 1 December. The army feared that the Commons was delaying the Remonstrance, and other reforms, indefinitely. It decided to march on London.[48]

The Commons, meanwhile, had been reconsidering the king's latest offer, including limited episcopacy. Though still not entirely happy with it, the Commons decided on 5 December by a majority of 129:83 that it could serve as a 'ground for the course to proceed upon for the settlement of the peace of the kingdom'. According to one report, Speaker Lenthall warned MPs that they had effectively voted to destroy themselves. To try and pacify the army, a committee was instructed to arrange a meeting with Fairfax, still its senior as well as its most moderate commander. The army summoned a Council of Officers at Windsor. Ireton and Harrison argued for the dissolution of Parliament. Others pressed for a purge, and their voices prevailed. The army then drew up a blacklist of MPs. At seven o'clock in the morning of 6 December, Colonel Pride and a band of soldiers stood by the House of Commons and barred over 100 members from entering. Many more, hearing of what was afoot, did not bother to turn up. Altogether the House was reduced from nearly 500 to just over 200. On the evening of the 6th, Oliver arrived back from the north; he was unaware 'of this design', he claimed, but since it was a done deed 'he was glad of it'. Pride and his men kept watch on the Commons until the 12th. Parliament was now at the army's mercy, and the army was master in England.[49]

On 15 December the army decided that the king should be brought to Windsor. Eight days later, Charles arrived. Yet still there were men even in the army, despite their conviction that the king should be held accountable for the wars and all the strife and misery, who baulked at the thought of putting him on trial for his life. A last ditch attempt at mediation by a group of peers to keep Charles as king, though with considerably reduced powers, was dismissed by Charles. This may have been the moment when Oliver swung irrevocably against the king. All the struggling in his soul was now over. On 27 December Thomas Brook preached to the newly purged Commons, and he took his text not from Romans 13 or the Sermon on the Mount, but from the Mosaic Law and the Book of Numbers – 'the land cannot be cleansed of the blood that is shed therein, but by the blood of him that shed it' (Numbers 35:33). Next day the Commons prepared an ordinance for the trial of the king. 'If any man whatsoever hath carried on the design of deposing the king', Oliver declared, 'he should be the greatest traitor and rebel in the world; but since the Providence of God hath cast this upon us, I cannot but submit to Providence.' But something else besides Providence was leading Oliver into realms unknown: Brook's revolutionary theology had entered into his heart and stuck fast in his mind, and nothing would ever drive it out again.[50]

The Lords, meanwhile, were shocked at the thought of the king being tried for treason. Yet even loyal peers had to resort to legal technicalities rather than emotional appeals to the sovereign's divine right. Suppose the king really was to blame for the war, pleaded Northumberland, 'we have no law extant that can be produced to make it treason in him to do so'. The Lords agreed and rejected the ordinance sent by the Commons. A resolution was then passed by the Commons:

> That the people are, under God, the original of all just power: that the Commons of England, in Parliament assembled, *being chosen by and representing the people, have the supreme power in this nation*; that whatsoever is enacted or declared for law by the Commons in Parliament assembled, hath the force of law, and all the people of this nation are concluded thereby, *although the consent and concurrence of king or House of Peers be not had thereunto* [italics mine].

The piercing irony of *this* Commons having a mandate from 'the people' would challenge even the satirical genius of Jonathan Swift. Only a few days before it had been purged by the army at the sword's point. Its claim to supreme representative authority was pure chimera. All real authority rested with the godly fighters of the New Model Army. But such is the language of all revolutionaries.

On 6 January, in the Commons, the ordinance became an act with the full force of law. It began with a swipe at Charles's predecessors, though it did not name anyone, who had made 'encroachments … upon the people in their rights and freedoms'. But it accused Charles of going far beyond this: of having 'a wicked design totally to subvert the ancient and fundamental laws and liberties of this nation, and in the place, to introduce an arbitrary and tyrannical government'; this stratagem he had pursued by 'fire and sword'.[51]

The Commons now ordered an impressive new seal. On one side was a map of England and Ireland, on the other an engraving of the Commons. The Lords was nowhere to be seen. 'In the first year of freedom, by God's blessing restored, 1648', ran the inscription alongside. The revolution was now forging ahead relentlessly. On 20 January, Algernon Sydney raised a point of law; he argued tamely that 'the king can be tried by no court'. Oliver, no longer striving with his conscience, retorted that 'we will cut off his head with the crown on it'. Yet legal scruples still stalked even Oliver. On the morning of 20 January, when he saw the king led towards the garden of Cotton House, he turned to his companions and reminded them that they would need an answer ready if the king demanded to know by what authority the court sat. After a moment's reflection Henry Marten replied: 'In the name of the Commons in Parliament assembled, and all the good people of England.'[52]

Oliver had anticipated well; Charles did indeed make his demand. Bradshaw, chief presiding judge, called on Charles to answer 'in the behalf of the Commons assembled in Parliament and the good people of England'. Before Charles could reply, a woman's voice cried out from the gallery: 'Not half, nor a quarter of the people of England. Oliver Cromwell is a traitor.' It was Lady Fairfax, and anyone other than the wife of the Parliamentary general would have been quickly despatched to prison. When order was restored, Bradshaw repeated his question. Charles replied that he was king by birth, not by consent of the people or any other institution. He scornfully dismissed the charge of treason and the right of the Commons to try him. 'If power without law may make laws', he argued, no subject in England would be safe.[53]

As almost all witnesses and historians have agreed, Charles was getting the better of Bradshaw. By what law had the army purged Parliament? By what law had the purged Commons put the king on trial, without the consent of the Lords? Law in England was now in thraldom to power. A small group of dedicated and hardy men, who had, beyond all doubt, just complaints against the king's policy and duplicity, had forcibly taken into their hands the whole law of the land.

Shortly before the court's inevitable verdict was pronounced, Oliver was trying to convince the Scots of the justness of the cause. According to a witness, Oliver did so as follows:

> He thought that a breach of trust in a king ought to be punished more than any crime whatsoever; he said, as to their covenant, they swore to the preservation of the king's person in defence of the true religion: if, then, *it appeared that the settlement of the true religion was obstructed by the king, so that they could not come to it but by putting him out of the way*, then their oath could not bind them to the preserving him any longer [italics mine].[54]

The revolution now under way was not just a revolution against Charles. This was a revolution against the Reformation. Thomas Cromwell and Thomas Cranmer had been condemned to the scaffold and the stake by a sovereign who rejected what they believed was the true religion; yet both would almost have abjured the faith for which they died sooner than see Henry or Mary brought to an earthly trial. The idea that the establishment of 'true religion' could conceivably involve the overthrow of the monarch, that ordinance of God on earth, was more in keeping with the spirit of Thomas Müntzer than the Protestant Thomases of the Tudor age.

On 27 January, Charles was brought to court for the last time to hear the sentence of death confirmed. The king bid a fond farewell to his children, Princess Elizabeth, aged thirteen, and the Duke of Gloucester, ten. He told them he was going to die for 'the laws and liberties of this land and the true Protestant religion'. For their comfort and spiritual edification, he commended the works of Andrewes, Hooker and Laud. Charles then prepared for 'my second marriage day', and on 30 January he departed this life. 'For the people', he declared in his last words:

> truly I desire their liberty and freedom as much as anybody whatsoever; but … their liberty and freedom consist in having government, those laws by which their lives and their goods may be most their own. It is not their having a share in the government; that is nothing appertaining unto them. A subject and a sovereign are clean different things.

His coffin was buried in the same vault that contained the remains of Henry VIII and Jane Seymour.[55]

As with Strafford and Laud, it may be said of Charles that he died better than he had ruled. Stubborn and duplicitous he was in life, regally serene at the hour of death. Though never loved by his people as Elizabeth had been, his dignified passing made sure that whatever regime succeeded him would begin with a huge handicap, and be unlikely ever to win the affection of the

nation. Yet neither the natural sympathy of the onlookers, nor the horrified
groan that arose from among them when the axe fell, could obscure the fact
that Charles was the author of so many of his own misfortunes. He had sadly
mishandled and antagonised Parliament in a way that no Tudor prince ever
did. Besides the ill-tempered dissolutions, the abortive attempt to arrest the
five members, the imprisonments of others who displeased him, he frequently
expressed in private his contempt of the Commons. He seemed unable to
understand its unique place in the constitution and the fabric of the nation.
Many feared, not without good reason, that he was turning the divine right
of kings into an earthly absolutism. As for the church, if he had only put a discreet distance between himself and Laud, then opposition to Laud would have
passed the king harmlessly by. Had Charles remained a good Elizabethan, he
could have used his kingly authority to allow, but also to keep under control,
a Laudian and a Puritan wing to the national church. By throwing in his lot
with the Laudians, Charles exposed himself to the same suspicions and charges
that Laud had aroused: the undermining of the Protestant Reformation and
a covert re-Catholisation of England. It would also have been far wiser for
Charles to let the Kirk go its own way.

But Charles could do none of these things. There was not enough flexibility or statecraft in his make-up. More than most of his predecessors and
successors, he was driven by conscience. Once he vowed in all things 'to look
to my own conscience in the faithful discharge of my trust as king'.[56] The
sacrifice of Strafford was a rare lapse, due to the king's powerlessness and fears
for the safety of his beloved queen. For his own part, for the sake of his conscience he would rather lose his corruptible, earthly crown than yield on a
matter of church or state.

Yet not even Charles at his most haughty and insensitive had dared to
assault Parliamentary rights with the ruthlessness of Colonel Pride and the
New Model Army, and these were the men who now wielded power in
England. So what kind of men were they, who had won the war and sent the
king to the scaffold? Oliver Cromwell was a pragmatic enough commander
to realise that he would have to recruit from all possible sources to swell the
ranks of his forces, but he left us in no doubt what sort of fighter he preferred.
Even though, in April 1645, Parliament had passed an ordinance forbidding
laymen to preach, and Fairfax was urged to ensure its enforcement throughout the army, Oliver was convinced that 'he that prays and preaches best will
fight best'.[57]

In the church of Elizabeth, as in the church of Charles and Laud, only
the ordained minister preached. Devout parishioners said their morning and
evening prayers in the privacy of their homes, and during services they joined
in the communal prayers of Cranmer's Prayer Book; but none of them led
the congregation in prayer, or did much praying from the heart in public.

Soldiers of the New Model Army, Oliver's godly warriors, his pride and joy, had no such inhibitions; they would pray, preach and rouse each other to godly fury. Many of them came, as noted already, from Independent churches, where preaching and praying were not the sole duty of the recognised minister. Besides Oliver, John Cook, the prosecuting lawyer at the trial of the king, belonged to one such church. One who has studied them closely, Murray Tolmie, has shown how gradually they and their radical brethren emerged as a powerful force as militant saints, active accomplices in the revolution and the execution of the king. They had not always sought such a prominent or destructive political role. When these movements first began, their main aim was civil and religious freedom and no more; affairs of state they were content to leave well alone. Two things had radicalised them. One was official intolerance and repression when the liberty of worship they wished for was denied them. The other, in part an outcome of the first, was the certainty that Providence was guiding them, even commanding them, to take the sword against all enemies of the truth, not sparing even the king himself. The execution of Charles, says Tolmie, was the 'climax of the revolution for the saints'. Letters from many of them to Oliver after the king's death rejoiced over the 'wonderful hand of God … in bringing down the proud and haughty ones, making them to drink the wine of the cup of His fury …'.[58]

Unless one side has the advantage of overwhelming odds, victory in war is invariably won by those with the stomach to fight and the will to win, essential martial qualities conspicuously lacking in many Stuart Englishmen. The neutrality pacts at the outbreak of the Civil War, the indecision of the gentry, the reluctance to take sides until forced to do so – such a spirit may appear understandable and even commendable to twenty-first-century readers, but it never stood a chance against Oliver Cromwell's disciplined and fearsomely motivated Ironsides.[59]

These were men spurred on by the certainty that they were called to do the Lord's avenging work. It may now be timely to ask how this conviction arose, what the source of it was, and what substance there might have been to it.

DIFFERENTLY DIVIDING THE WORD OF TRUTH

In the seventeenth century, to quote David Daniell, 'the English Bible was not a special file to be called up when one was feeling religious'. Indeed not. Christopher Hill, writing of the men and women of the Revolution, noted that the Bible was the 'point of reference in all their thinking … the source of virtually all ideas'.[60]

Perhaps. But what Hill says, surely, is also true of the men and women of the Reformation? They too devoured the sacred writings, no less than the generations that followed.Yet the Bible did not inspire them to revolution: on the contrary, they used it to condemn the revolutionary spirits of their time.

Luther and Tyndale translated the Bible. The Augsburg Confessions, Melanchthon's *Loci*, Calvin's *Institutes*, Cranmer's Homilies and Prayer Books are all essentially commentaries on Scripture from men who knew the sacred text just as well, and probably a lot better, than the militant saints. Elizabeth read a passage from the New Testament in the original Greek every day. Thomas Cromwell learned his Latin New Testament by heart on a visit to Italy, and he could read the Greek as well if he wished to. More than anyone else of his time, except the Bible translators themselves, he gave the English people the Bible in the English tongue and with the king's blessing. He had a command of Scripture powerful enough for him to debate with (and in my view get the better of) the scholarly Bishop John Fisher. Miles Coverdale, one of the translators, described the Great Bible project as 'your lordship's work' (Thomas Cromwell's work).[61] Persuading Henry to allow a Bible in every parish was, it could be said, the Tudor Cromwell's 'crowning mercy'. But Thomas did not simply know his Bible mechanically; he showed a keen sense of how to apply the Word effectively, not just recite from it at random. On two different occasions he told Bishops Fisher and Shaxton – one of the old faith and one of the new – that they were taking Bible verses out of context and getting the meaning all wrong.[62]

In the times of the Tudors, there was no lack of interest in or devotion to the Bible. So how, in that case, is it possible for the same book to inspire the mind and shape the aims of Luther *and* Müntzer, Whitgift *and* Cartwright, Laudians *and* Puritans, and both the Cromwells? How can the deferential Reformation of the first Cromwell, and the godly Revolution of the second, arise from the same source?

The different ways of handling Scripture on a whole range of subjects between the times of the two Cromwells is a theme well worthy of a doctoral thesis or other specialist study; here it can be discussed only briefly.

Though Oliver quoted abundantly from the Scriptures in his speeches and letters, unlike Thomas he did not always allow for the context. Oliver approved, for instance, Thomas Brook's address to the purged House of Commons, justifying the trial and execution of the king from the Book of Numbers, chapter 35. This passage sets out the procedure to be followed under the Mosaic Law when a murder has been committed. Two witnesses are required for proof of guilt, and if a ransom is offered for the life of the guilty man it should be refused: 'for blood it defileth the land; and the land cannot be cleansed of the blood that is shed therein, except by the blood of him that shed it' (Numbers 35:33 – see also p. 194). This is the historical context. 'We can now see', concludes Christopher Hill, 'that the Bible was primarily responsible for the execution of Charles I.'[63]

That all rather depends on whether Brook and his friends had accurately applied the text from Numbers; and whether the legal regulations for dealing with the crime of murder in ancient Israel, more than a thousand years BC, were a valid handbook for the trial of King Charles I in AD1649. Hill's statement suggests he thinks they were; but Thomas Cromwell would never have used Numbers this way. Reformers in his time divided the Word of Truth differently. They did not reject Numbers, or doubt its historical accuracy; like other narratives of the history of ancient Israel, it was full of interest and wholesome lessons. Nevertheless, it belonged to an era that had passed. The Law of Moses was chiefly a shadow of things to come, a tutor to bring us to Christ, not a blueprint for Christian societies (based on various texts including Colossians 2:14, 17; Galatians 2:19, 24). The choicest parts of the Old Testament were those looking on to the New, foretelling the coming of Christ. The Christian lived in the times of the New Testament, of the Kingdom of Heaven, of Romans 13 and the Sermon on the Mount, of obedience to princes, of rejection of rebellion, of suffering for Christ if the need demanded it. The books of the Bible were, in that sense, prioritised, and the New Testament took priority over the Old.

Over-simplified, this might be described as the 'most recent first' approach, and it is one that most of us use for almost every subject worth studying. If, for example, you are fairly new to Tudor history and you want to learn about, say, Thomas Cranmer, it is not advisable to begin with the *Letters and Papers … Henry VIII* and plough through nearly twenty weighty volumes one by one. It would be far more sensible to begin with Diarmaid MacCulloch's biography, which gathers all the relevant facts and narrates them in the historical context. After that you can consult the original documents on any points of special interest. In the same way, the Reformers would recommend a student coming to the Bible to begin with St Paul. The epistle to the Romans in particular is not only the most comprehensive treatise on Christianity, written by the chief New Testament apostle; it is also a guide to the Christian interpretation of much of the rest of Scripture. The story of Abraham, for instance, can seem a bit flat unless Romans 4 and Galatians 4:21–31 are read first.

So the Reformers used a commonplace, and common sense, methodology. This did not guarantee agreement on all points – the exact meaning of the Words of Institution, for example, could still be disputed. Nor does it make the Reformers objectively in the right. Who was right and who was wrong on these things is a subjective matter, like nearly everything else in church history. The point is that Reformers had a method, one that was easy to understand and easy to follow. Anyone, moreover, who did follow it, and keep faith with it, would not start a religious war or a rebellion: he would never invoke Numbers over the head of St Paul and the Sermon on the Mount on the subject of the Christian's relationship with his ordained king.

Sola Scriptura (Scripture alone) was a fundamental Protestant principle. But if there is no method of any kind applied to the handling of Scripture, then it is possible to find just about anything you like there, and this is what happened when Oliver and the saints turned the Reformation methodology on its head. Now the sixty-six different books of the Bible, written over a period of many hundreds of years, were, so to speak, levelled out, and any text anywhere could be pressed into use regardless of date, author or context provided it suited the mood. And the mood of the times warmed more to Mosaic justice and war stories than turning the other cheek or not resisting evil.

Oliver's soldiers carried with them into battle their pocket soldier's Bibles, a little book about the size of a modern passport. It contained nearly 150 verses, which, according to the specially prepared introduction, 'do show the qualifications of his inner man, that is a fit soldier to fight the Lord's battles'. Only four verses came from the New Testament. These included: 'Fear not them which kill the body; (Matthew 10:28), and 'Be strong in the Lord' (Ephesians 6:10). In both cases, minimal attention was given to the context. The first of these verses is an encouragement to disciples who risk death for their faith, while the second is a word on *spiritual* trials, 'for our struggle is not against flesh and blood'. Neither text has anything to do with a physical battle whatsoever.

Also from the New Testament was John the Baptist's directive to soldiers to 'do violence to no man, neither accuse any falsely, and be content with your wages' (Luke 3:14). Also, slightly incongruously for men in combat, there is 'Love your enemies' (Matthew 5:44). Alongside was the explanation that 'a soldier must love his enemies as they are *his* enemies, and hate them as they are God's enemies', with a reference to Psalm 139:21–2: 'Do I not hate them O Lord that hate thee?' All other verses were taken from the Old Testament, chiefly the wars of Joshua and the Israelites against the surrounding hostile nations in the books of Judges, Samuel and Kings.[64]

In Thomas Cromwell's day the deeds of these warriors were applied differently. As one example, take Joshua's conquest of the Promised Land and the destruction of the Canaanites. According to Tyndale, these were *divine* judgements on God's enemies, not something the believer should ever take in hand. Luther liked to see Joshua as a type of Christ leading His people to victory through the Gospel; but for the Christian under Christ, the victory is not won with swords and spears, but through 'faith in His Word'. The enemies are papists, monks and radicals; the idols and false gods of the ancient Canaanites become the false worship of popery and monasticism; but all the killing is done 'through the Word and the Spirit … this is not a material sword striking down bodies; it is the Word of God smiting consciences'. Luther and Tyndale, therefore, make a spiritualised application of the historical acts of Joshua and his men. But in Oliver's day this method was overturned, and these same stories were used to boost morale in an actual physical fight. Pace St Paul, the contest *was* with flesh and blood, and Israel's historical victories over her enemies were to be re-enacted by the new generation of the godly.[65]

Tyndale handles Numbers in a similar fashion to Luther on Joshua. Tyndale treats the book historically, but he likes to draw spiritual lessons for his own times. He notes the unbelief and false freewill of the Israelites, and he makes this topical by comparing it with the work righteousness of the papists. In Chapter 14 the unbelieving people go up to fight the Amalekites and Canaanites contrary to the Word of the Lord and of Moses; and Tyndale notes: 'Blind reason ... teacheth them now to trust in their own works.' In Chapter 16 Moses is falsely accused by the rebels of Korah and pleads to the Lord, 'I have not taken so much as an ass from them, neither have vexed any of them'; here Tyndale asks wryly: 'Can our prelates say so?' In Chapter 18 the Levites shall have no inheritance, but live off the tithes of the other tribes of Israel; to which Tyndale adds: 'Ours will have tithes and lands and rents and kingdoms and emperies [sic] and all.' On Numbers 35, unlike Oliver Cromwell and Thomas Brook, Tyndale sticks entirely to the historical meaning with a very brief explanatory note – 'The right use of the sanctuaries' – and nothing specific on verse 33. It would never have occurred to him to use this verse as the regicides did.[66]

Moses and Joshua, therefore, were full of interest to the first reformers, and they found much that was valuable in them; but their military deeds are not for the Christian to copy. 'Christ Himself', says Tyndale in his Prologue to the *Obedience of a Christian Man*, 'taught all obedience, how that it is not lawful to resist wrong ... how a man must love his enemy, and pray for them that persecute him ... and how all vengeance must be remitted to God.' Thirty years later, the Geneva Bible has this enigmatic note on Numbers 35:33: 'So God is mindful of the blood wrongfully shed and He maketh His dome [sic] creatures to demand vengeance thereof.' Note the contrast – we might say the contradiction – between Tyndale and Geneva. Tyndale leaves vengeance entirely to God; the Geneva introduces the thought of a demand for vengeance. But with Tyndale the Christian *cannot* demand vengeance; he cannot pray for a persecutor and call for vengeance on him at the same time. Vengeance is in God's hands, and in His alone. This was the Reformation credo, turned around 180 degrees at the Civil War, but a crucial point in the revolution was the Geneva Bible. This, incidentally, is one reason why the causes of the Civil War cannot be sought *only* in the Stuart age. No one would deny that Ship Money, tonnage and poundage, neo-absolutism, Parliamentary liberties and so on were important elements; but it is necessary to go back a little further to trace how the revolutionary mindset developed, which could overthrow the established order and condemn the king to death.[67]

Christopher Hill notes that his book, *The English Bible and the Seventeenth Century Revolution*, 'has turned out to be almost exclusively concerned with the Old Testament, apart from Revelation', which makes the point nicely.[68] The Reformation was primarily about the *New* Testament, especially St Paul; and because the New was believed to be the fulfilment of the Old, the Old was read through the lens of the New. The revolutionaries, fired by their unrefined zeal, threw this lens away.

OLIVER CROMWELL AND THE INTERREGNUM, 1650–58

THE MILLENNIUM

Although the execution of the king shocked the crowd that saw the deed done, many among the army and its supporters welcomed it as a sign that would usher in the end times, the destruction of all the ungodly kingdoms of the world, and the dawn of the millennium. This was not just an outbreak of radical fervour on the fringe, because one such man was John Owen, later Vice-Chancellor of Oxford, and a friend of Oliver Cromwell. When the rule of the saints was established, warned Owen, the Lord would 'shake all monarchies of the earth'. William Rowse wrote to Speaker Lenthall prophesying: 'Methinks I see the kingdom of Christ begin to flourish, while the wicked … do perish and fade.' John Spittlehouse warned the pope in Rome that Hugh Peter, a leading New Model Army chaplain, might yet descend on the papal city and 'preach in St. Peter's chair'. [1]

Millennialism – alternatively known as chiliasm – had a long history in Christendom. It was based on a certain interpretation of prophetic parts of Scripture, most significantly Revelation 20 and the thousand-year reign, and also the book of Daniel. It could claim highly respectable origins. The early-second-century Christian apologist, Justin Martyr, believed that Jerusalem, then in ruins after its destruction by the Roman armies following the Jewish revolt, would one day be rebuilt in glory. Justin admitted, however, that 'many who belong to the pure and pious faith, and are true Christians, think otherwise': obviously his view was far from a consensus and not an article of faith. Justin also believed, from Isaiah 66 and Revelation 20, that the church will live 1,000 years with Christ and the Patriarchs and all the pre-Christian faithful, with the New Jerusalem as the centre of the millennial kingdom, after which would come the general resurrection. However, St Augustine (354–430), arguably the greatest of the Western church fathers, abandoned the literal interpretation in favour of a more spiritualised one: he made the 1,000 years symbolic for the entire Christian era. Because of his huge influence, his view soon became Christian orthodoxy. But neither the authority of Augustine nor a succession of popes could suppress the appeal of chiliasm, and from time to time during the early church period, and well into the Middle Ages, various self-styled 'Messiah' figures appeared, announcing the imminent end of the world, and the beginning of a new golden age.[2]

Millenarian ideas and groups often sprung up in times of political crisis, uncertainty or revolution: for example, in the days of John Ball and his followers during the English peasants' revolt of 1381; or the early stages of the Hussite revolution in Bohemia in 1419–21; and also Thomas Müntzer and his 'League of the Elect' in the German Peasants' War of 1525. One of the most dramatic outbreaks of chiliast fervour during the sixteenth century occurred when streams of radical Anabaptists flocked to the city of Münster in the 1530s, persuaded that here, not in Israel, the New Jerusalem would be built. The city council was overrun, and quickly fell to Anabaptist control. A Dutchman known as John of Leiden announced that he had received a revelation from heaven confirming him as the Messianic King who would inherit the throne of David. Normally peaceable folk, best known for their rejection of infant baptism and any participation in civil government, the mood of the Anabaptists turned alarmingly militant and repressive. All 'non-believers' – about 2,000 Lutheran and Catholic citizens – were expelled, forced to leave their property and belongings behind. Anabaptist leaders enforced polygamy and abolished private ownership of money. Other strict rules included directives for employment and the death penalty for various offences besides the usual ones of murder and robbery; theoretically a disobedient child could be put to death. As king, John of Leiden renamed streets and gates, abolished Sundays and feast days, set up his harem, and dressed and lived splendidly. His subjects, however, were commanded to live aesthetically and in modest clothing, and houses were routinely searched for anything deemed superfluous or luxurious. Echoing Thomas Müntzer, Leiden proclaimed that the time had come for the saints to rise up against the godless, after which Christ would return and the avenging saints would reign with Him, no longer in poverty and suffering but in glory. A Reign of Terror began against all who sinned against 'the truth', and many were executed. But the millennial dream was doomed when Münster was besieged and captured by an alliance of Catholic and Lutheran princes, who restored control of the city to its former councillors, and hanged Leiden in chains.[3]

One reason why Luther so despised the 'unlearned mob of the Anabaptists' and other radical men was what he derisively called their 'great affection for the more obscure books, such as the Revelation'. The Reformation had given short shrift to millennial ideas. The Augsburg Confession brushed them aside in a couple of terse sentences, which may be one reason why Leiden and his followers at Münster condemned Luther as a false prophet, worse than the pope. In his German New Testament Luther set four books, one of them Revelation, apart from the rest because he was unsure whether they should be in the canon at all. With its jerky Greek and fantastic imagery, it seemed to him a world away from the lucid and uncomplicated writings of the apostles in the Gospels and the epistles. In later years he was not quite so dismissive, but he was never convinced that Revelation was the work of an apostle. In later editions of his Bible he did give a few brief thoughts on it, and in general it was a historical interpretation. On the famous twentieth chapter, Luther thought the 1,000 years had probably begun when the book was written; but he spent little time enlarging on it.[4]

By contrast, Luther had a high regard for the book of 'St Daniel', and he used it in a way far different from the chiliasts. Luther praised Daniel for his God-fearing life and faith in a pagan land. In chapters 4 and 5 the temporary fall of Nebuchadnezzar and the definitive judgement on Belshazzar served as consolation for all who suffer under tyrants. The moral, for Luther, was that the church should bear patiently with unjust rulers, and wait on God to deal with them in His own way (quite the opposite of some of the revolutionary spirits met in this story thus far). The visions of the future kingdoms in chapters 7 and 8 were for the Christian's consideration and instruction: but not a call to arms. Daniel's seventy weeks in Chapter 9, though fearsomely difficult exegetically, was as a prophecy of Christ and Calvary and the future resurrection (see especially 9:26–7; 12:2–3). Words from Daniel's intercessory prayer of the same chapter were later adapted by Thomas Cranmer and included in the Prayer Book for the communion service: 'We do not presume to come to this thy table, O merciful Lord, trusting in our own righteousness, but in thy manifold and great mercies ...' (Daniel 9:18). Luther praised Daniel as a man 'above all prophets', a prophet and prince of the world; 'among all the children of Abraham, none was so highly exalted'. He commended Daniel to all good Christians. There was far more to this book than visions of kingdoms falling apart (or adventures with lions).[5]

Luther set the tone for the mainstream reformers. From John Calvin the chiliasts and the 1,000-year reign received a sweeping Gallic dismissal – 'this fiction is too childish either to need or to be worthy of a refutation ... even a blind man can see what stupid nonsense these people talk'. In general Calvin followed Augustine and Luther. According to that doughty Elizabethan, John Whitgift, the rejection of chiliasm was one of the proofs that the doctrine in Elizabeth's church was 'much more perfect and sounder' than in the ancient church, when even many of the leading lights were 'infected' with millennial ideas. Henry Bullinger in Zürich, even Thomas Cartwright in England, had lectured and written on the Revelation. But just as Luther found Daniel edifying for the soul rather than a call to arms, so Bullinger managed to navigate his way through the Apocalypse, avoiding the deadly blasts of the trumpets and the vials of wrath, seeking out calmer waters like the consolations to the churches, the visions of the elders before the throne, the blessing promised to the martyrs, the promise of Christ's return, and the wonderful depiction of the eternal city descending out of heaven. Bullinger did not believe in a literal, futuristic 1,000-year reign of the saints.[6]

Later editions of the Geneva Bible, from 1599, reveal a growing interest in the Revelation, and the accompanying notes are more detailed than in the original edition of 1560. Notes to the early chapters are Christological and pastoral. Then comes an 'Order of the Time whereunto the contents of this book are to be referred', which offers the reader a historical interpretation. Sharp words are directed against the more notorious popes; but even here there is little to encourage the chiliasm of the Civil War years.[7]

It is not clear, therefore, what moved one of our scholars to say that the Reformation 'stimulated millenarian preaching'.[8] The Reformation did nothing of the kind; it condemned millennialism forcefully, scornfully, over and over again. The surge of chiliasm in the 1640s could even be called a *counter*-Reformation movement, though not one led by Jesuits or Dominicans, but emerging instead from within the ranks of the saints.

Apart from the very general comment that chiliasm had more than once revived in times of national conflict and crisis, it is not easy to explain how the increased attention given to the strange yet fascinating book of Revelation was transformed into millenialist fervour; or why and how the traditional historical interpretation gave way to a futuristic one. Besides, a national crisis is not enough on its own to kindle chiliasm. There was no sign of it when the Armada was bearing down on England. Because it appeared in Puritan and especially Independent companies, the search to clues for its sudden awakening must focus on them and their origins.

This subject may be worthy of more detailed study one day, but one undeniable factor was Laud's innovations and his anti-Puritan policy generally, as a result of which many of the godly felt compelled to leave the established church and set up on their own. In doing so, maybe they did not fully appreciate that they were turning their backs not just on Laud, but also on a great deal of accumulated Christian thought and learning. They were setting off on an uncertain spiritual journey. So was Luther over a hundred years before, some might say; but with a supportive elector and like-minded friends and colleagues, Luther had the benefit of a favourable spiritual and intellectual infrastructure to lean on and help him on his way, as did Calvin in Geneva a generation later. The godly in Stuart times were not so fortunate. More and more they thought and acted as they felt 'led' to think and act, either from impulse or pressure of contrary events whirling around them. Facing danger, uncertainty, even the risk of persecution, they turned for succour to the book of Revelation, with its dramatic visions of deliverance for the oppressed and vengeance on the oppressors. An aggressive chiliasm sprang up, holding out the prospect of freedom and power, especially for those who felt downtrodden under Charles and Laud. One of the most potent dynamics fuelling the Civil War and the Revolution was the craving for liberation, and the yearning to bring the corrupt order crashing down, and set up a purer one in its place. Before Marxism, chiliasm was the opium of the people.

In the 1640s chiliasm was pervasive among godly companies. A visiting Scotsman, Robert Baillie, noted in 1645 that 'most of the chief divines here, not only Independents … are express chiliasts'. As the Civil War loomed ahead, millennialism fused with militancy, even in the hearts of those who had not hitherto supported the principle of resistance or insurrection in a good cause. 'In vain are the high praises of God in your mouths without a twoedged sword in your hands', said one. 'He that dies fighting the Lord's battle dies a martyr', avowed another. One author wrote, in 1642:

> Millenaries are most frequent with us; men that look for a temporal kingdom, that must begin presently and last a thousand years … to promote that kingdom of Christ they teach that all the ungodly must be killed, that the wicked have no propriety in their estates … this doctrine filleth the simple people with a furious and unnatural zeal.[9]

This spirit has been met before in this story. It was not the spirit of Luther or Calvin, or Thomas Cromwell, Cranmer or Elizabeth. This was more akin to the spirit of John of Leiden and Thomas Müntzer. Leiden and his Anabaptist kingdom were invoked nostalgically and admiringly by some English revolutionaries, while others praised Müntzer, Luther's 'Satan of Allstedt', as a 'Champion of Truth.'[10]

The Fifth Monarchists were the most vigorous of millennial groups. Like Müntzer a century before, they saw contemporary society as part of the antiChristian fourth kingdom of Daniel 7, which had to be destroyed before the advent of the millennium. Thomas Harrison, one of Oliver Cromwell's foremost generals, was a Fifth Monarchist. At the battle of Langport, when Parliamentary forces had put the Royalists to flight after a perilous charge up a narrow lane, a witness heard Harrison 'break forth into praises of God with fluent expressions, as if he had been in a rapture'. Leading national figures like Oliver and Sir Henry Vane were millenialists, and although Oliver did not belong to the Fifth Monarchist group, he must have known that many of his soldiers and officers did. To the Scots in 1650, Oliver's men explained their reason for prosecuting the war against the king: it was 'the destruction of Antichrist, the advancement of the kingdom of Jesus Christ, the deliverance and reformation of His church … and the just civil liberties of Englishmen'. This clarion call was issued with Oliver's blessing.[11]

Two points ought now to be conceded. The first is that not all chiliasts were violent men, and a great many English people were not chiliasts at all. In troubled times, however, when the talk is all of war, of threats to liberties and true religion, a small band of dedicated, zealous men can easily provide the thrust that drives events forward, whether it commands widespread support or not. The army had purged Parliament and cut off the king's head, yet it had no mandate from the nation.

Secondly, it is of course true that there was nothing especially new in the belief that the end times were at hand. Many reformers since Luther had thought so. But they have no common ground with the saints of Stuart times on this account. There is a huge difference between believing that the end of the world is nigh according to Nicene Creed – the resurrection of the dead and the life of the world *to come* – and the setting up of a godly millennial kingdom in the *present* world under the rule of King Jesus and His servants, like Müntzer or Thomas Harrison. In the first, the church will be delivered from all her foes and dangers by divine power, and that same divine power will take care of the unpleasant task of meting out justice to the wicked. The redeemed, apart from enjoying heavenly bliss, do nothing very much. The new chiliasts were not so passive; they were eagerly looking forward to an active, avenging role in Christ's *earthly* reign. 'The saints shall judge the world … whereof I am one', declared one of them, George Fox. The rule of saints like these, says Christopher Hill aptly, would be a 'dictatorship of the godly'.[12]

For these godly revolutionaries, the hope of the church had ceased to be spiritual and heavenly. Pace St John's Gospel, Christ's kingdom *is* of this world. The saints were no longer content to wait for reward in heaven; they wanted glory and power now, in this age not the next. This ideology the Reformation had strongly rejected.[13] These saints were rebelling not just against King Charles, Strafford and Laud, but against Thomas Cromwell, Cranmer, Elizabeth, even John Calvin as well.

Be that as it may, the saints had won their famous victory. Now they had to win the peace.

THE COMMONWEALTH

The Parliament Colonel Pride had purged came to be known, unflatteringly and with little affection, as the Rump. It tried its best to establish its authority in the land. On 6 February 1649 a Commons committee passed a resolution pronouncing positively that the House of Lords was 'useless and dangerous', and should be got rid of. Next day came another announcement: the office of a king, not just Charles Stuart personally, had been shown to be 'unnecessary, burdensome and dangerous to the liberty, safety and public interests of the people of this nation'; for that reason, it too had to go. Both motions were quickly carried without division. A new Council of State was created with executive power, though subject to the Commons. Forty-one names, of judges, lawyers and officers, were elected to the new Council; these included Cromwell and Fairfax, though rather unexpectedly Ireton and Harrison failed to secure enough votes. By March all necessary legislation was passed, and England was formally declared to be 'a republic without King or House of Lords'.[14]

The Revolution had done its work thoroughly. In times past the monarchy had been damaged and humbled, but not destroyed. The barons had forced King John to sign the Magna Carta, and Simon de Montfort defeated King Henry III on the battlefield at Lewes, compelling the king to make unpalatable compromises. But John remained king, and although Lewes left de Montfort the effective ruler of England, just over a year later he was killed in battle and Henry restored to the throne. Bolingbroke and his allies had dethroned Richard II, and Henry Tudor overcame Richard III on Bosworth Field; but both these usurpers took the Crown themselves. The Stuart regicides, however, with their supporters in the Rump, swept away not just the present wearer of the crown, but the very institution itself.

The new government then proceeded to deal with five prominent men who had supported the king and fought alongside him. One of them, Lord Capel, provided the Royalist cause with another martyr. He dismissed the godly minister assigned to prepare him for his last hour. On the scaffold he declared that his faith was to be found in the Thirty-Nine Articles, 'the best he knew of'. He died unashamedly for his loyalty to the late king, 'the most religious of all princes in the world'.[15]

Estimates of the casualties of the Civil War – taking into account lesser skirmishes and sieges as well as major battles like Naseby – suggest that around 84,000 lives were lost between 1642 and 1651 in England and Wales. Less easy to calculate is the number who perished from diseases like typhus and dysentery in a besieged town, though one well-researched estimate puts the figure at approximately 100,000. Out of a population of around 5 million, therefore, 3.6 per cent may have died, compared with 2.6 per cent and 0.6 per cent respectively in the two world wars of the twentieth century. Even these figures do not allow for the plight of the homeless following the destruction of buildings, towns or villages.[16]

But there was to be little rest for a war-weary nation, and the republic now faced the risk of war on two fronts, or at least one front quickly after another.

Prince Charles was in The Hague, and he was not short of willing support-ers in Scotland and Ireland. The Scots had not been consulted about the king's trial or his execution, or the setting up of a republic; nor had they sworn alle-giance to the regime in London, which they soundly disliked. On 5 February in Edinburgh, Prince Charles was proclaimed 'King of Great Britain, France and Ireland', subject only to satisfactory agreements being reached with him on the church and constitutional affairs in England and Scotland.[17]

For Royalists in England, defeated and demoralised though they were, the prospect of being delivered from the republic by Scots Presbyterians was less than exhilarating. Like Royalists in exile, their best hopes lay in Ireland. Charles agreed, because he was just as loath as his father to make the commitments to Presbyterianism that the Scots demanded. Only after Oliver Cromwell's bru-tally efficient conquest of Ireland did Charles reluctantly make a pact of sorts with the Scots. It was an uneasy alliance. The Kirk's Commissioners, when they visited the prince on the continent, noted disapprovingly how 'many nights he was balling and dancing till near day'. For expediency's sake, how-ever, Charles was forced, via the Treaty of Breda, to endorse Presbyterianism, to sign the National Covenant and the Solemn League and Covenant, to recognise the authority of the Kirk and Parliament in spiritual and civil affairs, and to be ready to disown the Irish and the Scots who had fought for him and his father. English Royalists present at the Breda negotiations were not slow to notice the contrast between the prince and the late king, who would never have made such drastic concessions, even to save his life. 'Our religion is gone', wrote one of them; 'and within a few days is expected the funeral of our liturgy, which is gone already.'[18]

This may be one reason why, despite the unpopularity of the republic and the various abortive experiments in government throughout the Interregnum, there were few serious Royalist risings, or attempted risings, to restore the prince. Many English people may have longed for the days of the monarchy, a free Parliament, the old church and the Prayer Book; but how could they be sure that all this would be theirs once again if Prince Charles were restored? Even if, as many observers suspected, Charles detested and resented the terms that he was forced to sign at Breda, the likelihood that he would sign a treaty and then break it when it suited him was not the sort of thing to inspire loyal men and women to risk their lives on his behalf. It certainly did not endear the prince to the English people to see him, in early 1651, at the head of an invading Scottish force. Charles was, though perhaps understandably, too eager to recover his Crown and avenge his father's death. But the invaders were no match for the godly fighters of the New Model Army.

Oliver's victory over Charles and the Scots at Worcester completed his conquest of England, Ireland and Scotland. It had taken less than ten years. No king of England had matched this achievement; and it would be churlish to

deny Oliver the grossly overused word 'greatness' just because, unlike Henry
V, Marlborough and Wellington, he did not operate on the larger European
theatre. Often he enjoyed the advantage of numerically superior forces, but
not always: at Dunbar 3,000 English under Oliver outmanoeuvred and routed
11,000 Scots. Yet for this staunch Puritan general, his astonishing sequence of
triumphs could never be ascribed to military prowess alone. Until the Civil
War broke out he was a country gentleman who had never fought a battle.
He had little if any formal military schooling. The reason for his success lay
elsewhere. Every one of his victories was a blessing of Providence, a sure sign
that the Lord was with him. After Marston Moor he gave thanks that 'England
and the Church of God hath had a great favour from the Lord'. At Naseby
and Preston he saw clearly the 'hand of God'. Bristol was 'none other than
the work of God'; anyone blind to this 'must be a very atheist'. Drogheda in
Ireland was a 'righteous judgement of God upon these barbarous wretches,
who have imbued their hands in so much innocent blood'; that same 'righteous justice' was manifest again to Oliver at Wexford. 'The Lord has delivered
them into our hands', he cried at Dunbar, when he noticed the Scots army
advancing down the hill to their doom; and as the sun rose and the battle
began, he invoked the war cry of the Psalmist: 'Now let God arise and His
enemies be scattered' (Psalm 68:1). Worcester was the 'crowning mercy'. [19]

After Worcester, Oliver was eulogised by John Milton, the finest poet of his
age and arguably all ages:

> Oliver, our chief of men, who, through a cloud
> Not of war only, but detractions rude,
> Guided by faith and matchless fortitude,
> To peace and truth thy glorious way hast ploughed.

However, a lasting constitutional settlement was still needed. As Milton
continued:

> … yet much remains
> To conquer still; Peace hath her victories
> No less renowned than war. [20]

By the end of the year (1651) Oliver and many of the officers were unhappy
with the Rump, so a conference of officers, lawyers and carefully selected
MPs was arranged. One of the lawyers, Sir Thomas Widdrington, suggested
making the young Duke of Gloucester king. Oliver agreed that a settlement
'of somewhat with monarchical power in it would be very effectual'; but
it is not altogether clear from this guarded comment whether he felt that a
constitutional monarchy would be practicable or desirable with any king of

Stuart blood. England was now bristling with ideas for political regeneration. Gerard Winstanley wanted to sweep away lords and landlords as well as kings and bishops; he also demanded the abolition of money and the creation of a communal society. Oliver had little time for this sort of thing, though more radical men like Lilburne were attracted to it. There was also much discussion about the church. John Owen, who enjoyed Oliver's confidence, favoured a national Puritan church that would exist alongside non-conformist churches, though the consensus was that 'popery and prelacy' should not be permitted. ('Prelacy' is just another word for episcopacy, namely Laudianism.) Others wondered how the new religious groups and sects – the Baptists, Congregationalists, Quakers and Unitarians – would fit into the proposed new order; and even whether the Commonwealth should revoke the decree of Edward I and formally readmit Jews to England. The Rump, meanwhile, passed a number of bills, one for the sale of lands owned by leading Royalists, but it had been sluggish on broader constitutional and law reform. Worse, it had failed to bring about a full godly reformation that the saints longed for. Nor did it go unnoticed in the army and elsewhere that many MPs had lately become extremely rich, despite having done nothing exceptional in the service of church or state. The Rump had also, in May 1652, begun a naval war with the Dutch, provoked chiefly by commercial rivalry.[21]

Around this time it was noticed that Oliver seemed to be distancing himself from the more radical men. It was also rumoured that he was attracted to the idea of making the young Duke of Gloucester a king as a minor, with Oliver as Protector. However, in a conversation with Bulstrode Whitelocke in November 1652 over problems with Parliament, Oliver startled his companion with a blunt question: 'What if a man should take upon him to be king?' Whitelocke sensed at once that Oliver had himself in mind, and tried to dissuade him. 'You have full kingly power in you already, concerning the militia', he began, 'and although you have no negative vote in the passing of laws, yet what you dislike will not easily be carried.' The danger, Whitelocke went on, was that 'our friends' believed that the Commonwealth would secure more freedom in spiritual and civil affairs than a monarchy could ever do; so if Oliver were to take the title of a king, the central issue would be not whether England should be governed by a monarchy or a free state, 'but whether Oliver or Charles Stuart shall be our king and monarch'. Little more was heard on the subject, and Oliver's exact motives in raising it remain mysterious and disputed. On 7 December, however, Parliament decided to send the Duke of Gloucester to Flanders, on the grounds that his safety at Carisbrooke Castle on the Isle of Wight could not be guaranteed so long as England was fighting the Dutch.[22]

Away from the corridors of power, many in the country were slowly coming round to accepting the Rump as tolerable, if only because it served as a barrier against radicalism. Still, discontent in the army grew. But the army also had its factions, with men like John Lambert pressing for pragmatic Parliamentary government, based on virtually free elections with only notorious Royalists excluded, while others like Thomas Harrison eagerly awaited the rule of the godly. When impatient officers talked of dissolution, Oliver at first resisted. The Dutch war, meanwhile, made trading hazardous, leaving the merchants as restless as some of the soldiers. The Dutch had been chased out of the Channel but they were very active in the North Sea, disrupting cargoes of coal to and from Newcastle, causing the price of coal to rise threefold. Elsewhere the 'preaching party', as one news writer described the more voluble saints, watched the Rump's failure to create a more godly society with rising disapproval. The Rump was now suspected of scheming to safeguard its own survival; of drawing up a plan for partial elections only, to fill up the vacancies caused by Pride's Purge, an idea which would allow existing members to hold on to their seats indefinitely. When Oliver called for a general election, a republican MP retorted by calling for a new general for the army.[23]

These suspicions of the Rump's motives may have been mistaken, according to recent research. It now appears that the Rump was not after all making plans for elections only to vacant seats. Legislation was being prepared for a completely new Parliament to meet next November. The Rump's exact plans are unfortunately unclear because its bill for a new Parliament is lost, which means that the exact reasons for its dissolution are also uncertain. What is certain, however, is that the army had lost confidence in the Rump. Oliver feared that a new Parliament, called under arrangements to be supervised by the Rump, would be opposed to the ideals of the godly Commonwealth. There was also the vexed question of how to ensure the election of suitable members. Oliver was not worried about Cavaliers; keeping them out would be easy enough. He was worried lest an assembly dominated by Presbyterians might seek to impose their system on the church as vigorously as Laud had tried to impose his, to the detriment of Independents, to which Oliver and many officers were attached. The army also suspected that Rumpers, whatever declarations they might make for a free Parliament, were nevertheless somehow devising a way of keeping themselves in power, while excluding officers from a future Parliament.[24]

So on the morning of 20 April, Oliver marched to the House with a company of soldiers. He sat in the Chamber for some minutes listening to the debate; then he turned to Harrison, the Fifth Monarchist, who had gone with him. 'This', said Oliver, 'is the time I must do it.' He then rose to accuse the House of corruption and dishonesty: 'without a heart to do anything for the public good, to have espoused the corrupt interest of presbytery and the lawyers, who were the supporters of tyranny and oppression, accusing them of an intention to perpetuate themselves in power'. He spoke, according to one witness, 'with so much passion and discomposure of mind, as if he had been distracted'. Advancing to the middle of the House he announced that 'I will put an end to your prating'. He tramped up and down telling them: 'You are no Parliament, I say you are no Parliament; I will put an end to your sitting.' He barked out an order, and armed soldiers rushed into the chamber. Oliver's harangue of the House went on and on, and he singled out certain members for their vices: one he called a drunkard, another whoremaster. Finally he turned to the mace: 'What shall we do with this bauble? Here, take it away.' The shocked protests of the House availed nothing.[25]

That afternoon Oliver was relaxing with fellow officers, reflecting on the morning's events. 'When I went there', he said, 'I did not think to have done this: but perceiving the spirit of God so strong upon me, I would not consult flesh and blood.' Oliver has mingled together words from Isaiah, Christ and St Paul; it is almost needless to add that these texts have nothing at all to do with dissolving Parliaments. As so often, Oliver drew on Biblical imagery and language; but he did so randomly. He seldom bothered with the context.[26]

If this report is accurate, it is small wonder that the reason for the Rump's downfall, at that precise moment, is still uncertain and debated. According to Oliver's own words, he did *not* go to the Commons determined to dissolve it. Whatever the officers may have said among themselves, Oliver's mind was not made up when he strode into the House. So no dissolution had been formally agreed on. Something Oliver had heard in the Chamber, something he felt stirring within him, something that no amount of historical research is ever likely to satisfactorily discover, triggered the amazing scenes that followed. Nevertheless, the story is by no means unbelievable. It was a feature of many in the Independent churches to be 'led by the spirit' in praying or preaching rather than follow a regular order of service, and Oliver was not the kind of man to leave his religion in church: it was part of him, it animated him wherever he went and in whatever he did. It was normal for him to act and think as he was 'led'. A later, less godly generation of historians might ascribe this to impulsiveness or a fiery temper; but few of us have ever felt the 'spirit of God so strong upon me' as Oliver did, so we cannot analyse nor explain his psyche adequately.

Later that day John Bradshaw emboldened himself to take Oliver to task for getting shot of the Rump. 'You are mistaken', he told him, 'to think that the Parliament is dissolved; for no power under heaven can dissolve them but themselves.' Bradshaw was a lawyer, and in dry legal theory he was right. In the circumstances, however, he was merely whistling in the wind. Parliament really *was* dissolved, and by a power that Parliament could never control – the power of the sword in the hands of Oliver Cromwell, who, like some Old Testament warrior, felt the strength of the Lord surging up within him. But at least this time there was no anguished groan, as when the king died. 'This House to be let unfurnished', wrote a wag on the door of the Chamber. Oliver himself later noted that the Rump's demise caused 'not so much as the barking of a dog'.[27]

The underlying reason for the dissolution was made clear in the army's declaration, dated 22 April. After blessings of Worcester, Parliament 'had opportunity to give the people the harvest of all their labour, blood and treasure, and to settle a due liberty, both in reference to civil and spiritual things, whereunto they were obliged by their duty, their engagements, as also the great and wonderful things which God hath wrought for them'. However, it was a 'matter of much grief to the good and well affected of the land to observe the little progress which was made therein, who thereupon applied to the army, expecting redress by their means'. The army had tried by means of petitions to bring about 'justice and righteousness', but to little avail. Increasingly the Rump had been marked by 'much bitterness and opposition to the people of God, and His Spirit acting in them'. In too many of them was the selfish desire 'of perpetuating themselves in the supreme government'. To this end 'they resolved ... to recruit the House with persons of the same spirit and temper, thereby to perpetuate their own sitting'. It was clear to the army that the Rump 'would never answer those ends which God, His people, and the whole nation expected'. And so on in the same vein.[28]

Here is the main reason for getting rid of the Rump, whatever the uncertainties regarding the details and the timing: it had failed to meet godly expectations. No new Jerusalem was rising from the ashes of the Civil War. Instead, said Oliver bitterly, the 'liberties of the nation' were being handed over by default to those who had never fought for them. Observers noted his 'hate of rotten presbyters', and how he feared that the new Parliament the Rump was planning for 'would have been an inlet to that tyrannical, now sordid tribe' (Oliver's reported words).[29] Old rivalries, not just between the army and Parliament, but also between Presbyterians and Independents, were festering still, holding up the settlement of the nation. Oliver and the officers feared that a Presbyterian majority in a new Parliament would have been as great a threat to Independency as Laud had been; and after fighting a war against bishops, the army was not about to submit to the rule of elders.[30]

King, Lords, bishops, and now the Commons had been cleared away, leaving the English constitution, as Gardiner put it, 'but a sheet of white paper'. So what should be put on it? Harrison had his answer – the time had come for the rule of the saints. Other officers, like Lambert, were more pragmatic. Eventually the Council of Officers decided on a new assembly of the godly to be nominated by them (the officers). Many of the nominees, like many of the officers, were Independents. The list was subsequently approved by the Council of State, and by June the writs were sent out and the chosen ones summoned. Barebone's Parliament, which met in July, was so named after one of its most prominent members, the renowned Puritan, Praise-God Barebone. But it was not packed with religious zealots; out of a total of 140 members there were at most about thirteen Fifth Monarchists.[31]

Nevertheless, Oliver's opening speech rings with millennial fervour. He began by calling to mind the 'series of providences wherein the Lord hath appeared, dispensing wonderful things to these nations'. By 'godliness and religion' the late wars had been won. He reflected on the workings of Providence: 'the king removed, and brought to justice; and many great ones with him; the House of Peers laid aside; the House of Commons itself, the representative of the people of England, sifted, winnowed, and brought to a handful'. In all these things, not forgetting the 'pulling down of Bishops', Oliver saw a 'remarkable print of Providence'. He then justified at length the dissolution of the Rump. He hoped Barebone's would be altogether different. 'Truly God hath called you to this work by, I think, as wonderful providence as ever passed on the sons of men in so short a time.' He quoted Psalm 110:3: 'The people shall be willing in the day of thy power.' After this Oliver continued: 'I confess I never looked to see such a day as this … a day of the power of Christ.' Surely this assembly could be a fulfilment of the words of the prophet Isaiah: 'This people I have formed for Myself, that they may show forth my praise.' (Isaiah. 43:21). Oliver hoped he had not 'unfitly applied' the text to his hearers: 'God apply it to each of your hearts! You are as like the forming as ever people were.'

No longer was Oliver quoting haphazardly from the Bible. This was a carefully prepared address to a public assembly, not an off the cuff quote in the heat of battle or the spur of the moment.

The real significance of this passage, taken from Isaiah, is that traditionally it had been applied to the church as a whole, to the people redeemed from among the mass of the Gentiles from all walks of life: peasants, princes, artisans, nobles, yeomen, merchants; all the baptised from every tribe, tongue and nation. Never until now had it been applied to a nominated group of legislators in one country only. But Oliver was persuaded that there was 'never a people so formed, for such a purpose so called' as the gathering listening to him. On he went:

> Why should we be afraid to say or think that this may be the door to usher in the things that God has promised; which have been prophesied of; which he has set the hearts of His people to wait for and expect? We know who they are that shall war with the Lamb, against His enemies; they shall be a people called, and chosen and faithful. And God hath, in a military way – we may speak without flattering ourselves, and I believe you know it – He hath appeared with them and for them; and now in these *civil powers and*

authorities does He not appear? ... Indeed, I do think something is at the door, we are at the threshold ... You are at the edge of the promises and prophecies [italics mine].[32]

As others have pointed out, Oliver was not part of Harrison's Fifth Monarchists. There is, however, no mistaking the chiliast exuberance and expectation of the speech. He was not absolutely certain that this was *the* day, the last day before the end times. But he had high hopes that it might be. He gave a thoroughly millennial interpretation of the Old Testament, especially of Isaiah. He took a text which, until now, had been universally applied to the redeemed church scattered throughout the world; and he made a direct connection between that text and the assembly in front of him. And the idea that the end times will be ushered in by the coming together of an elect *civil* legislature shows how far English Puritanism had travelled from classic Protestantism since the days of the Reformation, which had roundly condemned the ideas of Müntzer and others, that 'before the resurrection of the dead the godly will take possession of the kingdom of the world'.[33]

Oliver then formally handed over supreme authority to Barebone's Parliament until November. This authority entitled the members to determine what assembly should come after them. This second assembly would sit for one year, during which time it would determine a further 'succession in government'.[34]

Barebone's Parliament was mercilessly ridiculed by Royalists for its affected saintliness and political naivety. Nevertheless, it briskly got down to work, with attendance figures far higher than was the case with the Rump. It began with a series of uncontroversial and generally useful affairs, including reforms to the administration of government, the law regarding wills, civil marriage, debts and solvency, and various beneficial measures to help creditors, the poor and the mentally impaired. A committee was appointed for the advancement of learning. The main problem areas were tithes for the clergy and law reform. Radicals objected to tithes on principle; they preferred to see preachers and pastors maintained by the voluntary offerings of their congregations. Trouble threatened when petitions were handed into the House to abolish tithes without compensation. The lively radicals in the House then managed to defeat a committee's recommendation to retain tithes. This worried the better-off classes in the country, especially those whose ancestors had bought church lands in Tudor times, because with the lands came the entitlement to receive tithes. Regarding law reform, most MPs agreed that changes were desirable, but here the consensus ended. Those of Levelling sympathies called for elected local magistrates to administer the law independently of professional lawyers. A few wanted to do away with common law, and replace it with the Mosaic Law.[35]

Although a great many words were spoken and documents drafted in committees in the House, no bill was actually presented to Parliament; and some of the proposals now emerging on law reform were too drastic for mainstream Puritan opinion as well as property holders and land owners. Then the radicals scored another success when they won a motion to abolish the court of chancery. This alarmed professional lawyers even though, despite much discussion and debate, no act was passed. By now Oliver's enthusiasm for this Parliament was fading. 'I never more needed all helps from my Christian friends than now', he sighed to his son-in-law, Major-General Fleetwood. Sadly he admitted that the saints 'are of different judgements … each sort most seeking to propagate their own'. Surely, he added wistfully, 'if the day of the Lord be so near (as some say), how should our moderation appear'.[36]

The war with the Dutch, begun in the days of the Rump, was another cause of friction. Oliver was understandably eager for peace with his fellow Protestant Dutch, and he presented detailed plans to them for a union between the two nations. When this idea was coolly received, he tried to interest them in a close alliance, which would be extended to include Sweden, Denmark, the German Protestant princes, and even France if the Huguenots were granted some liberty of conscience. England and the Netherlands, Oliver suggested, should divide the world between them in the interests of religion and commerce: the Dutch would take Asia, and England the Americas. War would be declared against Spain if necessary. The plan came to nothing, mainly because the more pragmatic Dutch did not share Oliver's visionary enthusiasm. The Dutch, however, had suffered losses at sea to the English, and they warmed to Oliver's overtures of peace, though not political union. This set Oliver against the radicals inside and outside the House, including the Fifth Monarchists, who despised the Dutch for being both Presbyterian and materialist, and were ardent supporters of the war.[37]

The end of Barebone's Parliament was drawing closer. When elections to the Council of State were held on 1 November, all 113 members present voted for Oliver. Harrison, the Fifth Monarchist, won fifty-eight votes, to appear thirteenth on the list. Though radicals like him were still a minority in the House, they were a sizeable minority and a source of irritation to the government and the property classes. They were highly motivated, and more assiduous in attendance than many of their colleagues, a fact which frequently made up for their numerical disadvantage. On 17 November the House debated a proposal to abolish lay patronage, a controversial topic because in some counties nearly two-thirds of parish livings were indebted to lay patrons. It was a system that could easily lead to abuse, though it did not always do so. Not for the first time in this Parliament, those opposed to abolition feared that religious and political radicals were threatening property rights and the social order. Nevertheless, opponents of patronage managed to secure a vote in favour of bringing in a bill for abolition. Rumours quickly started to spread that dissolution was imminent.[38]

The government had other troubles besides Parliament. A Royalist rising in the Highlands, the so-called Glencairn rising, renewed fears that Royalists in the Lowlands and in England might join forces and, with help from the continent, challenge the still insecure Commonwealth. Outside Parliament the Fifth Monarchists were more strident than ever. Christopher Feake was condemning even Reformed Churches as Babylonian, while Oliver himself had become the 'man of sin' and the 'Old Dragon'. Oliver's disappointment with Barebone's had alienated some of his more radical brethren. Long suffering as ever with such fiery spirits, Oliver tried to reason with them and soothe them, though to little avail. Inside the House, MPs sympathetic to radicals were in the habit of punctuating their speeches with statements like, 'He spake it not, but the Lord in him'; and this tendency to claim divine inspiration for political and social opinions increasingly irritated more pragmatic MPs and councillors, entertaining though it was to Royalists and foreign observers. The climax came when the House was debating the vexed subject of maintaining and financing the preaching ministry, and when it was obvious that even on this seemingly uncontroversial point, no agreeable consensus would emerge.[39]

John Lambert, Oliver's best general, and the most politically astute of the officers, had already decided that the nominated assembly was unworkable. For some weeks he had been preparing a new form of government. Oliver, too, was now convinced that his confidence in the gathering of the godly had been misplaced; and it greatly distressed him to see factions and divisions appearing among a company of members nominated by the army, and chiefly from the Independent churches. Later he would admit his 'weakness and folly' in imagining that Barebone's would usher in the promised kingdom and millennial righteousness. Fortunately for Oliver, Lambert came to his rescue by drafting the Instrument of Government. Lambert's allies in Parliament then effectively voted their own dissolution, and handed their power back to Oliver.[40]

Lambert's original plan was to offer Oliver the Crown. This was declined, despite the entreaties of Lambert's allies. This apart, the Instrument was similar to Ireton's earlier Heads of Proposals. Supreme legislative authority would reside 'in one person, and the people assembled in Parliament: the style of which person shall be the Lord Protector of the Commonwealth of England, Scotland and Ireland'. Executive government would be carried out by the Protector and the Council of State. The Protector 'shall dispose and order the militia', though in practice 'by the consent of Parliament'. (Following Pride's Purge, the forced dissolution of the Rump, and the 'voluntary' surrender of Barebone's, the idea that Parliament's 'consent' would be needed to control

the army might have brought a wry smile to the faces of Royalists, who were
for the most part still excluded from the government and future parliaments.)
No new law or tax was to be levied 'but by common consent in Parliament'.
Parliament would be summoned triennially. The office of Protector would be
elective, not hereditary, and he would be elected by the Council. All Christians
except adherents of 'popery and prelacy' would enjoy freedom of worship. Bills passed by Parliament would need the Protector's approval; but if,
within twenty days, he had given neither his consent nor any 'satisfaction' to
Parliament for not consenting, then the bills would become law so long as
they contained nothing contrary to the Instrument. Thus the right of veto, as
enjoyed by kings past, was withheld from the Protector. And here, as Gardiner
noted, lay a potential problem that had either slipped through unnoticed or
was knowingly overlooked: there was no body, such as a special constitutional
court, established to judge whether a bill was, or was not, contrary to the
Instrument.[41]

Nevertheless, on 16 December 1653 Oliver was installed as Protector.
Among officers elected to the new Council of State was John Lambert, but
not Thomas Harrison. Harrison's Fifth Monarchist brethren felt frozen out
and bitter. To them the Protectorate had neither legality nor morality. Their
preachers were now likening Oliver to Daniel's little horn and the malevolent
King of the North (Daniel 7:8, 20–7; 11:20–1, 28, 31). They were fortunate
that no quasi-military ruler has ever endured insults with the patience that
Oliver Cromwell showed. He was used to it by now, from Royalists, republicans and radicals. There was a phlegmatic side to his nature. 'Shall we quarrel
with every dog in the street that barks at us?' he once asked. Oliver then
proceeded with a number of conciliatory measures. No longer, for example,
was the oath of allegiance to the Commonwealth 'without King or House of
Lords' compulsory.[42]

But if Oliver was showing signs of mellowing on constitutional affairs, there
was another subject where the enthusiasm of earlier days was still very much
alive. Oliver decided he must improve the nation's morals. His government
banned public cock-fighting, not out of any great sympathy for cocks, but
because such occasions were 'commonly accompanied with gaming, drinking,
swearing' and other ungodly behaviour. Barebone's Parliament had already
banned bear-baiting for much the same reason, prompting the witty if slightly
unfair quip that what rankled with the Puritans was not the pain suffered
by the bears, but the pleasure enjoyed by spectators. In fact, Oliver and the
Puritans were not entirely hostile to the thought of people enjoying themselves, so long as they did so without ungodliness: he himself, at Hyde Park on
May Day, enjoyed watching a hurling match followed by Cornish wrestling.[43]

It took some time to organise elections to the first Protectoral Parliament,
and it did not meet until September 1654. Though Royalists were officially

disqualified, a few managed to evade the new constitutional barriers and get elected. Apparently unaware of these intruders, Oliver addressed the assembled members in grand style. All the hopes he once had in Barebone's Parliament he now transferred to this one: for 'you are met here on the greatest occasion that, I believe, England ever saw'. Oliver had not lost his revolutionary fervour; he recalled with satisfaction 'our first undertaking to oppose that usurpation and tyranny that was upon us, both in civils and spirituals'. But he also spoke scornfully of Levellers and the 'men of that principle', who 'would have cried up interest and property fast enough'; and although he admitted that some sincere men could be found among the Fifth Monarchists, he pointedly distanced himself from them. Oliver had tempered rather than abandoned his chiliasm; he now looked for the reign of Christ 'in our hearts', and he disowned those who were convinced of their moral entitlement to 'rule kingdoms, govern nations and give laws to people'. Almost contemptuously he dismissed demands for the Mosaic Judicial Law to replace 'known laws settled amongst us'.[44]

Oliver's speech set the tone for the Protectorate. It would be solid, mainstream Puritan, faithful to the cause for which they had fought, but rejecting alike political radicalism and religious fanaticism.

OLIVER PROTECTOR

Oliver commended the Instrument to Parliament, expecting it to be endorsed with little ado. The Commons, however, were not that compliant. Some MPs wanted to know whether the right of free speech in Parliament would extend to members who questioned the institution of the Protectorate itself. Only four days after the session began, the Instrument, instead of being dutifully approved after a debate, was referred to a committee. Opinion in the committee was divided. Some readily accepted the principle that government should rest in the hands of the Protector and Parliament; others argued that it should be substantially in the hands of Parliament only. Closer parliamentary control over nominations to the Council was also proposed. Oliver, still conciliatory, was prepared to accept changes to the Instrument, or even something that superseded it, provided certain points were inviolable, namely these: government should be in the hands of a single person and Parliament; the Protector would have the authority to prevent a single Parliament prolonging its existence indefinitely; control of the militia should be at least shared between Protector and Parliament; and liberty of conscience would be enjoyed by all except followers of 'popery and prelacy'.[45]

Determined to avoid the effective dictatorship of a single chamber, Oliver addressed the Commons again. In justifying the Instrument he pointed out, rightly, that it was the work of others and not himself, and he denied personal ambition. Most MPs listened favourably, apparently willing to accept the Instrument at least as a basis for discussion; but as the weeks dragged on it became clear that others were determined to amend it appreciably, if not fundamentally. The main points of concern were the size of the army and navy, and Parliament's wish that, in the event of Oliver's death, complete control of the army should pass to Parliament. In short, though Parliament would share control of the army with Oliver so long as he lived, it wanted to ensure its own supremacy thereafter. This was the first step towards making Oliver's successors a constitutional head of state, shorn of the power that control over the army would have guaranteed them. 'I think I may tell you', an observer wrote, in an intercepted letter dated 16 November, 'this Parliament will end without doing anything considerable.' He spoke well; the debates in the Commons rattled the army chiefs, and they lost no time in pledging their loyalty to the unaltered Instrument. This in turn annoyed the Commons; one member complained that the army was involving itself in the business of government 'as if it had been a second House'.[46]

The disagreements exposed the still live rivalry between Parliament and the army, an army that had fought and won Parliament's wars before turning on the same Parliament, barring and driving out members at the point of a sword. More seriously perhaps, the role and authority of a *future* Protector had become uncertain, a factor that risked undermining the fledgling post-monarchical constitution.

Oliver was also concerned when the House passed a vote allowing itself to proscribe heretical sects and 'damnable heresies', if necessary without the Protector's consent. Then Parliament began considering proposals to reduce both the pay of soldiers and the strength of the standing army and navy; this in spite of continuing rumours of subversive Royalist activity, and in spite of Oliver's Western Design, an expeditionary force that had just set sail for the Caribbean to attack Spanish possessions there. Opinion in Parliament then moved slowly towards the view, until now a minority one, that Parliament should exercise control over the army, and only grant supplies for a limited, specific period. Oliver saw instantly what this would mean. If Parliament – really the House of Commons – controlled the army, then the Commons could, if it so wished, keep itself in existence indefinitely, even to the point of assuming absolute power. This was just what Oliver and the officers had suspected the Rump of doing; it would make the Council of State largely irrelevant, and the Protector a mere figurehead. This Oliver could not accept. Five months after the first Protectorate Parliament began Oliver dissolved it, as he was entitled to do under the Instrument.[47]

So the problems of the Protectorate remained unresolved. Republicans and godly radicals were alienated, while Parliament and the army remained suspicious and resentful of each other. Royalists were frozen out and disaffected. Supporters of the Stuarts were not a potent force; in March 1655 a Royalist rising in Wiltshire, led by John Penruddock, was put down by Major-General Desborough with little difficulty. Other plots, small scale and not especially threatening, were uncovered, and a few ring leaders dealt with. Nevertheless, Royalists formed yet another discontented group. Even those who wanted nothing to do with abortive risings, and dreaded another civil war, were unlikely to be won over by a regime that excluded them from government and Parliament, and which required them to worship in secret.

From his troubles with the Commons, Oliver turned to the army, and the rule of the major generals. These officers were appointed in the interest of national security to enforce law and order, to disarm papists and Royalists, and to improve moral standards throughout the country. Each was assigned a group of counties to supervise and control. They had orders to 'encourage and promote godliness and virtue, and discourage and discountenance all profaneness and ungodliness'. They closed brothels and alehouses, punished immorality and swearing, and made sure the Sabbath was faithfully kept. 'Plays and interludes', along with 'horse races, cock fightings, bear baitings, or any unlawful assemblies' likely to be used as a cover for rebellion, were forbidden. They were commanded to punish idlers, but to help the genuinely poor. More fines were threatened, though probably seldom imposed, on Royalists who kept in their houses any priest or chaplain who used the Prayer Book.

The major generals were financed by a decimation tax on Royalists, which was levied even on those who had not taken part in any of the recent disturbances. Each officer was assisted by a team of specially appointed commissioners. Frequently these commissioners turned out to be zealous Puritans, who, unlike some of their neighbours, welcomed the generals enthusiastically, actively supporting the official policy of creating a truly godly nation. The commissioners particularly enjoyed the opportunity to wring the maximum amount of tax possible from known local Royalists, and often they complained that the government's threshold was too low. But the experiment in military rule did nothing to endear Oliver to the people. He is, reported the Venetian ambassador, 'more feared than loved' by the nation, and 'mortally hated' by Royalists.[48]

Soon Oliver was faced with a crisis uncomfortably like the one that had confronted Charles I: how was the increasingly heavy government expenditure to be financed without calling a new Parliament? The costs of keeping a large army and navy were huge, and Oliver had ambitious foreign policy plans. Britain also was at war with Spain, with whom Prince Charles, still trying by all possible means to recover the throne, had made an alliance. Loath to summon another Parliament so soon after his unhappy experience with the last one, Oliver was minded to increase the decimation tax to meet his financial needs. Later, however, he yielded to the advice of others and agreed to call Parliament; but this time all those elected would need an approval certificate from the Council before they could take their seats. The government's suspicions of the loyalties of the new influx of members turned out to be justified. Resentment against the major generals ensured that voters, in large numbers, ignored appeals from Puritan ministers to elect only godly candidates.[49]

In his opening speech to the new Parliament on 17 September 1656, Oliver adopted the tone more of chief pastor than chief magistrate. He commended Psalm 85, especially the tenth verse:'Mercy and truth are met together.' Much more followed in the same vein on the need for mercy, brotherly love and Christian charity. But when the speech was over, many MPs were in for a shock. The Council had carefully examined the list of those who had been elected, and nearly 100 were deemed to be unsuitable: some were Royalist sympathisers, others avowed republicans. Tickets were then issued to those who passed the scrutiny of the Council. All who failed to produce a valid ticket to the soldiers standing guard at the door of the Commons were sent away.[50]

The Commons was aggrieved by the forced exclusions, and in what remained of it a lively debate followed. Some MPs protested that this could be no proper Parliament at all. The House decided to ask the Council why so many had been barred. The Council replied that it had acted in accordance with the requirement in the Instrument, that MPs should be 'persons of integrity, fearing God and of good conversation'. The Commons was not entirely convinced. Nevertheless, after another debate a vote was taken, and the government's supporters won, hardly surprising as those most likely to oppose with any degree of vigour were now on their way home. Still, besides the original 100, a further fifty or sixty MPs left the House in protest. The broadly dependable Parliament that remained then proclaimed its loyalty to Oliver; it declared the justness of the war with Spain, and it passed an act making it treason to plot Oliver's death or to advance the cause of Charles Stuart.[51]

Though the exclusion of the MPs was deeply unpopular in the country, the government had cause for rejoicing when news arrived that Vice-Admiral Stayner had convincingly won a sea battle with Spanish forces off Cadiz. Unfortunately, the plunder he seized was not enough to finance the war, or to solve the government's mounting financial problems. The House, meanwhile, was occupied with unresolved constitutional matters, chiefly the succession. Some wanted Oliver to nominate his successor, to prevent a potentially damaging contest after his death; a few suggested he should be offered the Crown. On both points the army was divided. The Republican Party was naturally opposed, but it did not have the clout of the army; and with most of its leaders excluded from the House, republicans tended to look back to the Rump as the ideal constitutional solution, completely free from army control. The Fifth Monarchists still dreamed of a government of the saints, but their influence was declining.[52]

Away from his problems with parliaments, Oliver Cromwell has enjoyed the reputation of being a remarkably tolerant ruler for his time, particularly regarding the church. There was little state control over the church during the Protectorate. Local commissioners were authorised to supervise local churches, and if necessary, remove unsuitable ministers. The Directory had replaced the Prayer Book, and some parishes worked out for themselves something like a Presbyterian-style system. Independent and Baptist churches were thriving. Oliver was also eager to readmit the Jews to England, partly for their commercial expertise, but also because he was among those who believed in a national conversion of the Jews as a prelude to the end times. Where, Oliver demanded, was that conversion more likely to take place than in England, 'the only place in the world where religion was taught in its full purity'?[53]

But there were limits to this toleration, at least officially. To his Second Protectorate Parliament Oliver stated his special interest: 'men that believe the remission of sins through the blood of Christ and free justification by the blood of Christ, and live upon the grace of God, that those men are … members of Christ, and are to Him the apple of his eye'. Oliver wished freedom of conscience for 'whoever hath this faith, let his form be what it will if he be walking peaceably without the prejudicing of others under another form'.[54]

It reads finely. Except that, under Oliver, the Prayer Book was banned; and nowhere in the English tongue is the 'free justification by the blood of Christ' more eloquently and majestically set forth than in Cranmer's prose. It is clear from the context of Oliver's speeches on the subject of religious liberty, that what he really wanted was freedom for Presbyterians, Baptists, and Independents – freedom, in other words, for all *Puritan* Christians, but not necessarily *all* Christians. The ban on the Prayer Book meant that not only papists and Laudians, but also traditional Elizabethans, were, technically at least, proscribed under the Protectorate.[55]

Edward Fisher was a writer and amateur theologian, and typical of the 'Elizabethan' Protestants who had survived the Civil War. He was neither Laudian nor Puritan, but when compelled to make his choice after the fighting broke out, he rejected rebellion in principle, and supported the king. During the Interregnum, Fisher published *A Christian Caveat* … , which defended Christmas, now officially abolished, and opposed strict Sabbatarianism. Fisher turned the tables on the godly by accusing *them* of superstition for refusing to minister the Sacraments anywhere except in church and on Sunday, and also for their horror of harmless religious customs, like holly and ivy at Christmas, and ringing church bells. Fisher wondered what was so special about a 'toleration' that produced a multiplicity of strange sects while drowning out the Prayer Book. The *Caveat* was a best eller.[56]

Judging by the success of Fisher's work, there must have been a substantial number of traditional Elizabethans still living, so Oliver's exclusion of them must be one of the strangest decisions he ever made. Many of them had little time for Laud; and many sympathised with the Commons in its complaints that Charles had bypassed Parliament, contrary to Tudor and pre-Tudor law and custom. Many fought on the king's side only reluctantly. Nor could they be certain that Prince Charles, should he ever be returned to the throne, would break his promise at Breda and scrap the agreement to impose Presbyterianism, and in its place restore the Elizabethan church, liturgy and the Prayer Book. Fisher and those who eagerly read his book, therefore, were exactly the sort of people that the government, to broaden its base, needed to win round by concessions or inducements.

In practice, non-Puritans of all shades were largely free from persecution, though not from heavy taxation. A semi-underground network of loyal Anglicans ensured that ordinations continued in secret. Foreign observers noted that even Catholics, whatever the letter of the law might be, enjoyed more liberty of worship under Oliver than they had done under Charles I, though the fines were not relaxed. The same indulgence was extended to Prayer Book services, despite another government declaration in November 1655 against it and all clergymen who used it.[57] An indulgence, however, is not the same thing as a lawful right; and consequently even traditional Protestants, who believed as devoutly as anyone in the 'free justification by the blood of Christ', were not *officially* granted full liberty of worship. They were 'tolerated' under Oliver; but not as equals, or as full members of the community. Oliver turned a blind eye to them, but he made little effort to win their hearts and minds, or invite them into the Protectoral fold. It is no wonder they never felt any great love for him, or that his government lacked anything like broad support.

It speaks volumes for the English Revolution that the Prayer Book had become something to be indulged, or tolerated. It is also a tribute to the resilience and enduring appeal of Cranmer's work, that two years after the November declaration, Oliver was advised to examine two old-style clergymen, Mr Gunning and Dr Taylor, and call them to account for the 'frequent meetings of multitudes of people held with them, and cause the Ordinance for taking away the Book of Common Prayer to be enforced'. To official exasperation, many couples on their wedding day made no secret of their preference for the Prayer Book marriage service, some insisting on it.[58] As these people were, presumably, mainly young, it seems clear that the Protectorate was failing to win the allegiance of the rising generation. Making Cranmer's prose forbidden fruit was a bad mistake.

Meanwhile, as Fisher said, the sects were multiplying. Their origins are obscure, and the forms they took quite diverse. Some set aside the authority of Scripture, trusting instead in an 'inner light', or the 'primacy of the inner spirit'. Most wanted to see tithes abolished, along with Christmas and Easter festivities; many had women preachers, and many passionately supported the government's policy for a godly reformation in the country. Modern Quakers are peaceable and devout folk, but some of their early forefathers were far feistier. They made a name for themselves by refusing to doff their hats to social betters, and by interrupting church services. One individual once felt called to walk naked around Smithfield. Contemporary testimonies of groups such as the so-called 'Ranters' include these: 'a man baptised with the Holy Ghost knows all things even as God knows all things'; they 'set up the Light of Nature under the name of Christ in men'; they call men to 'hearken to the voice of Christ within them'. It was also alleged that they were consummate libertines, who 'committed whoredoms commonly', justifying themselves with a novel take on St Paul's words that 'to the pure all things are pure'. Others, more pantheist than Christian, believed that 'God is essentially in every creature'. Frequently the sects claimed to have attained a state of sinless-ness beyond the reach of ordinary believers.[59]

Modern churchgoers may not recognise some of these unconventional sects as Christian in any real sense of the word, and some contemporaries feared that the country might be sliding into apostasy. Oliver's reaction was to show inexhaustible patience. He invited George Fox, the fiery Quaker leader, to meet him, saying hopefully that 'if thou and I were but an hour a day together we should be nearer one to the other'. When a Fifth Monarchist preacher named Simpson told Oliver to his face that he was a traitor to the cause for which they had fought, Oliver merely told him to calm himself. Two of Simpson's brethren, Rogers and Feake, had been locked up for inflamma-tory preaching; but Oliver invited Rogers to meet him, and assured him that he had no wish to act like a tyrant, that he was merely trying his best to keep all godly factions at peace. Thomas Harrison and three fellow officers accused Oliver of having taken 'the crown off from the head of Christ and put it on his own' when he dissolved the Barebone's Parliament. When they were asked to moderate their language and give an assurance to live in peace, they refused. Oliver was then compelled, though reluctantly, to commit them to custody.[60]

The sects had no fear of any earthly power. Even the major generals could occasionally be taken to task for lapses into ungodliness. George Fox once rebuked General Desborough when he came upon him suddenly one day, and found him enjoying a game of bowls. Fox was a man with a wonder-ful way all of his own with the Scriptures. Where, he once demanded of a magistrate, does the Word of God command that hats should be removed? The bench went into a fluster, so Fox, who had prepared well for this, quoted

Daniel 3:21, where Shadrach, Meshach and Abednego were 'bound in their coats, their hosen, and their hats', and cast into the furnace. There, Fox concluded triumphantly, these godly men had kept their hats on all through their trial, and so would he.[61]

James Naylor was a former Independent who had served as a quartermaster in the New Model Army before flirting with the Quakers. He was one of those radicals who denied that the Bible was the Word of God. With his magnetic personality he was able to attract a large following, and when his more adoring disciples likened him to the Messiah, Naylor did little to discourage them. In autumn 1656, after a short spell in prison in Exeter, Naylor staged a parody of Palm Sunday by riding on a donkey into Bristol at the head of a large, ecstatic crowd. The spectacle provoked outrage inside and outside Parliament, with many MPs condemning the tolerance that had been extended to the sects. In defence, Naylor pleaded that he had acted according to a revelation, and he denied ever making Messianic claims for himself.[62]

The House was in no mood to listen to excuses. A few members were minded to treat Naylor as a crank, but most demanded exemplary punishment. The general feeling was that liberty of conscience had been taken to a horrible and ridiculous excess. 'If this be liberty,' said one staunch Puritan man, 'God deliver me from such liberty'. If the Instrument of Government had intended to protect the likes of Naylor, said another, 'I would have burnt it in the fire'. As the law stood, it was not easy to proceed severely against Naylor; nevertheless, the Commons were determined to make an example of him. To do so, MPs claimed that the judicial powers of the House of Lords had transferred automatically to the Commons when the Lords was abolished. So a quick Commons 'trial' was arranged, in which Naylor was denied the right of defence. Some members demanded the death penalty, a motion only narrowly defeated. Instead, Naylor was sentenced to a series of harsh punishments, including whipping, the pillory and branding, to be followed by a spell of hard labour.[63]

Oliver was shocked by Naylor's stunt, but the attitude of the Commons also disturbed him. Not for the first time he feared that Parliament might use its power to crack down not only on eccentrics like Naylor, but also on upstanding Baptists and Independents like him and many in the army. So he wrote to the Commons asking them 'to let us know the grounds and reasons whereupon they have proceeded'.[64]

Oliver had touched on a fine constitutional point. What right had the Commons to pass sentence on Naylor? The existing law was unclear, the prisoner was denied the right of defence, and the claim of the Commons that it had automatically acquired the judicial authority of the defunct Lords was, putting it mildly, questionable. Thus the Naylor affair brought to light two still unresolved problems of the Protectorate. First, there was no check or restraint on the Commons, nothing to stop it doing whatever it liked. Second – where did this leave the Protector, who was bound by oath to defend the lives and liberties of the people? Naylor brought home the uncomfortable fact that the constitution was still not properly sorted out. A satisfactory settlement to replace the old order had still not been reached.

The House was sitting on Christmas Day, 1656, the day Oliver wrote about Naylor, and some members were annoyed that in many parts of the country the day's traditional festivities were merrily kept. 'I could get no rest all night for the preparation of this foolish day's solemnity', grumbled one MP. Then Major-General Desborough introduced a bill that would effectively extend the decimation tax on Royalists in order to pay the costs of the standing army and navy. This was supported by most officers, though opposed by many MPs still fearful of the strength and influence of the army. But Desborough could make a fairly strong case, because during the winter Oliver had been the target of more than one assassination attempt. A plan to blow up Whitehall by Edward Sexby, a former agitator now in league with foreign Royalists, failed dismally when one conspirator panicked and confessed to Oliver personally. This, and rumours of other Royalist risings, and the fact that Charles Stuart was conspiring to invade England with Spanish help, strengthened the case of Desborough and his supporters. On 29 January, however, the bill was rejected by 124 votes to 88. It was a humiliating defeat for the army. The bill's opponents then tried to soften the blow by showing their loyalty to Oliver by voting £400,000 for the Spanish war.[65]

The opponents of the bill were motivated chiefly by fear of military rule and dislike of the major generals. Many were also preoccupied with the succession, even though Oliver still seemed in good health. According to the Instrument, the new Protector would be elected by the Council of State, which meant that, in the fairly foreseeable future, a major general would almost certainly succeed Oliver. For those inside and outside the Commons who distrusted the army, it was a gloomy prospect. It made the old, pre-revolutionary constitutional order seem attractive once more. Consequently, a new constitutional document, that came to be known as the Humble Petition and Advice, was drawn up mainly by the civilians in the Commons. It proposed government by a King, Lords and Commons, in keeping with the historic and well-tried constitution of England. And the king would be Oliver Cromwell, not Charles Stuart. Oliver was reluctant to take the Crown, but his former contempt for the Lords had gone, and he was eager to see it restored. Arguing his case to his officers, he reminded them of the unfortunate James Naylor: 'by the proceedings of this Parliament', he told them, 'you see they stand in need of a check or balancing power, for the case of James Naylor might be your case'.[66]

The army took Oliver's point, and most officers were reconciled to the idea of a reconvened Lords. They were less happy about the restoration of the monarchy. The civilians in the government and the Commons, however, pressed Oliver repeatedly to accept the Crown. They were encouraged when he seemed amenable to their main argument, that the monarchy was the form of government that the English people recognised, empathised with and instinctively understood. But eventually, after a great deal of soul-searching, he declined. He was guided by the same force that had always guided him when a momentous decision was required – Providence, or his interpretation of it. God, he believed, had 'laid this title aside … not only to strike at the family but at the name'. Not just the Stuarts, but the very institution of monarchy itself was rejected. God had 'not only dealt so with the persons and the family, but He hath blasted the title'. The Commons urged him to reconsider, and at one point it appeared as though he would accept after all. The final refusal came on 8 May, when he pleaded in conscience, that 'I cannot undertake this government with that title of king'.[67]

It was agreed, therefore, that Oliver would govern according to the Humble Petition and Advice, though as Lord Protector and not as King Oliver. The Petition had now replaced the Instrument as the country's main constitutional document. It was somewhat more legitimate in the sense that it was substantially the work of Parliament, whereas the Instrument was entirely the work of the army. This Parliament, however, with over 100 elected members arbitrarily excluded, was hardly a properly representative national assembly; so the new Protectorate, to quote Charles Firth, was 'just as much a stop gap as the old', and little more than a 'half way house to a monarchy'.[68]

Nevertheless, the political climate was encouraging for the government in the spring and summer of 1657. In May great rejoicing followed the news of Admiral Blake's victory over the Spanish fleet at Santa Cruz. Despite occasional rumours of plots, the regime seemed stronger than ever when, in June, Oliver was confirmed for the second time as Lord Protector, and Parliament was adjourned, amicably this time. Oliver was entrusted with choosing the men who would sit in the re-formed House of Lords; and in this he had a free hand because the Commons had obligingly voted not to insist on its right to approve appointments. Oliver spent much of November drawing up a list of suitable names. A sign of the placatory mood of the times was the wedding of Oliver's daughter Mary to Thomas Lord Falconbridge that same month, a service reportedly performed according to the Prayer Book rite. Oliver seemed genuinely to like his newest son-in-law, and despite his Royalist-Anglican connections, Falconbridge was one of those nominated to the new Lords.[69]

The full list of sixty-three was completed by 10 December. Besides nobility and the sons of noblemen, it included seventeen officers and a number of gentry. Oliver had tried to make the list representative of those who broadly supported the government; but this, unfortunately, left significant sections of the country, including Royalists and republicans, largely excluded and as disaffected as ever. The list ran into trouble almost straight away, and not only with the regime's usual opponents. Of seven English peers, only two obeyed the summons to attend. One who declined was Lord Saye, a man of traditional values, whose loyalties lay with the Lords of old, 'the peers of England, and their power and privileges in the House of Lords'; Saye had no time for a House 'chosen at the pleasure of him that hath taken power into his hands to do what he will'. Several members of the Commons had been hoping for a place in the new Lords, and inevitably many were disappointed. An opposition block of disgruntled MPs in the Commons now looked likely.[70]

Parliament, which had adjourned in June, reassembled in January 1658. When about thirty MPs from the Commons had been moved to the Lords, a number of republicans, originally excluded by the Council, were readmitted to the Commons after taking the oath required by the Humble Petition and Advice. Almost immediately the temperature rose, beginning with a dispute over what the new 'Lords' ought to be called. Some were content with the familiar title 'Lords'; some preferred the 'Other House', as in the Petition. This developed into a discussion about the rights and extent of the authority of the new Lords; now some MPs seized the opportunity to let off steam about the evils of the *old* Lords.[71]

Once more Oliver tried conciliation, in a speech to both Houses on 25 January 1658. Look across the Channel, he appealed, to the threat from the papacy, the House of Austria and Spain, all supporters of Charles Stuart. Against these dangers England needs a strong army and navy for her defence. Where necessary, and Oliver was sure it would be necessary, England must intervene in Europe in the interests of religion and commerce. At home all kinds of factions and sects strove for the upper hand, while the 'malignant episcopal party' was only waiting for the chance to rise again. Oliver stoutly defended the latest constitutional settlement – 'I mean the two Houses of Parliament and myself' – and he called for unity and concord to prevail.[72]

The speech made little impact. Few seemed roused by Oliver's grand overseas, imperial designs. The Commons carried on wrangling about the most suitable name for the Lords, and what its exact powers ought to be. In the political vacuum, a curious alliance began to form, comprising republicans inside and outside the Commons, Fifth Monarchists, dissatisfied officers and certain sects. A petition was drawn up, rehearsing all the evils of the old king and the old Lords, and implying that the quasi-monarchical Protectorate was little better. The petition called for supreme power to belong to Parliament (effectively the Commons). In no time fifty copies were printed, and many thousands of signatures obtained. The plan was to hand the petition to the Commons on 4 February, addressed to the 'Parliament of the Commonwealth of England', as if the Lords had no right to exist. This new movement was essentially a call to restore the republic, and according to rumour it had much support in the army. While this potentially seditious pressure group was gathering strength at home, Charles Stuart was mustering an army in Flanders. The government received intelligence that Royalists were stirring in Ireland, and waiting anticipatively for developments in England.

Oliver's response showed that his renowned flair for bold and decisive action had not abated with age. Acting on impulse as he so often did, and without consulting the Council, he set off for the House on 4 February to pre-empt the delivery of the petition. When General Fleetwood implored him to 'consider well' what he intended to do, Oliver rounded on him and called him a 'milk sop'; he vowed that 'by the living God I will dissolve this House'.[73]

Oliver then addressed the Lords and the Commons combined. As in his previous speech, he defended the restoration of the Lords, and the settlement based on the Humble Petition; in short, the Protector and two Houses. But 'a new business' had been brewing, encouraged by restless spirits in the Commons. Oliver did not blame the Lords, 'or whatever you will call them'; the blame lay in the Commons, where you have 'disquieted yourselves' and the nation, by stirring up trouble and threatening the stability of England, by 'playing of the King of Scots his game'. Nothing but 'blood and confusion' would result from such schemes; so 'if this be the effect of your sitting … I think it high time that an end be put to your sitting'. Oliver sent them away, calling on God to 'be judge between you and me'.[74]

Soon after the dissolution, Oliver cashiered six republican officers. Most of the rest quickly declared their support. The republican threat had been dealt with resolutely. The Royalist threat, such as it was, had also crumbled: an English naval force neutralised the danger from Flanders, and at home a Royalist plot was uncovered. That summer Oliver enjoyed one of his most impressive military gains abroad when an Anglo-French force defeated the Spanish at the battle of the Dunes, and Dunkirk was surrendered to English control.[75]

But Dunkirk would be a mixed blessing for Britain. On the one hand, it gave Oliver's impressive navy a base from which it could strike at any invading flotilla. It also gave him, as one of his officers enthusiastically put it, 'a sally port by which His Highness may advantageously sally forth upon his enemies'. At £70,000 a year, however, it proved burdensomely expensive to garrison. Finance was now Oliver's greatest worry, as intractable as his troubles with Parliament. His government was nearly bankrupt, and the pay of his soldiers badly in arrears. He had tried to meet the enormous costs of his army and navy by the sale of lands that had belonged to the Crown and the redundant bishops, and by swinging taxes on property, mainly of Royalists. Attempts to raise more revenue by increasing customs charges, and higher taxes on ale and beer, were predictably deeply unpopular. Overseas gains like Jamaica and Dunkirk resulted in more expenditure than income, and English trade suffered from the Spanish war. As Protector, Oliver had inherited a debt of £700,000 from the republic; this figure had now reached nearly two million, and it was still rising.[76]

But there was nothing Oliver could do about the crisis. By now his strength was ebbing away. His condition worsened critically after the death in August of his beloved daughter, Elizabeth. George Fox was shocked at his pallid appearance when he saw him one day, riding at the head of his guards – 'I saw and felt a waft of death go forth against him; and when I came to him he looked like a dead man'. Oliver died on 3 September 1658, shortly after naming his eldest son Richard as his successor.[77]

THE END OF GODLY RULE

There are no full stops in history, and unless the subject of a book is a biography, it is not always easy to select an entirely satisfactory starting and finishing point. The Protectorate survived two uncertain years before its demise, the Restoration of the monarchy, the victorious Cavalier Parliament, and the return of bishops to their palaces and lands. The Restoration, however, did not turn out to be the ideal 'solution' to the troubles of previous years, and tensions in church and state remained unresolved. But that is a separate subject. The theme of this work is the contrast between the pragmatic, constitutional Reformation begun by the first Cromwell, and the godly Revolution and rule of the second.

This book is not reviving the old 'long high road to Civil War' argument; it simply seeks to trace the cause of the disputes of the late 1630s to their roots.

Scarcely had the Reformation begun when a revolutionary movement began with it, running alongside it, rivalling it, snapping at its heels. Mainly because of men like Thomas Müntzer, so-called 'magisterial reformers' like Luther increasingly looked to the state to protect the Reformation from radicalism; and this, inevitably, led them to forge closer ties with the princes than they had intended or desired at the outset. This was the evangelical mainstream that Thomas Cromwell commended to King Henry, and tried to get established in England. The task was carried on by Thomas Cranmer in the reign of Edward, though in matters of doctrine the Edwardian church was closer to Zürich and Geneva than to Wittenberg. Nevertheless, following Zwingli's misfortune at Kappel, rejection of war for the Gospel's sake, rejection of rebellion, deference to princes, even cooperation with princes, had become a Protestant consensus. Obedience to divinely ordained princes as an article of faith passed its severest test in Mary's reign.

By the time of Elizabeth's accession, the first generation reformers had either passed away or were living out their final years (except Henry Bullinger, who lived on till 1575, dying aged seventy-one). A new generation was rising to the fore, some of whom had not known the spiritual struggles of their predecessors, who had made the often difficult transition from the old faith to the new. The new men were unhappy with the Elizabethan Settlement because it did not seem thorough enough; they longed to raise the level of godliness everywhere, and to see the English church swept systematically clean of all traces of its popish past. They were, perhaps, a little less willing than some of their spiritual fathers and tutors to bear with imperfections. More ominous from the government's viewpoint was the growth of militancy in some Protestant quarters, one result of persecution in France, the Netherlands and Mary's England. The principle of the divine right of kings was no longer quite as absolute as it had been. In the times of Cromwell and Cranmer the subject, at least the good Protestant subject, was expected to submit to the ordained prince, and if necessary to suffer for doing so, but never to resort to organised resistance. This view was now being modified: with an ungodly or idolatrous prince, there *was* a right of resistance, and according to some, even the duty of it. From this point onwards a revolution, though not inevitable, was always a possibility. Elizabeth was never in any personal danger from supporters of the new thinking, but she saw in this development a threat to civil order, stability and the divinely ordained rule of princes.

The question of how a Christian society should deal with a tyrant or a bad ruler was not, of course, new to the Reformation; it had exercised the minds of patristic and medieval writers long before Luther.[78] This book, however, is about Protestant thought between the two Cromwells. And besides, the Reformation had changed the nature of the issue: hitherto it had been the Christian's response to a tyrannical ruler; now it was to an ungodly one. The issue had become more subjective. Mary Tudor was no tyrant to English Catholics.

Meanwhile, church government turned out to be an unexpectedly thorny problem. Up to and including the Elizabethan Settlement, almost all English reformers followed Luther in this respect: church government was not a fundamental doctrinal point, and there was no binding divine command for one particular form. The existing episcopal organisation of the church was therefore acceptable, and consequently it did not go the way of the Mass, transubstantiation or clerical celibacy. This consensus broke down in the days of Beza and his English supporters in the 1570s. The Presbyterian system, it was argued, should be put into practice, not because it was more efficient or suitable, but because it had Scriptural warrant. A reaction against Presbyterianism specifically, and Puritanism generally, was led by men like Whitgift and Hooker, before being carried on to new levels by the Laudians.

According to them, episcopacy, not Presbyterianism, was a divine law. By the time of Charles I, there were two parties each advocating a different form of church government, and each side was claiming that it had a divine mandate. Laud also required more ceremonial in the church, when the Puritans were convinced that there was far too much of it already. Puritans feared that clandestine moves were under way to realign the English church with Rome. These may have been largely misplaced; but they were nonetheless understandable, because Laud was determined to reintroduce and absorb into the Church of England rites and traditions which, in the watchful eyes of the godly, were provocatively 'popish'.

Church government is not a subject likely to fire the imagination of modern minds. In fact, rarely in church history has it caused anything like as much controversy as it did in the late sixteenth and early seventeenth century. The minds of the church fathers, the medievalists and the first generation of reformers were, on the whole, occupied by more spiritual, theological themes. However, once church government was made an article of faith, and not just a largely practical matter, it was bound to take on scarcely less significance than justification, transubstantiation, clerical celibacy and the Mass. Those who disagree on these subjects seldom commune together now in the twenty-first century, never mind the seventeenth. The same point applies to images in churches, liturgy, sacred music and art, and much other ceremonial. If these things are optional, there is no problem: churches in different places are free to choose their own forms of worship and remain in communion with each other; and even those who dislike parts of the liturgy may put up with it for the sake of peace and quiet, with a clear conscience. If, however, certain rites must or must not be done, as if in obedience to a divine command, then this issue, too, is raised to the level of an article of faith; and if disagreements arise, church unity is threatened. The more divine laws men make, the greater the likelihood of discord and disunity. So the only realistic solution to the problems of the church in the times of the early Stuarts was something like the later Toleration Act of 1689. But that was neither practicable nor even barely thinkable in the 1630s.

The Puritan party then appeared to offer a ray of hope. The Long Parliament, though opposed to bishops by divine law, did not seem determinedly set on a Presbyterian system, and might have accepted a reformed episcopacy substantially slimmed down, working with lay commissioners, perhaps more subject to Parliamentary monitoring than royal patronage. But a reformed episcopacy was wholly unacceptable to King Charles. He saw it as a veiled attack on his divine right and Royal Supremacy, which would undermine the very principle of episcopacy, and open the door to Presbyterianism. The controversy, therefore, remained largely unaltered, and the king was too firmly allied with Laud to become an arbitrator. Yet another form of church government was introduced by the rise of Independency, though Independents and Presbyterians, along with Baptists and others, could make common godly cause against Laud.

Yet not even the most passionate Puritan or the most devoted episcopalian could argue that church government was a subject on which the eternal salvation of the soul depended, and this must account for the widespread reluctance to fight over it. Just as widespread was the feeling that the king and Parliament ought to be able to come to terms and resolve their constitutional differences. It is difficult to gauge public opinion entirely satisfactorily on this point; but it may be safe to say that whereas most people agreed in principle that the king should raise money through Parliament, and not by extra-Parliamentary means, most people also doubted whether it was an issue worth a bloody conflagration: hence the many neutrality pacts. During this 'uncivil war', recorded a Midlands vicar in his diary, 'I lived well because I lay low'.[79] Countless others tried to do the same. The war was fought, carried on, and eventually won, because there were enough men, most of them in the New Model Army, who despised the idea of laying low, who disdained the frame of mind of the Midlands vicar.

In the reigns of the two Stuarts, these constitutional issues concerning the Crown and Parliament were running alongside and exacerbating the quarrels in the church. Apart from the Royal Supremacy legislation, little has been said in this book about Tudor parliaments; partly because other scholars have already covered the subject, and partly because no really dangerous crisis occurred in them. As another has noted, Elizabeth's long and costly war with Spain was not only carried on with the support of the nation, but also financed for the most part by Parliament.[80] This is not to suggest that everything was always blissfully harmonious under the Tudors; nevertheless, problems were containable and invariably resolvable. Then came the change of dynasty, and with the death of Robert Cecil in 1612, the departure of the last outstanding Tudor minister. Relations between the Crown and Parliament deteriorated noticeably under James, and alarmingly under Charles. Attempts to bypass Parliament and rule without it offended not only sitting MPs, but many in the country as well.

Under the Tudors, as noted on p. 53, the prestige of the monarchy was raised higher than ever before; but not at the expense of Parliament. The role and prestige of Parliament also rose, because it was required to enact the momentous Supremacy legislation. This dual elevation of Crown and Parliament was a unique Tudor achievement, and especially that of the Tudor Cromwell. Witnesses spoke of Parliament's dignity and authority as 'absolute', and how it 'bindeth all manner of persons'.[81] Professor Elton has also traced how, during the days of Thomas Cromwell, the concept of the Crown *and* Parliament gradually turned into that of the Crown *in* Parliament, albeit with the king as the 'chief and principal part of the Parliament'.[82] Under Charles, even before the Civil War actually broke out, this had almost become the Crown *versus* Parliament. The problem went deeper than tonnage and pound-age or Ship Money. Parliament feared the erosion of its historic rights and liberties. The king seemed to have little respect for Parliament; he seemed to be treating it no longer as an integral part of the constitution, but as an irritant, a potentially seditious nuisance.

Occasionally in books on the Revolution the expression England's 'wars of religion' appears. It has not yet passed into common usage, which is understandable. Most 'religious' people – those who believed in God, went to church and broadly accepted the Christian faith preached to them – did not want to fight, so it does seem faintly bizarre to call the Civil War a religious conflict. Nevertheless, the crisis over church government – that contest for, effectively, the control of the national church – and the unorthodox use of the Old Testament, and the resurgence of chiliasm, were all powerful factors. Despite this, the parallel political controversy was probably more dangerous to the peace of the realm. Even if all had been quiet in the church, the struggle between the liberties of Parliament and the royal prerogative was likely to reach breaking point before long.

It has been said by others that conflict was not inevitable during the reign of Charles, even as late as the days of the Long Parliament. This may be so; but there is a difference between the inevitability of conflict, and the danger of conflict. It is not absolutely inevitable that a drunk driver will crash his car; nevertheless, the likelihood of a crash is high, the warning signs are there, and the cause of the crash when it happens is plain enough. So it was in Stuart Britain in the late 1630s and early 1640s, when no resolution to fundamental problems in church and state appeared in view. There may have been periods of quiet; but as Robert Cecil warned James when he feared that the king was despising Parliament, 'the storm comes before it breaks'.[83] There was also the occasional olive branch, as when the Puritans seemed willing to accept limited episcopacy. Charles himself appeared to yield to the Commons on Ship Money and the Triennial Act, though this was probably just a stalling tactic that did not come from the heart. In the main, however, the parties remained entrenched in rigidly opposing positions. There was not even the threat of a foreign invasion to unite them. Only outstanding statesmanship that commanded the respect of all sides could have avoided serious trouble. Unfortunately, Charles was unlikely to be able to provide it. Having sided with Laud against the godly, having angered and alienated the Commons, Charles was, as we say, part of the problem, not the solution.

These were the principal underlying causes, and as in most revolutions, events soon gathered an ugly momentum of their own as the country slid into war. Crucial factors include Charles's attempt to impose the Prayer Book on his Scottish subjects, his abortive arrest of the five most outspoken MPs, the rebellion in Ireland, and the rise of chiliasm that fuelled the mood of militancy among the king's more radical opponents. But for the king's efforts to buy time in the hope of winning support from abroad, and a common fear of war, the fighting might have started earlier than it did.

Though the Great Civil War overthrew the existing order, the victors struggled and ultimately failed to establish a lasting new one. One constitutional experiment after another had to be abandoned. The new rulers were able to secure outward compliance and sullen acceptance, but neither the republic nor the Protectorate had anything like broad popular support. This failure ensured that the Restoration was the only acceptable solution, even for those who had once opposed the policies of Charles I and his government. There were many who had hoped to see church and state reformed for the better; only a few wanted a revolution, regicide, and the rule of the saints.

To borrow and slightly adapt S.R. Gardiner: Ten years of Laud drove thousands of Englishmen into the parliamentary ranks; where, some reluctantly, others eagerly, they took up arms against the king. Ten years of godly rule drove them back again.[84]

In the 1530s, Thomas Cromwell was the minister chiefly entrusted with the all-important Royal Supremacy legislation. With the sole exception of Henry, he was the most powerful man in England. Oliver in the 1650s, though never an absolute dictator, and maybe not even a despot in the manner of Henry, was, in Milton's words, 'our chief of men'.

Unlike Thomas, Oliver was never the king's servant, so he had more freedom of action and authority to carry out his plans. Nevertheless, each Cromwell was the driving force when huge transformations were made to church and state. Yet neither man came from noble stock or the ruling class. Thomas was a layman of obscure and humble birth, raised by the king to the foremost place in the Council as Principal Secretary and Vice-Gerent; he was the chief reformer at the time of the greatest spiritual upheaval that Western Christendom has ever known. Oliver was a plain country gentleman who never fired a shot in anger before the age of forty; yet within a mere ten years he had conquered England, Scotland and Ireland, staking his place in England's military hall of fame as one of the greatest military commanders in the nation's history.

Both Cromwells were controversial men, arousing great admiration and deep hostility, though fair-minded opponents paid each man ungrudging tributes. Music appealed to them both, though Oliver did not approve of sacred art or music; and neither did he collect works of art or read the humanities as Thomas did, and he did not have Thomas's gift for languages. Nevertheless, both had the honour of being eulogised by the finest poets of their times, Thomas Wyatt and John Milton respectively. Each has been dubbed a tyrant, and accused of all kinds of evils – hypocrisy, corruption, blood guiltiness, ambition, ruthlessness, deception, and more. It has been said of Thomas Cromwell that he created something like a modern police state, while Oliver's more hysterical enemies dreamed up new words for him, like 'tyranipocrit'.[2] Such are the ravings of the ignorant, the wearisomely partisan or the plain stupid. Tudor justice could be tough, and the mid-1600s were turbulent times, but there was nothing remotely akin to a Reign of Terror in either period. Oliver was one of the most merciful revolutionaries ever; he may have taxed the Royalists heavily and shut them out of government, but there were no mass executions, gulags or concentration camps. A fool's reproach is a kingly title, which both Cromwells are proud to bear.

Each of them sought to reform the church of his day, because each was convinced that his king was wrong on essential aspects of the Christian faith. In this dilemma, Thomas did what he could, and thanks to an abundance of wit and guile he could do a great deal, and he went to the very limits of what was allowable under Henry. But further than this he would not go. Like Cranmer under Mary, Cromwell under Henry finally yielded and faced the consequences, each man trusting in the God he worshipped to put wrongs to right in His own time and His own way. Oliver did not do this; he and his revolutionary allies had to take matters into their own hands. Oliver fought, parleyed, negotiated, and was prepared to be reasonable; but when agreement proved unreachable, he returned to the battlefield, before finally resolving on the king's death. Like Zwingli a century earlier, Oliver took the sword.

So what were the consequences and what are the legacies of the two Cromwells?

It was chiefly due to Thomas Cromwell that the principal early Protestant statements – the Augsburg Confession, the *Apology* and Melanchthon's *Loci Communes* – were introduced into England, then translated and circulated throughout the land. Because there is little substantial difference between these writings and the Thirty-Nine Articles, still the foundation documents of the Church of England whatever glosses may be put on them, this makes Cromwell as much a founder of the future Protestant England as Cranmer and Elizabeth: he planted, they gave the increase. The increase did not come immediately; it rarely does. Few could have foreseen it in 1540 when Cromwell died and evangelical hopes seemed to be dashed. Nevertheless, its coming was not long delayed. Less than a generation after Cromwell's passing, Elizabeth was crowned queen, and a Protestant Settlement established that has lasted to the present day and spread through nearly all the world. Historically speaking, therefore, Thomas Cromwell as a reformer of the church was a huge success, far more so than he could have imagined in his lifetime.

As for Oliver, in his cherished aim of a national Puritan church and a society conformed to godliness, he failed. The Restoration accorded Oliver's chief enemies – Charles I and Laud – the status of martyrs, and the divine authority of both bishops and the monarchy became an integral part of the Church of England, which began to edge inexorably away from orthodox Calvinism. According to Dr Robert South in 1661, the Church of England 'glories in nothing more than she is the truest friend of kings and kingly government, of any other church in the world'; and 'they were the same hands that took the crown from the king's head and the mitre from the bishops'. Besides their mitres, all the lands that had been taken from the bishops were shamefacedly handed back to them, with barely a murmur of protest from landowners. Presbyterians as well as Baptists and Independents were now classed as Dissenters. Hundreds of godly clergymen and their lay supporters, who bore no culpability for the death of the late king, were deprived and forced to eke out a living as best they could. No one who did not take the Anglican Holy Communion was allowed by law to hold public office, a restriction that remained in force until the nineteenth century.[3]

The anniversary of the death of King Charles I – 30 January – was faithfully observed in parishes, cathedrals, schools and chapels as a day of fasting and prayer for 150 years after the Restoration. Anglican loyalists had begun this tradition during the Interregnum, some secretly, though others had risked appearing on that day in mourning dress in public. Charles was remembered as the suffering king. Charles, the man of blood according to Oliver and the regicides, was transformed into the Christ-like innocent, the martyred sovereign who, in the words of devoted followers, was 'enabled so cheerfully to follow the steps of his blessed Master and Saviour'.[4] The victorious episcopalians then turned the tables on the defeated saints with a vengeance by invoking the book of Revelation in support of the restored monarchy. According to the *Key of Prophecy,* published in 1660, the first four seals of Chapter 6 ended with John Huss, the fifth lasted from Huss to Mary; then the dreadful sixth seal, with its earthquake and convulsions in the heavens, was the dark era of Puritanism and radicalism, oppressing the nation until the blessed dawn of the Restoration. The persecuting dragon was the infernal amalgam of Puritans, Independents and all who had waged war against the king. Oliver Cromwell, not the pope, was the Antichrist; the two slain witnesses were Charles and Laud. Many other tracts followed in a similar vein.[5]

Besides restoring the king to his throne and the bishops to their palaces, the Restoration reopened theatres and taverns, and reintroduced maypoles, cock-fighting, public games, Christmas festivities, and other assorted activities proscribed or disapproved of under the Interregnum. No one symbolised the collapse of the Puritan republic more than the new king, arguably the most notorious philanderer and lover of pleasure ever to sit on the throne of England. In words that would bring tears to the eyes of godly preachers, the 'merry monarch' was once overheard grumbling about the 'disease of sermons', and giving thanks that sleep 'is a great ease to those who are bound to hear them'.[6]

So the godly revolution was utterly undone. The vanquished of the Civil War were now the victors. Nor was this reversal a temporary one, like the reign of Mary Tudor had been to the reforms of Thomas Cromwell and Cranmer. From the Restoration onwards the national church, though never entirely the church that Laud would have made it, bore more of the traits of Charles and Laud than of Oliver and the godly. Even the liberty of worship granted to Protestant Dissenters (mainly Puritans) under the Toleration Act of 1689 was not achieved until thirty years after Oliver passed away; and the principal *raison d'être* of this act was not to provide a memorial to the achievements of Oliver, but the fact that the new king of Britain was a Dutch Calvinist, William of Orange. Nor was this act quite the magnanimous reconciliation that its title suggests. Contemporaries called it an 'indulgence', because Puritan Non-conformists were tolerated in the sense that they were exempt from a list of penalties still legally in force.[7] This was, ironically, much the same kind of 'indulgence' that Oliver had shown to Anglicans and their Prayer Book services during the Interregnum.

Away from the church and in the political sphere, the paramount Tudor constitutional legacy was the growth of the concept of the Crown *in* Parliament – King, Lords and Commons – and the supremacy of statute. On this foundation, to quote Elton, the modern state rests.[8] No one is suggesting that Henry VIII and Thomas Cromwell invented this from nothing; the point is not the origin of it, but the development of it in their day, and the added dynamic they injected into it. The modern state is also obviously different in the sense that the roles and the practical authority of each component part has altered: the power of the Lords is not what it was; a party system of government and official opposition has emerged, the Crown does not veto bills, and so on. The future of the Lords is also often hotly debated, though it is a tribute to the durability of the Upper House that reforms invariably prove easier to talk about than put into practice. Much has indeed changed, and coming years will no doubt see many more changes. However, to adapt a thought of George Orwell, a child changes out of recognition when it becomes an adult – yet remains the same living being.[9] So it is with the Crown and Parliament – it is the same constitutional edifice as it was 500 years ago. It has greatly adapted over the centuries, but not into something unrecognisably different.

It was wounded near to death, though not quite to death, at the end of the Civil War. The conquerors could find nothing to replace it. All Oliver's experiments failed; one after another they had to be discarded. The monarchy and the Lords were abolished, and the Commons purged by the army. What remained of this Commons, the Rump, was dissolved by soldiers. Then the army nominated a single chamber, which was persuaded to give itself up barely six months later. Its replacement was the Instrument: government by the Protector and Parliament this time, though really only half of Parliament – the Commons on its own; and because Royalists and other undesirables were debarred, it was not even a properly representative Commons. This did not last either, and before long Oliver restored a rehashed Lords. After much soul-searching, he declined the offer of the Crown, despite hinting that he might accept. As one recent authority of the Stuart age has put it, the various forms of government between the death of Charles I and the Restoration were not experiments, but a 'succession of expedients, each rather hastily cobbled up to fill a hiatus in legitimate government or to avert a threatened breakdown of it'.[10] Oliver was not the first soldier of renown to find the art of government more frustratingly difficult than captaining armies in the field.

John Milton hailed Oliver's 'faith and matchless fortitude'; but a poet of a later age and different temperament admired him for other motives:

> Sylla was the first of victors; but our own
> The sagest of usurpers, Cromwell; he
> Too swept off senates while he hewed the throne
> Down to a block – immortal rebel![11]

Oliver the rebel! And for no other reason could this godly Puritan fire the imagination of an irreligious romantic libertine like Byron. Still, the poet wrote well. None of Oliver's problems with his Parliaments can deny him greatness on the battlefield; but his was a destructive greatness, like a storm or a tidal wave that sweeps away everything in its path, good or bad, leaving in its trail a mass of rubble and debris. Then the rebuilding must begin; but those who won the war were destroyers, not builders. The reforms of the Tudor Cromwell have survived for centuries, but during the Interregnum nothing really survivable was ever done at all.

Immortal he may be, but Oliver and his allies could not make their godly crusade a national one or an enduring one. Gardiner notes the sheer impossibility of a successful, durable settlement after the death of the king. Oliver's unsolvable dilemma was that so long as the army remained the dominant force in the land, no settlement was practicable without it, which meant that no satisfactory constitutional foundation commanding genuine popular support was likely to be laid.[12] Drawing the sword may sound more heroic than dignified acquiescence – Byron certainly thought so – but the aftermath brings the reckoning; and what was overthrown in 1649 was too strong, too embedded in English national life and consciousness to *remain* overthrown, unless something could be found to take its place that would win the consent of the nation as a whole. Tragically for Oliver, that was not so. He tried hard, desperately hard, and after a violent upheaval only a figure of outstanding ability could prevent disintegration into chaos and anarchy. To keep the Revolution ship afloat for as long as he did was no mean feat; but it was the 'achievement' of a great man fighting, and ultimately failing, in too flawed a cause.

Yet it is often claimed that Oliver, because he once said he favoured a settlement 'somewhat with monarchical power in it', was an early advocate of the constitutional monarchy.[13]

This argument may puzzle those who struggle to see how a man who would 'cut off the king's head with the crown on it', abolish the Lords, purge the Commons with armed musketeers, dissolve one Parliament after another, refuse the Crown when offered it because God Himself had 'blasted the title' – how such a man can, in any sense at all, be a harbinger of the constitutional monarchy. Besides, Oliver is legendary for changing his mind, and his comment (in the previous paragraph) has to be balanced with another that he made to the republican Edmund Ludlow, sometime in January 1648. Oliver,

says Ludlow, admitted he was convinced of the 'desirableness' of a republic, 'but not the feasibleness'. Oliver may have been just trying to conciliate
Ludlow; but it is hardly the language of a consistently principled constitutional monarchist.[14]

Nor is Oliver's record with his Parliaments an encouraging one. In vain
he sought, time and time again, to secure a consensus even within the godly
party itself. He excluded Cavaliers and Royalists from his Parliaments, which
meant that although a few managed to evade the military guardians of the
constitution and creep in, the Parliaments Oliver dissolved in righteous
anger were composed mostly of Puritans of various shades, usually selected
or approved by the government. Yet despite all the official vetting, relations
between Oliver and the Commons were constructive only in short spells.
By contrast, the first Cromwell, in a mere three years, successfully steered
the complex Supremacy legislation through both Houses, even though a lot
less than half of their members were Lutherans like himself. Whereas Thomas
Cromwell worked with Parliament almost as if his Maker had designed him
to operate that way, Oliver could barely work with it at all. Oliver was a
Parliamentary statesman chiefly in the sense that he kept persevering with
Parliament and trying his best with it, rather like a man gamely trying to sal-
vage something from an ill-matched marriage. It is significant that for one of
his most cherished aims – the creation of a godly society – he turned to the
army and the rule of the major generals.

It is also very questionable whether Parliament emerged from the
Revolution stronger and more independent than it had been before. Its
immediate history after the Restoration suggests that it did not.

The Cavalier Parliament lost little time in passing the Militia Act of 1661,
which restored to the Crown supreme control of the armed forces, as if settling the debates of the 1640s in the Crown's favour. Then one of Parliament's
constitutional victories over Charles I, the Triennial Act, was repealed in 1664
at the request of his son. One of this act's provisions was that Parliament must
be allowed to sit for at least fifty days before it could be dissolved; but the
Parliament of 1681 lasted only eight days before Charles II put an end to
it. In fact, despite Oliver's fits and starts with his Parliaments, that body still
managed to meet together more often in the 1650s than in the 1680s. And
after all the campaigning for Parliamentary liberties in the early Stuart age, it
was, ironically, Parliament itself, now vindictively pro-Royalist and pro-epis-
copalian, that restored the bishops, confirmed royal prerogatives, and passed a
glut of laws to rigorously penalise dissent. In David Ogg's judgement, Charles
II 'brought English kingship to its highest point of power', until his inept
brother threw it all away.[15]

Against this it needs to be noted that pressure from the Commons did
persuade Charles II to revoke his Declaration of Indulgence and also to pass

the Test Act, so Parliament was by no means a walkover.[16] This is a complex subject; but at least it can be said with confidence that the Revolution did not establish either Parliamentary ascendancy over the Crown, or the constitutional monarchy as it is understood today. Moreover, expansion in trade and increased prosperity, and the higher revenues from Customs and Excise in Charles II's later years, enabled him to become less dependent on Parliamentary grant. It was perhaps fortunate for him and the peace of the realm that the Cavalier Parliament in 1660, in the heady days of the Restoration, had granted Charles Customs and Excise for life: this meant that, when he used them liberally, he could never be accused of seeking to raise money without Parliament's agreement.[17] This way the Commons had gifted the king with a golden opportunity to be free of it to a degree that his father would have envied, and which Charles II came increasingly to rely on. It was also in the latter part of this reign that fears of popery and royal absolutism, which the Revolution was supposed to end forever, revived once more. They may have been exaggerated, but Charles's parliaments failed to persuade him to alter the succession laws and prevent his Catholic brother James becoming king. Revolutionary ideals were so thoroughly suppressed that sermons on non-resistance and obedience to princes prevailed even when James ascended the throne; and the Protestant succession was preserved thanks chiefly to the peaceful invasion of William of Orange, and James's obliging but largely unforced flight from England.

Sometime in the summer of 1647, when the king was in the army's keeping, Oliver was asked about his aims and his vision for the nation. He replied that 'no one rises so high as he who knows not whither he is going'.[18] This is true, and maybe profound. But it could also be one of Oliver's problems as a statesman.

By his own admission, Oliver was unsure where he was heading, which may be the reason why his policies frequently appear unstructured and make-shift. He preferred following wherever he sensed Providence leading him. Once he grasped the will of Providence he could act with irresistible force; nevertheless, the moment of decision was often a long time coming, mainly because the ways of Providence can be highly debateable, often baffling and invariably uncertain, reducing even a man of Oliver's vigour to indecisiveness. He floated the idea of 'taking it upon himself to be king' to Whitelocke. Then when offered the Crown under the Instrument of Government, he refused it. Later, offered it again, he was inclined to accept; then he changed his mind once more and turned it down. In between he summoned and dissolved a succession of Parliaments, and his high expectations of each new assembly were quickly abandoned. He was forever trying things out, sometimes to move with events, sometimes to control them; but never arriving on settled ground.

Because no one can see into the future, no one can say for certain that he knows exactly where he is going. Nevertheless, it is still possible to have clear, definable aims, as Thomas Cromwell did. He established the Royal Supremacy in church and state at the expense of Rome; he tried to persuade the king to accept the Augsburg Confession, and when he could not do that he managed, as opportunities arose, to spread as many Lutheran ideas around the country as he safely could. There is coherence to all of this, even though, as the king's servant and never a head of state, he had less freedom to operate than Oliver, and even though his evangelical program had to be carried on discreetly, as and when doors were opened to him. Thomas improvised on the details, but his overall strategy was clear.

Oliver ran the state and the government as if he was taking the field at the head of his beloved New Model Army. A seventeenth-century general advancing against the enemy may have a broad strategic plan, but he cannot carry it out until he actually takes the field. Then a hundred and one different things can happen to make him change his plan: bad weather has made the ground soggy hampering manoeuvrability; a messenger gallops up and brings unexpected news; reinforcements don't arrive when they are supposed to; a charge on the left flank is repulsed and something else must be tried, and fast; disagreements arise between junior officers, and a decision is needed immediately; and so on. In every case the commander must react quickly; a few moments' delay can be fatal. The ability to think and act at lightning speed, to overturn a prearranged plan and work out a better one on the spur of the moment, to notice and grasp an unexpected opportunity, can turn imminent disaster into glorious victory. Oliver had been through this many times with his soldiers. But his chopping and changing with the constitution had less satisfying results. An enemy beaten on the field is finished and cannot fight again; but when one parliament is dissolved, another one has to be called sooner or later.

Oliver, said Charles Firth, always acted in the interests of the 'Puritan minority', and he was 'too much the champion of a party', though Firth added that in 'serving his cause he served his country too'.[19] This, more than any constitutional rationale or political creed, was Oliver's real reason for restoring the Lords – to make sure that his godly allies would be protected against an over-powerful, unsympathetic and unchecked Commons. But it would be difficult to say that Thomas was *too* much the champion of the Lutheran party in the 1530s. A study of Cromwell's relations with the West Country by Dr Mary Robertson has shown how concerned he could be for the well-being of a region in which he had little vested interest. Yet he made no attempt to pack the Devon and Cornish benches or local authorities with loyal evangelical protégées. Another time, during a dispute between the evangelical Bishop Shaxton and an abbot of the old faith, that was referred to Cromwell for arbitration because the abbot had done nothing unlawful, Cromwell showed an even-handedness that left Shaxton bitter and irritated.[20]

Oliver's dependency on Providence, dare it be said, suggests that beneath the tough exterior and coat of mail, lay a susceptible, even an impressionable mind. For in spite of all his efforts to conciliate, he was won over completely by the speeches and sermons of Major Goffe, a junior officer, and Thomas Brook, condemning Charles as the man of blood (pp. 189–92) and justifying Pride's Purge, the death of the king and all that followed. This made the saints of the New Model Army more like Thomas Müntzer than Thomas Cromwell. Oliver was, admittedly, a more reluctant revolutionary; he was also a big-hearted man with admirable qualities not easily discernible in Müntzer, and Oliver certainly mellowed after the demise of Barebone's and his installation as Protector. Before this, however, flashes of the spirit of Müntzer had burst forth in Oliver from time to time: in the execution of the king, at the siege of Drogheda, at the dissolution of the Rump, where, 'perceiving the spirit of God so strong upon me, I would not consult flesh and blood' (see pp. 215–16). But there was not a trace of the fanatic in Thomas. He was calculating, thoughtful, rational; in church and state, the pragmatic reformer not the godly revolutionary, but no less religious for that. Nothing could be wider of the mark than to imagine that because Thomas, like Elizabeth, appeared more reserved on the outside than the passionate saints, he must have been less spiritually devout. Still waters run deep, nowhere more so than in spiritual things. Religious zeal comes easily. When the light dawns, and the heart feels, or imagines, itself awakened, unless time is allowed for it to develop and mature, it is all too easy to bubble over with frothy enthusiasm, to be puffed up with self-righteousness, to want to change the whole world instantly, and then get frustrated and angry when others do not respond as they are supposed to. The ability to show restraint, to wait on the king, on Parliament or on the people; to be patient and lead by persuasion; to move slowly when the impulse is to forge ahead rapidly; to bear disappointments and persevere in the hope of better times to come – all this is far more spiritually demanding, calling for far greater depth and maturity.

Under Thomas Cromwell, England was a European power of at best second rank, no match for France or the German empire. Under Oliver, with a powerful navy as well as one of the finest armies in Europe, England was a major force, esteemed and feared in continental courts. Even Oliver's opponents like Clarendon ruefully admitted that the Protector's 'greatness at home was but a shadow of the glory he had abroad'.[21] Appearances, however, can be deceptive. Under Thomas, England was at peace, and solvent, with an economy in a most satisfying state: inflation low, trade growing, the currency revalued.[22] By the end of Oliver's rule, and for all his greatness abroad, Britain was nearly bust.

Thomas was lucky, some may say: he had the wealth of the church to help himself to. But good government consists in making best use of whatever resources are available, and Oliver also had his sitting targets – the Royalists – and he taxed them just as rigorously as Thomas taxed the clergy. Besides, Oliver's financial difficulties were not due chiefly to lack of resources at home; they were caused by the high cost of a large standing army and navy, and a hugely ambitious foreign policy.

And nothing drains a nation's assets and wealth more than the love of glory, a point Thomas Cromwell understood long before he became the king's Principal Secretary. In his maiden parliamentary speech he opposed the designs of Henry and Wolsey to go to war against France. Instead, Cromwell urged the king to safeguard England's security by ending the long, historic rivalry with Scotland. Mindful perhaps of his own escapades as a foot soldier in his youth, he stressed the horrors of war, the slaughter and the 'most lamentable cries and sorrowful wringing of hands' when Christendom's princes wage war rather than seek peace. He saw clearly the danger of a country exhausting its resources by fighting at some distance from its own shores: problems with communications, extended supply lines, disruption to trade and commerce, the need to make deals with a lord or faction in enemy territory who might break his word, and so on.[23]

The foreign policy of Thomas Cromwell, when he became Henry's chief minister, was very simple, but wise and economical. To Ambassador Chapuys he pledged that 'I will never allow the king my master to carry war across the channel, or try to gain one more foot of land on the continent than he has already'. Cromwell was, of course, exaggerating his influence with his master, because he could not have stopped Henry from going to war across the Channel had the king been determined to do so. Nevertheless, this mild boast vindicates Foxe's judgement, who noted approvingly that during Cromwell's period England was never at war, and that his policy was to 'nourish peace' with the Emperor Charles V, King Francis of France, the Scots, even with Rome if the pope would be willing. Alliances with foreign powers were discussed from time to time. Cromwell was hoping he could persuade Henry to join the Schmalkaldic League; but the League was purely a defensive grouping of Protestant states. During negotiations with Ambassador Chapuys, Cromwell indicated he would be willing to help Charles against the Turks as part of an Anglo-Imperial treaty; but his main rationale for this was to make sure the emperor would never attack England. In both cases, his chief aim was the security of the realm and the prevention of war. Cromwell did his utmost to avoid the costly and mostly unproductive foreign ventures that had been a feature of Henry's reign in Wolsey's time, and would become so once again after Cromwell's fall. It was a foreign policy with clear aims, rather like those of the first Tudor king: to avoid conflict and keep England at peace, out of and free from continental dynastic and territorial quarrels, secure at home, and in sound economic condition.[24]

But Oliver, says Gardiner after an exhaustive analysis, 'embarked on foreign politics as upon an unknown sea, in which it was hard for him to find his bearings, and still harder to direct his course aright'. Some modern writers find this judgement too harsh, and it has been claimed that Oliver's foreign policy, if it did not begin particularly well, improved appreciably in later years, becoming more pragmatic and less idealistic.[25] Maybe; but still there remains more than a touch of naivety in Oliver's idea of Anglo-Dutch political union (it certainly baffled the Dutch), and also his support for Charles X of Sweden, when Oliver was hungering for a Protestant league while Charles, as most observers realised, was chiefly interested in replenishing the empty Swedish coffers. Oliver seemed to have difficulty understanding how keen commercial rivalry could exist between Protestant Sweden and the Protestant Dutch, or why the Swedes had to fight their fellow Lutheran Danes mainly over territorial claims. Oliver was filled with a godly longing for the 'advancement of the common interest of religion and the civil interest', and his Protestant League, unlike the Schmalkaldic League, would not be purely defensive. But as his envoy Jephson reflected after trying to make peace between the Scandinavian kings, 'religion amongst states is much oftener pretended for their own interests than really embraced for the honour of God'. Renewed conflict between Sweden and Denmark, and Sweden and the Elector of Brandenburg, proved, if proof was still needed, that Oliver's dreams of a Protestant alliance in Europe were doomed by territorial ambitions and rivalries of these supposedly Protestant princes.[26] All this surprised and disappointed Oliver, but the more equable and less idealistic Tudor Cromwell would have known it without having to learn it from experience.

Thomas Cromwell never gave his king a great foreign policy triumph like a major conquest or victory, the sort of transient glory that a showy prince like Henry would have treasured. By contrast, Oliver enjoyed his foreign policy successes like Dunkirk and Jamaica; but both came at a price, especially Dunkirk. There were humiliating failures as well, like Hispaniola, where supply lines were over-stretched, and startlingly little account was taken of the practical needs of an army fighting in near tropical conditions. To quote Gardiner again: 'Oliver, as ever, trusted in God. For once in his life he had forgotten to keep his powder dry.'[27] Thomas trusted in God too, but he preferred to keep his powder in England in reserve, to guarantee the defence of the kingdom against invasion. Foreign exploits held little attraction for him. It may be suspected, though it cannot be proved, that he would have been less than enthusiastic about the derring-dos of Drake, Hawkins and other adventurers in the Mediterranean, the West Indies and the Americas.

As John Foxe noted, however, the foreign policy of Thomas Cromwell was unusual for the time, while that of Oliver – interventionist, expansionist, imperialist – was more typical of English kings and statesmen, and it was followed by the later Stuarts, the Hanoverians and into the Empire days. So perhaps Oliver is more 'modern' than Thomas. It would seem so, according to a recent 'Greatest Britons' poll organised by the BBC, in which viewers were invited to vote for their favourite historic personality. As with all polls, a touch of healthy scepticism is advisable when poring over its findings, especially when in the top 100 we find Guy Fawkes, Richard III and Aleister Crowley, plus a predictable clutch of shallow celebrities. To add to the merriment there was a '100 worst' list as well as a 'best', and more than one name appears in both. But, it may still be a useful indicator of historical reputations. Of the major figures in the period covered by this book, Elizabeth I, William Shakespeare and Oliver Cromwell all made it into the top ten (Winston Churchill came first, Oliver tenth). Henry VIII would be irked to know that he ranked number 40, behind William Tyndale and Thomas More (26 and 37 respectively). But no place was found in the first 100 for Thomas Cromwell (or Thomas Cranmer either).

So Oliver is one of our all-time 'greats'. Charles I remains a martyr, seldom is the word 'Puritan' used as a compliment, and the influence modern English republicanism wields is minimal: yet still Oliver rides high. Historians call him 'God's Englishman', the sturdy, plain-speaking country gent who took on the establishment in a noble if slightly flawed cause, and won. Oliver's appeal has endured; and despite the failure of the Revolution to erect its own constitutional structure, its early ideals have also endured and show no sign of fading. For it was during the 1630s and 1640s that thoughts of popular sovereignty were put into words, hearts and minds as never before. After Naseby, Oliver and the officers endorsed the argument that government's 'foundation and supremacy is in the people', and it should be exercised through Parliament; but Oliver at this stage had not given up hope of reaching an agreement with the king, and he was still protesting loyalty to Charles.[28] This was Oliver before he became a regicide, before his own notorious clashes with his parliaments, Oliver before the firebrand revolutionary theology of Goffe and Brook had taken him captive. His dreams then, unfulfilled in his lifetime, are now reality. Seen in this admittedly slightly 'Whiggish' light, the Revolution may be remembered as the first step – albeit the first failed step, the immediate result of which was a stumble and a bad bruise – towards the abandonment of the old order of monarchical divine right, and its replacement by the constitutional monarchy. Thus, eventually, the ideals of the Revolution, when moderated and purged of their wilder elements, came to be grafted on to the robust constitution that Thomas Cromwell and the Tudors did so much to fashion. If so, then the first Cromwell stands for an era that for all its virtues, its glories and its fascination – and no age is more absorbing than that of the Tudors – is nevertheless an era that is past and will never be restored; while Oliver was a pioneer, a forbearer, a valiant founding father of the modern state. Between the two great Cromwells, let the reader be judge.

NOTES

Abbreviations used in the Notes

Abbott	*Writings and Speeches of Oliver Cromwell*, ed. W.C. Abbott
AC	Augsburg Confession ★
Apology	Philip Melanchthon's *Apology of the Augsburg Confession*
BSLK	*Bekenntnisschriften der Evangelisch-Lutherischen Kirche*
Brecht	Martin Brecht's biography of Luther
Burnet	Burnet's *History of the Reformation of the Church of England*
Calvin, *Inst.*	John Calvin's *Institutes of the Christian Religion*
CH	*Church History*
CJ	*Commons Journals*
Cranmer, *Misc.*	*Misc. Writings and Letters of Thomas Cranmer Writings*
CR	*Corpus Reformatorum*
CSP For.,	*Calendar of State Papers, Foreign*
CSP Span.,	*Calendar of State Papers, Spanish*
CSP Ven.,	*Calendar of State Papers, Venetian*
EHR	*English Historical Review*
Elton, *Policy*	G.R. Elton, *Policy and Police: The Enforcement of Reformation in the Age of Thomas Cromwell*
Elton, *Studies*	Elton, *Studies in Tudor and Stuart Politics and Government*
ET	*Epistolae Tigurinae*
Firth	C.H. Firth, *The Last Years of the Protectorate, 1656–1658*
Foxe	*Acts and Monuments of John Foxe*
Gardiner	S.R. Gardiner, *History of England … 1603–42*
Gardiner, *CP*	Gardiner, *History of the Commonwealth and Protectorate*
Gardiner, *CW*	Gardiner, *History of the Great Civil War*
Hall	E. Hall, *A Chronicle containing the History of England … to the end of the reign of Henry VIII*
HJ	*Historical Journal*
JEH	*Journal of Ecclesiastical History*
Kaulek	*Correspondence Politique de Mm. de Castillon et de Marillac … ed. J. Kaulek*

LCC	*Library of Christian Classics*
LP	*Letters & Papers, Foreign & Domestic, of the Reign of Henry VIII, 1509–47*
LW	*Luther's Works: American edn*
MBW	*Melanchthons Briefwechsel*
MW	*Melanchthons Werke*
Merriman	R.B. Merriman, *The Life and Letters of Thomas Cromwell*
OL	*Original Letters,* ed. H. Robinson
PS	Parker Society
Pelikan, *Creeds*	Pelikan and Hotchkiss, *Creeds and Confessions … vol 2: Part 4: Creeds and Confessions of the Reformation Era*
Shaw	W. A. Shaw's *History of the English Church during the Civil Wars and under the Commonwealth, 1640–1660*
SCJ	*Sixteenth Century Journal*
SP	*State Papers*
UP	University Press
WA	*Dr. Martin Luthers Werke* (Weimar edn)
WA, Br	*Dr. Martin Luthers Werke: Briefwechsel*
WA, DB	*Dr. Martin Luthers Werke: Deutsche Bibel*
WA, TR	*Dr. Martin Luthers Werke: Tischreden*
Wright	Wright's *Letters relating to the Suppression of Monasteries*

* The Augsburg Confession and other Lutheran Confessional Documents are printed in Pelikan, *Creeds* (see above). Students may also wish to use the Internet (Google or other search for 'Book of Concord').

1. THE EUROPEAN BACKGROUND, 1517–31

1. Brecht 1, pp. 470–5; Brecht 2, p. 1.
2. *LW* 48, p. 326.
3. Brecht 2, pp. 1–4, 29–33; *LW* 45, pp. 62–3, 67–8.
4. On the Tower experience, see discussions in Brecht 1, pp. 221–30; Lowell Green, *How Melanchthon Helped Luther Discover the Gospel*, especially pp. 40–1, 174.
5. Brecht 1, chaps 3–6.
6. *LW* 51, pp. 70–100; Brecht 2, pp. 59–61.
7. *LW* 3, p. 53; *LW* 24, p. 214; *LW* 45, pp. 114, 116, 120. Luther's main early work on this subject, on which the following discussion is based unless otherwise stated, is *Temporal Authority: To what extent it should be obeyed*, in *LW* 45, pp. 77–129.
8. *LW* 45, p. 121.
9. *LW* 51, p. 76.
10. Brecht 2, pp. 121–6, 129–35, 251–7.
11. *LW* 53, p. 316.
12. Brecht 1, pp. 306–22; Friesen, *Müntzer,* p. 6; LW 30, p. 285.
13. Friesen, *Müntzer*, pp. 5–6, 10–32.
14. Friesen, *Müntzer*, pp. 33–72, 168–70.
15. Baylor, *Radical Reformation*, pp. 1–10.
16. Friesen, *Müntzer*, pp. 125–30.
17. Friesen, *Müntzer*, pp. 130–1, 179–80.
18. Friesen, *Müntzer*, pp. 184–5.
19. English translation in Baylor, *Radical Reformation*, pp. 11–32; see also Brecht 2, pp. 153–4; Friesen, *Müntzer*, pp. 202–9.
20. Brecht 2, p. 154; Friesen, *Müntzer*, p. 211; *WA, Br* 3, p. 120 (27–36).

21. *LW* 40, pp. 45–59; Brecht 2, pp. 151–2.
22. Quotes and discussion in Friesen, *Müntzer*, pp. 149–53; full discussion in pp. 146–67.
23. Brecht 2, pp. 149, 154–5.
24. *Concerning the Invented faith*, 1524, quoted and discussed in Brecht 2, p. 148.
25. Brecht 2, p. 148; *LW* 51, p. 77.
26. Brecht 2, p. 154; Friesen, *Müntzer*, pp. 185–7, 214–16.
27. Brecht 2, pp. 154–6; Friesen, *Müntzer*, pp. 220–6; Scott and Scribner, *German Peasants' War*, p. 37.
28. Brecht 2, pp. 155–6; Friesen, *Müntzer*, pp. 203, 227; Müntzer's *Highly Provoked Defence* is printed in Baylor, *Radical Reformation*, pp. 74–93.
29. Friesen, *Müntzer*, pp. 229–32; Scott and Scribner, *German Peasants' War*, p. 38.
30. Brecht 2, p. 175; Stayer, *German Peasants' War*, pp. 21–2, 32–3; Scott and Scribner, *German Peasants' War*, pp. 6–14.
31. Brecht 2, p. 174; Baylor, *Radical Reformation*, pp. 231–41; Scott and Scribner, *German Peasants' War*, pp. 32, 251–7.
32. Brecht 2, p. 183; Friesen, *Müntzer*, pp. 233–9; Scott and Scribner, *German Peasants' War*, p. 238.
33. *LW* 46, pp. 5–43; discussed in Brecht 2, pp. 175–7.
34. Friesen, *Müntzer*, pp. 244–5; Scott and Scribner, *German Peasants' War*, pp. 145–8.
35. *LW* 46, pp. 47–55; discussed in Brecht 2, pp. 178–81.
36. Friesen, *Müntzer*, pp. 259–68; Scott and Scribner, *German Peasants' War*, pp. 290–1.
37. *WA, TR* 1, no. 446 (18–20); Brecht 2, p. 185.
38. Printed in Scott and Scribner, *German Peasants' War*, pp. 292, 322–4; see also Brecht's discussion in Brecht 2, pp. 185–91.
39. Brecht 2, p. 188; Richard, *Melanchthon*, pp. 147–51.
40. Luther's *Open Letter on the Harsh Book*: *LW* 46, pp. 59–85.
41. Potter, *Zwingli*, chaps 1–2; Gordon, *Swiss Reformation*, pp. 46–51. This overview of Zwingli is taken mainly from Potter and Gordon. Also much recommended for a detailed study of Zwingli's theology is Stephens, *Zwingli*.
42. Stephens, *Zwingli*, p. 5.
43. Potter, *Zwingli*, chaps 3–6; Gordon, *Swiss Reformation*, pp. 51–71.
44. Potter, *Zwingli*, chaps 8–10; Gordon, *Swiss Reformation*, pp. 86–115.
45. Potter, *Zwingli*, pp. 100–14; Gordon, *Swiss Reformation*, p. 242.
46. *LW* 51, pp. 81–6; Potter, *Zwingli*, pp. 114–15, 140; Stephens, *Zwingli*, pp. 37, 174.
47. *WA, TR* 2, no. 2545; TR 3, no. 3815; TR 4, no. 4192; Potter, *Zwingli*, pp. 207–8, 399–400; Gordon, *Swiss Reformation*, p. 246; MacCulloch, *Reformation*, p. 146.
48. For Luther on the Eucharist, see Brecht 2, pp. 293–325. Luther's original works are collated in *LW* 37, which has an extremely helpful index. See also Luther's *Large Catechism* in *BSLK*, p. 709 (10) = Tappert, p. 448 (10). For Zwingli on the Eucharistic presence and his exchanges with Luther, see Potter, *Zwingli*, pp. 156–8, 287–315; Locher, *Zwingli's Thought*, pp. 19–22, 180, 215–28; Stephens, *Theology of Zwingli*, pp. 180–93, 218–59.
49. Stephens, *Zwingli*, pp. 282–309. For examples of Luther getting involved in economic affairs, see Brecht 3, pp. 258–62.
50. Quote from Gordon, *Swiss Reformation*, p. 78.
51. Unless indicated, this and the following paragraphs on Zwingli's war policy are taken from Potter, *Zwingli*, Chaps 14–16; Gordon, *Swiss Reformation*, pp. 119–45.
52. On the details of the agreement, see Potter, *Zwingli*, pp. 415–16; Gordon, *Swiss Reformation*, p. 134.
53. Brecht 2, p. 423; *LW* 54, no. 1451.

2. THE TUDOR CROMWELL, HIS TIMES AND AFTERMATH, 1509–58

1. Quoted in Scarisbrick, *Henry VIII*, pp. 12–16.

2. Elton, *Studies* 1, p. 182; Fox and Guy, *Reassessing the Henrician Age*, pp. 165–6; Guy, *Tudor England*, pp. 104–5.

3. Swanson, 'The Pre-Reformation Church' in Pettegree (ed.), *Reformation World*, p. 13; Thompson, *Popes and Princes*, pp. 24–8, 52–3.

4. *LP* 3 (1) 1273–4. Fisher was one of Luther's ablest early opponents on justification – see Rex, *Theology of John Fisher*, pp. 116–28.

5. Henry VIII, *Assertion of Seven the Sacraments*.

6. Scarisbrick, *Henry VIII*, p. 111; Tjernagel, *Henry VIII and the Lutherans*, pp. 10–11; Henry VIII, *Assertion of Seven the Sacraments*, pp. 58–9.

7. Daniell, *Tyndale*, chap 8, 10; Daniell, *Bible in English*, pp. 133–59.

8. This is, of course, a very brief summary of Henry's Great Matter. It has been exhaustively covered many times. One of the best starting points remains Elton, *England under the Tudors*, chaps 5–6.

9. MacCulloch, *Cranmer*, pp. 44–6.

10. Schofield, *Cromwell*, pp. 45–8, 71–2 and sources there.

11. Foxe 1, pp. 309–10; MacCulloch, *Cranmer*, pp. 54, 59; Foxe and Guy *Reassessing the Henrician Age*, pp. 157–63. Also the pope's jurisdiction in England had been refuted in the days of Richard II (Foxe 3, pp. 316–17).

12. Schofield, *Cromwell*, chaps 2–3.

13. Elton, *Tudor Constitution*, pp. 350–3; Merriman 1, p. 343; Lehmberg, *Reformation Parliament, 1529–1536*, pp. 136–8.

14. Covered in great detail in Lehmberg, *Reformation Parliament*, pp. 139–54; Elton, *Studies* 2, pp. 107–35; Elton, *Tudor Constitution*, pp. 333–5; Elton, *Reform and Reformation*, pp. 151–6.

15. Schofield, *Cromwell*, pp. 50–4. For Francis's encouragement to Henry to marry Anne, the crucial original documents are *SP* 7, pp. 428–30, 434, 495.

16. Hall, p. 794; Chapuys: *CSP Span.*, 1531–3 *(cont)*, no. 1048, p. 602; no. 1053, p. 609; Cranmer: Cranmer, *Misc. Writings*, p. 246. Most writers prefer the January date. For Hall, however, see MacCulloch, *Cranmer*, pp. 637–8; Schofield, *Cromwell*, pp. 50–1.

17. Elton, *Tudor Constitution*, pp. 353–8; Elton, *Studies* 2, pp. 82–106; Lehmberg, *Reformation Parliament*, pp. 164–9, 174–9.

18. *LP* 6, no. 1070; *CSP Span.*, 1531–3, nos 1123–4, pp. 788–9.

19. *LP* 6, no. 1501, p. 607; *LP* 7, no. 152; *CSP, Span*, 1534, no. 9, p. 30.

20. Elton, *Tudor Constitution*, pp. 42, 53–6; Elton, *Reform and Reformation*, pp. 189–90; Lehmberg, *Reformation Parliament*, pp. 202, 206–7.

21. Elton, *Policy*, pp. 263–92; Elton, *Tudor Constitution*, pp. 62–4; Lehmberg, *Reformation Parliament*, pp. 196–205.

22. *SP* 1, p. 393.

23. *CSP Span.*, 1534–5, no. 178, p. 505; *LP* 8, nos 742, 1117; Merriman 1, pp. 416–19; 427–30.

24. Elton, *England under the Tudors*, pp. 169–70; *Reform and Renewal*, pp. 164–5.

25. On this and the next two paragraphs, see Schofield, *Cromwell*, chap. 6.

26. There is almost too much material on Henry and Anne to include in one footnote, and much of it is of little real value due to the prevalence of dismal conspiracy theories on Anne's fall. For an answer to the wild idea that Cromwell masterminded her ruin, see Schofield, *Cromwell*, chaps. 7–9.

27. *LP* 10, no. 793.

28. Burnet 1, pp. 316, 330, 332.

29. Schofield, *Cromwell*, pp. 135–8.

30. Holye, *The Pilgrimage of Grace and the Politics of the 1530s*.

31. Cranmer, *Misc. Writings*, p. 98; Youings, *Dissolution of the Monasteries*.

32. Brecht 3, pp. 48–58. Incidentally, Cromwell's Swiss contacts do not indicate that he was changing his mind on the Eucharist and anticipating Cranmer's later Eucharistic theology. As noted, the expectation was that the Swiss might move *away* from Zwingli to a Lutheran (or Phillipist) view, not the other way round. Besides, writing to Bullinger is not in itself enough to make a man a Zwinglian; otherwise Luther would be a Zwinglian too, because he and Bullinger were writing to each other in quite friendly terms around this time.

33. Daniell, *Tyndale*, pp. 361–84; Hall, p. 818.

34. Schofield, *Cromwell*, pp. 219–22; Daniell, *Bible in English*, pp. 204–5.

35. Kaulek, p. 189 = LP 15, no. 766.

36. *CSP Span.*, 1534–5, no. 205, p. 542.

37. *ET*, p. 10 = *OL* 1, p. 15.

38. Latimer, *Remains*, pp. 410–11.

39. Wright, pp. 77–8, 186; *LP* 10, nos 227, 835, 1257 (9); *LP* 11, no. 117; *SP* 2, p. 539.

40. Elton, *Policy*, pp. 6–8; *LP* 11, no. 841; *LP* 12 (1) nos 163, 853, 976, 1021 (5), and also Bush, *Pilgrimage of Grace*, Index under Cromwell, pp. 438–9.

41. *LW* 50, pp. 136–8.

42. For the following, see Schofield, *Cromwell*, chaps 15–17.

43. *MBW* 3, nos 2473 [3], 2474 [1], 2479 [3], 2483 [2], 2484 [2] = *CR* 3, cols 1070–71, 1075–7.

44. AC: see summary at the end of Article 21, and also at the end of the entire work in *BSLK*, pp. 83 (1), 134 (19–20, 24) = Pelikan, *Creeds*, pp. 76–7, 117 [5]. The German text is *Christliche Kirche*, so Melanchthon has used Christian and Catholic (in this sense) interchangeably. *Variata: MW* 6, pp. 36 (17–27), 79 (16–19). Cranmer's later work on the Eucharist is the *Defence of the True and Catholic Doctrine of the Sacrament*: Cranmer was contending for the *Reformed* doctrine, arguing that this was the one held by the ancient church. For Cromwell's last words and prayer, see Foxe 5, pp. 402–3.

45. *Quam vere dixit ille in Tragoedia, non gratiorem victimam Deo mactari posse quam tyrannum. Utinam aliquo forti viro Deus hanc mentem inserat. MBW* 3, no. 2479 [3] = *CR* 3, col. 1075. See also *MBW* 3, no. 2483 [2] = *CR* 3, col. 1076.

46. Elton, *Studies* 2, p. 32.

47. MacCulloch, *Cranmer*, pp. 309, 325; Ryrie, *Gospel and Henry VIII*, pp. 43, 47, 197–8; *King's Book*, ed. Lacey, p. 11.

48. Cranmer, *Misc. Writings*, p. 116. See also the discussion in MacCulloch, *Cranmer*, pp. 278–9, 576–7, and how this would later embarrass Cranmer at his trial.

49. Fuller account in MacCulloch, *Cranmer*, pp. 297–321.

50. Catherine Parr, *The Lamentation of a Sinner* 1, pp. 286–313; *LW* 42, pp. 5–14.

51. Foxe 5, pp. 553–61. For Catherine as an evangelical patroness, see Ryrie, *Gospel and Henry VIII*, pp. 166–7.

52. Ridley, *Henry VIII*, pp. 364–400; Scarisbrick, *Henry VIII*, pp. 433–57.

53. Daniell, *Bible in English*, p. 229; Foxe 5, pp. 563–4, 692; *LP* 21 (1), no. 1526.

54. Scarisbrick, *Henry VIII*, pp. 482, 490, 496; Foxe 5, p. 689.

55. Cranmer, *Misc. Writings*, p. 127.

56. Images: MacCulloch, *Tudor Church Militant*, pp. 69–74, 134–6. The Eucharist: MacCulloch, *Cranmer*, pp. 180–4, 232–4; 354–5; 379–83; 390–2; 406–8, 614–16; Brooks, *Thomas Cranmer's Doctrine of the Eucharist*, pp. 3–37.

57. Cranmer: MacCulloch, *Cranmer*, pp. 427–8, also index refs, p. 687. Calvin: Wendel, *Calvin*, pp. 266, 273–5, 280; Niesel, *Calvin*, pp. 164–5. Bullinger: J. Wayne Baker, 'Henry Bullinger and the Reformed Tradition in Retrospect', *SCJ* 29/2 (1998): 371–5. Melanchthon: Schofield, *Melanchthon*, pp. 33, 36–7, 52–4, 64–5.

58. MacCulloch, *Cranmer*, pp. 410–11.

59. MacCulloch, *Tudor Church Militant*, pp. 23–36; MacCulloch, *Cranmer*, pp. 472–3.

60. Bush, *Protector Somerset*, pp. 1–30; MacCulloch, *Reformation*, pp. 256–7.

61. Bush, *Protector Somerset*, pp. 101–2, 112–26.

62. MacCulloch, *Tudor Church Militant*, pp. 43–8; Fletcher and MacCulloch, *Tudor Rebellions*, pp. 52–64.

63. Loades, *Northumberland*, pp. 94, 124, 129–87.

64. MacCulloch, *Cranmer*, pp. 504–12.

65. MacCulloch, *Cranmer*, pp. 525–8.

66. MacCulloch, *Tudor Church Militant*, pp. 39–41; Loades, *Northumberland*, pp. 232–71; Foxe 6, pp. 385–6.

67. Foxe 6, p. 384.

68. MacCulloch, *Reformation*, p. 258; Whitelocke and MacCulloch, 'Princess Mary's Household and the Succession Crisis, 1553', *HJ* 50/2 (June 2007): 265–89; *CSP Span.*, 1553, pp. 72–3, 83, 85, 98.

69. Foxe 6, pp. 384–9; *CSP Span.*, 1553, pp. 106.

70. *CSP Span.*, 1536–8, no. 70.

71. Schofield, *Cromwell*, pp. 133–4; Duffy and Loades, *Church of Mary Tudor*, pp. 12–17.

72. *CSP Span.*, 1553, pp. 116–9, 216–19.

73. Cranmer, *Misc. Writings*, p. 189; Fletcher and MacCulloch, *Tudor Rebellions*, pp. 90–101.

74. MacCulloch, *Reformation*, p. 283.

75. The doctrine of transubstantiation had been defined at the Lateran Council of the Church in 1215. It stated that the substance of the bread and wine in the Eucharist service, when consecrated, is transformed into the body and blood of Christ, and only the outward appearance – the so-called 'species' or 'accidents' – of the bread and wine remain. This distinction between the 'substance' and 'accident' of a being or thing is derived chiefly from the great Ancient Greek thinker and scholar Aristotle (384–322 BC): though a pagan who died 300 years before Christ, he was the medieval church's most revered authority on scientific and philosophical subjects. The substance of bread is what bread essentially is – the food made from flour, yeast or meal – while its accidents are its non-essential aspects, like whether it is white or brown. Ironically from the fourteenth century Aristotle's theories of substance and accidents were progressively being discarded, especially by theologians and philosophers of the so-called 'Nominalist' school. Because transubstantiation was a consensus of the church, however, the Nominalists made no challenge to it. At the Reformation Luther *did* challenge it. It clashed with Scripture and St Paul ('The bread we break …Who eats this bread': 1 Cor. 10:15; 11:26–8). Luther believed Christ to be present in the Eucharist, but in a way indefinable by man, neither by Aristotle nor the pope. 'We are not commanded to inquire how it may be that the bread becomes and is the body of Christ. God's Word is there, that speaks. With that we remain, believing.' (*LW* 40, p. 216). In Henry's day the English Protestant movement under Cromwell accepted transubstantiation, albeit glumly and out of deference to Henry; but the English in Edward's reign rejected it bitterly. Cranmer accused the papists of making and worshipping a different Christ from the One born of Mary: 'for whereas, at His Incarnation, He was made of the nature and substance of His blessed mother; now, by these papists' opinion, He is made every day of the substance of bread and wine … O what marvellous metamorphosis and abominable heresy is this' (*Work of Thomas Cranmer*, ed. Duffield, p. 103). Passions were running extremely high, for and against.

76. Fenlon, *Heresy and Obedience in Tridentine Italy*; Mayer, *Reginald Pole*, chap. 4.

77. Quotes and discussion in Duffy and Loades, *Church of Mary Tudor*, pp. 47, 244–5.

78. MacCulloch, *Reformation*, p. 284.

79. Loades, *Mary Tudor*, pp. 240–2.

80. See discussion in Duffy and Loades, *Church of Mary Tudor*, chap. 8.

81. Duffy and Loades, *Church of Mary Tudor*, p. 29.

82. Foxe 6, pp. 354–5; Ridley, *Nicholas Ridley*, p. 303. To make these points is not to suggest that denying the real presence was entirely a novelty. Some English Zwinglians had been burned under Henry, but those unfortunate casualties were never among the leaders of the evangelical movement. Besides, Henry also burned Thomas Hitton in 1530 for smuggling a New Testament and other forbidden evangelical literature into the country, and ten years later he burned three Lutheran men for preaching justification by faith, even though they held broadly acceptable views on the Eucharist. (Foxe 5, pp. 438–9; 8, pp. 712–15.) The point is that under Mary the chief test of orthodoxy was not whether justification is by faith alone, or the English Bible, but what remains in the bread and wine after consecration.

83. See discussion and examples in Daniell, *Bible in English*, pp. 263–70, 289 (quote on p. 264); More quoted and discussed on p. 248.

84. Duffy and Loades, *Church of Mary Tudor*, pp. 195–7; see also Pettegree, *Marian Protestantism*, pp. 156–62.

85. *CSP Ven*, 1556–57, no. 884, pp. 1058–60. I have taken the liberty of paraphrasing some rather cumbersome prose in the *CSP*. Quoted verbatim it reads as follows: Mary's hatred was 'increased by knowing her (Elizabeth) to be averse to the present religion, she having not only been born in the other, but being versed and educated in it; for although externally she showed, and by living catholically shows, that she has recanted, she is nevertheless supposed to dissemble, and to hold to it more than ever internally'.

86. Ibid. pp. 1074–6.

87. Haigh, *English Reformations, passim*.

88. *CSP Ven.*, 1557–58, no. 1274.

89. MacCulloch, *Reformation*, pp. 284–5; Mayer, *Reginald Pole*, p. 314.

3. ELIZABETH, 1558–1603

1. *LP* 19 (2), no. 744; *King's Book*, ed. Lacey, p. 11.

2. *CSP Ven*, 5, no. 934, p. 539; Giles, *Works of Roger Ascham* 1, pp. lxiii–lxiv, 164, 174, 191–2; *ET*, p. 49 = *OL* 1, p. 76. Also on Elizabeth's piety, see *ET*, p. 183 = *OL* 1, pp. 278–9.

3. Foxe 6, pp. 415–24.

4. Macaffrey, *Elizabeth*, pp. 18–19.

5. Elizabeth also knew her Bible well, and she could hardly have failed to notice examples of dispensations apparently granted in exceptionable circumstances. Naaman the Syrian, though converted to the Jewish faith, was allowed to return and serve his pagan king with the blessing of Elisha the prophet (2 Samuel 5).

6. Ryrie, *Gospel and Henry VIII*, chap. 2. See also discussion at the end of chap. 13.

7. MacCulloch, *Cranmer*, p. 551. On the subject of conformity, see also Pettegree, *Marian Protestantism*, chap. 4.

8. Calvin: Wright, 'Marian exiles and the legitimacy of flight from persecution', *JEH* 52 (2001): 200–43; Luther: *LW* 23, pp. 300–4.

9. *CSP Ven*, 4 (2), 1556–57, no. 884, pp. 1059–60; *CSP For*, 1575–77, no. 1236, p. 505.

10. Sharpe, 'Representations and Negotiations: Texts, Images and Authority in Early Modern England', *HJ* 42 (1999): 870.

11. MacCulloch, *Later Reformation*, pp. 26–7. The words to be spoken at communion fused Cranmer's 1549 and 1552 Prayer Books, as follows: 'The body of our Lord Jesus Christ which was given for thee, preserve thy body and soul unto everlasting life [1549]. Take

and eat this in remembrance that Christ died for thee, and feed on him in thy heart by faith with thanksgiving' (1552). For detailed discussion on the Convocation, see Haugaard, *Elizabeth and the English Reformation*, especially chaps 1 and 2.

12. Hardwick, *History of the Articles of Religion, 1536–1615*, pp. 125–7; Gibson, *Thirty-Nine Articles*, index refs under 'Confession', p. 794; *CSP Span*, 1558–67, no. 29, pp. 61–2. For the Act of Uniformity, see *Documents of the English Reformation*, ed. Bray, pp. 329–34. The standard work on the act's passage through Parliament is Jones, *Faith by Statute*. Jones, however, seems to want to play down Elizabeth's Protestantism: on this, and Melanchthon's influence on her, see Schofield, *Melanchthon*, chap. 12. On the comment that Elizabeth's pro-Lutheran statements were made in a diplomatic context and should therefore be treated with caution (Jones, p. 58), note her letter to Catherine Parr, and the testimony of Hooper and Ascham: there was nothing diplomatic about these. She also told a certain John Spithovius of her admiration for Melanchthon, and Spithovius was not a diplomat either; he was a former pupil of Melanchthon who travelled to England and for a time served as one of Elizabeth's tutors (*MBW* 7, no. 7348; *CSP For.*, 1558–59, nos 232, 502). Besides, a statement made in a diplomatic context is not automatically and necessarily unreliable. Whilst it is possible that such statements may not be quite the whole truth, this would have to be tested and proved on a case-by-case basis. But there is no reason to suspect that Elizabeth was merely jesting when she told the Spanish ambassador that she would like to take the Augsburg Confession 'or something like it' (*CSP Span*, 1558–67, no. 29, pp. 61–2). There is no evidence either that she was insincere when she sent letters to John Frederick II of Saxony, Augustus of Saxony, Albert of Prussia and Philip of Hesse assuring them that she would do her utmost to support and recommend the Augsburg Confession to her people, or when she authorised Christopher Mont to invite a Lutheran delegation to England (*CSP For.*, 1558–59, nos 730, 912, 916, 918, 920, 939, 1194; Kouri (ed.), *Elizabethan England and Europe: 40 unprinted letters*, p. 23). If all this was just pretence, it would have achieved nothing apart from an undesired reputation all over Europe for downright untruthfulness.

13. Lewis, *English Literature*, p. 39.

14. Cameron, *European Reformation*, pp. 348–9; MacCulloch, *Reformation*, pp. 274–5.

15. Jouanna, *La France du XVIe Siècle*, pp. 354–6, 365–6, 372–3, 389–90.

16. Ridley, *Bloody Mary*, pp. 175–8, 188; Mason (ed.), Knox, pp. 70–1, 169–70; Ridley, *Knox*, p. 280.

17. Quoted and discussed in Ridley, *Knox*, pp. 186–7, 275–6.

18. Quoted in Ridley, *Knox*, pp. 303–5, 311–12.

19. Mason (ed.), *Knox*, pp. 140, 143, 146–7.

20. Ridley, *Knox*, p. 527; Parker, *Correspondence*, pp. 60–1.

21. Quoted in Niesel, *Theology of Calvin*, p. 239; see Niesel's discussion on pp. 238–45, based on Calvin, *Inst.* 4.20. 'Evil rulers must not be resisted', Tyndale had insisted: quoted and discussed in Daniell, *Bible in English*, p. 222.

22. Calvin, *Inst.* 4.20.30–1. Another interesting passage from Calvin, from his commentary on Daniel 6:22 may be worth noting: 'For earthly princes lay aside their power when they rise up against God, and are unworthy to be reckoned among the number of mankind. We ought, rather, to utterly spit on their heads (*conspuere in ipsorum capita*) rather than obey them' – *CR* 41, p. 25. It is not clear what he meant practically by 'spit'; maybe it was a figure of speech for pious disdain rather than any kind of revolutionary resistance.

23. Augustine, *City of God* 1.21.

24. *Geneva Bible*, ed. Berry. On the Geneva Bible generally and its circulation, see Daniell, *Bible in English*, pp. 291–319; MacCulloch, *Reformation*, p. 588. On the Knoxian influence specifically, see Ridley, *Knox*, pp. 287–90.

25. Ridley, *Knox*, chap. 17; Ryrie, *Origins of the Scottish Reformation*, chaps 7–8.
26. Ridley, *Knox*, chap. 18; 'mingle mangle' quoted from Mason (ed.), *Knox*, p. 175.
27. Ridley, *Knox*, pp. 375–6: see also comments in MacCulloch, *Reformation*, pp. 292–5; Cameron, *European Reformation*, pp. 385–6; Pettegree (ed.), *Reformation World*, chap. 23. Figures of deaths from Todd, *Culture of Protestantism*, p. 2.
28. Quoted in Ridley, *Knox*, p. 390.
29. Ridley, *Knox*, pp. 438–9, 446–7, 464–73; MacCaffrey, *Elizabeth*, pp. 103–5.
30. MacCulloch, *Reformation*, pp. 309–13; Pettegree, *Reformation World*, chap. 20; *CSP Elizabeth*, 1558–67, no. 380, p. 577.
31. Jouanna, *La France du XVIᵉ Siècle*, pp. 452–4; Pettegree (ed.), *Reformation World*, chap. 19; Elizabeth quoted in MacCaffrey, *Elizabeth*, p. 153. However, it is not being too cynical to note that in 1584, when a Protestant prince became heir to the throne of France, writers who had previously talked the language of Knox switched back to the inviolability of the divine right of kings: see Mousnier, *Assassination of Henri IV*, p. 97.
32. *CSP Elizabeth*, 1558–67, no. 358, p. 552.
33. For Hooper, see footnote 2 above.
34. Parker, *Correspondence*, pp. 263, 272.
35. Collinson, *Elizabethan Puritan Movement*, pp. 347–9; Pilkington quoted in Collinson, *Religion of Protestants*, p. 203.
36. Collinson, *Elizabethan Puritan Movement*, pp. 358–9, 363–9; Collinson, *Godly People*, pp. 297–8.
37. Quoted in Collinson, *Godly People*, p. 301.
38. Quoted in Collinson, *Religion of Protestants*, p. 201.
39. Melanchthon: *CR* 21, pp. 506–8. See also Luther: *LW* 12, pp. *220*, 234–5, 39
40. Todd in Pettegree (ed.), *Reformation World*, p. 376.
41. See discussion of Puritans, predestination and a Covenant theology of works in MacCulloch, *Later Reformation*, pp. 74–9. See also Wayne Baker, 'Henry Bullinger and the Reformed Tradition in Retrospect', *SCJ* 29/2 (1998): 359–76; Avis, 'Moses and the Magistrate: A Study in the Rise of Protestant Legalism', *JEH* 26 (1975): 149–72.
42. *CR* 21, cols 415–19.
43. Melanchthon, Romans: *tales imaginationes falsae sunt et impiae, quia calumniantur et corrumpunt has promissiones*: *MW* 5, pp. 162 (1–8). *Quid aliud est quaerere de electione quam promissionem in dubium vocare. Id autem vere est abrogare evangelium et Deum accusare mendacii. Tantum mali habet haec curiositas: scrutatur Deum sine verbo, postea vocat in dubium promissionem divinam, ita et abicit evangelium et accusat Deum mendacii*: *MW* 5, p. 252 (16–22).
44. *LW* 34, pp. 50–1, 92; *BSLK*, pp. 463–4 = Tappert, *Book of Concord*, pp. 316–17.
45. Lutheran confessions refer to *one* ministry only, which the Augsburg Confession calls the 'The Office of *the* Ministry' (italics mine). In translation it is slightly misleading because no legal or official office is meant. *The* ministry is the proclamation of the Gospel through the Word and Sacrament, exercised in practice by called and ordained pastors (not by anyone who happens to feel led to do so). These Confessions do not specify any form of church government as binding, and Luther had no difficulty with an episcopal organisation in principle. See AC 5. This singleness is clear in both the German and Latin texts but especially the German: *Solchen Glauben zu erlangen, hat Gott das Predigamt eingefest, evangelium und Sacrament geben*; Latin: *ministerium docendi evangelii et porrigendi sacramenta*. See *BSLK*, p. 58 = Pelikan, *Creeds*, p. 61. On the calling to the ministry, see Article 14 (Pelikan, *Creeds*, p. 66). On bishops, see Article 28 (Pelikan, *Creeds*, pp. 107–16). The proclamation of the Gospel is the 'foundation for all other functions' (such as deacons, helpers, governing the church and so on): see *LW* 40, p. 36.
46. Calvin, *Inst.* 4.3.4; 4.10.30, discussed in Wendel, *Calvin*, pp. 302–3.

264 Cromwell to Cromwell: Reformation to Civil War

47. Calvin, *Inst.* 4.3.4–9, discussed in Wendel, *Calvin*, pp. 303–5, 309; Niesel, *Theology of Calvin*, pp. 201–2. For the elders and deacons, see Romans 12:7–8; 1 Corinthians 12:28.
48. Collinson, *Elizabethan Puritan Movement*, pp. 81–2, 101–10; Lake, *Anglicans and Puritans*, pp. 3–4, 77–8.
49. Collinson, *Elizabethan Puritan Movement*, pp. 112–13, 122.
50. Quotes in Collinson, *Godly People*, pp. 101, 105; Lake, *Anglicans and Puritans*, pp. 83–4.
51. Parker, *Correspondence*, pp. 418–19. Other quotes in Collinson, *Godly People*, p. 336; Collinson, *Religion of Protestants*, pp. 200–1.
52. Whitgift, *Works* 1, p. 16. See also the entertaining, if biased, section in Lewis, *English Literature*, pp. 445–9.
53. Whitgift, *Works* 2, pp. 425–6; AC 7 (Pelikan, *Creeds*, p. 62); CR 21, p. 507.
54. Quoted in Collinson, *Godly People*, p. 71.
55. Udall quoted in Lewis, *English Literature*, p. 44; for Cartwright, see Lake, *Anglicans and Puritans*, p. 57.
56. Collinson, *Elizabethan Puritan Movement*, pp. 126–9, 168–76, 191.
57. Collinson, *Elizabethan Puritan Movement*, pp. 195–7, 243–62; Daniell, *Bible in English*, p. 295.
58. For fuller coverage and discussion, see Lake, *Anglicans and Puritans*, pp. 13–66.
59. Whitgift, *Works* 1, p. 6.
60. Whitgift, *Works* 3, p. 315.
61. Whitgift, *Works* 3, pp. 314, 316.
62. Whitgift, *Works* 3, pp. 326–8.
63. Quoted from Neale, *Elizabeth and her Parliaments, 1584–1601*, p. 70.
64. Collinson, *Elizabethan Puritan Movement*, pp. 303–16.
65. Collinson, *Elizabethan Puritan Movement*, pp. 385–90, 404–31.
66. Tolmie, *Triumph of the Saints*, p. 2; White, *English Separatist Tradition*, pp. 2–19, 71, 84–9.
67. There are many editions of Hooker's Laws: I have used *Of the Laws of Ecclesiastical Polity* (2 vols, Everyman's Library, London: Dent 1968–9). Recommended select reading on Hooker includes: Lake, *Anglicans and Puritans*, pp. 145–230; Lake, 'Business as Usual? The Immediate Reception of Hooker's Ecclesiastical Polity', *JEH* 52/3 (2001): 456–86; MacCulloch, 'Richard Hooker's Reputation', *EHR* 117 (2002): 773–812; Voak, *Richard Hooker and Reformed Theology*.
    Hooker has become sufficiently controversial for questions to be raised about his Protestant orthodoxy. It is claimed that his view of the Fall was somewhat less grave than that of Luther, Melanchthon or Calvin. Hooker talks, for example, of the will 'being weakened' (*Laws* 1.7.7). I am willing to be corrected on this, but as I understand Hooker he is, at this point in the *Laws*, discussing the capacity of the will in a very *general* sense, not specifically the effect of the Fall on man's *spiritual* state and his subsequent need for salvation entirely by grace. However, those wishing to study this further should also read the above works on Hooker, especially Lake, p. 150; Voak, pp. 138–57.
    On justification, at least according to an earlier work of his, Hooker seems sound enough. On Rome's doctrine of justification, infused righteousness and satisfactions: 'This is the mystery of the man of sin.' True justification is imputed; the believer is accepted for Christ's sake. This Rome denies, and in so doing 'doth pervert the truth of Christ'. Taken from Hooker's *A Learned Discourse of Justification, Works, and how the Foundation of Faith is Overthrown*, printed in *Laws* 1, pp. 14–76; see especially sections 5–6. This work was composed sometime in the mid-1580s, before the first editions of the *Laws* appeared in 1593, but there is no evidence that Hooker had radically changed his mind in between. On Hooker and the Fall (see also above), it seems to me that anyone who accepts the Protestant imputed righteousness, as Hooker does here, must also have the Protestant view of the Fall and its consequences. They

are the two sides of the same coin. The whole point of imputed righteousness is that because man is so spiritually ruined by the Fall, saving righteousness cannot be either inherent or infused; so it *has* to be imputed.

On whether papists may be saved, a touchy subject with some of the godly, Hooker shows an ecumenical spirit; charitably, if slightly ingeniously, he distinguishes between practising a heresy and teaching a heresy. Heresy is only really heresy 'by such as obstinately hold it after wholesome admonition'. Of this sort, 'their condemnation, without actual repentance, is inevitable'. But many followed their leaders and guides, innocently if wrongly imagining they did God service. Even among Rome's leaders, there are degrees of error. There are those in the Roman church who 'hold the foundation which is precious, though they hold it but weakly, and as it were by a slender thread'; and such will be saved. The Foundation is Christ, the Saviour of the world: whoever denies this 'doth utterly raze the foundation of our faith'. This the Roman church, whatever her faults, does not do; many papists, when dying, called on 'Christ my Saviour, my Redeemer Jesus'. See Hooker's *Learned Discourse*, sections 11–12, 14, 16–17, 19, 21.

68. *Laws* 1.2.3, 5; 1.3.4.
69. *Laws* 1.10.2–3; 2.1.2; 2.7.9; 2.8.3–6.
70. *Laws* 3.8.10–11, 18; Schofield, *Melanchthon*, pp. 28–31.
71. *Laws* 3.9.1; 3.11.16.
72. *Laws* 4.1.3; 4.6.1; 4.8.1; 4.10.1; 4.13.3.
73. *Laws* 3.1.3–4; 3.1.8–12. Unlike Calvin, Hooker would baptise papists' children (3.1.12).
74. *Laws* 5.16.2.
75. *Laws* 1.14.5.
76. *Laws* 5.21.3–4; 5.22.1; 5.22.10; 5.22.19.
77. *Laws* 5.25.3; 5.28.3.
78. *Laws* 5.38.1; 5.49.1; 5.49.3.
79. For the influence of Melanchthon and Bullinger, see Milton, *Catholic and Reformed*, p. 390, fn 42. For these men on predestination and universal grace, see chap. 2 For Elizabeth's opposition to the Lambeth Articles of 1595, which endorsed predestination, see Tyacke, *Anti-Calvinists*, pp. 5, 103, 267. More on Hooker on predestination in Lake, *Anglicans and Puritans*, pp. 182–97.
80. *Laws* 5.50.3; 5.57.3–4; 5.67.2–3, 5–6, 9.
81. For Tyndale, see Daniell, *Bible in English*, p. 150; compare *Laws* 5.67.6.
82. McCullough, *Sermons at Court*, pp. 76–8; Collinson, *Godly People*, pp. 131–2.
83. MacCulloch, *Reformation*, pp. 511–12; Croft, 'The Religion of Robert Cecil', *HJ* 34 (1991): 787–9.
84. Lake, *Anglicans and Puritans*, pp. 89–98.
85. See discussion in Gibson, *Thirty-Nine Articles*, p. 744.
86. Quoted in Neale, *Elizabeth I and her Parliaments, 1559–1581*, p. 192.
87. Fletcher and MacCulloch, *Tudor Rebellions*, pp. 102–16.
88. Elton, *Parliament of England*, chap. 14; MacCaffrey, *Elizabeth*, pp, 364–9; Graves, *Tudor Parliaments*, *passim*.
89. MacCaffrey, *Elizabeth*, pp. 369–71; quote from Elton, *England under the Tudors*, pp. 464–5.
90. *Macbeth*, Act 1, scene 2.

4. JAMES, 1603–25

1. Coward, *Stuart Age*, pp. 118–19.
2. Coward, *Stuart Age*, p. 120.

3. *CSP Ven.*, 1603–1607, no. 739, p. 513.

4. Coward, *Stuart Age*, pp. 119–24; Croft, *James*, pp. 1–9.

5. Bacon, *Letters and Life*, 3, p. 103, discussed in Gardiner 1, pp. 12, 147.

6. *Letters of James*, pp. 110–11. Millenary Petition discussed in Collinson, *Elizabethan Puritan Movement*, pp. 448–67.

7. Ridley, *Knox*, p. 525; McIlwain (ed.), *Political Works of James I*, p. 126; Mason (ed.), *Knox*, p. 222.

8. James quoted in Collinson, *Godly People*, p. 155; Melville in Russell, *Fall of British Monarchies*, p. 29.

9. Collinson, *Elizabethan Puritan Movement*, pp. 464–7; Lake, *Anglicans and Puritans*, pp. 239–50.

10. *Letters of James*, p. 221.

11. Gardiner 1, pp. 195–201.

12. Quoted in Mason (ed.), *Knox*, p. 156.

13. McIlwain (ed.), *Political Works of James I*, p. 126; MacDonald, 'James VI and I, The Church of Scotland and the British Convergence', *HJ* 48/4 (2005): 885–903.

14. McCullough, *Sermons at Court*, pp. 114–15, 126–7, 129.

15. McCullough, *Sermons at Court*, pp. 147–55; *CSP Ven.*, 1603–1607, no. 313, 341, p. 219; no. 739, p. 511.

16. Gardiner 1, p. 97; Okines, 'Why was there so little government reaction to the Gunpowder Plot?', *JEH* 55/2 (2004): 275–92; MacCulloch, *Reformation*, pp. 472–3, 493.

17. *CSP Ven.*, 1607–1610, no. 376, p. 195.

18. Quoted in Elton, *England under the Tudors*, p. 455.

19. Mousnier, *Assassination of Henri IV*, p. 127.

20. McIlwain (ed.), *Political Works of James I*, pp. 61–3.

21. Elton, *Studies* 3, pp. 8–9.

22. Croft, *James*, pp. 73, 78; Gardiner 2, pp. 108, 110.

23. Quotes from Croft, *James*, pp. 80–2. In his will Cecil summed up his faith 'which I have always lived and hoped to die in'. However, Pauline Croft has argued for a shift in Cecil from the orthodox Protestant to the emerging religion of Andrewes and Neile: see Croft, 'The Religion of Robert Cecil', *HJ* 34 (1991): 773–96: quote on p. 794.

24. This and the following paragraph from Gardiner 2, pp. 227–48.

25. *CSP Ven.*, 1615–1617, no. 456, p. 315.

26. Schofield, *Cromwell*, pp. 168–73; Connors, 'Surviving the Reformation in Ireland (1534–80), *SCJ* 32/2 (2001): 340–1. Bingham quoted in Ford, *Protestant Reformation in Ireland*, p. 44.

27. Ellis, *Ireland*, p. 199; MacCulloch, *Reformation*, p. 395.

28. Ford, *Protestant Reformation*, chap. 2; Lyon quoted on p. 37.

29. Gardiner 1, pp. 373–4.

30. Gardiner 1, pp. 384–8.

31. Gardiner 1, pp. 388–91; Ford, *Protestant Reformation in Ireland*, pp. 49–58.

32. Gardiner 1, pp. 392–5.

33. Gardiner 1, pp. 397–401.

34. Gardiner 1, pp. 402–6.

35. Gardiner 1, p. 418.

36. Gardiner 1, pp. 423–33.

37. Woolrych, *Britain in Revolution*, pp. 47–8; Ford, *Protestant Reformation in Ireland*, chap. 8.

38. Ford, *Protestant Reformation in Ireland*, pp. 191–3; Croft, *James*, p. 152.

39. McIlwain (ed.), *Political Works of James I*, p. 344.

40. Gardiner 3, pp. 248–51; Parker, *English Sabbath*, pp. 149–54, 158.

41. Parker, *English Sabbath*, pp. 42–5, 49–50, 57–9.

42. Parker, *English Sabbath*, pp. 161–4.

43. Tolmie, *Triumph of the Saints*, chap. 1.

44. Tyacke, *Anti-Calvinists*, chaps 4–5: quote from Andrewes on p. 103.

45. Kilby and Earle quoted in Collinson, *Religion of Protestants*, pp. 191–2; others quoted in Coward, *Stuart Age*, pp. 85, 87–8.

46. Quoted in Todd, *Culture of Protestantism*, p. 407.

47. Parker, *Thirty Years War*, passim.

48. Gardiner 3, pp. 326–7; 4, pp. 117–18.

49. Gardiner 4, pp. 30–4; Croft, *James*, p. 111; *CSP Ven., 1619–1621*, no. 749, pp. 580–1.

50. Gardiner 4, pp. 126–31, 140.

51. Gardiner 4, pp. 242–3, 248–51, 254–7.

52. Gardiner 4, pp. 258–62.

53. Gardiner 4, pp. 263–4; Roskell, 'Perspectives in English Parliamentary History' in Fryde and Miller (eds), *Historical Studies of the English Parliament 2*, pp. 296–323.

54. Gardiner 4, pp. 265–7.

55. MacDonald, 'James VI and I, The Church of Scotland and the British Convergence', *HJ* 48/4: 899; MacCulloch, 'Richard Hooker's Reputation', *EHR* 117 (2002): 786; *Letters of James*, p. 384.

56. Gardiner 5, pp. 183.

57. Gardiner 5, p. 191, 197–9, 230–1.

58. Gardiner 5, pp. 234–5. James reminded the House that he had asked for a clause to be added to a subsidy bill stressing his commitment to recovering the Palatinate; but they, added the king accusingly, 'had made the preamble without his advice', and consequently he felt he was 'forced to alter it, and set his marginal note upon it'. In the event the Subsidy Act was not altered, though why James changed his mind is not clear.

59. Gardiner 5, pp. 246, 258–64.

60. Gardiner 5, pp. 278–9.

61. Quoted in Houston, *James I*, p. 115.

62. Exeter quoted in Collinson, *Religion of Protestants*, p. 90.

5. CHARLES I, 1625–42

1. Sharpe, 'Private Conscience and Public Duty in the Writings of Charles I', *HJ* 40/3 (1997): 643–65.

2. Gardiner 5, pp. 317, 326, 334.

3. Gardiner 5, pp. 342–5.

4. Gardiner 5, pp. 348–9, 370–3.

5. Gardiner 5, p. 377.

6. Gardiner 5, pp. 397–8.

7. Gardiner 5, pp. 405–11.

8. Gardiner 5, pp. 417–30.

9. Gardiner 6, pp. 19–23, 32–4, 37.

10. Gardiner 6, pp. 59–63.

11. Gardiner 5, pp. 73–82.

12. Gardiner 6, pp. 85–7, 109–14, 120–1.

13. Gardiner 6, pp. 131, 149–50.

14. Gardiner 6, pp. 159–62, 171.

15. Gardiner 6, pp. 231–5.
16. The closing stages of the third Parliament are narrated in massive detail in Gardiner 6, pp. 230–339: see especially pp. 268, 273–4, 311–14. For a concise summary see Woolrych, *Britain in Revolution*, pp. 57–8.
17. Gardiner (ed.), *Constitutional Documents*, p. 69.
18. Gardiner 5, p. 364.
19. Gardiner 6, pp. 323–5; Gardiner (ed.), *Constitutional Documents*, p. 73.
20. Gardiner 6, pp. 326–9.
21. Gardiner 6, pp. 349–55, 59.
22. Gardiner 7, pp. 1–4, 34; Woolrych, *Britain in Revolution*, p. 59.
23. Gardiner 7, pp. 38–42.
24. Gardiner 7, pp. 65–76; Gardiner (ed.), *Constitutional Documents*, p. 83.
25. Gardiner (ed.), *Constitutional Documents*, p. 87; Gardiner 7, p. 77, 81, 119–22.
26. Gardiner 8, pp. 306–7; MacCulloch, *Reformation*, p. 518.
27. Trevor-Roper, *Laud*, p. 49.
28. Laud: 'For that Christ died for all men is the universal and constant doctrine of the Catholic Church of all ages … Almost all of them (the Puritans) hold that God from all eternity reprobates by far the greater part of mankind to eternal fire, without any eye at all to their sin: which opinion my very soul abominates.' See Laud, *Works* 3, pp. 304–5; *Works* 6, pp. 132–3. See also discussion in Tyacke, *Anti-Calvinists*, pp. 181–5, 266–70.
29. Como, 'Predestination and Political Conflict in Laud's London', *HJ* 46/2 (2003): 263–72; Gardiner (ed.), *Constitutional Documents*, pp. 66–8.
30. Trevor-Roper, *Laud*, pp. 104, 110–11, 144. For an unflattering survey of the character of many Laudian bishops, see pp. 171–89. For Laud's attempts to extend control to foreign churches, see chaps 5, 7.
31. The offer: Trevor-Roper, *Laud*, p. 146; Laud quoted in Gardiner 7, p. 301.
32. Collinson, *Elizabethan Puritan Movement*, pp. 356–71; Milton, *Catholic and Reformed*, pp. 496–7.
33. Tyacke, *Anti-Calvinists*, pp. 199–200; MacCulloch, *Reformation*, p. 520.
34. Montagu, *New Gag*, pp. 300, 303; Gardiner 7, p. 255.
35. See the fine discussion in Milton, *Catholic and Reformed*, pp. 454–70.
36. Milton, *Catholic and Reformed*, pp. 464–5. Episcopal succession, Laud agreed, had to be accompanied by true doctrine and faith; but although Laud never specifically ruled out the possibility of true faith existing independently of Episcopal succession, he does not seem to have made much allowance for it. See Milton, *Catholic and Reformed*, pp. 305–6, discussing Laud *Works* 2, pp. 422–6.
37. Quotes from Milton, *Catholic and Reformed*, pp. 314, 316. For Normanton, see Milton, pp. 311, 318.
38. Quoted in Milton, *Catholic and Reformed*, p. 439. I have taken this slightly out of context – Whitelocke was writing in 1654. But the same point is valid for the 1630s.
39. Quoted in Milton, *Catholic and Reformed*, pp. 439–46.
40. Milton, *Catholic and Reformed*, pp. 75–6, 183–6, 192–208, 211–15, 220–1.
41. Milton, *Catholic and Reformed*, pp. 245–6, 529–30; Montagu, *Appello Caesarem*, p. 88.
42. Article 11, printed and discussed in Gibson, *Thirty-Nine Articles*, pp. 388–406.
43. Trent, Canon 9, printed in Schaff, *Creeds of Christendom* 2, p. 112. See also Canons 11–12, 14.
44. Montagu seems to have been well practised in the art of carefully selecting quotes from leading Protestant works without always taking the context into account. From Melanchthon's *Saxon Confession* he quoted this line approvingly: 'When the will accepts the Holy Spirit, it is not idle' (*voluntas statim accepto Spiritu sancto non est iam ociosa*). Here Montagu was enlisting Melanchthon against predestination, a fair

polemical tactic perhaps. However, Montagu failed to mention that the main reason why Melanchthon wrote the *Saxon Confession* was to defend justification by faith alone against Trent; and that at the end of the work Melanchthon confirms that the Saxon churches disagree with Trent. Montagu, *Appello Caesarem*, p. 88; Melanchthon, *Saxon Confession: MW* 6, pp. 106 (15–16), 110 (32–3), 166 (14–18). In a similarly artful vein Montagu could say of the Lord's Supper that 'the difference betwixt us and the popish writers is only about the *modus*, the manner of Christ's presence in the blessed Sacrament'. Agreement, he suggested, would be possible 'but for the factious and unquiet spirits on both sides'. Montagu quoted Calvin completely out of context, saying that Christ is 'substantially received' in the Sacrament. Montagu may sound sweetly reasonable and commendably ecumenical, but he was just being disingenuous. He skirted round the obvious point – that Calvin, like the Puritans, denied any real presence of Christ *on the altar*; in other words, he denied transubstantiation, which the Roman Church insisted on. Only a fool – and Montagu was not a fool – could imagine Calvin and the Catholics agreeing on the Eucharist. Catherine de Medici tried this in the previous century, but failed (chapter 3). Montagu must also have known that two of the most ecumenical men on either side of the Reformation divide – Philip Melanchthon and Gasparo Contarini – could not come to an agreement on the Sacrament when they met for a conference at Regensburg in 1543. See Montagu, *Appello Caesarem*, pp. 288–90. For Regensberg, see Matheson, *Cardinal Contarini at Regensburg, passim*.

45. Cosin, *Works* 2, pp. 26, 29; see also discussion in Tyacke, *Anti-Calvinists*, pp. 128, 153, 172–80. Melanchthon's *Responses: MW* 6, pp. 286–7, 292–3. The queen's chapel: Gardiner 8, pp. 131–2.
46. See, for example, Reynolds, 'Predestination and Parochial Dispute in the 1630s', *JEH* 59/3 (2008): 407–25.
47. Gardiner 8, pp. 130–8.
48. Gardiner 8, pp. 138–53; Milton, *Catholic and Reformed*, pp. 221–7. Heylyn quoted and discussed in Milton, *Catholic and Reformed*, p. 528.
49. Laud, *Works* 4, p. 60: quoted with a fine discussion in Gardiner 7, pp. 126–7.
50. Gardiner 8, p. 107.
51. Gardiner 5, p. 359.
52. Gardiner 5, p. 360.
53. Melanchthon's *Loci Communes*, 1521: *MW* 2 (1), p. 142 (31–7), 146 (23–4) = *LCC* 19, pp. 134, 137; *MW* 2 (1), p.109 (28–31) = *LCC* 19, p.107. Luther: *LW* 33, p. 16. Montagu quoted in Tyacke, *Anti-Calvinists*, p. 239.
54. Anti-Laud satires: Pierce, 'Anti-Episcopacy and Graphic Satire in England, 1640–45', *HJ* 47/4 (2004): 809–48. Quotes on Laud from Collinson, *Religion of Protestants*, p. 90, and Daniell, *Bible in English*, pp. 295, 412. Anti-Puritan satires: Questier, 'Arminianism, Catholicism and Puritanism in England during the 1630s', *HJ* 49/1 (2006): 73–4.
55. Article 17: Gibson, *Thirty-Nine Articles*, pp. 76–7, 459–91. Montagu, besides denying double predestination from Article 17, also claimed that it was consistent with the doctrine of the Church of England to say that a justified man may fall from grace. He mischievously reminded the Puritans that the Lutherans condemned predestination 'with such vehemence, as their custom is, in everything to be vehement and violent'. Montagu, *Appello Caesarem*, pp. 51, 57, 89.
56. Laud, *Works* 6, p. 57; see also discussion in Tyacke, *Anti-Calvinists*, p. 202.
57. Gibson, *Thirty-Nine Articles*, p. 661; Schofield, *Melanchthon*, pp. 197–201; Litzenberger, 'Richard Cheyney, Bishop of Gloucester: An Infidel in Religion', *SCJ* 25 (1994): 580–82. Elizabeth's Prayer Book: see chapter 3, note 11.
58. Gardiner 6, p. 65.

59. Russell, *Fall of the British Monarchies*, p. 15.
60. McIlwain (ed.), *Political Works of James I*, p. 24.
61. *CSP Ven.*, 1621–1623, no. 603, pp. 452–3; McCullough, *Sermons at Court*, pp. 208–9; MacCulloch, 'Richard Hooker's Reputation', *EHR* 117 (2002): 791, 795–6. As MacCulloch notes, however, Hooker himself was no champion of absolute divine right monarchy or episcopacy by divine law.
62. Gardiner 5, p. 364; 6, p. 206–7; 7, p. 142; Tyacke, *Anti-Calvinists*, pp. 161, 166–7, 266–7.
63. Milton, *Catholic and Reformed*, pp. 523, 526.
64. Trevor-Roper, *Laud*, pp. 156–8.
65. Trevor-Roper, *Laud*, pp. 292–4.
66. Parker, *English Sabbath*, pp. 190–6, 199–201, 208–9. Also on the Book of Sports, see chap. 4. Luther: AC 28 (Pelikan, *Creeds*, pp. 109–14 [33, 44, 53, 57–64].)
67. M. Questier, 'Arminianism, Catholicism and Puritanism in England during the 1630s', *HJ* 49/1 (2006): 53–78.
68. See discussion in Gardiner 8, p. 128.
69. Tolmie, *Triumph of the Saints*, pp. 9, 12–26.
70. Tolmie, *Triumph of the Saints*, chap. 2 (quotes from pp. 28–9); Durston, 'By the Book or with the Spirit', *Historical Research* 70, no. 203 (Feb. 2006): 50–74 (quotes from 50–54).
71. Tolmie, *Triumph of the Saints*, p. 31.
72. *CSP Ven.*, 1636–1639, no. 261, pp. 242, 246, 300.
73. Baillie quoted in Russell, *Fall of British Monarchies*, p. 27.
74. Trevor-Roper, *Laud*, pp. 140–1; Gardiner 7, pp. 281–6, 298.
75. Footnotes in this section are mainly from Gardiner. Moderns who have also covered the period include Fletcher, *Outbreak of Civil War* and Russell, *The Fall of the British Monarchies*.
76. Gardiner 8, pp. 103–4.
77. Gardiner 8, pp. 147–8.
78. *Letters of Stephen Gardiner*, ed. Muller, p. 399; Schofield, *Cromwell*, p. 152.
79. Examples: Schofield, *Cromwell*, pp. 61, 248–9.
80. Henry quoted in Elton, *Studies* 2, p. 32. See also chap. 2.
81. Gardiner 8, pp. 200–3.
82. Gardiner 8, pp. 206–9, 226–34, 269–70; Russell, in Todd (ed.), *Reformation to Revolution*, pp. 118–19, 127–8; Russell, *Fall of the British Monarches*, pp. 10–11.
83. *CSP Ven.*, 1636–1639, no. 329, pp. 297, 300. For more popular reaction to Laudianism, see Walter; "Affronts and Insolencies": The Voices of Radwinter and Popular Opposition to Laudianism', *EHR* 122, no. 495 (Feb. 2007): 35–60.
84. Gardiner 8, pp. 314–24 (Baille quoted from p. 321).
85. Gardiner 8, pp. 274–5.
86. Gardiner 8, pp. 327–8.
87. Gardiner 8, pp. 330–34, 338, 344: (quote from p. 334).
88. Coward, *Stuart Age*, p. 519; Gardiner 8, pp. 278–80; Clarendon 1, p. 72.
89. *Lycidas* was written in 1637 and first appeared the following year: *Poems of John Milton*, ed. Carey and Fowler, pp. 232, 238–9, 247–9. Also on the engine, see Gardiner 8, pp. 245–6.
90. Gardiner 8, pp. 373, 375.
91. Gardiner 9, pp. 75–6.
92. Gardiner 9, pp. 99–106, 116.
93. Gardiner 9, pp. 143–6.
94. Gardiner 9, pp. 173–5.
95. Gardiner 9, pp. 195, 207–8, 214.
96. Shaw 1, pp. 6–20; Gardiner 9, pp. 249, 265; Gardiner (ed.), *Constitutional Documents*, pp. 137–55.

97. Gardiner (ed.), *Constitutional Documents*, pp. 155–6.
98. Army plot: Russell, *Fall of British Monarchies*, pp. 291–3; see also Gardiner 9, pp. 354, 357, 362, 369.
99. Gardiner 9, pp. 126, 230–1, 240–1, 333, 364–8.
100. Shaw 1, pp. 65–74; Gardiner 9, pp. 382–3, 389, 400, 404; Gardiner (ed.), *Constitutional Documents*, pp. 163–6; Russell, *Fall of British Monarchies*, pp. 353–4. The Root and Branch Bill, meanwhile, remained in committee after August and never went to the Lords. By now its chief proposal was not the replacement of episcopacy by a full Presbyterian system, but by lay and clerical commissioners appointed by Parliament. Whether these proposals would have been viable is debatable, but it is noticeable and quite remarkable that demands for formal Presbyterianism seemed muted in the Long Parliament, only to revive dramatically in just over two years. On this, see Shaw 1, pp. 99–102.
101. Gardiner 9, pp. 375–6, 415–18. See Russell, *Fall of British Monarchies*, pp. 303–4, for the suggestion that Charles really wanted the Scots to simply leave England alone so that he could reassert his authority in England.
102. Gardiner 10, pp. 6–9.
103. Gardiner (ed.), *Constitutional Documents*, pp. 197–8; Gardiner 10, pp. 14–17; Shaw 1, pp. 107–8.
104. Gardiner 10, pp. 24–9. That the king had some knowledge of the Incident seems almost certain: see Russell, *Fall of British Monarchies*, pp. 322–8.
105. Gardiner 10, pp. 51–8; Woolrych, *Britain in Revolution*, pp. 192–8; Russell, *Fall of the British Monarchies*, pp. 373–9.
106. Gardiner (ed.), *Constitutional Documents*, pp. 206–7; Gardiner 10, pp. 53–79; Morrill in Todd (ed.), *Reformation to Revolution*, pp. 145–6. Not just a popish plot: Pym and his allies may have suspected that the king was in league with the Irish rebels, see Russell, *Fall of British Monarchies*, p. 419. Russell rejects this.
107. Gardiner 10, pp. 83–4; Gardiner (ed.), *Constitutional Documents*, pp. 201–2.
108. Gardiner 10, pp. 88, 95–8, 106–10, 113, 116–20.
109. Gardiner 10, pp. 122–5.
110. Gardiner 10, p. 124.
111. Gardiner 10, pp. 128–40; Russell, *Fall of British Monarchies*, pp. 447–8.
112. Gardiner 10, pp. 153–4, 163, 166–8, 171; Russell, *Fall of British Monarchies*, p. 472.
113. Gardiner 10, pp. 173–6.
114. Gardiner 10, pp. 178–80, 182, 193–7; Russell, *Fall of British Monarchies*, pp. 503–5, 514–17. Nineteen Propositions printed in Gardiner (ed.), *Constitutional Documents*, pp. 249–55; quote from Russell, *Fall of British Monarchies*, p. 515.
115. Gardiner 10, pp. 206, 208, 213.
116. Gardiner 10, pp. 217–20; Walter, 'Popular Iconoclasm and the Politics of the Parish in Eastern England, 1640–42', *HJ* 47/2 (2004): 261–90; Parker and Whitelocke quoted in Woolrych, *Britain in Revolution*, pp. 224, 228 resp.

6. CIVIL WAR, 1642–49

1. Maltby, *Prayer Book and People*, chaps 3–4; Fincham and Lake, 'Popularity, Prelacy and Puritanism in the 1630s: Joseph Hall explains himself', *EHR* 111/2 (1996): 856–81. The petition in question was the Kentish Petition: see chap. 5.
2. Clarendon 2, p. 469; Morrill, in Todd (ed.), *Reformation to Revolution*, pp. 148–50; Fletcher, *Outbreak of Civil War*, chaps 8, 12.
3. Gardiner, *CW* 1, pp. 4–6.
4. Gardiner, *CW* 1, pp. 31, 168.

5. Fuller quoted in Gardiner, *CW* 1, pp. 277–81. Luther: see chap. 1.

6. Gardiner, *CW* 1, p. 282.

7. Gardiner, *CW* 1, pp. 61–2, 78–80, 84; Shaw 1, pp. 120–1. Episcopacy was not officially abolished till three years later: Spurr, *Restoration Church*, p. 3.

8. Gardiner, *CW* 1, pp. 142–3.

9. Quoted in Woolrych, *Britain in Revolution*, p. 249; see also Morrill, in Todd (ed.), *Reformation to Revolution*, p. 152.

10. Gardiner, *CW* 1, pp. 14–15, 66, 302, 309; Morrill (ed.), *Oliver Cromwell and the English Revolution*, p. 226; Shaw 1, p. 113; Parker, *English Sabbath*, p. 218.

11. Gardiner, *CW* 1, pp. 148–9, 226–36; Shaw 1, pp. 109–10, 39–44; Gardiner (ed.), *Constitutional Documents*, pp. 267–73.

12. Gardiner, *CW* 1, pp. 290–3, 301.

13. Abbott 1, pp. 287–9.

14. Gardiner, *CW* 2, pp. 3, 23, 59.

15. Gardiner, *CW* 2, pp. 99–102.

16. Gardiner, *CW* 2, pp. 106–7.

17. Gardiner, *CW* 2, pp. 106–8; Shaw 1, pp. 145–9, 352–3.

18. Gardiner, *CW* 2, pp. 109–14; Durston, 'By the book or with the Spirit', *Historical Research* 70, no. 203 (Feb. 2006): 55–69.

19. Gardiner, *CW* 2, pp. 115, 125, 129, 155.

20. Gardiner, *CW* 2, pp. 258–9, 301.

21. Gardiner, *CW* 2, pp. 303–4, 313.

22. Gardiner, *CW* 2, pp. 319–20; Abbott 1, pp. 377–8.

23. Gardiner, *CW* 3, p. 72.

24. Gardiner, *CW* 3, pp. 78–9, 116.

25. Tolmie, *Triumph of the Saints*, chap. 5. Carter quoted on p. 108; Walwyn on pp. 185–6.

26. Shaw 1, p. 25; Gardiner, *CW* 3, p. 135.

27. Gardiner, *CW* 3, pp. 166, 213–14.

28. Gardiner, *CW* 3, pp. 216–20.

29. Gardiner, *CW* 3, pp. 225, 229–31.

30. Gardiner, *CW* 3, pp. 250, 253, 260, 271–2.

31. Gardiner, *CW* 3, pp. 280, 293–5, 298, 301, 304.

32. Gardiner, *CW* 3, pp. 306–8.

33. Gardiner, *CW* 3, pp. 330–3; Gardiner (ed.), *Constitutional Documents*, pp. 316–26.

34. Gardiner, *CW* 3, pp. 340–41, 354.

35. Gardiner, *CW* 2, pp. 328–9. Richard Baxter had formerly noted that the 'greatest part' of the soldiers 'were ignorant men of little religion', many formerly the king's prisoners, who 'would do anything to please their officers'. Obviously he had observed a change in the soldiers as the war went on.

36. Gardiner, *CW* 3, pp. 366–7, 378, 380–1.

37. Gardiner, *CW* 3, p. 386.

38. Gardiner, *CW* 4, pp. 1–6, 10, 15–19.

39. Gardiner, *CW* 4, pp. 31, 38–40, 43; Gardiner (ed.) *Constitutional Documents*, pp. 347–52.

40. Gardiner, *CW* 4, pp. 45–8; Gardiner (ed.), *Constitutional Documents*, p. 356.

41. Gardiner, *CW* 4, pp. 57–9.

42. Gardiner, *CW* 4, pp. 59, 69, 94–8.

43. Gardiner, *CW* 4, pp. 111–12, 114, 118.

44. Abbott 1, pp. 598–9; Gardiner, *CW* 4, pp. 119–20.

45. Gardiner, *CW* 4, p. 124; Abbott 1, p. 638.

46. Gardiner, *CW* 4, pp. 217–24.

47. Gardiner, *CW* 4, pp. 233–7, 241.

48. Gardiner, *CW* 4, pp. 243–7, 263.

49. Gardiner, *CW* 4, pp. 266, 269–73; Woolrych, *Britain in Revolution*, pp. 427–8; Underdown, *Pride's Purge, passim.*

50. Gardiner, *CW* 4, pp. 278, 280, 286, 288; Brook quoted in Coward, *Stuart Age*, p. 236.

51. Gardiner, *CW* 4, pp. 289–90; Gardiner (ed.), *Constitutional Documents*, pp. 357–8.

52. Gardiner, *CW* 4, pp. 294–7. For records of the king's trial, the charges against him and the proceedings, see Gardiner (ed.), *Constitutional Documents*, pp. 371–80.

53. Gardiner, *CW* 4, pp. 300–1.

54. According to the evidence of a witness, Lieutenant-General Drummond, who heard Oliver speak and who later related it to Gilbert Burnet. Gardiner, *CW* 4, pp. 306–7; Abbott 1, p. 746.

55. Gardiner, *CW* 4, pp. 319–24.

56. Sharpe, 'Private conscience and public duty' in the writings of Charles I', *HJ* 40/3 (1997): 653.

57. Gardiner, *CW* 2, p. 193; Abbott 2, p. 378.

58. Quotes from Tolmie, *Triumph of the Saints*, pp. 188–90.

59. Ironside, the singular, began as a nickname for Oliver Cromwell personally, not his forces. However, after Oliver's siege of Pontefract in August 1648, his men became known as Ironsides, the plural: Gardiner, *CW* 2, p. 1; *CW* 4, p. 179.

60. Daniell, *Bible in English*, p. 461; Hill, *English Bible*, p. 34.

61. Coverdale, *Remains*, p. 492.

62. Schofield, *Cromwell*, pp. 14, 20, 67–8, 195–7.

63. Hill, *English Bible*, p. 329. I do not want to appear to be gratuitously fault-finding with Christopher Hill's stimulating book, but one or two statements in it jumped out at me while reading it and almost cried out for a reaction.

64. Calamy, (ed.), *Cromwell's Soldier's Bible*; Daniell, *Bible in English*, pp. 471–2.

65. Among the verses quoted in the Soldier's Pocket Bible are Deuteronomy 20:1, 4; 23:9; 28:25. Tyndale's prologue on Deuteronomy in *Tyndale's Old Testament*, ed. Daniell, pp. 254–6. Luther on Joshua: *LW* 9, *passim*, especially pp. 43, 130–1, 203–6. This is Luther, as always, treating the historical books of the Old Testament as narrative, but also drawing lessons suitable for Christian times; it is an allegory *of* history, not *bare* allegory. In his preface to his work on Deuteronomy Luther defines a 'proper allegory': namely when teachers and expositors find in the text 'the ministry of the Word or the progress of the Gospel and of faith' (pp. 7–8).

66. Tyndale's *Old Testament*, ed. Daniell, pp. 191–8, 221, 224, 228, 251.

67. Prologue to *Obedience of a Christian Man*, printed in 'Work of William Tyndale', ed. Duffield, p. 335; *Geneva Bible*, ed. Berry.

68. Hill, *English Bible*, p. 440. Henry VIII, of course, based the case for his divorce on Leviticus: but Henry was no Protestant.

7. OLIVER CROMWELL AND THE INTERREGNUM, 1650–58

1. Quotes from Capp, *Fifth Monarchy Men*, pp. 50–1, 53, 55.

2. Justin, *Dialogue with Trypho*, chaps 80–81 (see also Irenaeus, *Against Heresies*, 5.32–6); Augustine, *City of God*, 20.7–9; Cohn, *Pursuit of the Millennium*, pp. 41–52. The belief in the so-called 'Rapture' of the church forms part of a doctrine known technically as 'dispensational pre-millenialism'. A variation on early millennial ideas, dispensationalism began in England in the nineteenth century, from where it spread throughout the UK and to America, where today it commands a dedicated though not a majority following among pietistic Protestants. It is usually non-aggressive, unlike many of the seventeenth-century men, and some believers are effectively pacifists. Its most comprehensive outline can be found in the *Scofield Reference Bible*

(no relation to the author of this book). For an examination and critique of dispensationalism from a more orthodox Protestant point of view, see Allis, *Prophecy and the Church*.

3. Cohn, *Pursuit of the Millennium*, pp. 261–80, 284.

4. The other three books were Hebrews, James and Jude: Brecht 3, p. 34; AC 17 (Pelikan, *Creeds*, p. 68); *LW* 2, p. 150; *LW* 35, pp. 400–9.

5. *LW* 35, pp. 294–316.

6. Calvin, *Inst.* 3.25.5; Whitgift, *Works* 2, p. 434; O' Banion, 'The Pastoral Use of the Book of Revelation in Late Tudor England', *JEH* 57/4 (2006): 693–710; I. Backus, *Reformation Readings of the Apocalypse*, pp. 108–11; Firth, *Apocalyptic Tradition*, esp. chap. 7.

7. Daniell, *Bible in English*, pp. 369–75.

8. Hill, *English Bible*, p. 298.

9. Quotes from Tolmie, *Triumph of the Saints*, pp. 87, 89; Capp, *Fifth Monarchy Men*, pp. 38–40, 43.

10. Capp, *Fifth Monarchy Men*, p. 146.

11. Capp, *Fifth Monarchy Men*, p. 131; Gardiner, *CW* 2, p. 272. Army's statement quoted in Woolrych, *Commonwealth to Protectorate*, pp. 13–14.

12. Fox quoted in Hill, *English Bible*, p. 305.

13. Melanchthon's *Variata* puts the point more strongly than the Augsburg Confession: the pious should not seek to control the world; in this life the church is under the cross, waiting a *future* glorification. The words are Philip's, but until recently this had been a Protestant consensus. *Variata*, Article 17: *MW* 6, p. 23.

14. Gardiner, *CP* 1, pp. 3–5; *CJ* 6, pp. 132–3, 138, 166, 168; Gardiner, (ed.), *Constitutional Documents*, pp. 384–8.

15. Gardiner, *CP* 1, p. 11.

16. Morrill (ed.), *Impact of the English Civil War*, pp. 19–20. For a detailed study of the effects of the wars, see Carlton, *Going to the Wars*.

17. Gardiner, *CP* 1, pp. 17–18, 21.

18. Gardiner, *CP* 1, pp. 20–2, 197, 203, 235–7.

19. Abbott 1, pp. 287, 360, 377, 638; Abbott 2, pp. 127, 142, 317–18, 463.

20. *Poems of John Milton*, ed. Carey and Fowler, pp. 326–7.

21. Gardiner, *CP* 2, pp. 75–9, 96–101, 228.

22. Gardiner, *CP* 2, pp. 229, 232; Abbott 2, pp. 589–90.

23. Gardiner, *CP* 2, pp. 236, 245–8, 251, 253–5.

24. Worden, *Rump*, part 5; Woolrych, *Commonwealth to Protectorate*, pp. 3–4, 68–87; Woolrych, *Britain in Revolution*, pp. 532–5.

25. Abbott 2, pp. 641–3.

26. Abbott 2, p. 644. Same quote, with only minor variations, in Worden, *Rump*, p. 356. More than one account of that meeting seems to have survived, but the substance is the same. Scripture texts: Luke 4:18; Isaiah 61:1; Galatians 1:16.

27. Abbott 2, p. 646; 3, p. 453; Gardiner, *CP* 2, p. 265.

28. Gardiner, (ed.), *Constitutional Documents*, pp. 400–1.

29. Abbott 2, p. 641; Worden, *Rump*, p. 357.

30. See full discussion and analysis in Woolrych, *Commonwealth to Protectorate*, chaps 2–3; Worden, *Rump*, part 5.

31. Gardiner, *CP* 2, pp. 266, 268; Woolrych, *Commonwealth to Protectorate*, pp. 110–23, 128, 136–7; Woolrych, *Britain in Revolution*, p. 540. Fuller analysis of those who made up this assembly in Woolrych, *Commonwealth to Protectorate*, chap. 7.

32. Abbott 3, pp. 52–4, 60, 63–4. See also discussions on Abbott's text in Woolrych, *Commonwealth to Protectorate*, pp. 145–8; Woolrych, *Britain in Revolution*, p. 542. I have followed Woolrych on the disputed parts of the text.

33. AC 17 (Pelikan, *Creeds*, p. 68). See also discussion in section 1 of this chapter.
34. Gardiner, *CP* 2, pp. 287–8.
35. Woolrych, *Britain in Revolution*, p. 547; Woolrych, *Commonwealth to Protectorate*, pp. 157–60, 237–43, 262; for the quality of the House, see chap. 6.
36. Woolrych, *Commonwealth to Protectorate*, pp. 273, 295–8; Abbott 3, p. 89.
37. Gardiner, *CP* 3, pp. 48–51; Woolrych, *Commonwealth to Protectorate*, pp. 284–8.
38. Woolrych, *Commonwealth to Protectorate*, pp. 312–20.
39. Woolrych, *Commonwealth to Protectorate*, pp. 321–8, 339–40.
40. Abbott 4, p. 489.
41. Gardiner, *CP* 2, pp. 319, 332; Gardiner, (ed.), *Constitutional Documents*, pp. 405–17.
42. Gardiner, *CP* 3, pp. 2, 5; Capp, *Fifth Monarchy Men*, p. 133; quote from Gardiner, *CW* 3, p. 321.
43. Gardiner, *CP* 3, p. 18.
44. Gardiner, *CP* 3, pp. 173–4; Abbott 3, pp. 434–8.
45. Gardiner, *CP* 3, pp. 178–87, 192, 199.
46. Gardiner, *CP* 3, pp. 205–9, 218–19.
47. Gardiner, *CP* 3, pp. 222, 236–9, 244–52.
48. Gardiner, *CP* 3, pp. 315–46; Abbott 3, pp. 844–8; Durston, 'Settling the Hearts and Quieting the Minds of all Good People', *History* 85, no. 278 (April 2000): 247–67; *CSP Ven.,* 1655–6, no. 403, pp. 311–12.
49. Gardiner, *CP* 4, pp. 253–5, 266.
50. Abbot 4, p. 278; Firth 1, pp. 12–13.
51. Firth 1, pp. 13–16, 41.
52. Firth 1, pp. 53–6, 64–7.
53. Abbott 4, p. 52.
54. Abbott 4, pp. 271–2.
55. Gardiner, *CP* 3, p. 23; Fletcher, 'Oliver Cromwell and the Godly Nation' in Morrill (ed.), *Oliver Cromwell and the English Revolution*, pp. 209–33.
56. Durston, 'Edward Fisher and the Defence of Elizabethan Protestantism', *JEH* 56/4 (2005): 710–29. See also Spurr, *Restoration Church*, chap. 1 for a survey of the traditional church under the Interregnum.
57. Gardiner, *CP* 3, pp. 334–5; *CP* 4, pp. 19–21; Firth 1, pp. 74–9; Spurr, *Restoration Church*, pp. 9–10, 14–15.
58. Abbott 4, p. 691; Spurr, *Restoration Church*, p. 17.
59. Gardiner, *CP* 3, p. 259; Cohn, *Pursuit of the Millennium*, pp. 150, 292–332; Hill, *English Bible*, pp. 233–6.
60. Spurr, *Restoration Church*, pp. 23–4; Gardiner, *CP* 3, pp. 262–8.
61. Gardiner, *CP* 4, pp. 7, 9.
62. Firth 1, pp. 84–8; Hill, *English Bible*, p. 234.
63. Firth 1, pp. 89–94.
64. Abbott 4, p. 366.
65. Firth 1, pp. 108, 117–19, 125–6.
66. Firth 1, p. 126; Abbott 4, p. 417.
67. Abbott 4, pp. 473, 512–14; Firth 1, pp. 175, 190–3.
68. Firth 1, p. 199. Petition printed in Gardiner (ed.), *Constitutional Documents*, pp. 447–64.
69. Firth 2, pp. 7, 9, 11, 14; Abbot 4, pp. 664–5.
70. Firth 2, pp. 10–16.
71. Firth 2, pp. 19–22.
72. Abbott 4, pp. 712–21.
73. Firth 2, pp. 30–6; Abbott 4, p. 728.
74. Abbott 4, pp. 728–32.
75. Firth 2, pp. 44–6, 74–82.

76. Firth 2, pp. 210, 218, 257, 263–4, 268; Hutton, *Restoration*, pp. 12–13.

77. Firth 2, pp. 299–300, 305.

78. For a good survey, see Mousnier, *Assassination of Henri IV*, Book 2, chapter 1.

79. Quoted in Woolrych, *Britain in Revolution*, p. 247.

80. Croft, *James*, p. 183.

81. Quotes and discussion in Elton, *Tudor Constitution*, p. 236; see also p. 248.

82. Elton, *Studies* 2, pp. 32–5: quote from Christopher St Germain, a writer whose ideas Cromwell used and developed.

83. Quoted in Croft, *James*, p. 82.

84. Gardiner 3, p. 257.

EPILOGUE: THE REFORMER AND THE REVOLUTIONARY

1. Preface to Roberts, *Gustavus Adolphus*.

2. Abbott 4, p. 878.

3. MacCulloch, *Reformation*, pp. 529–31; Hutton, *Restoration*, pp. 175–7; South quoted in Coward, *Stuart Age*, p. 295.

4. Lacey, 'The Office of King Charles the Martyr', *JEH* 53/3 (2002): 510–26.

5. Johnston, 'The Anglican Apocalypse in Restoration England', *JEH* 55/3 (2004): 467–501.

6. Charles quoted in Spurr, *Restoration Church*, p. 221.

7. Spurr, *Restoration Church*, p. 376.

8. Elton, *England under the Tudors*, p. 168.

9. Orwell's essay, *England your England*, section 1.

10. Woolrych, *Commonwealth to Protectorate*, p. 391.

11. Milton: see chapter 7; Byron: McGann (ed.), *Lord Byron: The Complete Poetical Works* 2, p. 152–85

12. See discussion in Gardiner, *CP* 1, pp. 1–2.

13. Quote (not the claim) from Gardiner, *CP* 2, p. 76.

14. Gardiner, *CW* 4, p. 59.

15. Ogg, *Charles II*, pp. 139, 198, 450; Woolrych, *Britain in Revolution*, pp. 699, 788.

16. Ogg, *Charles II*, pp. 366–8, 379, 384–6; Coward, *Stuart Age*, pp. 309–10.

17. Ogg, *Charles II*, pp. 421–2, 454.

18. Gardiner, *CW* 3, p. 316.

19. Firth, *Oliver Cromwell*, pp. 485–6.

20. Robertson, 'The Art of the Possible: Thomas Cromwell's Management of West Country Government', *HJ* 32/4 (1989): 793–816; Schofield, *Cromwell*, pp. 183, 195–7.

21. Clarendon, *History* 6, p. 94.

22. Schofield, *Cromwell*, pp. 174–6.

23. Schofield, *Cromwell*, pp. 15–17.

24. Foxe 5, p. 395; *CSP Span.*, 1534–5, no. 142, p. 427; for Cromwell and the Imperial alliance negotiations in 1536, see Schofield, *Cromwell*, chapter 9.

25. Gardiner, *CP* 3, p. 164; Woolrych, *Britain in Revolution*, pp. 636–7.

26. Gardiner, *CP* 4, pp.194, 206; Firth 1, pp. 314–15, 328–9, 339; Firth 2, pp. 281–9.

27. Gardiner, *CP* 4, p. 145.

28. Gardiner, *CW* 3, p. 386; see also chapter 6.

BIBLIOGRAPHY

PRIMARY SOURCES

Augustine, *City of God against the Pagans*

Calendar of State Papers, Domestic, Edward VI, Philip and Mary, Elizabeth (9 vols, H.M.S.O., 1856–72)

Calendar of State Papers, Foreign (23 vols, H.M.S.O., 1863–1950)

Calendar of State Papers, Spanish, ed. P. de Gayangos *et al.* (15 vols in 20, H.M.S.O., 1862–1954)

Calendar of State Papers, Venetian, ed. R. Brown *et al.* (9 vols, H.M.S.O., 1864–98)

Correspondence Politique de Mm. de Castillon et de Marillac …, ed. J. Kaulek (Paris, 1885)

Die Bekenntnisschriften der Evangelisch-Lutherischen Kirche, herausgegeben im Gedenkjahr der Ausburgischen Konfession 1930 (7 Auflage, reprint Göttingen, 1976)

Calamy, E. (ed.), *Cromwell's Soldier's Bible* (London: Elliot Stock, 1895)

Calvin, J., *Institutes of the Christian Religion*

Clarendon's *History of the Rebellion and Civil Wars in England*, ed. W. Macray (Oxford: Clarendon, 1888)

Constitutional Documents of the Puritan Revolution, 1625–1660, ed. S.R. Gardiner (Oxford: Clarendon, 1906)

Corpus Reformatorum, ed. C.G. Bretschneider *et al.* (100 vols to date)

Cosin, John, *Works of* (5 vols, Oxford: John Henry Parker, 1843–55)

Cranmer, Thomas, *Works of Archbishop Cranmer …*, vol. 1 on the Lord's Supper, ed. J.E. Cox (Cambridge: PS, 1844)

—— *The Work of Thomas Cranmer*, ed. G.E. Duffield (Courtenay Library of Reformation Classics, Appleford: Sutton Courtenay Press, 1964)

—— *Miscellaneous Writings and Letters of Thomas Cranmer*, ed. J.E. Cox (Cambridge: PS, 1846)

Cromwell, O., *Writings and Speeches of Oliver Cromwell*, ed. W.C. Abbott (4 vols, Cambridge: Harvard UP, 1937–47)

Documents of the English Reformation, ed. G. Bray (Cambridge: James Clarke, 1994)

Elizabethan England and Europe: Forty unprinted letters from Elizabeth I to Protestant Powers,
    ed. E. Kouri (London: University of London, 1982)
Epistolae Tigurinae de rebus potissimum ad ecclesiae Anglicanae Reformationem ....
    (Cambridge: PS, 1848)
Foxe, J., *Acts and Monuments of John Foxe,* ed. Josiah Pratt (8 vols, 4th edn, London:
    Religious Tract Society, 1877)
Gardiner, S., *Letters of,* ed. J.A. Muller (Cambridge: Cambridge UP, 1933)
Geneva Bible, A Facsimile of the 1560 edition, ed. L. Berry (Madison: Wisconsin UP,
    1969)
Giles, J.A., *The Whole Works of Roger Ascham* (London: John Russell Smith, 1865)
Hall, E., *A Chronicle containing the history of England ... to the end of the reign of Henry
    VIII* (London: J. Johnson, 1809)
Hearne, T., *Sylloge epistolarum, a variis Angliae scriptarum ...* (Oxford, 1716)
Henry VIII, *Assertion of the Seven Sacraments Against Martin Luther,* trans. T.W. Gent
    (Heversham Tracts, vol. 5, London: N. Thompson, 1687)
Hooker, R., *Works,* Folger Library edn, ed. W. Speed Hill *et al,* (7 vols, Medieval and
    Renaissance Texts Studies, Tempe, Arizona: 1998)
—— *Of the Laws of Ecclesiastical Polity* (2 vols, Everyman's Library, London: Dent,
    1968–9)
Hooper, J., *Early Writings,* ed. S. Carr (Cambridge: PS, 1843)
—— *Later Writings,* ed. C. Nevinson (Cambridge: PS, 1852)
King James VI & I, Letters of, ed. G. Akrigg (Berkeley, LA: University of California Press,
    1984)
—— *Political Works of,* ed. C.H. McIlwain (reprint, New York: Russell and Russell, 1965)
King's Book, ed. T.A. Lacey (London: SPCK, 1932)
Latimer, H., *Sermons,* ed. G.E. Corrie (Cambridge: PS, 1844)
—— *Sermons and Remains,* ed. G.E. Corrie (Cambridge: PS, 1845)
Laud, *Works of William Laud,* ed. J. Bliss and W. Scott (7 vols, Oxford, 1847–60)
Luther, M., *Dr Martin Luthers Werke: Kritische Gesamtausgabe* (61 vols, Weimar: Hermann
    Böhlaus, 1883–1983)
Luthers Werke, Briefwechsel (18 vols, Weimar: Hermann Böhlaus, 1930–85)
Luther's Works: American edn, ed. J. Pelikan (55 vols, Philadelphia and St Louis: Fortress
    Press and Concordia, 1955–86)
Melanchthon, P., *Philippi Melanchthonis Opera Quae Supersunt Omnia,* ed. C.G.
    Bretschneider (28 vols, Halle, 1834–60)
—— *Melanchthons Briefwechsel: Kritische und Kommentierte Gesamtausgabe,* ed. H. Scheible
    (15 vols to date, Stuttgart-Bad Cannstatt: Frommann-Holzboog, 1977–)
—— *Melanchthons Werke in Auswahl,* ed. R. Stupperich (7 vols to date, Gütersloh: Gerd
    Mohn, 1951–)
Milton, J., *Poems of,* ed. J. Carey and A. Fowler (London: Longman, 1968)
Montagu, R., *A Gagg for the New Gospel? No. A New Gag for an Old Goose* (London:
    Lownes, 1624)
—— *Appello Caesarem: A just appeal from two unjust informers* (London: Lownes, 1625)
Müntzer, Thomas, *The Collected Works,* ed. P. Matheson (Edinburgh: T & T Clark, 1988)
Original Letters Relative to the English Reformation, ed. H. Robinson (2 vols, Cambridge:
    PS, 1846–7)
Parker, M., *Correspondence of,* ed. J. Bruce and T. Perowne (Cambridge: PS, 1853)
Parr, Catherine, *The Lamentation of a Sinner* (Harleian Miscellany, vol. 1, London:
    Robert Dutton, 1808)
Pelikan, J. and Hotchkiss, V. (eds), *Creeds and Confessions of Faith in the Christian Tradition,
    vol 2: Part 4: Creeds and Confessions of the Reformation Era* (New Haven: Yale UP, 2003)

Records of the Reformation: The Divorce, 1527–1533 ed. N. Pocock (2 vols, Oxford: Clarendon, 1870)

State Papers Published under the Authority of His Majesty's Commission, King Henry VIII (11 vols, 1830–52)

Tappert, T. (ed.), *The Book of Concord: The Confessions of the Evangelical Lutheran Church* (Philadelphia: Fortress Press, 1959)

Tyndale, W., *Work of*, in Courtenay Library of Reformation Classics, ed. G. Duffield (Appleford: Sutton and Courtenay Press, 1964)

—— *Tyndale's Old Testament*, ed. D. Daniell (London: Yale UP, 1992)

Whitgift, J., *Works of*, ed. J. Ayre (3 vols, Cambridge: PS, 1851–3)

Wright, T. (ed.), *Three Chapters of Letters relating to the Suppression of Monasteries*, (Camden Society, vol. 26, (London: John Bowyer Nichols, 1843)

Zurich Letters, ed. H. Robinson (2 vols, Cambridge: PS, 1842, 1845)

SECONDARY SOURCES

Allis, O.T., *Prophecy and the Church* (Philadelphia: Presbyterian and Reformed Publishing Co., 1964)

Avis, P., 'Moses and the Magistrate: a study in the rise of Protestant legalism', *JEH* 26 (1975): 149–72

Backus, I., *Reformation readings of the Apocalypse: Geneva, Zürich and Wittenberg* (Oxford: Oxford UP, 2000)

Baker, J. Wayne, 'Henry Bullinger and the Reformed Tradition in Retrospect', *SCJ* 29/2 (1998): 359–76

Baylor, M.G. (ed.), *The Radical Reformation* (Cambridge: Cambridge UP, 1991)

Brecht, M., *Martin Luther*, trans. J.L. Schaff (3 vols, Philadelphia and Minneapolis: Fortress Press, 1985, 1990, 1993) …

—— 1, *His Road to Reformation, 1485–1521*

—— 2, *Shaping and Defining the Reformation, 1521–1532*

—— 3, *The Preservation of the Church, 1532–1545*

Brooks, P.N., *Thomas Cranmer's Doctrine of the Eucharist* (London: MacMillan, 1965)

Burnet, G., *History of the Reformation of the Church of England*, ed. N. Pocock (7 vols, Oxford: Clarendon, 1865)

Bush, M.L., *The Government Policy of Protector Somerset* (London: Edward Arnold, 1975)

—— *The Pilgrimage of Grace: A study of the rebel armies of October 1536* (Manchester: Manchester UP, 1996)

Cameron, E., *The European Reformation* (Oxford: Clarendon, 1991)

Capp, B., *The Fifth Monarchy Men: A Study in Seventeenth-century English Millenarianism* (London: Faber, 1972)

Carlton, C., *Going to the Wars: The Experience of the British Civil Wars, 1638–1651* (London: Routledge, 1992)

—— *Charles I: The Personal Monarch* (2nd edn, London: Routledge, 1995)

Clement, C.J., *Religious Radicalism in England, 1535–1565* (Carlisle: Rutherford, 1997)

Cohn, N., *The Pursuit of the Millennium: Revolutionary millenarians and mystical anarchists of the Middle Ages* (London: Pimlico, 1993)

Collinson, P., *The Elizabethan Puritan Movement* (London: Jonathan Cape, 1971)

—— *Archbishop Grindal, 1519–1583: The Struggle for a Reformed Church* (California: University of California Press, 1979)

—— *The Religion of Protestants: The Church in English Society 1559–1625* (Oxford: Clarendon, 1982)

—— *Godly People: Essays on English Protestantism and Puritanism* (London: Hambledon, 1983)

Como, D., 'Predestination and Political Conflict in Laud's London', *HJ* 46/2 (2003): 263–94

Connors, T., 'Surviving the Reformation in Ireland (1534–80): Christopher Bodkin, Archbishop of Tuam, and Roland Burke, Bishop of Clonfert', *SCJ* 32/2 (2001): 335–55

Coward, B., *Oliver Cromwell* (London: Longman, 1991)

—— *The Stuart Age: England 1603–1714* (3rd edn, London: Longman, 2003)

Croft, P., 'The Religion of Robert Cecil', *HJ* 34 (1991): 773–96

—— *King James* (Basingstoke: Palgrave, 2003)

Cunningham, A. and Grell, O.P., *The Four Horsemen of the Apocalypse: Religion, War, Famine and Death in Reformation Europe* (Cambridge: Cambridge UP, 2000)

Daniell, D., *William Tyndale: A Biography* (New Haven and London: Yale UP, 1994)

—— *The Bible in English* (London: Yale UP, 2003)

Davies, J., *The Caroline Captivity of the Church: Charles I and the Remoulding of Anglicanism, 1625–1641* (Oxford: Clarendon, 1992)

Dickens, A.G., *The English Reformation* (2nd edn, London: Batsford, 1989)

Duffy, E., *The Stripping of the Altars: Traditional Religion in England 1400–1580* (New Haven and London: Yale UP, 1992)

—— and Loades, D. (eds), *The Church of Mary Tudor* (Aldershot: Ashgate, 2006)

Durston, C., 'Settling the hearts and quieting the minds of all good people: The Major Generals and the Puritan Minorities of Interregnum England', *History* 85, no. 278 (April 2000): 247–67

—— 'Edward Fisher and the Defence of Elizabethan Protestantism during the English Revolution', *JEH* 56/4 (2005): 710–29

—— 'By the book or with the Spirit: the debate over liturgical prayer during the English Revolution', *Historical Research* 70, no. 203 (Feb. 2006): 50–74

Ellis, S.G., *Ireland in the Age of the Tudors, 1447–1603* (London: Longman, 1998)

Elton, G.R., *Policy and Police: The Enforcement of Reformation in the age of Thomas Cromwell* (Cambridge: Cambridge UP, 1972)

—— *Reform and Renewal: Thomas Cromwell and the Common Weal* (Cambridge: Cambridge UP, 1973)

—— *Reform and Reformation* (London: Edward Arnold, 1977)

—— *Tudor Constitution: Documents and Commentary* (2nd edn, Cambridge: Cambridge UP, 1982)

—— *Studies in Tudor and Stuart Politics and Government* (3 vols, Cambridge: Cambridge UP, 1974, 1983)

—— *The Parliament of England, 1559–1581* (Cambridge: Cambridge UP, 1986)

—— *England under the Tudors* (3rd edn, London: Routledge, 2001)

Fenlon, D., *Heresy and Obedience in Tridentine Italy: Cardinal Pole and the Counter Reformation* (Cambridge: Cambridge UP, 1972)

Fincham K. and Lake P., 'Popularity, Prelacy and Puritanism in the 1630s: Joseph Hall explains himself', *EHR* 111/2 (1996): 856–81

Firth, C.H., *Oliver Cromwell and the Rule of the Puritans in England* (London: Putman, 1901)

—— *The Last Years of the Protectorate, 1656–1658* (2 vols, London: Longmans, 1909)

Firth, K., *The Apocalyptic Tradition in Reformation Britain, 1530–1645* (Oxford: Oxford UP, 1979)

Fletcher, A. and MacCulloch, D., *Tudor Rebellions* (5th edn, Harlow: Pearson, 2004)

Fletcher. A., *The Outbreak of the English Civil War* (London: Edward Arnold, 1981)

Ford, A., *The Protestant Reformation in Ireland, 1590–1641* (2nd edn, Dublin: Four Courts Press, 1997)

Fox, A. and Guy, J., *Reassessing the Henrician Age: Humanism, Politics and Reform, 1500–1550* (Oxford: Blackwell, 1986)

Friesen, A., *Thomas Müntzer, a Destroyer of the Godless: The Making of a Sixteenth-Century Religious Revolutionary* (Berkeley: California UP, 1990)

Gardiner, S.R., *History of England … 1603–42* (10 vols, London: Longman, 1905)

—— *History of the Great Civil War* (4 vols, London: Longman, 1901–5)

—— *History of the Commonwealth and Protectorate* (4 vols, London: Longman, 1903)

Gibson, E.C.S., *The Thirty-Nine Articles of the Church of England* (2nd edn, London: Methuen, 1898)

Gillespie, R., Devoted People: Belief and Religion in Early Modern Ireland (Manchester: Manchester UP, 1997)

Green, C. Lowell, *How Melanchthon helped Luther discover the Gospel: The Doctrine of Justification in the Reformation* (Fallbrook, California: Verdict, 1980)

Gordon, B., *The Swiss Reformation* (Manchester: Manchester UP, 2002)

Graves, M., *The Tudor Parliaments: Crown, Lords and Commons, 1485–1603* (London: Longman, 1985)

Haigh, C., *English Reformations: Religion, politics and society under the Tudors* (Oxford: Oxford UP, 1993)

Hardwick, C., *A History of the Articles of Religion, 1536–1615* (Cambridge: Deighton, Bell and Co. 1859)

Haugaard, W.P., *Elizabeth and the English Reformation: The Struggle for a Stable Settlement of Religion* (Cambridge: Cambridge UP, 1968)

Heal, F., *Reformation in Britain and Ireland* (Oxford: Oxford UP, 2003)

Hill, C., *The English Bible and the Seventeenth-Century Revolution* (London: Allen Lane, 1993)

Houston, *James I* (2nd edn, London: Longman, 1995)

Hoyle, R.W., *The Pilgrimage of Grace and the Politics of the 1530s* (Oxford: Oxford UP, 2001)

Hutton, R., *The Restoration: A Political and Religious History of England and Wales 1658–1667* (Oxford: Oxford UP, 1998)

Johnston, W. 'The Anglican Apocalypse in Restoration England', *JEH* 55/3 (2004): 467–501

Jones, N.L., *Faith by Statute: Parliament and the Settlement of Religion* (London: Humanities Press, 1982)

Jouanna, A., *La France du XVIe siècle, 1483–1598* (Paris: Presses Universitaires de France, 1996)

Lacey, A., 'The Office of King Charles the Martyr in the Book of Common Prayer', *JEH* 53/3 (2002): 510–26

Lake, P., *Anglicans and Puritans? Presbyterianism and English Conformist Thought from Whitgift to Hooker* (London: Unwin Hyman, 1988)

—— 'Business as Usual? The immediate reception of Hooker's Ecclesiastical Polity', *JEH* 52/3 (2001): 456–86

Lehmberg, S.E., *The Reformation Parliament: 1529–1536* (Cambridge: Cambridge UP, 1977)

—— *The Later Parliaments of Henry VIII: 1536–1547* (Cambridge: Cambridge UP, 1977)

Lewis, C.S., *English Literature in the Sixteenth Century, excluding Drama* (Oxford: Clarendon, 1954)

Loades, D., *Mary Tudor: A Life* (Oxford: Blackwell, 1989)

—— *The Reign of Mary Tudor: Politics, government and religion in England, 1553–58* (2nd edn., London: Longman, 1991)

—— *John Dudley: Duke of Northumberland, 1504–1553* (Oxford: Clarendon, 1996)

—— see also under Duffy, E. (eds)

Locher, G.W., *Zwingli's Thought: New Perspectives* (Leiden: Brill, 1981)

MacCaffrey, W., *Elizabeth I* (reprint London: Edward Arnold, 2001)

MacCulloch, D., *Thomas Cranmer: A Life* (New Haven and London: Yale UP, 1996)

—— *Tudor Church Militant: Edward VI and the Protestant Reformation* (London: Allen Lane, 1999)

—— *The Later Reformation in England, 1547–1603* (2nd edn, Basingstoke: Palgrave, 2001)

—— 'Richard Hooker's Reputation', *EHR* 117 (2002): 773–812

—— *Reformation: Europe's House Divided* (London: Allen Lane, 2003)

MacDonald, A.L., 'James VI and I, The Church of Scotland and the British Convergence', *HJ* 48/4 (2005): 885–903

Maltby, J., *Prayer Book and People in Elizabethan and early Stuart England* (Cambridge: Cambridge UP, 1998)

Manschreck, C.L., *Melanchthon, The Quiet Reformer (reprint Westport, Connecticut: Greenwood, 1975)*

Mason, R. (ed.), *John Knox and the British Reformations* (Aldershot: Ashgate, 2000)

Matheson, P., *Cardinal Contarini at Regensburg* (Oxford: Clarendon, 1972)

Mayer, T., *Reginald Pole, Prince and Prophet* (Cambridge: Cambridge UP, 2000)

McCullough, P., *Sermons at Court: Politics and Religion in Elizabethan and Jacobean preaching* (Cambridge: Cambridge UP, 1998)

McEntegart, R., '*Henry VIII, The League of Schmalkalden and the English Reformation* (Woodbridge: Boydell Press, 2002)

McGann, J. (ed.), *Lord Byron: The Complete Poetical Works* (7 vols, Oxford: Clarendon, 1980)

McGrath, A., *Reformation Thought: An Introduction* (3rd edn, Oxford: Oxford UP, 1999)

Milton, A., *Catholic and Reformed: The Roman and Protestant Churches in English Thought, 1600–1640* (Cambridge: Cambridge UP, 1995)

Morrill, J. (ed.), *Oliver Cromwell and the English Revolution* (London: Longman, 1990)

—— *The Impact of the English Civil War* (London: Collins & Brown, 1991)

Mousnier, R., *The Assassination of Henri IV*, trans. Joan Spencer (London: Faber and Faber, 1973)

Neale, J.E., *Elizabeth I and her Parliaments, 1559–1581* (London: Jonathan Cape, 1953)

—— *Elizabeth I and her Parliaments, 1584–1601* (London: Jonathan Cape, 1957)

Niesel, W., *The Theology of Calvin* (Grand Rapids: Baker Books, reprint 1980)

O' Banion, P., 'The Pastoral Use of the Book of Revelation in Late Tudor England', *JEH* 57/4 (2006): 693–710

Ogg, D., *England in the Reign of Charles II* (2nd edn, Oxford: Oxford UP, 1972)

Okines, A., 'Why was there so little government reaction to the Gunpowder Plot?', *JEH* 55/2 (2004): 275–92

Olivier, D., *The Trial of Luther* (trans. J. Tonkin, Oxford: Mowbrays, 1978)

Parker. G. (ed.), *The Thirty Years' War* (2nd edn, London: Routledge, 1997)

Parker. K., *The English Sabbath: A study of doctrine and discipline from the Reformation to the Civil War* (Cambridge: Cambridge UP, 1988)

Pettegree, A., *Marian Protestantism* (Aldershot: Scolar Press, 1996)

—— (ed.), *The Reformation World* (London: Routledge, 2000)

Pierce, H, 'Anti-Episcopacy and Graphic Satire in England, 1640 – 45', *HJ* 47/4 (2004): 809–48

Potter, G.R., *Zwingli* (Cambridge UP, 1976)

Questier, M., 'Arminianism, Catholicism and Puritanism in England during the 1630s', *HJ* 49/1 (2006): 53–78

Rex, R., '*The English Campaign against Luther in the 1520s', in Transactions of the Royal Historical Society*, 5th series, 39 (1989), pp. 85–106

—— *The Theology of John Fisher* (Cambridge: Cambridge UP, 1991)

—— *Henry VIII and the English Reformation* (Basingstoke: MacMillan, 1993)

Reynolds, M., 'Predestination and Parochial Dispute in the 1630s: The case of Norwich Lectureships', *JEH* 59/3 (2008): 407–25)

Richard, J.W., *Philip Melanchthon: The Protestant Preceptor of Germany, 1497–1560* (reprint New York: Burt Franklin, 1974)

Ridley, J.G., *Nicholas Ridley: A Biography* (London: Longmans Green, 1957)

—— *John Knox* (Oxford: Clarendon, 1968)

—— *Henry VIII* (London: Constable, 1984)

—— *Bloody Mary's Martyrs: The Story of England's Terror* (London: Constable, 2001)

Roberts, M., *Gustavus Adolphus and the Rise of Sweden* (London: English Universities Press, 1973).

Roskell, J.S., 'Perspectives in English Parliamentary History' in Fryde, E. and Miller, E. (eds), *Historical Studies of the English Parliament* (Cambridge: Cambridge UP, 1971)

Russell, C., *The Fall of the British Monarchies, 1637–1642* (Oxford: Clarendon, 1991)

Ryrie, A., *The Gospel and Henry VIII: Evangelicals in the Early English Reformation* (Cambridge: Cambridge UP, 2003)

—— *The Origins of the Scottish Reformation* (Manchester: Manchester UP, 2006)

Scarisbrick, J., *Henry VIII* (London: Eyre and Spottiswoode, 1968)

Schaff, P., *The Creeds of Christendom, with a History and Critical Notes* (3 vols, Grand Rapids: Baker, reprint 1977)

Schofield, J., *Philip Melanchthon and the English Reformation* (Aldershot: Ashgate, 2006)

—— *The Rise and Fall of Thomas Cromwell: Henry VIII's Most Faithful Servant* (Stroud: History Press, 2008)

Scofield, C.I., *The New Scofield Reference Bible* (Oxford: Oxford UP, revised edn, 1967)

Schwiebert, E.G., *The Reformation* (Minneapolis: Fortress Press, 1996)

Scott, T. and Scribner, R. (eds), *The German Peasants' War: A History in Documents* (Humanities Press: New Jersey, 1994)

Scribner, R.W., *Popular Culture and Popular Movements in Reformation Germany* (London: Hambledon, 1988)

Sharpe, K., *The Personal Rule of Charles I* (London: Yale UP, 1992)

—— 'Representations and negotiations: texts, images and authority in early modern England', *HJ* 42 (1999): 853–81

—— 'Private conscience and public duty in the writings of Charles I', *HJ* 40/3 (1997): 643–65

Shaw, W., *A History of the English Church during the Civil Wars and under the Commonwealth, 1640–1660* (2 vols, London: Longman, 1900)

Spitz, L.P., *The Religious Renaissance of the German Humanists* (Cambridge, Mass: Harvard UP, 1963)

Spurr, J., *The Restoration Church of England, 1646–1689* (London: Yale UP, 1991)

Stayer, J., *The German Peasants' War and Anabaptist Community of Goods* (Montreal: McGill-Queen's UP, 1991)

Stephens, W. P., *The Theology of Huldrych Zwingli* (Oxford: Clarendon, 1986)

Thompson, W.J. Cargill, *The Political Thought of Martin Luther* (Brighton: Harvester, 1984)

Thomson, J.A.F., *Popes and Princes, 1417–1517: Politics and Polity in the Late Medieval Church* (London: George Allen and Unwin, 1980)

Tjernagel, N.S., *Henry VIII and the Lutherans* (St. Louis: Concordia, 1965)

Todd, M. (ed.), *Reformation to Revolution: Politics and religion in early modern England* (London: Routledge, 1995)

—— *The Culture of Protestantism in Early Modern Scotland* (London: Yale UP, 2002)

Tolmie, M., *The Triumph of the Saints: The Separate Churches of London 1616–1649* (Cambridge: Cambridge UP, 1977)

Trevor-Roper, H., *Archbishop Laud, 1573–1645* (3rd edn, London: MacMillan, 1988)

Tyacke, N., *Anti-Calvinists: The rise of English Arminianism c. 1590–1640* (Oxford: Oxford UP, 1987)

Underdown, D., *Pride's Purge: Politics in the Puritan Revolution* (Oxford: Clarendon, 1971)

Voak, N., *Richard Hooker and Reformed Theology: A study of Reason, Will and Grace* (Oxford: Oxford UP, 2004)

Walter, J., 'Popular Iconoclasm and the Politics of the Parish in Eastern England, 1640–42', *HJ* 47/2 (2004): 261–90

—— '"Affronts and Insolencies": The Voices of Radwinter and Popular Opposition to Laudianism', *EHR* 122, no. 495 (Feb. 2007): 35–60

Watts. M., *The Dissenters, vol 1: From the Reformation to the French Revolution* (Oxford: Clarendon, 1978)

Wendel, F., *Calvin: The Origins and Development of his Religious Thought*, trans. P. Mairet (London: Collins, 1963)

Wernham, R.B., *Before the Armada: The Growth of English Foreign Policy, 1485–1588* (London: J. Cape, 1966)

White. B., *The English Separatist Tradition: From the Marian Martyrs to the Pilgrim Fathers* (Oxford: Oxford UP, 1971)

White, P., *Predestination, Policy and Polemic: Conflict and consensus in the English Church from the Reformation to the Civil War* (Cambridge: Cambridge UP, 1992)

Whitelocke A. and MacCulloch D., 'Princess Mary's Household and the Succession Crisis, 1553', *HJ* 50/2 (June 2007): 265–89

Woolrych, A., *Commonwealth to Protectorate* (London: Phoenix, 1982)

—— *Britain in Revolution, 1625–1660* (Oxford: Oxford UP, 2002)

Worden, B., *The Rump Parliament 1648–1653* (Cambridge: Cambridge UP, 1974)

Wright, J. 'Marian exiles and the legitimacy of flight from persecution', *JEH* 52 (2001): 200– 43

INDEX